3111481400

D0303880

BISMARCK

BISMARCK
THE WHITE REVOLUTIONARY

VOLUME 2
1871–1898

Q
43.07
092
BIS

Lothar Gall
translated from the German by
J. A. Underwood

POPLOAN

30084

London
UNWIN HYMAN
Boston Sydney Wellington

This translation © George Allen & Unwin (Publishers) Ltd, 1986
This book is copyright under the Berne Convention.
No reproduction without permission. All rights reserved.

Published by the Academic Division of
Unwin Hyman Ltd
15-17 Broadwick Street, London W1V 1FP, UK

Unwin Hyman Inc.,
8 Winchester Place, Winchester, Mass. 01890, USA

Allen & Unwin (Australia) Ltd,
8 Napier Street, North Sydney, NSW 2060, Australia

Allen & Unwin (New Zealand) Ltd in association with the
Port Nicholson Press Ltd,
Compusales Building, 75 Ghuznee Street, Wellington 1, New Zealand

This translation first published in 1986
Originally published under the title
Lothar Gall, *Bismarck Der Weisse Revolutionär*,
© 1980 by Verlag Ullstein GmbH, Frankfurt am Main.
First paperback edition 1990

British Library Cataloguing in Publication Data

Gall, Lothar.
   Bismarck: the white revolutionary.
   1. Bismarck, Otto, Fürst von   2. Statesmen –
Germany – Biography
   I. Title
   943.08′092′4   DD218
   ISBN 0–04–943040–8 (hb) Volume 1
   ISBN 0–04–445778–2 (pb)
   ISBN 0–04–943053–X (hb) Volume 2
   ISBN 0–04–445779–0 (pb)

Library of Congress Cataloging-in-Publication Data

Gall, Lothar.
   Bismarck: the white revolutionary.
   Contents: v. 1. 1815–1871 – v. 2. 1871–1898.
   Translation of Bismarck.
   Bibliography: p.
   Includes index.
   1. Bismarck, Otto, Fürst von, 1815–1898.   2. Statesmen –
Germany – Biography.   3. Germany – Politics and
government – 1871–1888.   4. Prussia – Politics and
government – 1815–1870.   I. Title.
   DD218.G2213 1986   943.08′092′4 [B]   85–26658
   ISBN 0–04–943040–8 (hb) (v. 1)
   ISBN 0–04–445778–2 (pb)
   ISBN 0–04–943053–X (hb) (v. 2)
   ISBN 0–04–445779–0 (pb)

Set in 10 on 12 point Bembo by Oxford Print Associates Ltd
and printed in Great Britain at the University Press, Cambridge

for Claudia

'We cannot for one moment doubt
that he was a born revolutionary.
For revolutionaries are born
just as legitimists are born,
with a particular cast of mind,
whereas chance alone determines
whether the circumstances of his life
make of the same person
a White or a Red.'

Ludwig Bamberger,

Monsieur de Bismarck (1868)

CONTENTS

PART THREE

The Sorcerer's Apprentice   1

10   *New Constellations, New Conflicts*   3

The shadow of success – Break with the past – The forces of the new – The political starting-position – The 'battle for civilization' – The question of motives – The nature of the Centre Party – The beginnings of the conflict – Bismarck's attitude – The background to Centrist opposition – The first shots in the battle: abolition of the 'Catholic Section' – 'The 'Pulpit Article' – The School Inspection Bill – The reaction of those concerned – Falk – Consequences of Bismarck's policy – Problems of the same – Commitment to the liberals – Alienation of the conservatives – The legation in Rome – 'We shall not go to Canossa' – Significance of the 'Kulturkampf' for domestic policy – Economic policy – Bismarck's role and responsibility – Social threats – The lessons of experience – The Commune uprising – Initial plan of campaign – The means employed – The problem of Bismarck's domestic policy after 1871

11   *The Reich and Europe*   40

The starting-position – Austria – Russia – The Three Emperors' Agreement – The 'Is War in Sight?' crisis – New avenues: the eastern crisis – Neutrality and challenges – The Kissingen Dictate – New perspectives – Bismarck's speech of 19 February 1878 – The world of the Congress of Berlin – Fresh problems

12   *A Change of Course at Home*   60

The crisis after 1873 – Relations with liberalism – The clash with Lasker at the beginning of 1873 – Estrangement from the liberals – The fight over the military budget – Bismarck's motives – The compromise – Long-term plans? – Possibilities – An attempt at demarcation: the Imperial Press Law – The amendment to the criminal code – The economic crisis – The question of protective tariffs – Bismarck's reluctance – Motives – Pressure group action – The parties – The *Kreuzzeitung* attack and Bismarck's reply – Re-foundation of the Conservative Party – Delbrück's resignation – Heightened disagreement over the course to be pursued – Bismarck's position – Power-seeking opportunism – The pressure groups increase their pressure – Alternatives? – Bennigsen's 'ministerial candidacy' – The liberal left plays poker – The 'chancellorship crisis' of 1877 – The change of course in economic policy – Bismarck loses his parliamentary base – An agreement with the Centre Party? – Disastrous situation of the government – The Deputization Bill – Attempts on the emperor's life – The first Anti-Socialist Bill – The second assassination attempt and the dissolution of the Imperial Diet – Motives and perspectives – The 1878 election – The Anti-Socialist Law – Failure of attempts to provoke a split – Agitation for protective tariffs – The fight against the liberal left – Bismarck's speech of 2 May 1879 – The crucial confrontation and the break – The change of course – Drawing up a balance-sheet – The new programme – Its inherent problems – The attitude of the Centre Party

13   *Foreign Policy Reorientation, Domestic Policy Choices*   117

The problem of choice – 'The "Slap-in-the-face Letter"' – Bismarck's reaction – Motives behind the choice – Resistance and restrictions – The outcome – Domestic policy at a standstill – Pressure groups – The attempt to de-politicize the parties – Practical steps – The National

Economic Council – Social policy – Background, presuppositions and motives – Reaction of the parties and the public – The Accident Insurance Law – The debate in the Imperial Diet – Bismarck's reply – Lohmann – The shadow of the election – Bismarck's speech of 5 May 1881 – Perspectives – The landslide election of 1881 – Plans for a coup? – An escape into foreign policy? – The problem of Bismarck's colonial policy

14   *New Paths to Old Objectives*:
     The Foreign Policy of the 1880s   140

The starting-position – Reversal of relations with Britain and France – The limits to a German-French rapprochement – Ultimate objectives – Failure of the attempt to reach a settlement with France – Foreign policy alternatives? – Rejection of a choice between west and east – The eastern crisis of 1885 – The alliance position at the outset – Extension of the Three Emperors' Treaty – Russian initiatives in the Balkans – The Bulgarian rebellion – Bismarck's reaction – The situation worsens – Re-erection of the system of alliances – The danger of Russian-French co-operation – The Mediterranean Agreement – The Reinsurance Treaty – The Bismarckian 'system' and its problems – Alternatives? – Prospects

15   *The 'Stopgap' System*:
     Domestic Policy after 1881   160

The connection with foreign policy – The situation after the 1881 election – Bismarck sticks to his 'state-socialist' programme – Attempts at unification by the liberals – Bismarck counters – Failure – Dangers from the right – Social policy – Its failure – The National Liberals set a new course – Bismarck's reaction – The 1884 election – A new situation? – Conservative-liberal consolidation – The end of the 'Kulturkampf' and overtures to the Centre Party – The national rallying-cry – Bismarck's Polish policy – He invokes threats from abroad – The attempt to reach a settlement with the church and bypass the Centre Party – Economic policy – The army question used to step up the policy of national consolidation – Bismarck's speech of 11 January 1887 – The Cartel – Internal problems thereof – The conservative right breaks away – Spirits tax and grain tariffs – The change of sovereign – William II

16   *The End*   197

The starting-position – Death of Frederick III – Bismarck's battle with the liberal mythologization of Frederick – Differences over social policy – The miners' strike of May 1889 – The question of extending the Anti-Socialist Law – Bismarck gets himself in a tangle – The conflict comes to a head – The Crown Council meeting of 24 January 1890 – Apparent reconciliation – The election of 20 February 1890 – Prospects for the future – The final break – Bismarck's letter of resignation – A look ahead

17   *The Shadow of the Past*   219

'Chancellor without Office'? – The past as weapon – Bismarck elected to the Imperial Diet – The trip to Vienna in 1892 – Bismarck an alternative? – A past without a future – The 'reconciliation' – The battle for his inheritance – The revelation of the Reinsurance Treaty – Johanna's death – The end – *Thoughts and Reminiscences* – A tentative summing-up

NOTES   239

SOURCES AND LITERATURE   251

INDEX OF NAMES   271

PART THREE
The Sorcerer's Apprentice

[10]

New Constellations, New Conflicts

'I am weary, and while still bound up with the life of this world I begin to appreciate the attractions of peaceful repose. What I should like most is to leave the stage for a seat in one of the boxes.'[1] This was not the Bismarck of the late 1880s writing, a septuagenarian at the end of a long career. The words were penned by the newly appointed Chancellor of the recently founded German Reich, a man universally regarded as having reached the very climax of a political career that might last no one knew how long. For nine years now he had led the state of Prussia, a state that had steadily expanded under his leadership and enormously increased its influence and its importance in terms of European power politics. He had gone on to become chief minister first of the North German Confederation and then of the Reich, for the internal and external policy of which he was now as directly responsible as he was for those of Prussia. As head of the nascent imperial executive, as Minister-President and Foreign Minister of Prussia, as the effective voice of Prussia as chief power in the Federal Council, as chairman of the latter, and not least as 'founder of the Empire' ('Reichsgründer'), with all the prestige that that conferred, he held in his hands such a wealth of power as at his age, and given his character, suggested anything but retirement, renunciation and self-effacing resignation. And he did indeed remain in office for a further eighteen years, with this concentration of power combined with the great weight of his increasingly inflexible personality constituting an ever more oppressive burden on the nation and on the forces within it that were striving to unfold and to shape circumstances in their own way and on their own responsibility.

Yet it was no mere coquettish whim of the moment that was expressed in those lines written to Catherine Orlov on Christmas Day 1871, as in many others written around that time. Granted, there were various external reasons for his feeling that way: a protracted and at one point seemingly dangerous illness suffered by his wife, his own susceptibility to ill health, early signs of advancing age, even a certain weariness of success. But there was something else hidden behind all this, something of which much of it was merely symptomatic.

From his early years he had lived in a state of protest, as it were, against

3

the regimentation and discipline of the life of modern man and against the resultant ossification and impoverishment of human existence. Over and over again he had broken out in order to escape such constraints and not be a slave to the world purely in terms of a job, office, or profession. Freedom, independence, individuality – everything the writers of his youth, Shakespeare, Byron, Heine, the young Goethe, had invoked – remained a fundamental need for him, one that kept coming demandingly to the fore. It was also a crucial element in his religious life and in his belief in a personal God who ruled men in freedom.

In the life of a diplomat who had risen to high office by an unusual route he had enjoyed what he had at first regarded as a scarcely conceivable degree of freedom. He had further been able constantly to remind himself that the whole thing was on a temporary basis, that it might be exchanged at any time for the independent existence of the country squire, but that the way upwards, as it were, was also permanently open, the post of Foreign Minister having been mentioned as a possibility from the outset. Subsequently, however, he had come increasingly 'under the yoke', as he called it. At first he had still had to reckon with his days as chief minister in Prussia being very probably numbered. Again this had enabled him to see everything in terms of an experiment, a momentary harnessing of forces in a specific direction, a purely temporary one-sidedness, as it were. Who knew how soon he would be 'turning [his] back on this unremitting river of ink and living quietly in the country', he kept asking. Without such a prospect the 'bustle of life' was downright 'unbearable'.[2] Then, however, with success and the consequent strengthening of his position it became ever clearer that, as happens to everyone in such a situation, he had in a way become a slave to that success and to that position. During those years the individual, the private person, was increasingly obscured by the politician, the diplomat, the minister, by the problems that preoccupied him and the manifold tasks with which he was confronted in ever-changing forms.

Bismarck's whole make-up was such that he always retained a keen awareness of the process whereby private gradually became dissipated in public life. 'One has simply to renounce one's private life when one becomes a public personage', he summed up resignedly on one occasion in the 1880s.[3] Unlike many, he found this a very high price to have to pay for success – even at times of the most intense involvement and concentration, when he was almost wholly taken up with the tasks of office. Politics, he complained repeatedly, was 'dessicating' everything in him; 'neither hunting, nor music, nor company gave him pleasure any more'.[4]

The idea of freeing himself from all this, of living his own life once again, kept its power of attraction over the years, and not just in periods of illness, despondency, or aversion to work. It constituted a kind of counterpoint to his public life. It enabled him, for all his ambition, all his passionate commitment and all his highly developed taste for power, to maintain a certain detachment, a sense of never being inextricably involved – and to do so even and indeed especially at moments of crucial importance as far as his political existence was concerned. This in turn enabled him to stake his all each time, including his whole political position. His many offers to resign, though for the most part purely tactical in intention, in essence embodied a readiness, indeed almost a secret inclination to send himself *qua* public being into retirement. For him this was the expression and confirmation of that 'autonomy of private life' of which he had dreamt as a young man that he would be able to carry it over 'into the public sphere'.[5]

The 'autonomy of private life' was an ideal. But in Bismarck's level-headed pragmatism it meant at the same time securing the material foundations of a private livelihood. Since learning what it meant to live by politics and be dependent on career and success he had striven continually to broaden the narrow base that his paternal inheritance provided for him outside his official position.

He had done so, moreover, with extraordinary success. The fact that a heavily indebted country squire owning two relatively small estates became in the space of a few decades a man of means who left his children assets running into millions of marks already provoked speculation among Bismarck's contemporaries. Such speculation has never entirely ceased to this day. However, a meticulous, expert and wholly unprejudiced examination of Bismarck's fortune has meanwhile come up with what is probably definitive proof that there can be no question of any irregularities here, not even in the indirect sense of taking advantage of official information.[6]

Bismarck's prosperity rested on two things, and there was nothing secretive or dubious about either of them. One was the fact that in an age of sustained boom conditions and rapid economic growth he found in the Frankfurt-based Meyer Carl von Rothschild, and later and more particularly in Gerson Bleichröder, bankers who administered his revenues and property with the utmost skill. The other was the fact that the state of Prussia manifested extreme generosity towards its first citizen. In February 1867 he received an endowment of 400,000 taler in cash, a sum amounting to several million marks in today's currency. Shortly afterwards, in April 1867, he used it to purchase from Count Blumenthal the domain of Varzin, between Köslin and Stolp in East Pomerania (Koszalin and Słupsk in what is now Poland), an estate of more than 14,000 acres that comprised seven villages. And in 1871 a further endowment brought him the Sachsenwald in the duchy of Lauenburg, just east of Hamburg, a forest of almost 16,000 acres. This, together with a further 1,250 acres of land and a hunting lodge, albeit a derelict one, constituted an asset that was likewise worth many millions of marks in present-day currency. Recently created a hereditary prince, Bismarck was now one of the biggest landowners in Germany. Moreover, he contrived to increase his holdings systematically, manifesting an insatiable appetite for land despite Bleichröder's demonstrating to him on numerous occasions that the yield from such acquisitions, even given improved administration, was far inferior to what could be obtained in other sectors of the economy. In Bismarck's eyes, the only man who was beholden to nobody was the man who owned land.

Only the fact that he owned land allowed him to lead the one kind of life he considered worthwhile. Before 1871 he had tried in vain to combine the life-style of an estate-owner and country squire with the demands and commitments arising out of his various offices. But Schönhausen had become too small for him and Varzin was too far away and above all too difficult of access. The Sachsenwald, however, had the Berlin–Hamburg railway running right through it, with a stop at Friedrichsruh, a tiny place consisting in the main of a hotel-restaurant for excursionists, the Specht, which Bismarck purchased in 1879 as his future residence.

So from 1871 on the Sachsenwald and Friedrichsruh formed the true centre of his life, the 'refuge', as he wrote, that he was unfortunately 'condemned' far too often 'to contemplate with the eyes of Tantalus'.[7] This was where, realizing the aspirations of his youth, he felt his earthly life to be firmly rooted, as it were, far from the city and its sea of houses, that architectural symbol of the regimentation of all life, that 'stony ice' that 'will not melt', as he once wrote to his wife from St Petersburg,[8] far too from an ever more prevalent bourgeois life-style from which he was able to gain nothing either in a positive or in a negative sense – if we except his furniture, which, suggesting a total lack of interest in this regard, was that of a wealthy bourgeois with no taste. Here he could spend hours in the saddle or on foot in the midst of nature, following its growth, observing the cycle of the seasons and reflecting on the ways in which man depends on change and harmony, on the ordinary and on the extraordinary aspects of his natural surroundings. He often found it more important to jot such things down in his devotional and commonplace books than to record what the day had brought in the way of politics and human intercourse. Here he could organize his day as he liked and as he had been in the habit of doing from an early age, sleeping late, obeying sudden whims, but also sitting down to a particular problem for hours on end without being disturbed, burying himself in the writing of a memorandum or the drafting of a Bill. Here, even more than in Berlin, everything was arranged to suit his desires and preferences, including the remarkable eating habits that never failed to astonish guests at the Chancellery, the tendency to stuff himself indiscriminately with herrings and sweetmeats, roasts and nuts, sausages and pickles, and then wash it all down with two or three bottles of red wine, champagne, or even beer. People spoke of whole turkeys being consumed at a sitting by this gigantic but also increasingly corpulent man – until in the early 1880s Dr Schweninger put a partial stop to such excesses by prescribing a strict diet.

Friedrichsruh brought to an end twenty years of a nomadic existence in which Bismarck had always seen an element of the artificial, an element that at the very deepest level ran counter to his true nature. Granted, since his tour in St Petersburg he had lived all the time with one foot on his estates, as it were; only to a limited extent had he settled into his official residence at Wilhelmstrasse 76 – with good reason, as many people believed, in view of his initially precarious political position. Nevertheless, even outwardly he had led the life of the modern breed of mobile civil servant tied to no particular place other than capital and court, a life he had been inclined to mistrust so deeply, not least on account of this peculiar lack of ties. His three children, Marie, Herbert and Wilhelm, had grown up in the city. They were children of a top civil servant, a minister of the Crown, not primarily children of a Prussian nobleman; their conscious minds but also their whole lives were, like his own, more bound up with the city than with the rural aristocracy, making them more Mencken than Bismarck.

Twenty years earlier this had seemed to him inconceivable. 'A state that cannot, as a result of a salutary thunderstorm, tear itself free from a bureaucracy such as ours', he had written to Hermann Wagener in June 1850, 'is and remains doomed to extinction.' He had added: 'Bureaucracy is cancerous in head and limbs; only its belly is sound, and the laws it excretes are the most straightforward shit in the world.'[9] He himself, he had been convinced, would never become the kind of bureaucrat he so loathed, the man who at every stage of his career tended to see everything in accordance with the files and with 'general principles' and usually even rearrange it to fit. Nor did he ever become one in that sense; all the same, his attitude and ideas had changed a great deal in this respect as well.

At one time he had included the Prussian reformers among bureaucrats of this stamp and fulminated against them for having, in the name of an abstract idea of reason and of the state, done violence to tradition and to the social order as an organic growth. Now he had in many ways become an advocate of that kind of development himself. The state as intervening in and altering ever broader areas of social life and organization had not been pushed back at all during his period of office hitherto; it had been enormously strengthened.

Much of this, of course, particularly in the economic sphere, came under the heading of removing a wide variety of constraints, releasing individual forces and promoting the free development of society and the various groups within it. But that disguised and concealed what was really going on, namely the step-by-step construction of the modern interventionist state. This made its greatest steps forward precisely in the guise of the liberalizing, reforming state. That was true of the era of 'enlightened despotism', it was true of the revolution of 1789 and it was true of the Prussian reforms of the post-1806 period. The process continued all over Europe throughout the nineteenth century. After eight years of collaborating with liberalism and liberal reformist policies in broad areas of the economy and society, the Prussian Minister-President soberly remarked on one occasion in 1874 that the Prussian bureaucracy was spreading 'after the fashion of groundwater, everywhere finding the same level'.[10]

From his arch-conservative viewpoint Bismarck had once had far too sharp an eye for this aspect of developments not to have been aware of the extent to which he had himself meanwhile become a protagonist of this very process of an increasing bureaucratization and nationalization of broad areas of existence. When he occasionally remarked that the growing opposition of a large number of his fellow aristocrats and former political friends to himself and to his policy ultimately reflected only their envy at his success, at his meteoric rise up the social ladder to the rank of prince, that kind of reduction of profounder issues to purely human considerations shows one thing above all else: it shows that, convinced though he was of the inevitability of the process, he had what one might almost call instinctive misgivings about the whole thing; he knew exactly what his fellow aristocrats, his 'quarrelsome cousins', as he bitterly dubbed them on one occasion in 1873,[11] reproached him with.

Not that he seriously disturbed the supremacy enjoyed by the nobility in the diplomatic and officer corps and in the higher ranks of the civil service. The trend was towards increasing middle-class influence in all these spheres, but it was one he consistently opposed, even during the period of close collaboration with the National Liberals, and in the 1880s, in the so-called 'Puttkamer Era', named after the famous/notorious Prussian Minister of the Interior who took office in 1881, he fought systematically against it. At the same time his own policy was in fact further undermining the position of the nobility as a class, and he made a crucial contribution towards strengthening and extending the foundations of modern economic society with its levelling effect.

The process that he helped along with the policy for which he was responsible seems in retrospect to have been so ineluctable and so inevitable that attention tends in fact to become concentrated solely on the obstacles that Bismarck himself increasingly placed in its path. Yet many contemporaries still saw things in a very different light. This applies primarily to those areas and those strata of society, particularly east of the River Elbe, among which the forms and customs of economic life were still in many instances bound up with the forms and customs of the traditional social order and where the latter still largely determined the way people thought. Here the apparent arbitrariness of the laws passed and the measures taken by the state, the element that allegedly served a particular political line and its social objectives, stood out very clearly with either a positive or a negative connotation. It often obscured the element of simple reaction to the pressure of circumstances; this can be deduced from the impassioned debates about local government reform as much as from many other political disputes of the period. The upshot, however, was that those who felt 'got at' saw Bismarck, to a very much greater extent than is often appreciated today, as a kind of traitor – a traitor to his class, to the party to which he owed his career and his political position, and even to his own convictions.

To start with, in the period immediately after 1866, this had been the opinion of only a few. But since then it had been steadily gaining ground. For all the glamour conferred by his success, Bismarck found himself more and more isolated: the loneliness of the powerful was aggravated by the loneliness of the man who appears to adopt a position outside his social group, outside his class. To that extent there was something very artificial about his life on his Sachsenwald estate: it was a private invocation of a form of existence in which in reality he no longer had any part – not only because of his position but also, and above all, because of what he had meanwhile come personally to represent.

To someone who from an early age had so consciously wanted to be a 'nobleman', someone who for all his pronounced contempt for most members of his class had for deeply personal reasons so emphatically opted for that class, this could not, all criticism and self-criticism notwithstanding, be a matter of indifference. 'It is a severe test of the nerves of a man of mature years', he observed in his memoirs, 'suddenly to break off relations with all or nearly all the friends and acquaintances he has frequented hitherto.'[12] It brought him face to face with the inevitable question whether in pursuing a particular power-political objective he had not after all made himself too dependent on the means and forces of which he had availed himself without much hesitation and without much scruple whenever they offered. Was he, while appearing to act with such mastery, in fact a free agent at all? Was he not, to an extent even exceeding what he had regarded from the outset as inevitable, in thrall to a development that he had himself helped to launch?

The real secret of his success hitherto, on top of very obviously favourable circumstances and his ability to take both shrewd and energetic advantage of them, had been his extraordinary skill at building up around him as it were a ring of equilibrium situations: between the old and new forces in society, between federalist and centralist elements, between lower and upper houses of parliament, between monarchy and the sovereignty of the people. In many cases this had been possible only as a result of his making major concessions to just those up-and-coming new forces and tendencies, to the middle class and its interests, to nationalist but also to democratic ideas. Among his intimates and for the benefit of those directly affected in each case this kind of thing could at first be represented as purely tactical in intention, an attempt to stabilize the existing situation by making superficial concessions. But the longer Bismarck was in office and the longer people were able to measure what he had originally said was his objective against a rapidly changing reality, the more clearly the opportunist and purely power-seeking nature of this governmental principle emerged.

As Bismarck's conservative critics inevitably saw the situation, it was not the convictions of the man in charge and of the colleagues he had chosen accordingly, not a firmly grounded political and social philosophy that, governed by that principle, determined the policy of the executive; it was a process of social development taking as it were its natural course, a gradual shifting of the centre of gravity of the prevailing forces and interests. In other words, the state was obviously becoming exactly what the liberals had always wanted it to be: an executive organ of society and of the social process. That meant it was no longer, in the spirit of conservatism, a bulwark against upheaval and revolution, including the creeping kind, a guarantor of tradition and of the existing order.

Striking proof of this appeared to be furnished particularly by the role to which the new Imperial Diet promptly laid claim, citing the expectations of its electorate, the nation as a whole. Despite much flexing of political muscle by the monarchical forces and despite a federalism that still put the emphasis very much on decentralization, after 1871 nearly every eye was trained on this central parliament of the new national state. It was expected to redeem the manifold hopes that had become associated with the idea of national unification in the different sections of society. Nor was that all. The belief that this was now where everything else would originate in terms of legislation and the internal development of the Reich immediately received a very clear political orientation.

People have often, looking back, quoted a remark made by the historian

Heinrich von Sybel, a right-wing National Liberal, when very much under the spell of the founding of the Reich he contemplated the prospects for the future. 'How have we merited God's grace that we should be permitted to live through such great and mighty events? And how shall we live in days to come?' he wrote to his Karlsruhe colleague Hermann Baumgarten on 27 January 1871. 'What for twenty years formed the substance of every desire, every endeavour, is now fulfilled in so infinitely splendid a fashion! Where in my lifetime are we to find fresh substance for our life to come?'[13] But that was not at all, at the time, the prevailing opinion among those who on 3 March 1871, in the first election following the founding of the Reich, made Sybel's party, the National Liberals, the strongest group – with 125 seats and a third of the votes – in the newly elected parliament. And even less was it the opinion of those who by voting for the candidates of the German Progressive Party helped the liberal members of the Diet as a body, including the group of those who had stood as independents but were plainly to be classified as liberals, to a clear overall majority – amounting to 202 of the total of 382 seats. On the contrary, most of them agreed with the views expressed by the leader of the Baden liberals, the lawyer Carl Eckhard from Offenburg, during the negotiations over the treaty between Baden and the North German Confederation aimed at establishing the Reich: it was time, he had said, 'to go on with the great work and eventually achieve for our now united Germany what will finally and supremely consecrate the work of unification – a sound development of the whole constitutional life of the German state. As German warriors, hurrying from victory to victory, made possible the unification of Germany, so with God's help, and given the same valour on the part of the political combatants, freedom too will make its triumphal entry into the newly created Empire.'[14] It was a question, as Eduard Lasker said in blunter terms, of 'refining the constitution of the German Empire of the slag of its origins'.[15]

A very similar view, though with the emphases placed rather differently in many respects, was held by the political group that had very surprisingly, not many weeks after its official foundation, become at its first attempt the second-strongest party in the new Diet, winning sixty-three seats and almost one-fifth of the votes, namely by the Centre. This was an extremely heterogeneous coalition of the most diverse forces and interests. Socially it embraced elements from all strata of society, and its somewhat diffuse social and economic policy platform offered scope for tendencies ranging from the far right to the extreme left. But what held it together and gave it a surprising amount of appeal and political impact was its firm determination, as set down in its programme, to protect the rights of the Catholic section of the population – now in a minority in the new Reich – and of the Catholic Church by parliamentary means and by writing them into the constitution.

In formal terms this corresponded entirely with the ideas of the liberal electorate as well. Parliament was to become the true political creative centre of the nation, the forum of its self-responsibility and self-government. In other words, at least three-quarters of the electorate – and a universal suffrage electorate at that – gave express assent to the basic ideas of the liberal constitutional state and its social presuppositions. And anyone looking not just at the current holders of political authority, at the distribution of weight currently obtaining in the context of the immediate decision-making process, but also at the emerging and in many cases already prevailing trends of development, at the systemic character of the whole, inevitably received a strong impression that things had already gone a long way in this direction. German liberalism, it might appear, had at least in substance, albeit by remarkably circuitous routes, already achieved its objectives in many respects, while in others it was on the verge of doing so. When one day in the not too distant future the old emperor – he was over seventy – was succeeded by his liberal-minded, British-oriented son, the liberal majority would take the final step, the step that would bring them direct political responsibility through the possession of power. And what, in the final analysis, did that make Bismarck, the cry went up in the conservative camp: the lackey of liberalism, the man who, in the German phrase, 'held the stirrup' for something he had ostensibly first come forward to combat.

Things turned out quite differently, as we know. The so-called liberal period of the Reich came to a swifter end than anticipated. People's hopes of the crown prince remained bound to the fact that he was doomed to spend almost his entire life standing before the throne rather than sitting on it, for he survived his father by only ninety-nine days. But we cannot properly understand and assess the way in which the Reich developed and the course that Bismarck as its leading statesman adopted unless we are quite clear in our minds about the situation at the outset, following the founding of the German national state in 1871. At the time Bismarck was seen in a very specific fashion as the man of the age. He was seen as the man who, whether in full awareness or half unawares and to some extent unwillingly, had helped the future to triumph over the past.

Not, of course, by any means to the same extent in every sphere. The almost total relaxation of controls over economic and social forces and trends of development was not yet matched in the narrowly political realm. The institutional framework still stood in need of improvement in many respects; the constitutional state needed to be developed and consolidated, education needed to be made independent of ecclesiastical influences in particular and the institutions and forms of expression of modern culture and science needed protection against patronizing interference on the part of reactionary forces. In short, from the liberal standpoint the national state was felt to be in many ways not yet perfect. In the eyes of some this was true of its outward form as well, for the fact that large numbers of people of German extraction and language in central Europe and in Austria were excluded from the German national state was accepted by many liberals only with reluctance.

The accent everywhere, however, was on the 'not yet'. The prevailing attitude in all quarters was one of tremendous optimism. And Bismarck was almost universally regarded as the real driving force behind the whole process. The often embarrassing insistence with which National Liberal historians began to extol the 'Reichsgründer' immediately after 1871 reflects this as much as do the citations conferring the many honorary citizenships with which the urban middle class finally made its peace with the former 'Konfliktminister'. 'Filled with ardent patriotism, guided by a sure sense of history, borne along by the creative power of his genius', he had set 'the highest goals for Prussian policy', prepared, 'in his wisdom, the ways to their achievement', and pursued 'with unswerving courage the paths thus opened' – that was the burden, for example, of the one drawn up on 27 March 1871 by the selfsame city council of Berlin as, backed by the overwhelming majority of its citizens, had for years been among his fiercest political opponents.[16]

Anyone in the middle-class liberal camp who still had his doubts and required further confirmation that the new Chancellor had indeed undergone a Pauline conversion was seemingly furnished with it by Bismarck immediately after the founding of the Reich. In the struggle that, following a prelude in the south German states during the 1860s, now flared up in Prussia and the Reich as well against the Roman Catholic Church and its partisans – against ecclesiastical tutelage and reaction, as the liberals saw it – he resolutely brought the power of the Prussian and now of the new German state to bear in favour of the liberal middle class. He himself became a staunch champion of what the liberals called 'the achievements of modern civilization'; he became a 'Kulturkämpfer'.

The motives that drove Bismarck, so soon after the founding of the Reich, to become involved in a bitter struggle with the Catholic Church and the forces that supported it, indeed positively to provoke such a struggle, have been the object of much speculation. Attempts to account for them range from quite fundamental considerations of principle arising out of diametrical differences of opinion, particularly with regard to the role of the state, to considerations of foreign policy, specifically Bismarck's supposed fear of a Catholic coalition directed against the Reich, and even to considerations of a purely tactical nature: Bismarck's main aim, this argument runs, was by stirring up antagonisms to commit the liberal majority as it were passively to himself and in this way make it obedient to his will in other areas as well.

As is nearly always the case with such fundamental questions, the sources leave the historian almost completely in the lurch. In furnishing evidence for every explanation they in fact allow only two conclusions: either Bismarck deliberately disguised his true motives or his behaviour was governed by the whole gamut of motives that has been unravelled by contemporaries and by scholars looking back, each laying his own particular emphasis and attaching importance where he saw or sees fit – and of course emphasis and importance cannot be assessed in blanket terms but depended on the situation and specific circumstances obtaining at the time.

An overall appraisal of Bismarck and his policy and of the course of the so-called 'Kulturkampf' or 'battle for civilisation' makes the second conclusion appear the more plausible of the two. It is the one that best fits the basic pattern of Bismarckian policy, which was to seize on and exploit existing and immediately available conflict material with no great scruple and no long-term considerations with regard to the future. The Chancellor did this in the belief that friction and conflict were the very stuff of politics, so to speak, and that anyone who did not take an active, aggressive role would very quickly become a mere object of historical evolution. All his successes to date rested essentially on this approach. And it was one of his strongest political convictions that the man who leaves the choice of battlefield and weapons to others will soon number among the defeated.

Bismarck's experiences with the so-called 'Catholic group' in the Prussian House of Deputies, which had become loosely established in the early 1850s and now constituted an important part of the new Centre Party in the Imperial Diet, had scarcely been of a negative kind up to now. The group had by no means counted among his most determined opponents during the constitutional conflict; in fact it had repeatedly sought a compromise. Moreover, not a few of its members had come out openly in favour of his conservative, anti-liberal line. On the other hand he had been suspicious of the non-Prussian element in its ranks from the start, that is to say of the Hanoverians under Ludwig Windthorst and even more so of the Catholic groups in southern and south western Germany. In his view they also exerted a powerful influence on the people of the Rhine province, among whom there was still strong resistance to the Prussian- and Protestant-dominated central government.

This south and south-west German section of the new party – as, surprisingly, is often left out of account in assessments of this whole episode – had already, at a crucial stage of his policy, crossed swords with him in a manner as unexpected as it was embarrassing. This had been in 1867–8, when for reasons of both domestic and foreign policy he attempted to bring the popular, democratic element into play in the south as well. Here he had come up against what he saw as a most alarming blend of anti-Prussian feeling, opposition to essential basic trends in modern political and economic life and a pronounced anti-modernism in many spheres. 'Given the way things have worked out in southern Germany', he wrote in a directive to the Prussian envoy in Rome, Count Harry Arnim, in mid-April 1868, 'we cannot deny that those people are right who see the Catholic Church as it exists there as a danger to Prussia and northern Germany and warn strongly against anything that might foster or promote that church or in any way increase its influence.'[17]

It looked as if what was emerging here was a conservative Catholic party with a broad popular base and a permanent and solid internal structure in the shape of the Catholic hierarchy and the many different organizations for Catholic lay people. But that was just the kind of party that Bismarck was not at all keen to see emerge. It questioned the very concept on which his power crucially rested, namely that he and the executive he headed were the really decisive bulwark of tradition and the existing order in view of the shaky and imperilled position of the rest of the conservative forces, not least at the party-political level. A conservative alternative threatened to emerge here such as had virtually ceased to exist in Prussia.

During the 1860s it was hampered, at least as far as Prussia and large parts of northern Germany were concerned, by the group's decidedly anti-Prussian stance and its clear sympathy for Austria and the idea of a Greater Germany. This changed radically when, having forged a further, organizational link with the old 'Catholic group' in the Prussian House of Deputies, it took its stand on the newly founded Reich. Instead of continuing to criticize the new creation from outside, so to speak, as it had the North German Confederation, and making Prussia the focus of their criticisms, its representatives now demanded that certain Prussian legal and political traditions should actually be preserved. For example, they particularly extolled the Prussian constitution passed during the reactionary period of the 1850s; its basic rights, they thought, made it the ideal model for the constitution of the Reich as well, and they demanded that the relevant sections be adopted in order to protect the Catholic minority in the new state. This was their platform in what turned out to be a thoroughly successful election campaign for the first Diet of the newly founded Reich: with its appeal to the Prussian constitution of 1850 the Centre presented itself expressly as the 'party of the constitution'.

One of the chief spiritual fathers of this policy was the Bishop of Mainz, Wilhelm Emmanuel von Ketteler, whom Bismarck had known slightly in his student days. In 1848, already a priest, Ketteler had been elected to the Frankfurt National Assembly, and there as well as subsequently as Provost of St Hedwig's, Berlin, and Bishop of Mainz he had made a name for himself far beyond the confines of the church for his determined espousal of the economic and social interests of broad strata of the population. Bismarck had tried in vain to appoint him to the archbishopric of Posen-Gnesen in 1865 as a counter-weight to the dominant influence of the Polish nobility. In 1867, in a highly regarded essay entitled 'Germany after the War of 1866', Ketteler had called upon all non-Austrian German Catholics to accept the new situation, all their often justified criticisms of Prussia and its internal relations notwithstanding. They were to support the formation of a Lesser German national state and pursue their own demands on that basis and in the context of a German national parliament.

For the Chancellor of the North German Confederation this had constituted welcome support in respect of both foreign and national policy. It had been materially responsible for Austria's demand for a revision of the decision of 1866 giving way with such surprising swiftness to a sober reassessment of the Austrian national interest. But Bismarck had not, as a result, lost sight of the other demand for an internal reorganization of the new national state and its constitution as soon as the external work of unification had been completed. After all, on the one hand the Customs Parliament elections had confronted him with the substance of those demands and on the other hand the clashes between liberals and the Catholic movement in the south German states had shown him that what the Catholic movement – the 'Catholic People's Party', as it called itself in many areas – aspired to politically was to use the process of parliamentary democracy to cut the ground from under the liberals' feet. In other words, it had resolved to tread the path that Bismarck and his political friends had trodden twenty years earlier, in 1848–9. Even the goal – as Bismarck, now looking at things from a fundamentally different standpoint, registered very uneasily – was the same: the establishment of a conservative centre of power that was independent of the government of the day.

An occasion for considering the whole thing in concrete terms had presented itself to the Chancellor of the newly founded Reich even before the end of the war. On 18 February 1871, a month after the proclamation in the Hall of Mirrors and eight days before the provisional agreement with France, Ketteler had turned up at headquarters and handed the Prussian Minister-President a kind of petition on behalf of fifty-six Catholic members of the Prussian House of Deputies. In it the new German emperor was asked to come out emphatically in favour of the restoration of the Papal States, currently occupied by Italian troops.

Bismarck may have been struck on this occasion by the thought that here was a great political opportunity. What, it was possible to ask for public consumption, was a declaration of loyalty to emperor and empire worth in reality if one sought immediately to drive the empire into difficulties and unforseeable entanglements on the foreign policy front purely in order to help the pope recover a tiny piece of secular territory? Was this a conservative party loyal to king and country if its ultimate allegiance, even in earthly terms, was not to the Crown but to the head of the Catholic hierarchy? Were the forces at work here conducive to the maintenance of the authority of government? Was it not rather their opponents from the liberal camp that were to be regarded as such, having in their struggle against the Catholic threat repeatedly emphasized the absolute precedence of state and Crown over the church?

This was how Bismarck argued over and over again in the years that followed. Although there were undoubtedly elements of sincere conviction involved here, elements that stemmed principally from the tradition of the Protestant established church, what he was mainly pursuing with such arguments was a tactical political objective: a conservative party that was independent of him and therefore in his eyes suspect from the start and that was now organizing itself on a parliamentary basis was to be manoeuvred thus into the political wilderness, as it were out of reach of any coalition even on the political right.

Accordingly he had the *Kreuzzeitung* declare in mid-June 1871 that the government could not regard the leaders of the Centre Party 'as its friends'. It was quite nonsensical that the Centre should pose as 'protector of Germany's conservative interests' and seek in this way to disguise its true character.[18] That character was very clear. 'The Centre increases the dangers threatening society from Communism', he wrote ten days later in a severe warning to the Vatican that virtually amounted to a declaration of war on the new party. It fostered 'the subversive tendencies hostile to all authority. The alliance of Black and Red must be detrimental to the Church. The government is compelled to defend itself. If the Vatican does not break with this Centre and block its onslaughts, the government refuses to accept responsibility for the consequences.'[19]

Bismarck would not have been the politician he was, of course, had he limited his own scope for manoeuvre more than absolutely necessary and laid himself too wide open to attack. The real adversary of the Catholic movement and almost all its endeavours stood ready to hand, as was obvious to everyone. It was liberalism of very nearly every shade from the right wing through to the most uncompromising spokesmen of left-wing liberalism – and not just in Germany but throughout Europe. In other words, its representatives needed only to be given some encouragement for a double outcome to be as good as certain. For one thing, public interest could be expected to concentrate to a great extent on the party-political and ideological aspects of the conflict. And the other thing that could be foreseen was that the liberals would immediately rally round a government that supported them on this question and provided them with the requisite means of power. Both things were so obvious after what had happened in the south German states, in Italy, in France and now under rather different auspices in Britain too that it required no special degree of political Machiavellism or imagination to hit on them – particularly if like Bismarck you were in the habit of examining every conceivable domestic or foreign policy conflict in terms of how it could be exploited.

However, we should beware of pinning Bismarck down, as it were, to this kind of tactical plan. Undoubtedly he had a keen eye for this aspect of things. But like every truly great pupil of Machiavelli he was only too well aware of the limits and pitfalls of Machiavellism. Long-term tactical plans of the kind a certain school of history is fond of teasing out were something Bismarck was inclined to consider poor politics. In his view they underestimated both the opponent concerned and the element of the unexpected in historical evolution and took too sanguine a view of what was feasible or could be manipulated. Tactical considerations, he believed, must necessarily be of a short-term nature, otherwise they threatened to become an absurdity, a kind of rigid opportunism 'on principle', as it were. 'Politics is a job', he summed up aphoristically in his old age, 'that can really be compared only with navigation in uncharted waters. One has no idea how the weather or the currents are going to be or what storms one is in for. In politics there is the added fact that one is also largely dependent on the decisions of others, decisions on which one was counting and which then do not materialize; one's actions are never completely one's own. And if the friends on whose support one is relying change their minds, which is something one cannot vouch for, the whole plan miscarries.'[20]

The fact is, here too we must not underestimate the element of spontaneous motivation in his policy, the element that was born of the moment and bound to the moment. The older he became and the longer he worked in top-level politics, he told the Free Conservative deputy Lucius in May 1871, the shorter the terms he set for his objectives.[21] 'Short-sighted and long-sighted eyes both give incorrect vision', he had written to Gottfried Kinkel two years earlier, 'but for a *practical* statesman I regard the latter failing as the more dangerous because it makes him miss the things that are right in front of him.'[22]

Precisely because there was a very large and indeed progressively increasing measure of opportunism in his policy, he was literally thrown back on seeking self-affirmation and the preservation of his power in improvization and in keeping things in a constant state of flux. Only in that way could he hope to avoid himself becoming a victim of opportunism. For the cynical recognition of that kind of opportunism as a principle was something he could hardly expect of William I. And he knew very well that there were large numbers of people, ranging from many Prussian conservatives via the empress right through to the liberal camp, who were trying to undermine his position on this very score.

So for all the various political prospects that Ketteler's appearance in Versailles opened up, Bismarck refused to let himself be carried away, and there can certainly be no question of any definite commitment on the issue raised. For the time being he played a waiting game, taking apparently well-disposed if non-committal note of the address of the Catholic deputies and leaving it to others to mark out the fronts.

This happened a mere month and a half later. Shortly after it assembled the Imperial Diet had to decide on a motion proposed by the new Centre Party to the effect that a series of basic rights be incorporated in what was in effect the old constitution of the North German Confederation, this having been revised in purely formal terms and presented as such to be voted on. The move could be seen as a call for a substantive revision of the constitution and a harking back to the ideals of the liberal constitutional state and the model of the original, unrevised 1849 constitution. However, in limiting itself, partly through conviction and partly to avoid arousing the suspicions of potential political allies, to quite specific basic rights that it saw as indispensable for the free development of the Catholic Church and the Catholic movement, the Centre discredited its motion in the eyes of most political groups and a substantial section of the public. It was seen as arising not out of a demand on grounds of principle for greater and more assured freedom for all but out of a desire for a kind of particularist isolation. It looked as if privileges were being demanded for forces and for a direction that entertained a sceptical if not dismissive attitude towards the new state.

Accordingly the motion found no support outside the Centre; rejected by everyone from the conservatives right through to the Progressive Party and the two Social Democratic members, it was eventually thrown out by an overwhelming majority. Although in the final division on the whole constitution the Centre voted in favour to a man, the episode confirmed the already widely held opinion that the new party was deeply opposed and indeed hostile to the new Reich.

Many things had contributed to that opinion: Rome's blunt challenge to fundamental trends in the modern state and modern society, culminating in the *Syllabus errorum* of 1864; the attitude of the Catholic movement in southern Germany in the 1860s, which had not only been largely along these lines but had at the same time been bound up with determined opposition to a Prussian-led Lesser German unification solution; the pope's proclamation of a church governed by the ecclesiastical hierarchy and almost completely independent of the state as a bulwark against 'the principal errors of our so lamentable age', as the encyclical *Quanta cura* put it;[23] and finally the Vatican Council of 1870 with its pronouncement of the dogma of papal infallibility.

The scope of that dogma was of course often overestimated by liberals and Protestants and fostered in both camps quite grotesque visions of plans for world supremacy on the part of the pope and the Catholic Church. On the other hand the fact that the German episcopate and the German clergy had contested the dogma with particular vehemence and bowed to it only under protest was largely disregarded. Only the outright dissidents were loudly acclaimed by the liberal public, with some of them – the Bavarian theologian Ignaz Döllinger, for example – being cast in the role almost of new reformers. A groundswell of zeal swept aside all the nuances and differences of viewpoint that existed within the Catholic camp. It was matched by a secular sense of mission that was in many instances guided by a thoroughly nebulous conception of modern civilization and that in the cocksure optimism of its apostles and of their belief in progress not infrequently bordered on the ridiculous.

Behind all this, however, there were considerations of a more solid kind. The Catholic movement in the south had not only been a partisan of the pope and of the church hierarchy. It had also, almost incidentally at first but then in a more and more pronounced fashion, given a political voice to the groups and strata of society that found their traditional livelihood threatened by the course of economic and – directly bound up with it – social development: namely the rural population, including not only the poorer peasantry, small traders and craftsmen but also the lower and middle ranks of the nobility as well as many traditional professional groups. This protest potential grew steadily in importance as the process of change continued to make rapid strides. A further factor in its finding a natural catchment basin in the Catholic movement was that the Catholic upper class in central Europe, excepting Silesia and the Rhineland for the moment, had adapted to the modern liberal-capitalist economy to a very much lesser extent than had the Protestant upper class, principally the nobility of the districts east of the Elbe. Whereas the Protestant upper class, all political antagonisms notwithstanding, found itself in an obvious alliance of interests with the propertied middle class at the economic level, in the Catholic areas this relationship was for the most part much less developed. Instead, here the nobility and sections of the old urban upper classes were able in this respect too to place themselves at the head of forces that were dissatisfied with the new order of things and were pressing for changes, that in other words represented a potentially revolutionary element, albeit one with its eyes on the past.

On the other hand the extent to which the movement soon became a forward-looking one is shown by the efforts on behalf of the working class that are associated above all with the name of Ketteler; the attempts to formulate a Catholic social doctrine also belong in this context. It was these efforts that Bismarck followed with as much vigilance as mistrust, deducing from them what he alleged to be a readiness to come to terms with socialist forces. The 'desire of the ultramontane party to replace the modern state by a medieval theocracy', he wrote in a directive to the ambassador in Vienna towards the end of January 1873, was 'so impetuous that it . . . is seeking contact, with a view to joint action, with the party that intends to realize its ideals on the ruins of State and Church'.[24]

If we are properly to appreciate the depth and passion of the conflict that, following the prelude in the south, now flared up throughout the Reich, we must bear constantly in mind the character of the Centre Party as a multi-class counter-movement directed against the forces of middle-class liberalism and their political plans and aspirations. The forms assumed by and the outward course taken by the conflict were undoubtedly determined to a great extent by the governments of the Reich and of Prussia, that is to say by Bismarck himself and later above all by Adalbert Falk, who at the beginning of 1872 replaced the arch-conservative von Mühler as Prussia's Minister of Culture, Education and Church Affairs. But its actual substance was given in advance, as it were, and was by no means exhausted by the issues and topics superficially concerned. This explains both the detachment that, for all his undeniable involvement and responsibility, Bismarck was able to maintain throughout, even at the height of the conflict, and also the fact that it was possible in the end to settle the conflict without the so-called 'Kampfgesetze', the anti-Catholic legislation, being materially revised: in essence it was a conflict between the middle-class liberals and the Catholic movement. In it the state, the monarchical executive, admittedly took sides. Yet not only did it manage to preserve its independence in doing so; it even, in the end, contrived to reinforce it.

For us, looking back, there is undoubtedly a great temptation to infer from this outcome the innermost aim and actual intention of the campaign. But if the proposition that reality never chimes with what was intended – and vice versa – applies anywhere, it is here. For the real victor was in the end not Bismarck and not the Catholic Church and the Centre Party, none of which had done more than hold their own. The real victor was an all-embracing, supra-personal trend to which all those involved, the liberals, the Catholic movement and Bismarck himself, had declared themselves more or less determinedly opposed: the trend towards ever more radical intervention on the part of the state in all individual and social relations.

That trend was very considerably furthered by the 'Kulturkampf'. The strong reservations with which the liberal spirit of the age regarded the modern interventionist state were broken down by it just as much, although at first this happened as it were behind the backs of contemporaries, as were those entertained in the conservative camp. The process is directly reflected in the defiant 'The State can' that Bismarck wrote around this time in the margin of a document making the classic liberal claim that the state simply could not do this, that, or the other thing.

Bismarck himself had of course at one time very firmly held the view that the state must not be allowed to take over ever wider areas of existence. Absolutism's progressive overpowering of society by the state, so he and his conservative associates had once believed, had been the root of all evil. The fact that, compared with what was now emerging, the absolutist state had in many ways been very much a 'night-watchman state', imposing a minimum of duties on its citizens, was one that even he could scarcely conceal from himself in moments of detachment from day-to-day politics and its struggles.

The interventionist state, in Germany as throughout Europe, was undoubtedly, in the form it subsequently assumed, the product of other forces: of economic problems that suddenly became very much more acute,

19

and of the social question, the material poverty of large sections of the population and the negative prospects for the future of which they became increasingly aware in the wake of the economic crisis. But it was the 'Kulturkampf' that first broke down crucial opposition here. Through it people became more and more accustomed to the state intervening in ever broader areas of social life. This places the campaign in a context with which, as it is usually portrayed – with the emphasis on content and intention – it appears to be only very loosely and superficially connected.

The first piece of intervention by the executive power in the conflict between the Catholic and middle-class liberal movements, a conflict that with the debate on the Centre Party's constitutional motion was now being waged at the level of the newly founded Reich as well, may have seemed comparatively innocuous at first. It concerned the abolition of the so-called 'Catholic Section' of the Prussian Ministry of Culture. This had been set up by Frederick William IV in 1841 to draw a demonstrative line under what had become known as the 'Cologne Troubles', a protracted dispute between the Prussian state and the Catholic Church in the western provinces. Manned by Catholics loyal to the church, it had the job of engineering a balance between the interests of state and church and promptly and unobtrusively removing potential bones of contention.

It had worked very well for thirty years. On the other hand this kind of institutionalized representation of special interests conflicted with what was emerging more and more strongly as the modern political ideal of the bureaucratic institutional state focused on and committed to a concept of the general interest. This was felt not only by most liberals but also by the majority of conservatives. Indeed among conservatives in particular this kind of representation of special interests was increasingly seen as being incompatible with the idea of the 'state above party' on which they repeatedly laid such emphasis, not least vis-à-vis the political left. Consequently they felt more and more in sympathy with the liberals' demand, first made in the mid-1860s, that the section be abolished.

What really brought the question to the fore, however, was when the section, from being a specific organ of conciliation between state and church, threatened to become a bridgehead for the new political opposition within the apparatus of the state, a kind of 'Ministry of State for Papal Affairs in Prussia', as Bismarck once put it on a later occasion.[25] The decision to disband the section, a decision taken by the Prussian Cabinet at Bismarck's instigation towards the end of June 1871, was intended to nip this development in the bud.

An additional factor was that the government was currently faced with the difficult decision as to what to do about those Roman Catholic professors of theology who, while refusing to give allegiance to the decisions of the Vatican Council, in particular to the dogma of infallibility, nevertheless continued as civil servants to lay claim to their teaching posts. A separate ministerial section consisting of Catholics staunchly loyal to Rome would, it was possible to argue, serve only to aggravate this highly unusual situation. It would make it harder for the government to judge matters from a position of neutrality. The same was true with regard to the allegedly pro-Polish leanings of most of the members of the section, notably its head, Albert Krätzig. Krätzig had been in the service of Prince Radziwill before entering the Prussian civil service, and in Bismarck's opinion he still did more for Polish national interests than for those of Prussia. In short, the whole thing could be represented as an act of demarcation, a precaution against – among other things – potential conflicts overflowing their banks.

That was exactly what the man actually responsible, Culture Minister von Mühler, did when at the suggestion of the king he justified this step in an article in the official gazette, the *Staatsanzeiger*. Mühler disagreed with Bismarck completely over this and had resisted the measure to the last. When he then, relying on his reputation for being anything but a partisan of liberalism, himself sought to justify it, he did so in the hope of thereby cushioning much of the blow. The attempt was wholly unsuccessful, however, and shortly afterwards Mühler drew the consequences and resigned.

Against the background of the earlier conflict in southern Germany, the election campaign of early 1871 and a mood of growing mistrust of the Protestant and liberal majority in the new Reich, the move was immediately interpreted as an act of hostile partisanship on the part of the Prussian government, which at the top was identical with the government of the Reich. The general impression was that the Reich was mobilizing against the Catholic Church and its Rome-oriented following in the name of the modern concept of the state and everything that was summed up by the term 'modern civilization'.

Nor indeed did the government, in the person of Bismarck, do anything to counter that impression. On the contrary, a mere six months later it took a further step, the underlying hostility of which could this time scarcely be glossed over. The step consisted in adding to the new criminal code that had just been passed an article threatening with imprisonment 'any priest or other servant of religion' who in the exercise of his office dealt in a sermon or discussion with 'affairs of state' in what it described as 'a manner endangering the public peace'.[26]

Granted, this so-called 'Pulpit Article' – a clear case of an exceptive law, in flagrant disregard of the demand for equality inherent in the idea of the constitutional state – was suggested by the Bavarian government and moved by it in the Federal Council in the middle of November 1871. But the Bavarian initiative was of course undertaken with Bismarck's consent and with his full approval. Moreover, it was quite clear what he was after. Those who were in his eyes the actual officers of the Catholic movement were to be muzzled, and it was to be made clear to the church that the government he led denied it any kind of secular mandate and any kind of autonomy in non-ecclesiastical matters and demanded of it unconditional loyalty in all such questions.

The unspoken objective behind all this was that the church – by which was meant not only the Roman Catholic but also the Protestant Church as well as every other religious community – should either see itself as being, in all worldly affairs, an instrument of the state or alternatively confine itself strictly to the spiritual sphere in the narrowest sense. In view of the militant self-assurance of the Catholic Church and the way in which its wide-ranging demand for a say in things had been registered in many quarters in recent years, the former was hardly to be expected of it. That meant that the constructive objective was established in advance. It governed the nature and direction of the 'Kulturkampf' and its repressive measures from the outset: in place of the historically evolved and in many instances also institutionally anchored collaboration between state and church, between the secular and the spiritual powers, there was to be strict division and demarcation, if possible in all spheres of life.

With this intention Adalbert Falk, who was appointed to succeed von Mühler as Minister of Culture on 23 January 1872, began only days after taking office by presenting a School Inspection Bill on the south German model. This first decisive assault on the structure of the old relationship between state and church promptly raised the conflict to an entirely new level in political terms as well. The principle of an exclusively state-run school inspection system and hence of the purely secular character of the school system as a whole had of course been proclaimed by the Prussian reformers decades before this. However, given the close co-operation between state and church in the ensuing restoration period and the decided interest that the traditional ruling classes had in that alliance, little had changed in practice. The only thing that was different was the legal title by virtue of which the local clergyman and to a lesser extent his spiritual superiors continued to inspect schools and hence to exercise a not inconsiderable influence on the content of education. It was in the nature of a commission carried out on behalf of the state, the point being that both sides deliberately avoided getting involved in any kind of discussion of principles. Now, however, not only was the principle being taken seriously; the state was very determinedly drawing the consequences.

This inevitably commanded the attention of all who whether from direct interest, from conviction, or from a mixture of the two felt committed to the traditional order of things. And they were very much more numerous than those immediately concerned, namely those who held office in the two churches. They included all who suspected that this attack on the office was in reality an attack on the substance, that with the *de facto* church-run school inspection system the Christian character of the schools themselves and of the fundamental principles of education was in jeopardy, that the educational system was being 'dechristianized', as people put it, alluding to what the French Revolution and the Jacobins had tried to do.

After 1789 people had taken this road with a view to breaking the enduring power of the old order. It had been a question of destroying the spiritual as well as the material foundations of that order, which rested not least on the close association between clergy and church and the traditional ruling classes, in particular the nobility but also a section of the landed middle class. The question that now went round the conservative camp and was asked especially by the East Elbian nobility and landed gentry was whether the same considerations were not at work again here. Instead of the local clergyman, who often enjoyed a lifelong association with the family and was highly sympathetic to its interests and its political views, it was now the often anti-aristocratic, 'progressive' schoolteacher and the anonymous state authorities in sympathy with him who would be laying down the law in education. What the political revolution had been unable to do as yet would now be accomplished by a 'mental revolution' starting with the country's children: the undermining and eventual overthrow of the traditional order, the victory of materialism and the rule of half-educated masses who would be strangers to Christian teaching and morality. Ludwig von Gerlach spoke openly of a tendency towards a 'relapse into the grossest heathendom and the tyranny that goes with it'.[27]

The man on whom all such fears were focused, as were all the positive expectations of the other side, was not so much Bismarck, though he left it in no doubt that everything was happening with his unreserved approval; it was the new Minister of Culture, Adalbert Falk. Later on, when he found himself in an impasse and wished to change direction, Bismarck used that fact to shift the actual responsibility on to Falk. He, Bismarck, he hinted then, had merely gone along with things in obedience to the spirit of the age and in response to the pressure of external circumstances.

A Silesian by birth, Falk was 44 when he took office. Previously he had held a senior post in the Ministry of Justice and in that capacity had represented Prussia on the Federal Council. Here Rudolf von Delbrück, the head of the Imperial Chancellery, who later recommended him to Bismarck as von Mühler's successor, had got to know him better and to appreciate his qualities. Falk, like Delbrück himself, was the epitome of what had become known in the south as a 'Geheimratsliberal' – as we might say, an 'Establishment Liberal' – a reform-minded civil servant who was receptive to the ideas and trends of the time but for whom the state and the preservation of its authority and organization remained at all times the supreme criterion. A member of the House of Deputies since 1858, inclining towards the right wing of the liberals, he had quit his ministry job at the time of the conservative reshuffle of the Prussian Cabinet in 1862 and gone to Glogau in Lower Silesia as an appeal court judge. But he had taken only a hesitant part in the conflict over the army and the constitution. At the time of his appointment, when the king threatened to make trouble over Falk's activities as a liberal deputy during the conflict period, Bismarck was even able to cite a speech by his candidate in which the latter had pronounced in favour of approving the additional military expenditure demanded.

This had not been a case of opportunism or half-hearted vacillation. It had been dictated by Falk's concern that the authority and power of the state as the basis of all guaranteed order, including the whole legal system, might otherwise suffer harm. This concept of the *Rechtsstaat*, the constitutional state governed throughout by the rule of law, was the beacon that Falk allowed to guide all his actions. However, caught up in the Enlightenment tradition of bureaucratic political thought, he gave it a very specific interpretation, as did many of his contemporaries in Germany. In this the concept of an order or system of organization embracing all and binding upon all clearly outweighed the principle of the legal rights of the individual having their origin and justification outside the state. He could not conceive, for example, of that principle ever taking precedence over the concept of order and the power interests of the state. Thus it was that Falk was eventually able, in the name of the law and the ideal of the rule of law, to draft legislation during the 'Kulturkampf' that materially contradicted that ideal in many respects.

Bismarck himself, both at the time and subsequently, had nothing but irony for this aspect of the matter. As he remarked on one occasion in March 1874, Falk was 'daydreaming' again in company with the other lawyers who were 'more concerned about the public façade of their precious body of laws than worried about the practical requirements of government'.[28] He was quite familiar with politicians making increasing use of the weapon of the law in the course of political disputes, thus further emphasizing its relativity and dependence on power. He objected only when such a law affected him personally in some unwelcome manner. But that a man should take something that he, Bismarck, regarded as politically necessary and dress it up as being legally irrefutable, giving it an almost metaphysical or at least metapolitical quality in the process, merely struck him as grotesque. It was in this sort of context that he later made that mischievous remark about 'Rechtsstaat' being a 'technical term invented by Robert Mohl' with no real meaning.[29]

It can scarcely be claimed, however, that he had not come across this kind of approach and attitude before meeting Falk and that it genuinely took him by surprise. He had become only too familar with it at the time of the constitutional conflict, and there is no doubt at all that he knew exactly what he was doing when, talking to Falk before his appointment, he answered the latter's question about what his chief task would be with the words: 'To re-establish the rights of the State vis-à-vis the Church.' What this amounted to was an appeal to restore, with the rights of the state, nothing less than the majesty of the law. And when he added: 'And to do so with a minimum of fuss', he was further stressing that it should be done not in the rough-and-tumble of day-to-day politics but on the basis of universally valid laws.[30]

This was precisely how Falk understood his brief. For his part he did everything, just as Bismarck wished, to involve the liberals in what was purportedly a battle of principles. It was as if a play was being enacted without one of the parties involved knowing that he was in a play and that his deepest beliefs were simply being used by his partner as lines and characterization. Falk on the government side gave the whole thing the kind of passionate earnestness and solemn militancy, that faith in making a stand for a higher law, for the future and for progress that characterized many of the protagonists in the 'Kulturkampf'. Such motives were largely foreign to Bismarck. They served his concrete power interests, however, and for that reason suited him very well.

Bismarck once again made the power interests that guided him very clear when on 30 January 1872, exactly a week after Falk's appointment, he took the floor of the Prussian House of Deputies for an apparently spontaneous statement of principle. The outward occasion was provided by a debate, which at times became very heated, between the Centre Party deputies von Mallinckrodt and Windthorst on the one hand and the new Minister of Culture and Wehrenpfennig speaking for the liberals on the other. Discussion centred on the motives behind the abolition of the 'Catholic Section' of the Prussian Ministry of Culture. As far as Bismarck was concerned the debate was also a purely outward occasion in that he had not even been present for most of it and had heard only the end of the last speech, that of Windthorst. From this he picked out the statement that the Catholic element was notably underrepresented in the higher ranks of the civil service and in the ministries and now in the Ministry of Culture as well – a fact, Windthorst claimed, that reflected very clearly the partisan, indeed hostile attitude of the present Prussian government towards the Catholic population.

Without seriously going into the substance of this claim, Bismarck trimmed the argument to apply purely to the current composition of the college of ministers and then simply turned it round: how, in a constitutional state in which the requirement was for 'ministries of a majority that broadly supports our line', could a Catholic be appointed minister at the present time who leaned towards the Centre Party? Did Windthorst seriously believe that the government 'would then receive the backing of a majority'? Surely the opposite was the case? The blame for that, however – and here after only a few sentences he had the essential point in his sights – rested with no other body than the newly formed Centre Party and its parliamentary group.

He had been 'brought up to regard it as one of the most monstrous things that could occur in the political arena that a denominational party should form in a political assembly, a party against which, were all other denominations to adopt the same principle, one need only set the totality of a Protestant parliamentary group: then we should all of us be on an incommensurate footing, for we should be bringing theology into public assemblies to make it an object of platform debate'. If instead of shared politico-social views denomination alone were to become the formative principle of political parties and people were to make their 'political stance primarily dependent on their religious affiliation', his unspoken conclusion was that it would no longer be political bargaining but the character of the current denominational majority relations that governed the nation's overall political course – and did so permanently. Could the Centre Party and its leadership, he asked rhetorically, really be blind to that fact? Of course not, and with that the true nature and objectives of the new party stood revealed.

There followed a sharply worded declaration of war on the Centre Party that made a remote prospect of any possibility of a compromise. 'On my return from France', he went on, bringing out the heavy artillery straight away, 'I was unable to see the formation of this group otherwise than in the light of a mobilization of the party against the State', that was to say the state in its newly created internal and external form. Since then he had had this view repeatedly confirmed. Whatever the occasion, the party always turned against the state, against the government. Instead of 'maintaining respect for the government, even when believing the government is wrong,

25

among all circles, particularly among those of the politically less well informed common man, among the masses', the Centre Party had appealed in election speeches and in the press 'precisely to the passions of the lower classes, of the masses', in order to 'stir them up against the government'. Instead of supporting the Reich and its internal organization, even while criticizing details, it had seized upon 'willing elements' that were 'notorious for their constant opposition on principle to the Prussian State and to the German Empire and used those elements to strengthen itself'.

Though verbally dissociating itself from them, the party had with inner logic found 'approval and recognition . . . among all those parties that, whether from the national or from the revolutionary standpoint, are hostile to the state': Poles, Danes, Guelfs, Alsatians, Lorrainers and not least those advocates of political and social upheaval, the socialists. In short, the party was obviously ready to seize on any and every means of revolutionizing the Reich and its system of organization, both of which stood in the way of its claim to power on behalf of the Catholic Church.

Those means, Bismarck went on to say, evidently included the still extant areas of interplay between state and church. These must therefore be got rid of, although such a course ran counter to the original, deliberately pro-church attitude of the government. That attitude had always been adopted with regard to the Roman Catholic Church as well, with which the government had endeavoured to live in perfect harmony. 'We cannot', he said in this connection, outlining the whole programme of future reform legislation, 'concede the constant claim of the spiritual authorities to exercise a part of the powers of the State, and in so far as they possess such powers we feel obliged, for the sake of peace, to restrict them in order to leave us room to operate side by side, to enable us to live together in tranquillity and to give us as little occasion as possible to concern ourselves in this place with matters of theology.'

Measures directed towards this end, such as the abolition of the 'Catholic Section' of the Prussian Ministry of Culture, were not acts of aggression. They were defensive measures forced upon the state and the government by the utterly hostile and itself aggressive and power-hungry policy of the Catholic party. It was that party and the forces that favoured it within the Catholic hierarchy itself that had done what they accused the government of having done: it was they who had taken the offensive. 'The quarrel is more in the field of conquest for the endeavours of the hierarchy', he declared to the applause of the majority, 'than in the field of defence.'[31]

Bismarck's speech had touched on all the elements and furnished all the cues that were to play a part in the conflict and dominate future discussions. He had talked about both denominational and national antagonisms and made reference to matters both legal and social. The constitutional problem had been mentioned, and so had the question of cultural identity and of course party-political differences of opinion. In all these areas his speech had, if not ordered mobilization, at least sanctioned it. And in so doing, no matter how he was subsequently to represent things, he had assumed full responsibility for the whole campaign.

The closing passage of his speech once again made clear what the

Chancellor had in mind here. He wished to achieve something that in the field of foreign policy he had with good reason never attempted and that even in domestic policy he had hitherto contemplated only at times when a conflict had become really critical: to sustain the military idiom of his speech, he wanted to destroy the enemy. In concluding with an appeal to the well-intentioned majority of Catholics to oppose the policy pursued by the Centre Party, in calling upon the Catholic Church to return to its traditional policy of dealing directly with the state, and in leading into action against the Centre Party all the prevailing trends and forces of the period he intended systematically to deprive it of any kind of base.

The objective proclaimed in barely disguised fashion in his speech of 30 January 1872 was one that, as we know, Bismarck completely failed to achieve. On the contrary, as a result of his policy the Centre Party became more and more solidly established; it became a factor that, for decades to come, no government could ignore, one that from then on, whether constructively or obstructively, exerted a decisive influence on the course of German politics. More than that: in his fight against the Centre Party Bismarck roused and gave a boost to forces over which he never regained control.

Windthorst's reply might already have warned him.[32] Windthorst, probably the most important leader of parliamentary Catholicism in the nineteenth century, declined to go into details and offered no rectification and certainly no justification. Instead, forcefully demonstrating that he was the Chancellor's equal in the field of parliamentary debate, he adopted the thoroughly Bismarckian tactic of seizing programmatically on three points calculated to cast an entirely different light on the Chancellor's attack and at the same time break the ring of isolation that the latter was seeking to throw round the new party like a fever belt.

Having been placed in office with the confidence of the Prussian king, the Minister-President had, Windthorst claimed, expressly appealed to the parliamentary principle, in other words to the principle that it was not the monarch but the majority in parliament that was the deciding factor in the body politic. In doing so he did not, however, enjoy the support of the Centre Party, allegedly such a danger to the state. The Centre, Windthorst went on, was in reality a conservative party that was not by any means confined to the Catholic element. And as such it had no intention of participating in 'the move to the left' at the 'brisk pace' struck up by the parliamentary majority and its clearly loyal follower, the Chancellor. Windthorst's third argument was that if Bismarck, given this one-sidedly leftist policy, further claimed to all intents and purposes to represent the state, he could only counter: 'The Minister-President is not the State, and never has any minister yet dared to say that *his* enemies are also enemies of the *State*.'

This was tantamount to saying: Bismarck is a slave of the liberal majority; he is betraying the monarchical principle he was appointed to defend, and he is trying to disguise the fact by gratuitous attacks on a party that for its part is a loyal supporter of the throne and of the traditional order. Bismarck's heated reaction during the course of the next day's budget

27

debate,[33] which again got right down to principles, showed how powerfully he had been affected by a counter-attack skilfully geared to the political situation as a whole and to the growing mood of mistrust among Prussian conservatives – a counter-attack that the *Kreuzzeitung* subsequently took up in a number of programmatic articles.

His attempt to dismiss it as a wholly fabricated defensive assertion on the part of a body representing purely denominational interests and aggressively pursuing objectives inimical to the state was enthusiastically applauded by the liberal majority as well as by many Protestant conservatives. But there were many, too, who secretly asked themselves, some in jubilant and others in pensive mood, whether there was not something in Windthorst's interpretation and whether Bismarck's behaviour did not indeed reflect a growing dependence on the liberal majority in the Imperial Diet. 'We shall now, after all that has happened, have to drink the liberal cup to the dregs', wrote Moritz von Blanckenburg, to whom Bismarck had offered the Ministry of Agriculture as a sop to the conservatives, in a letter to Roon that dates from around this time. 'There is no alternative, unless Bismarck changes direction completely. A conservative centre party (of the kind he dreams of) is an absurdity.'[34]

The theory that Bismarck fell into increasing dependence on the liberal majority in the Imperial Diet during these years is one that has been rejected pretty well unanimously by a school of historiography heavily influenced by Bismarck-worship and by the course taken by developments after 1878–9. Even the Chancellor's critics have largely followed this trend. A kind of common denominator here is the tendency to place a very low value on the political potency, tactical abilities and real aspiration to power of the liberal majorities in Prussia and the Reich. But were those majorities and their leaderships really so naïve politically, so easily distracted and so little capable of seriously grasping and exploiting the power-political opportunities available to a parliamentary majority? Is this not in profound contradiction to the similarly widespread interpretation to the effect that the right wing of liberalism, later to become the National Liberal Party, allowed itself to be blinded by success in 1866–7 and by the prospect of participating in it and in power and that in so doing betrayed its principles?

What has happened is that a number of different and ultimately irreconcilable elements have come together here to distort our view of historical reality: first, a tendency to charge the objectives and policies of the liberals of that time with the observer's own expectations, which differ from person to person; secondly, the temptation to draw a connection between the liberals' failure and the non-fulfilment of such expectations as projected into the past; and finally, a preparedness – albeit often disputed and denied – to pin the blame for that (fictitious) connection on individual culprits.

Once all this has been discounted, the reality of the situation in many ways presents itself in a soberer and more sobering light. The commitment to the campaign against the Catholic Church and the Catholic movement that had emerged in earnest with Bismarck's speech to the Prussian House of Deputies on 30 January 1872 and the introduction of the School

Inspection Bill not only bound both sides, the government and the liberal majority, more and more closely together. It inevitably raised the question of who would primarily benefit from success in such a campaign. And there the liberals, for all their alleged political naïvety, were capable of working a certain amount out for themselves. Because whichever way one looked at it there was no doubt at all that the Catholic Church and the Catholic movement were indeed, so far as their leading representatives were concerned, genuine supporters of the monarchical principle and the traditional order, as Windthorst had stressed. To oppose them and attempt to weaken them was inevitably to strengthen the counter-forces.

Bismarck's tactical motives were a matter of relative indifference to the liberals. Undoubtedly his behaviour was largely governed by the assumption that his position was under greater threat from a well-organized party of the right and potential coalition partner for other groups and forces at that end of the political spectrum than from the National Liberals, with whom he had been collaborating more or less openly for years. But eliminating competition from the right necessarily meant placing the middle of the spectrum and the left, namely the liberals of various shades of opinion, at an advantage.

It was a game with a thoroughly uncertain and perhaps highly problematic outcome that Bismarck was embarking on here. To the liberals, leaving aside all matters of principle, it offered an unmistakable opportunity of gaining ever greater influence over the government and in fact binding it firmly to their cause. It was no accident that both the French and the Italian liberals of the period adopted the same tactics. And if, in the end, the expectations of German liberalism were not after all fulfilled, the factors to blame were ones nobody could have predicted at the time. They had to do primarily with the crisis of liberal thought and of the liberal order in the economic and social spheres that was precipitated by the drastic slump of 1873 and the period of economic stagnation that followed.

At first, however, there was great optimism in the liberal camp. More strongly than ever before they felt themselves to be in a large measure of practical agreement with the Chancellor and his governments in the Reich and in Prussia. At the same time they increasingly received the impression – indispensable to them in political terms – that there was no serious substitute for them as legislative and hence indirectly as government majority. That impression was further confirmed in the occasionally very heated debates about the School Inspection Bill. Here Bismarck found himself in violent disagreement with the majority of his former colleagues on the conservative benches, accusing them of 'treachery . . . over the Catholic question',[35] indeed of 'deserting the flag . . . of Throne and Gospel'.[36] In the end he appeared finally to have crossed the Rubicon of dissociating himself from the 'Romano-Germanic squirearchy',[37] as he scornfully called it on one occasion: 'The bulk of this party', we read in a note about the origin of the 'Kulturkampf' that Bismarck drew up for the tsar early in 1874, 'consists of people who think little and work not at all.'[38]

This could be seen as being in line with the fact that internationally too the Chancellor was abandoning his old policy of consideration for the forces of Catholic conservatism. To applause not only from German but above all from Italian liberals and from many like-minded people throughout Europe, he adopted an increasingly brusque attitude towards the papacy. When in the autumn of 1871 the man who had headed the recently opened German legation to the Holy See, Count Harry Arnim, went to Paris as ambassador, Bismarck immediately took up his suggestion of appointing as his successor a strongly establishmentarian and 'anti-Jesuit' prince of the church, Cardinal Prince Gustav von Hohenlohe-Schillingsfürst, a brother of the man who had been Minister-President of Bavaria in the late 1860s.

This, however it was dressed up and justified, was an insult of the first order. The reaction of the Curia could be predicted, particularly since the whole thing was presented as a *fait accompli*, as a firm appointment without the usual prior request for the Curia's approval. Offering, instead of a diplomat, a member of the Catholic hierarchy – and in many respects a dissenting one at that – meant not only divesting the relationship between the Reich and the Catholic Church of its quasi-intergovernmental character and further questioning the supra-governmental autonomy of the church; it could at the same time be seen as a form of meddling in the church's internal affairs. For it looked very much as if an attempt was being made to provide a specific and now very much a minority school of thought in the church with a sort of stronghold of its own at the supreme headquarters of the church. So when the Curia chose a relatively mild form in which to couch its refusal, in view of all this the gesture could be regarded as conciliatory. Instead of withholding the requisite *agrément*, which according to diplomatic usage would have been an 'unfriendly act', it merely refused to grant the prince the permission that, as a member of the Catholic hierarchy, he needed before he could take public office.

That happened on 2 May 1872. Twelve days later, on 14 May, the leader of the National Liberals expressed the hope, during a debate on the Foreign Office budget in the Imperial Diet, that in view of recent events and of the treatment that the German emperor had received at the hands of the pope the legation would soon be given up altogether. Undoubtedly the speech reflected the highly outraged mood of the liberal public in Germany. But we can also be fairly sure that this was a prearranged move between the leader of the majority group in the Diet and the Chancellor of the Reich in order to provide the latter with his cue. At any rate, Bismarck immediately took it up, not in substance but in terms of its general drift. In a statement of principle he once again put the position of his government, culminating in the words that were afterwards to be quoted so often: 'Have no fear: *We shall not go to Canossa* – either in body or in spirit!'[39]

With this catchy formula he once again invoked the fiction put about by the liberals that the church of the Vatican Council and of the dogma of infallibility was preparing to overthrow everything modern, to seize temporal power for the purposes of a thoroughgoing reaction against all the achievements of modern civilization in state, economy and society. A state forced on to the defensive and therefore compelled to take strong defensive measures – that was the distorted picture that hung over the whole 'Kulturkampf'.

It was also, as formulated and put about by the liberals, a tactical weapon that made it possible to push the political competition into the far right-hand corner, indeed to pronounce it a danger to the state and subversive in the reactionary sense. In adopting it as his own Bismarck not only bound the liberals to himself but also himself became dependent on them. Thus his famous 'We shall not go to Canossa' was a fundamental declaration of political intent going far beyond the actual object that occasioned it; it was tantamount to a long-term coalition pledge to the liberals.

It might therefore be asked, in view of all this, whether in fact either partner, Bismarck or the liberals, was seriously interested in a quick victory and a swift settlement of the conflict that had now come right out into the open. For that sort of success would have removed a mainstay of their collaboration, a collaboration in which both sides had the strongest interest, expecting from it as they did enormous benefits in terms of their own power and political prospects.

Such a question would of course be entirely hypothetical. In fact there was absolutely no chance of a swift and decisive victory. The Centre Party, after all, was the very embodiment, so to speak, of resistance to politico-social trends and developments that one partner, namely the liberal camp, enthusiastically greeted and encouraged and that the other, namely Bismarck, increasingly regarded as ineluctable and unavoidable, trends that were clearly, in one form or another, going to be a matter of dispute for many years to come. What was at issue behind the fiction of the modern state and the forces supporting it having been challenged and thrown on to the defensive was in fact a specific system of 'modernity', the driving forces of which were located not so much in the state as in society, where they were changing existing values and behaviour patterns with every-accelerating speed. It was Bismarck's becoming, in alliance with the liberals, the *accoucheur* of this system that was the real stumbling-block, not only from the standpoint of the Centre Party but also from that of the conservative camp as a whole. The government's anti-church policy appeared to fit neatly into this picture.

Accordingly, what systematizing historians have separated into liberal reform measures and reforming legislation on the one hand and the 'Kulturkampf' and the governmental and legislative initiatives behind it on the other belonged inseparably together so far as contemporaries were concerned and must in fact be treated as a single entity. Seen in this perspective, the insertion of the so-called 'Pulpit Article', the first of the 'Kulturkampf' laws at Reich level, in the newly adopted criminal code, a code dictated by the liberal idea of the constitutional state enjoying the rule of law, appears in a rather less preposterous light, despite the inherent contradiction between that article and the general trend of the new legislation. On the contrary, it reveals how 'absolutist' even the liberals were when it was a question of implementing what they regarded as constitutive elements of their own politico-social system. A formal infringement of the principle of equality before the law was seen as justifiable when it was to prevent representatives of the old order from using that principle to undermine what it stood for.

31

Of course, this view of the law as being also the power to implement the new, regardless of whatever principles still stood in the way, brought those who took it alarmingly close to a purely power-oriented mentality. This constituted the bridge, as it were, by which Bismarck and the majority of the liberals, although starting from quite different presuppositions, came closer and closer together – this shaping of a new reality and a new order that seemed conducive to both power and freedom and to their own interests as bound up with both.

This was true primarily in the economic sphere, where the close collaboration inaugurated after 1866 and profoundly affecting existing conditions was continued after the founding of the Reich. Once again, as at the time of the North German Confederation, the actual legal justification for all changes was the need to standardize and to create a common economic order that was binding upon all. And once again that justification was used, as it had been then, to reshape actual conditions along liberal lines or more precisely along the lines of a free trading and at the same time industrially oriented capitalism.

The victory over France and the founding of the Reich had primarily benefited the non-agrarian sectors of the economy. For one thing the common national market became further consolidated and was now finally secure. And the other factor was the enormous war indemnity that Paris poured into the coffers of the German governments. Bavaria, for example, received 90 million taler, the remaining states a total of some 700 million taler. Most ministries had used the war indemnity to clear such debts as their states had incurred on the capital market and to implement long-cherished construction and development plans. This gave a further powerful impulse, in terms of both capital and orders, to an economy already enormously stimulated by the prevailing boom and by the prospect of national unification.

It triggered off a kind of frenzy, an almost boundless confidence in the economic potential of the future. At the same time legislature and administration vied with one another to remove all remaining obstacles to the free flowering of economic initiative and even further improve conditions for economic growth, which was already rampant. With the aid of a law standardizing the currency, the establishment of a national central bank, the almost complete abolition of all external tariffs, the continuation of the mammoth task of standardizing the law and the many and various indirect encouragements given to firms by an administration already suitably disposed and now instructed to this effect from above, the legal and institutional framework for the full development of the liberal economic system was consistently extended and elaborated.

The responsibility for all this lay directly with the Imperial Chancellery and its president, Rudolf von Delbrück. However, he worked very closely both with the economy itself and with the liberal majority in the Diet, which was here led principally by Ludwig Bamberger, the co-founder of the Deutsche Bank in 1870 who because of his knowledge of the French terrain had been one of the Chancellor's advisers during the war of 1870–1 and had since then had direct access to him.

As after 1866, Bismarck took a direct part in discussions of these matters only in exceptional cases. One such case arose out of the suggestion, first put forward by the liberal majority, that an important part of the transport system and one that was becoming steadily more so, namely the railways, should bit by bit be brought under official jurisdiction and eventually pass into the ownership of the Reich. Here the Chancellor thought he glimpsed an opportunity of providing the Reich with an urgently needed additional source of income, so giving it a greater degree of independence vis-à-vis the individual states. But although he left most of the rest to Delbrück and his experts, this is not in any way to say that developments passed him by at all – and certainly not, even with regard to mere details, that they occurred against his will.

On the contrary, the only reason why Bismarck intervened so rarely was that he knew things were evolving precisely along lines that had his approval both politically and in substance. It follows that the argument about the extent of his economic expertise and particularly of his ability to make adequate and appropriate allowance for the economic sphere as well in the context of his political calculations and projections is in some degree superfluous and indeed in many respects misleading. Such an argument arises out of a notion of expertise that is in essence deeply unpolitical. In this the way in which expert decisions are dependent on political values and objectives is obscured by what is usually a very inadequate concept of their serving their purpose or even being right or wrong. In reality, of course, decisions regarding political values and objectives always take precedence; these are already given, as it were, in the individuals and groups of people concerned, and it is they that dictate the individual expert decisions, ruling out fundamental alternatives. Those decisions may individually turn out to have been incorrect, to be unsuited to the prescribed objective. But that lies at another level: it is a recruitment problem, a problem of which experts are called in to advise and appointed to execute. It is not one that can be solved by requiring detailed expert knowledge and meticulous practical supervision on the part of the politician responsible.

In short, there is no doubt whatever that in this sphere too it was Bismarck who made the real decisions, the decisions of principle, in full awareness of their political and – at least in the short and medium terms – also of their social import, and that Delbrück's administration by and large took its bearings strictly from them. The theory that the liberals had a *laissez-faire* attitude to the economic sector, indeed that they deliberately turned their backs on a field they allegedly regarded as being of minor importance, is one of history's legends. In fact we must go a step further and say that at this time too, as in the period immediately following 1866, the economic policy of liberalism was not, so far as Bismarck was concerned, in any way confined to purely tactical considerations of a party-political or parliamentary nature. On the contrary, his support for it arose out of his firm belief that it offered the only way of permanently securing economic prosperity and consequently political stability. This meant, however, that in this respect too he allied himself very firmly with the middle-class liberals and that he did indeed, as his conservative critics

33

rebuked him for doing, become a champion of the middle-class order in economic and social affairs.

To be sure, as a politician who in his basic attitude always allowed for events taking a negative course, Bismarck recognized the threat to that order earlier and more acutely than the overwhelming majority of his middle-class contemporaries, believing as they did firmly in progress and revelling as they were in economic successes. This was not true as regarded the hidden market and structural weaknesses of the liberal economy; when these suddenly and very clearly emerged in the wake of the crisis of 1873–4 he was as surprised as were almost all the experts. But it was true of the social sphere, for the new structure of society that was becoming more and more sharply defined.

In his search for potential counter-weights to the middle-class liberals' bid for power he had always paid particular attention, right from the start of his political career, to social differences, what they were based on, how they expressed themselves and the directions in which they might be expected to evolve. Evidence of this kind of thinking, this kind of sounding and political probing, is extraordinarily abundant. It ranges from his socio-political activities in the period 1847–50, through the carefully recorded experiences of his Frankfurt years in a world of which he had hitherto known little, to the celebrated conversations with Ferdinand Lassalle. This whole preoccupation culminated in what was at times very intensive examination of actual economic and social conflict situations, actual labour struggles in individual firms and branches of industry in the Prussia of the 1860s. As a pragmatist he found the study of such problems incomparably more important than the wide-ranging theoretical considerations that Lassalle lectured him on.

In this way he had formed a very clear picture of the divergences of social and economic interest within middle-class society and its economic order. He was not alone in this, of course; such things were obvious to everyone with eyes to see. But unlike the vast majority of his contemporaries in the middle-class camp he was only very marginally inclined to adopt a harmonizing approach. Inside that camp people were very ready to make light of such problems as being purely transitional phenomena, adaptive difficulties that with the inexorable progress being made in all spheres of life would soon resolve themselves without any help from outside. Bismarck, on the other hand, used to analysing all relationships and potential conflict situations in terms of their political exploitability, became convinced at an early stage that the true situation was being played down in this way and that here was dynamite lying ready to be used by forces that were prepared to blow the entire middle-class order sky-high.

The great object-lesson seemed to him to be the rebellion of the so-called 'Commune' in Paris in the spring of 1871, a popular movement embracing a broad section of the population of the French capital and directed against the middle-class republic then being set up. As a treaty partner of the government concerned, on whose victory war and peace crucially depended, and as head of the government of the power occupying a part of France, Bismarck had followed and studied this development very closely indeed.

A great many elements had conspired to form this highly heterogeneous coalition of left-wing opponents of the new republican government and the majority in the Versailles-based National Assembly that backed it: opposition to what was held to be excessive knuckling-under to the Prusso-German victor; concern about a possible return to the upper-middle-class politics of the 1830s and 1840s; fear of a clerical, legitimist reaction; and finally the conviction that only an act of revolutionary self-help could secure the social republic and so save the capital from being overwhelmed by the restorationist provinces. But the real driving force behind the Commune was a massive protest against the whole existing social order, by which many people felt in one way or another disadvantaged and even threatened. That protest was capable of being drawn to many different banners and mobilized for a wide variety of ends. Among many others to do so, for example, one of the two leaders of the 'Social Democratic Labour Party' in Germany, August Bebel, laid claim to the Parisian movement for himself and for the objectives of his party. On 25 May 1871, at the height of the bloody fighting in Paris, he referred to the Commune uprising in the Imperial Diet as 'a minor outpost engagement' in the struggle of the European proletariat against the existing social and economic order. 'The main issue in Europe' was, he prophesied, 'yet to come'.[40] This had in turn confirmed Bismarck in his basic appraisal of the whole phenomenon. 'That challenge of the Commune', he said in the autumn of 1878 during the debate in the Diet on his Anti-Socialist Law, had thrown a 'ray of light' on the situation: 'From that moment I recognized the Social Democratic elements as an enemy against which state and society are obliged to defend themselves.'[41]

Nor was that the only occasion on which Bismarck referred to the Commune uprising and the demonstrations of sympathy with the Parisian movement organized by the extreme left; there were many others. And every time he invoked the dangers that threatened to accrue to the existing order from the exploitation of its inherent conflicts of interest and social problems by clever agitators and revolutionary wire-pullers if no one put a stop to their game in time. As early as the beginning of July 1871 he wrote in a directive to the Prussian envoy in Vienna, von Schweinitz, of the need for 'recognition of the principle', in the international sphere as well, 'that Socialist threats to life and property, as they materialized in Paris, come under the heading of common rather than political crimes'.[42] And in a memorandum of 21 October 1871 addressed to the Prussian Minister of Commerce, von Itzenplitz, regarding a conversation with Count Beust, the Austrian Chancellor, he coupled a request to initiate appropriate preliminary groundwork with an outline of his whole programme in this field. He agreed with Beust on two points, he said: '1. Meeting the demands of the working classes by legislative and administrative means so far as is compatible with the general interests of the state. 2. Suppressing agitation dangerous to the state by means of prohibitions and penal laws.'[43] This was the only way, he argued in a detailed letter to Itzenplitz written four weeks later, of 'putting a stop to the Socialist movement in its present state of aberration and guiding it along more wholesome paths in particular by *realizing what appears to be justified in the Socialist demands* and is capable of being realized in the context of the present political and social order'.[44]

Unlike Beust, however, the vast majority of politically influential people in Germany did not share the anxieties and the assessment of the socio-political situation that prompted these reflections, or did so only to a very limited extent. Indeed they saw Bismarck's hints and suggestions primarily as an attempt to press the parties, by invoking supposed dangers from the left in what was already a tried and tested manner, into supporting his government – and dropping their own demands. A great many historians have followed them in this. Bismarck, they say, was here constructing a bogyman that could also be used on the international stage, as witness his talks in this connection, first with Austria and subsequently with Russia as well. The fear of revolution, of social upheaval, which for decades past had been an important bonding agent between the eastern great powers, was thus deliberately focused on a fresh object. For the old bogyman, they point out, namely the liberal and national movement, was no longer up to the task, having meanwhile become a partner of the government, both in Austria and in Germany.

Undoubtedly Bismarck had a keen eye for this aspect of the matter. Nor can it be overlooked that he made repeated use of the social question and the fear of upheaval as a policy instrument, nationally and internationally. But again it is to exaggerate the Machiavellian element in his policy to seek to portray him in this context too as the creator of the thing he made use of. The social problems of an emergent industrial society undoubtedly, in this transitional phase, constituted a powder keg. And it is beyond question that at least some of those who invoked them in a denunciatory manner were also disposed to lay a fuse to that powder and completely blow up society as it existed. We must not, as sometimes tends to happen, see things in the light of the fact that a section of the organized working class subsequently became reconciled to the so-called 'bourgeois state' and above all to the principles of a liberal capitalist economic order and the social order to which it gave rise. Such interpretations misjudge the historical reality of Germany in the 1870s and 1880s. They push the real causes of the developing conflict between the state and organized labour into the background, favouring a one-sidedly personal reading of history. Instead of the reality of steadily worsening social tensions and conflicts of economic interest during the transition to modern industrial society, suddenly we have Bismarck appearing as the man who stood in the way of an early reconciliation between labour and the middle-class liberal order.

In fact the possibility of any such reconciliation was extremely remote at the time. For a compromise that would have gone even some way towards satisfying the rapidly expanding industrial proletariat and its spokesmen, not only was any willingness on the part of the economy and its key representatives lacking; so, above all, were the material prerequisites in the shape of correspondingly increased financial profits. For that reason there is no country in the world where such a compromise was effected at this stage of the development of industrial society. And since the prerequisites were lacking and there was no real prospect of a conciliation of interests, those who were not imbued with an unshakable optimism and unlimited faith in social progress were thoroughly justified in their fear of revolution.

Bismarck was most certainly not so imbued. It is entirely credible, therefore, that anxieties and fears in this regard should have seized him earlier than the vast majority of the liberal middle class, which began to grow increasingly pessimistic only after the slump of 1873–4 and in the wake of the structural crisis that set in at that time.

However, the means by which the German Chancellor had in mind to dispel the 'nightmare of revolutions'[45] and to 'reconcile the majority of workers to the existing order', as he expressed his objective towards the end of 1871,[46] turned out to be of no more use than those he employed against the Centre Party. His first major political opponent, liberalism, he had managed if not to defeat at least to subdue politically by placing himself at the head, in many ways, of the forces, interests and aspirations that went to make it up – economically, nationally, legally and now also in terms of cultural and denominational policy as well as to some extent socially. All this was ruled out from the start in relation to the movements and forces now at issue. Neither the Catholic movement nor the labour movement cherished objectives that, except for details and individual elements, allowed of adaptation to an overall political plan that even someone as flexible as himself could advocate and pursue. Both took him to his political limits, limits that it was impossible for him to overstep: on principle, for one thing, because it would have meant sacrificing key elements of his individuality and of his understanding of himself as a Protestant Christian, a Prussian Junker and a spokesman and defender of a political order built on historical, legitimist foundations; and also for tactical reasons, because he would then have been in danger of finally forfeiting all credibility.

Trapped within those limits, Bismarck reacted in both cases in such a way that failure was, according to all historical experience, a foregone conclusion. He tried to combine direct repression on the one hand with outward concessions and an apparently co-operative attitude towards the supporters of the party concerned on the other. And all without being either able or willing to abandon a politico-social system that made any genuine concessions or serious co-operation impossible.

That system was based on a balance, characteristic of the German Reich of 1871, between the traditional and the newly emergent, bourgeois ruling classes and their respective expectations, ideas and interests. Granted, it favoured one side more than the other, particularly in Prussia, but it never left the other really dissatisfied. On that system, to which he largely owed his successes hitherto, the Bismarck of the period after 1871 believed that he could always fall back. He considered that what was capable of being achieved in his generation and by himself had now been achieved and that the important thing henceforth was to secure and extend it and to defend it against enemies at home and abroad.

This tendency has always been recognized in his foreign policy after 1871 in the switch from an aggressive questioning and adjusting of the status quo to a policy of 'satiety', of attempting to consolidate the new order of things while dropping all further ambitions entertained within his own camp. But it applies equally and indeed particularly to the sphere of domestic policy. Here the securing of what had been achieved on the basis of the constellation of forces and interests that had made it possible now likewise took absolute precedence over everything else.

In both domestic and foreign policy the ground for this switch had already been laid in the foregoing years, the years of dramatic changes and ever new combinations and manoeuvres. In both spheres reference to the limits that would be observed at all costs, together with the care with which Bismarck had avoided anything that might cast serious doubts on the credibility of his assurances to this effect, had been fundamental conditions of his success. Nor had he ever lost his awareness of the fact that the scope he enjoyed for a while in both spheres depended not only on luck and skill but above all on his being regarded as a conservative, a man of forward defence. In both spheres, however, that scope was exhausted by the achievements of 1871. The argument of offensive defence threatened to become less and less credible. This had been true of the annexation of Alsace and Lorraine, and in domestic affairs it was especially true now of the campaign against what was in essence a conservative party, the Centre.

The process marked a turning-point in Bismarck's political career. Granted, the preservation and defence of the internal and external order that had been attained by 1871 were in many respects a logical consequence of the development that had led to the new order and the means, methods and basic approach that had determined it. Yet the switch to them involved something that was in sharp contradiction to Bismarck's policy hitherto and led, at first only superficially and in terms of method but as time went on in substance as well, to a crucial loss of continuity.

Before 1871 Bismarck, a man of the establishment, a conservative, had repeatedly backed the forces of change. He had used them, done deals with them, pretexted them and set them against one another in order to achieve the changes that he wanted precisely in the context of what was established and within the limits beyond which change threatened to place everything in jeopardy. In a way he had enjoyed the advantage of the loyal younger son who avoids all blame when, while acknowledging that context, he seeks his own advantage and his own position, even if things temporarily become a little confused in the process. Now, however, he was in the position of a man for whom movement and change represented not so much opportunity as danger and who must rectify shifts in the distribution of weight, parry thrusts, defuse tensions – in short, preserve as such the system in which, allowing for and exploiting the corresponding endeavours of others, he had once moved so freely.

From now on, if we look deeper and do not, like many contemporaries, let ourselves be blinded by mere activity, action was outweighed by reaction. Not that the former had ever been entirely free, of course, but it had been a great deal more independent and productive and not bound by circumstances and a situation that had at all costs to be preserved. So that while Bismarck seemed – now especially – to be controlling the whole thing most impressively in a series of constantly surprising new moves and actions, in reality the initiative was passing more and more to those forces and tendencies that threatened to question or change it. Little by little they brought about a metamorphosis of the existing order that in the end harmonized ill with its laboriously preserved internal structure. To change that structure and adapt it to the new conditions was a task that exceeded Bismarck's ability. This was not so much a matter of waning flexibility and dynamism; it was due mainly to the fact that his personality and the image of that personality that had become fixed in the public mind imposed natural limits on him in this respect.

This change in political approach, mode of reacting and method is made very evident by a comparison of Bismarck's behaviour towards Ferdinand Lassalle and his General German Workers' Association in 1863–4 with his treatment of the new Centre Party in 1871–2, although the two political movements were not in themselves at all comparable. The Lassalle encounter, although in the end nothing went beyond the realm of speculation, was dominated by an atmosphere of possibility, of new opportunities and new solutions. In the case of the Centre Party, Bismarck was on the defensive from the start. He saw the new party as nothing but an interference factor, a threat to the newly created order. And the same was true subsequently and to an even greater extent of the socialists, Lassalle's successors in the field of labour politics, and their soon dominant Marxist rivals. Overthrowing the old political alliances and instigating a radical reorientation were courses he never, at this stage, even began to contemplate.

His earlier 'Acheronta movebo', his readiness, in pursuit of his own objectives and trusting in his own strength, to enter into alliances even with sworn enemies of the existing order, now came a very poor second to his desire to consolidate the new and to shield and secure it against further change. His policy became increasingly a status quo policy – quite literally, being focused on the internal and external order of 1871. After the turbulent events of the 1860s, of course, it was only at a very late stage, if at all, that many contemporaries became aware of this.

This is particularly true with regard to domestic policy, where rapid changes, principally in the economic and social spheres, together with the political reactions to which they gave rise very soon obscured the initial basic tendency towards the preservation of what had been achieved, above all of the political constellation of 1866–7, and eventually thrust it into the background. But it is also true of foreign policy.

[11]

The Reich and Europe

Immediately after 1871 and the conclusion of the Treaty of Frankfurt Bismarck gave the word that Prussia, as enlarged to form the German Reich, was now definitely 'sated'. It had no further demands of any kind and from now on aspired only to preserve the existing order. There can be no doubt, in retrospect, that he meant entirely what he said. All ideas and desires to the contrary, for example among population groups of German extraction in eastern-central Europe, he henceforth rejected unequivocally and sometimes quite fiercely. At the time, however, many of Europe's politicians were still inclined, after the experiences of the 1860s, to question his sincerity in this respect.

Moreover, a large section of European public opinion agreed with them, invoking – and not just in France – the dangers of a Pan-Germanism that would soon overrun the 1871 frontiers. In the main this was a response to the sort of thing that had been said in Germany in 1870–1 in connection with the demand for the annexation of Alsace and Lorraine. Granted, Bismarck could continue to assume with some justification that the relevant members of the Cabinets of Europe were not seriously going to regard him as an advocate and partisan of an expansive nationalism. His whole conduct hitherto precluded such a view. Even discounting the concrete situation and the objectives he was pursuing in it, it was wholly in accordance with his inner conviction that he wrote to von Schleinitz, the envoy in Vienna, following the outbreak of the war, that he considered 'any policy of Germanic conquest . . . a piece of folly quite beyond all political reason'.[1] But he quite obviously underestimated at first the misgivings that the emergence of the new power in central Europe aroused even among level-headed diplomats and coolly calculating politicians. Europe, he once claimed jokingly in 1872, could now 'always be dealt with, brushed and combed in ten to fifteen minutes at first breakfast'.[2]

Probably the most dramatic expression of those misgivings had been voiced in a speech in the British House of Commons only a few days after the Franco–German armistice. On 9 February 1871 the leader of the conservative opposition, Benjamin Disraeli, commenting on the imminent end–result of developments on the continent, said: 'This war represents the German revolution, a greater political event than the French Revolution of last century . . . There is not a diplomatic tradition which has not been

40

swept away . . . The balance of power has been entirely destroyed and the country which suffers most, and feels the effects of this great change most, is England.'[3]

Undoubtedly this was not only a dramatic but also a dramatizing exaggeration. Bismarck, however, was treating matters too lightly when he reduced such utterances essentially to their tactical motivation in terms of domestic policy. Whether the speaker or writer concerned was giving expression to genuine fears of his own or whether he was merely invoking such fears in his listeners or readers made no great difference. What mattered was the fact that such fears existed and the pressure that, given the chance, they might exert.

In the case of Austria Bismarck acknowledged that they were understandable. The problems of that multi-nation state in a world in which the principle of the national state continued to make headway were familiar to him. It had not been long since he had himself toyed with the idea of disintegrating that state by mobilizing and giving encouragement to its separate nationalities. It was in the nature of things that Vienna should now fear lest the formation of the German national state should inspire a movement in the German districts of Austria in favour of joining that state, a movement that Berlin might turn to its own advantage. As a result there was a risk of the Austrian government seeking safety in an anti-German coalition, even if such a coalition would have been as unpopular in the country as it had been before 1870.

Bismarck therefore concentrated his foreign policy efforts from an early stage on allaying Vienna's fears regarding possible national aspirations on the part of the new Reich and on drawing the Austrian Empire closer to Prusso-Germany. He had already, as soon as the treaties with the south German states were concluded, conveyed to the Austrian government his 'hopes regarding the future of the historically grounded friendship between Austria and Germany'.[4] At the time his motives may still have appeared essentially tactical, as being dictated by his desire to keep Austria neutral. But subsequently it became more and more clear that the Prussian Minister-President was really serious about this. In all sorts of ways he expressed the view that, with their respective spheres of interest and influence now conclusively defined, Berlin and Vienna were natural partners. Following the final conclusion of the peace treaty with France, for example, he succinctly informed the Viennese government once again: 'The aspirations of the group that seeks to incorporate into Germany the German patrimonial lands in Austria do not accord with the goals of our policy.'[5]

Bismarck's partner in the effort, which now went ahead very swiftly, to achieve not only a permanent settlement but also a close association between the two central European empires was, of all people, Count Beust – until then one of his fiercest political opponents. After 1866 Beust had worked for a revision of the decisions of Königgrätz and Nikolsburg and to this end had for a time sought a rapprochement with the now defeated France; he had even, while the war was still going on, toyed with the idea of intervening. If in the end no binding agreements or clear decisions had come of all this, among the many determining factors had been the realization that

41

the kind of preparedness to go to war that such a revision attempt ultimately required was, for a variety of reasons, lacking virtually throughout the empire.

Consequently Count Beust, whom Bismarck had meanwhile begun to court in the most flattering terms, had himself come round to working for a resumption of close relations between the two great powers of central Europe on the fresh basis of recognizing the situation that now existed. Since Bismarck's initial approach in late November 1870 the rapprochement had been making steady progress. It reached its first climax with the meetings between the two emperors that were staged in Ischl and Salzburg in August 1871.

However, those meetings once again brought out very clearly what from the Austrian point of view was the somewhat threatening and for a Greater Germany man such as Beust the particularly painful background to the whole business. At them the German emperor and his Chancellor received an extraordinarily friendly and at times even tumultuous welcome from the overwhelming majority of the population. And there could be little doubt that that welcome was not so much intended for the final reconciliation now beginning to materialize as addressed to the representatives of the new German national state.

So it suited Bismarck very well when in November 1871 Beust came to grief over the highly controversial question of a settlement with the Czech section of the population and had to resign. He was succeeded by the then Hungarian Minister-President, Count Julius Andrássy, a man of 48 years of age who, condemned to death for his part in the Hungarian revolution of 1848–9, had been pardoned only in 1858, had afterwards spent many years abroad, in London and Paris, and had then become one of the chief spokesmen and supporters of the Austro-Hungarian Settlement of 1867. One of the few politicians for whom Bismarck had a degree of personal sympathy, Andrássy had spoken out strongly, unlike the vacillating Beust, against a further federal division of the empire to place Bohemia on an equal footing with Hungary. And, as here in domestic policy, so also in foreign policy, not least in the interests of Hungary, Andrássy was a man of the status quo as constituted in 1866–7 and 1870–1, a rigorous opponent of all efforts at revision.

As such he was the ideal partner for Bismarck, and it is with his name that all the steps on Austria's part were associated that led in the 1870s to a growing rapprochement between Austria-Hungary and the German Reich – up to and including the famous Dual Alliance of October 1879, which brought to a climax the principle of the special relationship between the two central European great powers. The German Chancellor acknowledged Andrássy's personal contribution to this in a most unusual manner, namely in a speech to the Imperial Diet: 'Such a relationship is most auspicious when one's opposite number is a minister with respect to whom, when he gives his word that a thing is true, one is utterly convinced of its being so.'[6]

Far less understandable than the fears expressed by Austria – or so it seemed to Bismarck from the very beginning – were the alleged anxieties of the Russian government and a section of the Russian people. When his eastern neighbour warned of the possibility of the new Reich wishing to expand further and spoke of a threat to the European balance of power, Bismarck smelled, first and foremost, compensation demands of the sort that Russia had successfully advanced only recently in connection with the Straits question. He also identified a desire on the part of the Russian Chancellor, Prince Gorchakov – a man noted for his vanity – to draw attention to himself. As Bismarck said of him: 'He is incapable of stepping over a puddle without examining his reflection in it.'[7]

Here too the German Chancellor was immediately prepared, in accordance with his new policy line, to give Russia binding assurances with regard to the eastern frontier of Prusso-Germany and to remind the Baltic Germans of their obligation of loyalty towards the Russian government and the tsar. For example, he told the former civil governor of Livonia, von Oettingen, at the end of 1872 that, 'despite all [his] sympathy for the Balts', it was 'absolutely impossible' for him 'to do anything at all for the Germans there. If I could, I would put a premium on the emigration of every German from the Baltic provinces to this country.'[8] In conversation with a group of deputies early in 1873 he was even blunter: 'At best we could only get more Poles, and we've yet to digest the ones we have.'[9] Unlike with Austria, however, he was reluctant for the moment to commit himself to anything more than repeated assurances to the effect that, for Berlin, the 'Russian Baltic provinces' were of 'no political consequence'.[10] And he found it distinctly irritating that Russia immediately and violently interfered with the emerging entente between the German Reich and Austria-Hungary: it was not a pleasant thing for him, the tsar declared with feigned ingenuousness, 'when his best friend . . . gets together with someone else and he must wait outside his friend's door, as it were, while the other two consort within'.[11]

Bismarck was afraid that Russia might make use of a resurrected alliance of the three eastern powers, although the distribution of power within it would now be different in order once again, as after 1848, to increase its influence in central Europe. This time too the Russian government took its stand on the idea of the conservative solidarity of the three great monarchies of the east, an idea it had been using since 1815 as a tool and as a tie to bind the alliance together and hold it, not only externally but internally as well, on an arch-conservative course.

Granted, Bismarck had often operated along such lines himself. In his recent discussions with Beust regarding measures to combat the socialist threat there had been talk of the need for solidarity and co-operation between the three empires in the interests of preserving the established order. But the German Chancellor had meanwhile moved far away, both in theory and in practice, from the construction that the Russian government continued to put upon that idea, notwithstanding the changes that had taken place in Russia too since the abolition of serfdom and the reforms of the 1860s.

Forces that in Russia were still operating largely underground, subject to persecution by an autocracy whose powers were still unfettered by any constitution, had meanwhile become, in the Reich, acknowledged partners of the government and indeed pillars of the state and of the monarchy: namely liberalism, the middle-class intelligentsia and the national movement. The same was the case in the Habsburg monarchy. The two states, for all their other differences, had grown to resemble each other very closely in terms of their domestic systems and political practice. In fact they represented something in the nature of a specifically central European type of political order and constitution. This was as distinct from the parliamentary, party-political system of western Europe as it was from the autocratic, police-state system obtaining in Russia.

This similarity in internal structure gave rise, in addition, to a kind of natural affinity between the two great powers of central Europe. As a result of the remarkably parallel development of the two countries' domestic affairs, this lasted right up until the First World War and greatly fostered the rapprochement between them, over and above all calculations at the level of power politics.

It also drew a natural line of demarcation against the autocratic great power to the east, that line being further reinforced in the subsequent course of events by economic and power-political antagonisms in the Balkans – a fact that the flood of First World War propaganda, with its attempt to stress the common interests of the three eastern powers, very largely obscured.

So it was not only his fear of a possible attempt by St Petersburg to start exerting more influence on central Europe once again that prompted Bismarck to hold aloof from Russia's increased endeavours to achieve a rapprochement and to expand what was as yet a wholly informal entente between Germany and Austria into a triple alliance. It was also his awareness that, with no immediate occasion and no immediate objective, such an alliance would have no real substance in present circumstances. On top of that there was his fear of its possibly being misunderstood, both at home and in the forum of west European – particularly British – public opinion. For these reasons, while granting the tsar's urgent wish to be included in the Berlin meeting, planned for September 1872, between the German and Austrian emperors, Bismarck made sure that the declarations and resolutions of the three monarchs and their ministers remained largely non-committal.

The same was true of the 'Three Emperors' Agreement' that came into being on 22 October 1873, when William acceded to the Schönbrunn Convention signed by Tsar Alexander II and the Austrian emperor, Francis Joseph, on 6 June. This consisted of no more than a mutual pledge by the monarchs concerned 'to consolidate the peace currently prevailing in Europe', to do so by means of 'direct, personal negotiation between sovereigns' and above all to stand together 'on the ground of principle'. This last point invoked the spirit of the past once again without investing what was meant with any more solid content than the vague assertion that the principles concerned were 'alone capable of safeguarding and if necessary enforcing the peace of Europe against all convulsions, from whatever quarter they may come'.[12] This, as Bismarck very deliberately placed on record, was the sole objective. The purpose of the agreement was 'to ensure peace . . . on a long-term basis', not, 'as in the former Holy

Alliance, to oppress the peoples through the medium of an understanding among their rulers'.[13]

These assurances notwithstanding, in the minds of the European public and the rest of Europe's Cabinets the meeting and the agreement between the three emperors almost inevitably gave rise to certain fears and expectations and to estimates of the future policy of the Reich that, while they contradicted one another in many respects, contributed as a whole towards further increasing the atmosphere of insecurity and mistrust. Was Bismarck seeking to resume the policy of forming a reactionary bloc, they asked themselves – the kind of policy that Metternich and after him primarily the tsar's governments had pursued? What about his plea for freedom to form foreign policy coalitions without regard to the domestic relations and systems of government obtaining in individual countries – had that been mere tactics, and was the true nature of his policy only now becoming apparent? Or was all this simply a fresh manoeuvre, yet another bold move to pave the way for a further expansion of Prusso-German power? The speculations were endless, not only among the public but also among diplomats and those in positions of political responsibility. However, for all their inconsistency and mutually contradictory character, there was one thing those speculations had in common: they centred without exception on the Reich and on Bismarck. It was in Berlin that people sought the key to future developments, not in St Petersburg, Vienna, Paris, or London; it was Berlin that people expected to produce the crucial initiatives, make the decisive thrusts.

This was the new situation after 1871, and it took the man most immediately affected by it, the Chancellor and Foreign Minister of the German Reich, some considerable time, for all his experience, properly to adjust to it and to the consequences that flowed from it. He was accustomed to the power for whose foreign policy he was responsible operating as one power among many, whereby he was not infrequently able to shelter in the lee of the power that was tacitly regarded as dominant. The deliberate ambivalence of relationships, the diffuse question of where loyalties lay, the difficulty of distinguishing between reaction and initiative in this tangled situation, the multiplicity of almost equivalent interests – that was the field in which he had learnt to move with such consummate skill. That was where he had gained his great successes. Now, however, he found that he and the Reich were suddenly at the centre of the action. He was now seen as virtually calling the tune as far as the European system was concerned, as representing the power that was regarded from henceforth as the number one threat to the balance of power in Europe.

From this viewpoint, sometimes entirely contradictory interpretations of one and the same process led to the identical end-result. An example was when many people in London were inclined to see the bloc formation allegedly represented by the Three Emperors' Agreement as the prelude to an offensive policy of German hegemonic expansion, whereas St Petersburg looked upon the restraint evinced by Germany in the relevant negotiations as indicating a desire to retain a free hand for future initiatives. This was capable, subsequently, of leading to reactions that in the pre-1871 power-political constellation, the one to which Bismarck had been accustomed and from which he still half-unconsciously took his bearings, would almost certainly not have ensued.

Such a case occurred in the spring of 1875. It taught Bismarck his big lesson for the future. After it he very firmly and deliberately proceeded to adapt himself to the new situation and the new circumstances. The occurrence was the so-called 'Is War in Sight?' crisis, which owed its name to a sensational article that appeared under that headline in the Berlin *Post*, a paper regarded as being close to the government, on 8 April 1875. This represented the culmination of German efforts to put pressure on France, which had recovered its strength with surprising speed, and in particular to deter it from further enlarging its army. Whether the article, like the earlier one entitled 'New Alliances' in the *Kölnische Zeitung* of 5 April, was or was not directly inspired by Bismarck is relatively unimportant. At any rate it was entirely in line with his policy and intentions and was, as he said himself, 'likely . . . to have a beneficial, peaceful effect'.[14]

Universal compulsory military service had been reintroduced in France shortly after the conclusion of the Treaty of Frankfurt, and now a law passed by the French National Assembly on 13 March 1875 had placed the organization of the French army on an entirely new basis. That law upset a great many of the calculations of the German general staff. France had already forced an early withdrawal from the occupied areas by speeding up payment of the war indemnity, prompting doubts as to whether the old enemy's material strength had been correctly appraised and warnings to that effect to the political leadership. Now, however, the task of maintaining permanent military superiority over a diplomatically isolated France seemed scarcely feasible any more. Consequently there was quite open talk in the German camp of the possibility of a preventive war. This was to reduce the military and material strength of France once and for all to a level where it ceased to represent a danger to the Reich.

Unlike the chief of the German general staff, Count Moltke, Bismarck probably never really gave the idea serious consideration. But he was clearly determined not only to exert the most massive pressure but also to take the opportunity of reminding France of its isolation among the European powers and conclusively proving to it how hopeless were its efforts to secure revenge. 'All Europe' ought now to 'appreciate', he declared, 'that these Redskins in their patent-leather boots are and will very likely always be incorrigible disturbers of the European peace'.[15]

The plan completely miscarried. In the capable hands of Duke Louis de Decaze, French foreign policy even managed in a skilful counter-move to break out of its old isolation for the first time. Both Britain and Russia let it be known, albeit with much diplomatic polish and in cautiously reserved terms, that they would not allow France to be weakened any further. The joint suggestion was that, were Germany to continue its policy of confrontation, a serious situation threatened to arise.

The German Chancellor was thus put firmly in his place. What he found particularly irritating was the behaviour of his Russian counterpart, Prince Gorchakov. Gorchakov was unable to resist drawing particular attention to his own part in the whole affair. In a telegraphed circular to Russia's diplomatic missions that he sent out following a routine visit by the tsar to Berlin in the middle of May 1875 and the contents of which he repeated in various semi-official pronouncements, he intimated that it was only as a result of Russian pressure and his own personal skill that peace had been maintained. Gorchakov, said Bismarck in his memoirs, had rewarded him as 'a trusting and unsuspecting friend' by 'suddenly and insidiously' leaping on his shoulders 'there to stage . . . a circus performance' at his expense.[16]

His irritation was such that in retrospect, manifesting his usual relaxed attitude to his sources, he had Gorchakov express himself in even stronger terms than he had in fact done. At the time, however, in 1875, it did not prevent him from making a sober analysis of the really crucial supra-personal elements and aspects of the new international situation that had now emerged with great clarity and drawing from it certain overdue conclusions. It was a situation that the German Chancellor had already envisaged very clearly as much as two-and-a-half years before. 'Our chief danger for the future', he had written to William I early in December 1872, 'will begin the moment France is once again regarded by the royal courts of Europe as a potential ally.' Back in 1872 his bet had still been that 'in its present uncertain and disrupted situation' France was not yet so regarded. It was in the light of that situation that he had warned against intervening in France in favour of a restoration of the monarchy, as the ambassador in Paris, Count Harry Arnim, had urged in the interests of the monarchical idea. 'To the allied monarchies of Europe', Bismarck had said then, 'the Parisian crater represents absolutely no danger; they consider it will burn itself out and do the rest of Europe the service of providing it with yet another terrifying instance of what is happening to France under republican democracy.'[17] Now, however, it had been shown that, in view of the altered power-political situation, even a republican France could count on the support of the other powers. New ways must therefore be found of preventing dangerous coalitions from forming that might one day come to include France.

Bismarck now saw clearly that, if he did not want shortly to find himself once again in the same sort of situation as in April and May 1875, he must not only take into account the peculiarly exposed position of the Reich at the heart of Europe, between east and west in the political as well as in the geographical sense. He must also make increased allowance for the mistrust and the fears that the emergence of this new power in central Europe had aroused in many quarters. The policy of the Reich, Bismarck now realized, must henceforth proceed with the utmost caution. It must try to avoid anything that might even remotely suggest to the most hyper-critical observer intentions of an aggressive nature.

A maxim of this kind was not of course the same thing as a practical policy, let alone anything amounting to a foreign policy system. There was also a risk that, applied too starkly and conspicuously, it might lead the Reich into the kind of arch-conservative opposition to all progress that could spell problems for the government at home as well and might even, in certain circumstances, render it vulnerable to political blackmail from all quarters. Over and above the day-to-day business of diplomacy, therefore, Bismarck was much preoccupied in the weeks and months following the 'Is War in Sight?' crisis by the question of what constellations of the European powers, what alliances and options might be most likely on the one hand to reassure the Cabinets of Europe and European public opinion regarding the intentions of the Reich and on the other to safeguard the country from excessive dependence in any one direction and ensure that it retained the necessary freedom of action.

As always in his political life, Bismarck arrived at the foreign policy system that was to preserve and maintain to his advantage the decisions of 1866 and 1870–1 not at his desk, not by any purely theoretical route, but through the actual course of historical developments. That course was determined by something that, while not unexpected in the long term, now supervened very abruptly, namely a fresh flare-up of the situation in the Balkans, the so-called 'Eastern Question'. Coming shortly after the 'Is War in Sight?' crisis, this once again focused the attention of almost all the European great powers on the south-eastern part of the continent – and did so in a way that Berlin found most welcome.

'The Eastern Question', Bismarck had stated aphoristically not long after taking office as Prussian Foreign Minister, 'is an area in which we can help our friends and harm our enemies without being inhibited to any great extent by direct interests of our own.'[18] Events in connection with the war of 1870–1 had subsequently confirmed this estimate. Unlike the other four great powers of Europe, each of which was heavily committed in one way or another by concrete interests in the Balkans, Prusso-Germany had nothing directly to gain in that part of the world, nothing that would even have been 'worth the healthy bones of a single Pomeranian musketeer', as Bismarck put it on one occasion towards the end of 1876.[19]

This fresh crisis in the Balkans gave German policy, which was thus in the priveleged position of the largely uninvolved third party, the chance to influence the balance of power in Europe. It further provided it with an opportunity of, if not entirely dispelling, at least considerably diminishing the prevailing climate of mistrust concerning the Reich and the man responsible for its foreign policy. Not only did Bismarck make vigorous use of that opportunity; he also derived from it the basic pattern of his future foreign policy in terms of method and objective.

This was the fourth flare-up of the Eastern Question since the beginning of the century, and like all those that had gone before it had its origins in the clearly inexorable internal collapse of the Ottoman Empire. The spark in this instance was provided by rebellions in Bosnia and Herzegovina. The inhabitants of both districts, which had been under Turkish rule for centuries, had meanwhile been 'awakened' nationally by appeals to their history, language and religion. In the spring of 1876 Bulgaria followed suit. And when shortly afterwards the already largely autonomous Serbia, in alliance with Montenegro, formally declared war on Turkey, practically the entire Balkan Peninsula was in flames.

It seemed obvious to everyone of any perception that behind the demands of the Balkan peoples for independence and self-government and at least indirectly aiding and abetting them was Russia. Citing a double title as natural leader of the Slav nations and protecting power of Orthodox Christianity, St Petersburg was believed to be seeking by this means to extend its sphere of influence in the direction of Constantinople and the Mediterranean.

Up to now Britain, France and to an increasing extent Austria too had based their resistance to Russian expansionism on the principle – repeatedly invoked in international treaties – of the territorial integrity of Turkey. However, with the emergence of ever stronger and more self-assured national independence movements in Turkey's European territories the compromise formula aimed at preserving the balance of power in Europe had become increasingly problematic. It too obviously conflicted with the principles of the right of self-determination that the two western great powers in particular, which with their parliamentary governments were involved in a continuing process of internal democratization, found it hard to repudiate where European territories were concerned. The efforts of France and Britain were therefore initially directed, in concert with those of Austria-Hungary, at persuading Turkey to make voluntary concessions. The intention was to avoid giving Russia any reason to intervene directly.

The Pforte, however, would have none of it, particularly as its army soon had the rebellions under control. Constantinople was convinced that in Paris and more especially in London the argument of self-interest would once again prevail in the end, making it appear to the two western governments urgently necessary that, in order to protect their own positions in the eastern Mediterranean, they should work for the preservation of the Ottoman Empire in its present form.

Under pressure from a steadily mounting wave of anti-Turkish feeling at home, the Russian government declared war on the Pforte at the beginning of April 1877. In alliance with Romania, which had had a Hohenzollern on the throne since 1866, and in the name of the rights and demands of the tsar's Slav co-religionists in the Balkans, Russia forced the enemy into submission within a year. In March 1878, at the gates of Constantinople, St Petersburg imposed peace terms on Turkey through the Treaty of San Stefano that took almost no account of the interests of the other European great powers. By setting up a Princedom of Greater Bulgaria entirely dependent on itself, Russia made itself virtually master of the Balkans all the way to the shores of the Aegean. This, however, was a situation that neither Britain nor Austria-Hungary was prepared to accept, so that in the spring of 1878 a major European conflict looked imminent.

Up until this point German policy, while keeping a most careful eye on developments in all their ramifications, had maintained the strictest neutrality. Even now it made it clear that Berlin had no thought of siding with anyone. Bismarck had laid down the posture to be adopted by the Reich as early as October 1876: 'The more acute the situation becomes, the more clearly, in my opinion, we must remember and in our diplomatic dealings give expression to the fact that our main interest lies not in this, that, or the other arrangement of the circumstances of the Turkish Empire but in the position in which the powers friendly to us are placed with regard to ourselves and one another. The question of whether, as a result of the Eastern troubles, we end up on permanently bad terms with Britain, even more with Austria, but most of all with Russia, is of infinitely greater importance for the future of Germany than all Turkey's relations with its subjects and with the European powers.'[20] The sole but nevertheless very decided interest of the Reich, so the Chancellor informed everyone, was that a settlement should be found and an armed conflict avoided. For that he was personally prepared to make every effort and to bring all his influence to bear. At first Bismarck characterized his potential role as being that of 'mediator' – an allusion to Goethe's *Elective Affinities* – and ultimately as being that of the 'honest broker' whose one aim is to make sure that 'the deal really comes off.'[21] Not, of course, that his attitude was quite as disinterested and lacking in personal objectives as that. No one expected it to be. But although no one was quite sure what it boiled down to, either, it did appear not to be in outright conflict with the interests and aspirations of any of the powers involved.

This had been put to the test on more than one occasion over the past two years, most persistently by Russia. German policy had itself provided the opportunity here. As its commitment to the rebel peoples of the Balkans grew, so did St Petersburg's fear that the Reich might take this opportunity, possibly in conjunction with Austria-Hungary, to stab it in the back. In order to reassure Russia, early in September 1876 Berlin had dispatched the notoriously arch-conservative and Russophile Field Marshal Edwin von Manteuffel to the court of the tsar, currently residing in Warsaw, with a personal letter written in the emperor's own hand. William's letter had included the sentence: 'The memory of your attitude towards myself and my country from 1864 to 1870–1 will govern my policy towards Russia, come what may.'[22]

That attitude had been one of benevolent neutrality. And that was exactly the prospect that William wished for his part to hold out to the tsar. It was a question, as Bismarck put it in a dicate drawn up at the end of August, of a renewed assurance 'that we will under no circumstances be a party to hostile or even merely diplomatic manoeuvres against Russia'[23] – not, however, of the converse, namely a guarantee of active support. But the wording was so general as to be easily capable of being misunderstood, particularly by someone who was anxious to do so. And this was how Russian policy did in fact make use of it to ask Berlin, with brutal frankness, the crucial question.

This would scarcely have been possible by normal diplomatic channels. However, the court of the tsar included a special German military plenipotentiary who, as someone enjoying particular trust, was also used as a kind of diplomatic short cut for informal contacts at the highest level. And that military plenipotentiary, one General von Werder, allowed himself to be 'misused' by Gorchakov for Russian ends, as Bismarck put it in a state of high irritation. He sent a telegram from Livadiya on 1 October to say that, 'should it come to war with Austria', the tsar expected 'His Majesty the Emperor to behave exactly as he [the tsar] did in 1870'. The tsar, he added, spoke of this 'almost daily' and desired 'urgent confirmation'.[24]

This had placed Berlin in an extremely delicate situation, for a reply in the negative would inevitably have been interpreted as taking sides against Russia. That would in turn have mobilized everyone's mistrust of the Reich afresh and probably forced Berlin into commitments that conflicted with its own interests and threatened to make it forfeit independence for no discernible gain. Bismarck had attempted to extricate himself from this situation by declining 'to reply, *in abstracto*, without any reference to actual circumstances',[25] to so 'theoretical' a question[26] – in other words, to write Russian policy what amounted to a blank cheque. This had not been particularly convincing, nor had it been the sort of answer to allay mistrust of the Reich's real motives. But at least it had not destroyed all hope of support in the future. When news leaked out – with the active assistance of the Reich and its diplomatic corps – that Berlin was reacting in a similar manner to corresponding approaches from other parties, this refusal to take sides or enter into any commitments had eventually been accepted, so to speak, for want of anything better. It did at least seem to leave everything open as far as the future was concerned.

But it had been a long haul, during which the Reich had found itself not only subject to constantly renewed diplomatic pressure but also exposed to the danger of total isolation and the possibility of the powers uniting behind its back. The central question that had arisen out of this – and preoccupied Bismarck more and more after the Russian approach in the autumn of 1876 – was this: was the Eastern Question sufficiently explosive and were the antagonisms between the various European powers sufficiently great, if not to preclude such a danger, at least very substantially to reduce it?

Even on the basis of a scepticism that had been enormously enhanced by the experience of the 'Is War in Sight?' crisis and that in the words of a French journalist had led to what was literally a 'cauchemar des coalitions', a nightmare of hostile alliances, the German Chancellor did eventually arrive at a cautiously positive answer to that question. Nor was that all. He derived from it the general direction and objectives of his future foreign policy. All this is encapsulated in a note that he dictated to his son Herbert during an extended stay at the north Bavarian health resort of Bad Kissingen at the height of the Russo-Turkish War. This not only defined – in terms that rightly became famous – the estimate that he had meanwhile arrived at with regard to the European power constellation and the possibilities it contained for the Reich. It also sketched in broad outline the long-term conclusions that he believed must be drawn from that estimate as far as the policy of the Reich was concerned.[27]

Even in their outward form the thoughts contained in the four sections of the so-called 'Kissingen Dictate' of 15 June 1877 reflected what in Bismarck's eyes was the most important basic fact of European politics and hence of world politics. They began and ended with remarks concerning the relationship between Britain and Russia. The conviction underlying all the rest was that it was this, rather than anything else, that governed the question of war and peace and consequently the preservation of the status quo in Europe. The Chancellor assumed with complete confidence that the antagonism between these two powers, rivals in many parts of the world, was ultimately insuperable and that the 'Whale' and the 'Bear', as they were respectively known at the time would never really reach an understanding, at least not in the foreseeable future. So a regional settlement between them in the eastern Mediterranean not only held no threats but was on the contrary highly desirable. 'I want us', Bismarck said at the beginning of this document, 'without being obtrusive about it, actually to encourage the British if they have designs on Egypt.' He went on: 'If Britain and Russia were to agree on the basis of the former having Egypt and the latter the Black Sea, both would be in a position to content themselves with the preservation of the status quo for a long time to come and would nevertheless, as far as their wider interests are concerned, be plunged once more into a rivalry that makes them virtually incapable of participating in coalitions against us, quite apart from Britain's internal difficulties in that regard.'

For the present, then, they were safe from a coalition taking in Russia and Britain at the same time. But they must constantly allow for the possibility of a triple coalition including either power separately: one 'based on the Western powers with Austria acceding' or, 'possibly even more dangerous', one on a 'Russo-Austro-French' basis. There was also the fact that 'a high degree of intimacy between two of the three last-named powers' would 'provide the third at any time with the means of putting very painful pressure on us'. So if there had been talk in France of this 'cauchemar des coalitions', all he could say was: 'That kind of nightmare will long and possibly always remain a very legitimate one for a German minister.'

The outcome of the present eastern crisis might, however, offer some hope of a substantial alleviation of the nightmare. Looking beyond the details, Bismarck summarized his expectations in this regard under five headings: first, an eastward shift in the focal points of both Austrian and Russian interests; as a result of this, 'occasion for Russia to adopt a heavily defensive posture in the East and along its coasts and to need us as an ally'; thirdly, a partial agreement between Britain and Russia along the lines indicated; fourthly, 'separation of Britain from a France still hostile to us because of Egypt and the Mediterranean'; and fifthly, 'relations between Russia and Austria making it difficult for them both jointly to put together the anti-German conspiracy against us to which centralist or clerical elements in Austria might, for example, be disposed'. And he went on, summing up once again his analysis of the situation and his projection of his goal in a particular case and at the same time proceeding to draw generally valid long-term conclusions: 'If I were fit for work I could complete and elaborate the picture I have in mind: not that of any acquisition of lands but that of an overall political situation in which all powers except France have need of us and are as far as possible kept from forming coalitions against us by their relations with one another.'

These words have since been quoted hundreds of times as representing perhaps the most precise summary of his foreign policy objectives, of his 'system' during the 1870s and 1880s, and beyond that as embodying a classic statecraft transcending the narrow confines of the immediate present. Both quite rightly, no doubt. But Bismarck, unlike many of his later admirers, never for one moment lost sight, in these entirely action-oriented meditations that grew out of his first-hand perceptions and experience, of the *rebus sic stantibus* and the limits of the feasible. He came back once again, persistently and in a thoroughly sceptical spirit, to relations between Britain and Russia and the future policy and development of their two enormous empires: the Straits would remain a sore spot even after a British occupation of Egypt because London would always be afraid of the Russians advancing further. Even a formally established 'double-locking system with the Dardanelles for Britain and the Bosphorus for Russia' was probably unsatisfactory as far as the British were concerned, containing as it did 'the risk for Britain that its Dardanelles fortifications could possibly be more easily taken by land forces than defended'. He added: 'The same mental reservation will probably obtain on the Russian side, and for a generation they may perhaps be content with the closure of the Black Sea.' What form the whole thing would ultimately take and how long it would last were 'matters for negotiation' and depended on further developments: 'The overall outcome, as I envisage it, could equally well emerge after as before the decisive battles of this war.'

We see clearly here how close together opportunity and danger were for Bismarck in what he saw as the most desirable constellation of powers as far as the Reich was concerned. He was fully aware of how quickly, particularly in the case of Russia and Britain, the dynamics of power interests could upset all his calculations. He clung to the view that even in the extreme case of war between Britain and Russia the policy objective of the Reich must remain the same, namely 'to procure, at Turkey's expense, a peace satisfactory to both'. But it was an open question whether such a readjustment would succeed. The same was true of whether the powers concerned would allow themselves to be tied into the European system on a long-term basis and submit to its traditional control mechanisms and modes of procedure.

Behind all this, albeit only in vague outline, was a very much more critical problem as far as the future was concerned: was the basic structure of European power relations with its concentration on the actual continent of Europe and its tendency to speak in terms of peripheral powers, peripheral areas and shifting conflicts out to the periphery – was this really still equal to the realities of the situation or rather to the new reality now emerging? Was it not the truth of the matter that the old European system was gradually giving way to a kind of world political system, the hidden centres of which must of necessity be quite different? In other words, was the 'official' reality, so to speak, with its problems, conflicts and apparent solutions, simply covering up another reality, unofficial as yet but in fact of enormous import for the future?

In his circling round relations between Britain and Russia one senses in Bismarck something of the feeling that behind the constantly changing situations and current centres of conflict with which he was familiar a metamorphosis of the European system was taking place. This threatened to lead to a far more radical change in all relations than everything that appeared to jeopardize it acutely and in part at the moment. Not that this was more than a presentiment as yet. But it was sufficient to heighten his awareness that, given the position of the Reich, any foreign policy was a tightrope walk in which even the tiniest step must be undertaken with the greatest care and attention. 'Not for us a policy like that of Frederick II at the start of the Seven Years' War – of suddenly falling on the enemy as he prepares to attack', he told the Free Conservative deputy Lucius a few days after composing the Kissingen Dictate. 'That would indeed be to smash the eggs from which very dangerous chicks might emerge.'[28]

Bismarck's now famous speech in the Imperial Diet on 19 February 1878 made this very clear to a German public that was still in many ways luxuriating in a sense of its own power. It was delivered after the armistice but before Russia had dictated the Treaty of San Stefano, a 'victor's peace' that was highly provocative towards Britain and very nearly led to war between the two powers – an eventuality that Bismarck had not ruled out as early as the middle of 1877.[29]

Replying to an interpellation from the ranks of the two liberal parties and the Free Conservatives regarding the attitude of the Reich government towards the Eastern Question, he sought at first to place the most innocuous interpretation possible on the armistice terms. Only then did he go into the part Germany might play at the kind of European great power conference that Vienna had meanwhile suggested. Under himself as director of German foreign policy it would be neither that of an 'arbiter' nor 'merely' that of a 'schoolmaster'. Rather it would be very strictly confined to that of an intermediary, 'an honest broker who wants to see that the deal really comes off'.

One requirement for such a part was a good relationship with all the powers concerned, which because of its policy hitherto the Reich was fortunate enough to enjoy. And the second requirement was a readiness to extend a welcome to every solution conducive to agreement and understanding, in other words to be committed to nothing substantive in advance. Even at the conference table German policy must avoid giving any impression that its desire to get this or that compromise accepted was greater than its impartiality: 'If instead of arguments reference is made to the balance of power', it might be possible to get such a compromise through. However, the party affected would 'make a note of this and charge it' to the appropriate account. As a state that from the point of view of its interests was wholly uninvolved, Germany would eventually pay for such a course by one day having to pick up part of the bill for the compromise arrived at.

Probably no one but Bismarck, given a nation in which thinking in terms of power had meanwhile become so prevalent, not least as a result of his own policy and his own successes, could quite openly have imposed upon it a policy of extreme restraint and called upon it deliberately to renounce any kind of demonstration of strength and influence. That very fact, of course, enormously enhanced his personal standing in the international sphere. In the eyes of St Petersburg, London, Vienna and even Paris he now increasingly became the man who was not only prepared but was probably alone in being in a position to keep within bounds, for the sake of peace in

Europe and an order acceptable to all the powers, German demands for power and prestige and the forces of German nationalism.

The troublemaker of Europe, whom both the British and the Russian governments had only recently believed must be put in his place, had in the space of a few years become a kind of guarantor of the European order. Bismarck and the Reich now appeared to embody the basic principles and regulators of that order. They had come to represent the 'lead trimming . . . that always brings the figure back to the upright position', as Bismarck had once put it with regard to the relationship between Germany and Austria.[30]

This was the Europe of the existing order, of the status quo, of the established powers. It was not surprising, therefore, that his policy was strongly criticized by all who were unwilling to accept the existing order and who after the experiences of the last few decades expected external changes to be accompanied by changes at home. They included the Centre Party, which accordingly made common cause with Austria for the formation of an anti-Russian bloc. And they included above all the Social Democrats, whose spokesman, Wilhelm Liebknecht, called in that same session of the Diet on 19 February 1878 – wholly in the spirit of Karl Marx, incidentally – for a determined and active policy of containment vis-à-vis Russia. Otherwise, said Liebknecht, there would 'come a time when peace is no longer possible, when the power of Russia asserts itself in such a way that the sword has to be drawn'.[31] But surreptitious voices could already be heard saying the same thing in the liberal camp as well. They spoke of the need offensively to maintain Germany's position in what were emerging as the new dimensions of a world political system, and at the same time they looked for some change at home.

What critics of Bismarck's post-1871 foreign policy repeatedly pointed to as its fixation on the status quo could of course serve only as an additional recommendation in the present situation. In fact the kind of criticism that sought to brand it as having no future was positively welcome to Bismarck in the circumstances. The fact was, over and above the ever present need in every system of powers to safeguard the status quo against change, on the home front as well nearly all the European powers had at that time swung behind a policy of strict preservation of the existing order.

In Britain a conservative Cabinet under Disraeli had replaced Gladstone's liberal reform ministry in 1874 and had now clearly thrown the helm right round, particularly regarding social policy, despite certain concessions in matters of detail. In France the republicans had in fact, albeit with great difficulty, beaten off an attempt by the right to restore the monarchy in 1877; but the majority of the Republican leadership was convinced that the only way to make their victory stick was to grant increased concessions to the demands of the right and to resist all leftward tendencies. And in Austria too the period of liberal ascendency was clearly nearing its end – not to mention Russia, where all the tendencies towards a liberal relaxation that had marked the 1860s had long since been abandoned and where now in particular the autocratic government of the tsar found itself facing the onslaught of revolutionary forces.

Trends of development were emerging throughout Europe that were crucially to influence the politics of the 1880s. They found their first expression in a preference for a foreign policy dedicated to the unconditional preservation of the existing order and catering to the need to maintain external power intact. That was exactly the policy of Bismarck. With it he once again showed himself to be a man who possessed a highly developed feeling for the prevailing tendencies of his day, for its expectations, hopes and fears, and was able as it were directly, without ruminating too much about his reasons for doing so, to translate them into terms of practical policy.

It was this, over and above all points of detail, that formed the basis of his paramount position at the congress of European powers that met in Berlin from 13 June to 13 July 1878. Another factor, surely not to be underestimated, was that the congress took place in a situation of heightened domestic crisis in the Reich, following two attempts on the emperor's life. This strikingly underlined once again the fears and anxieties that lay behind such a policy.

The Congress of Berlin, which found Bismarck at the apogee of his influence in European affairs, precisely on account of his extreme caution and restraint, came at the end of a long, long road. Predictably, Britain in particular had categorically refused to accept the results of the Treaty of San Stefano, which contrary to previous usage had not been agreed upon between the great powers in advance. The negotiations that, with Bismarck's cautious assistance, were promptly initiated between London and St Petersburg had for long periods teetered on the brink of military conflict. And it had taken the most vigorous efforts on the part of the chief Russian negotiator, the London ambassador Count Shuvalov, to get the compromise that was finally arrived at accepted by the hawks at home, who were led by the Russian ambassador in Constantinople and virtual author of the treaty in question, Count Ignatiev.

That compromise rested on what to Bismarck was the very welcome condition that the key points should already have been settled in bilateral agreements prior to the congress of European powers that, at the prompting of Andrássy, it was now proposed to hold. The whole thing was then simply to be placed before the congress for its blessing. In this way British policy wished to ensure in advance that the congress did not – for example, by way of a change of course possibly being imposed on the Reich and a reactivation of the Three Emperors' Agreement of 1873, which was after all still in existence – become a tool of Russian policy.

So it was beforehand, on 30 May 1878, that London and St Petersburg agreed that part of the 'Greater Bulgaria' called into being at San Stefano, namely the province of Eastern Rumelia, should be returned to Turkey, albeit under a Christian governor to be appointed with the approval of the great powers. Five days later, on 4 June, under a treaty that was at first kept secret, Britain took as a reward for its successful championship of the Turkish cause the right to occupy the island of Cyprus – the 'key to western Asia', as Disraeli called it.[32] And, to ensure that Austria-Hungary agreed to these arrangements, on 6 June, likewise before the congress opened, Vienna was granted the right to occupy Bosnia and Herzegovina.

All this was pure power-political wheeling and dealing. The principle of the territorial integrity of Turkey was now finally abandoned, with all three interested powers appropriating parts of the Ottoman Empire. But the rival principle too, that of the right to national self-determination, was observed only to a very limited extent here, namely in so far as it happened to fit the power-political equation. The demands of power were now finally and quite openly declared to constitute the sole guideline of all foreign policy dealings. There was no longer even a pretence of the power of a state being required, in foreign affairs as well, to serve an ideal and be harnessed to higher ends. Power itself became an ideal; it became an end in itself, an ideology. Virtually the only limits to the spread of a nation's power and power-seeking that were now deemed worth acknowledging lay in the rival and equally legitimate power interests of others, in what rational calculation saw as invincible enemies or enemy alliances.

But what if, in the wake of developments that could no longer be successfully controlled or offset, that status quo began to slip? What if, influenced by internal changes or dangers in individual states, coalitions did after all once again begin to form that were governed by other elements than purely external, power-political interests? That was the worry that, as the representative of a power whose very geographical position appeared to make it particularly vulnerable in such an eventuality, Bismarck had constantly before him. It even overshadowed his outward triumph at the Congress of Berlin.

Although the basic decisions had already been taken before the leading representatives of the European great powers met in Berlin under the chairmanship of the Chancellor of the German Reich, many details still needed to be finalized. Russia was expecting the backing of Germany particularly over the frontier questions that still awaited settlement. Nor was that all. Doubtless St Petersburg had still not altogether given up hope of regaining the upper hand during the course of negotiations. The tsar's government was banking on the Reich, all its declarations of principle notwithstanding, when faced with a choice between the British and Russian proposals, opting for the Russian in the interests of covering its rear in future, chiefly against France.

Bismarck disappointed Russia's hopes virtually all along the line; indeed for the sake of his plan he had to disappoint them if he was not to make nonsense of all that had gone before. Doing so was made considerably easier for him by the growing conflict of economic interests in the agrarian sector of which the people who had hitherto been the chief supporters of a pro-Russian policy, namely the landed aristocracy of the districts east of the Elbe, were beginning to bear the brunt. But that was simply an additional element; it was not the decisive one. What was at issue here was the preservation of the European balance of power on which the security and power of the Reich so crucially depended, as did Bismarck's own position at home and the policy he was pursuing there. And he agreed with his opponents on the domestic policy front, even including Liebknecht, that at the moment that balance was under the greatest threat from Russia.

Any suggestion of concrete concessions, which St Petersburg might mistake for encouragement, must in his opinion be scrupulously avoided. That meant, however, even if Bismarck repeatedly sought to disguise the fact, that the Reich leaned towards the British position on every point at issue. In the end, therefore, Britain became the real beneficiary of the entire crisis. As Disraeli triumphantly remarked, London could now confidently assume that the loose Three Emperors' Agreement of 1873 was finally a thing of the past and that with it the danger of an ominous anti-British coalition had been removed for the foreseeable future. 'Our great object', the British statesman wrote two years later, 'was to break up, and permanently prevent, the Alliance of the Three Empires, and I maintain there never was a general diplomatic result more completely effected.'[33]

In the end, in fact, the Russians were more than disappointed with the attitude of the German Chancellor, whom everyone was courting. This was true not only of the politicians involved, with the prestige-seeking Prince Gorchakov at their head. It was especially true of Russian public opinion. Under growing pressure from that quarter St Petersburg quite soon decided to present Berlin with a choice between joining with Russia in a firm alliance, not to say a kind of bloc, and facing the permanent hostility of the tsardom.

Not only did this appear finally to have robbed the alliance between the three eastern powers of any kind of basis. It also seemed to have destroyed the fundamental assumption of Bismarck's foreign policy plan as laid down in the Kissingen Dictate. Proceed how it might, there could no longer be any question of Berlin having a free hand in foreign affairs and certainly none of 'an overall political situation in which all powers except France have need of us and are . . . kept from forming coalitions against us by their relations with one another'. On the contrary. The eventuality that Bismarck had spoken of as constituting his nightmare in 1877 now seemed almost inevitable: a triple alliance against the Reich either 'based on the Western powers with Austria acceding' or on a 'Russo-Austro-French' basis. A constellation threatened to emerge that would in essence be determined solely by the worldwide antagonism of Britain and Russia and by the mutual interests of their two major empires.

There were already many people, both on the right and on the left, who believed that this was in any case going to be the constellation of the future and that the Reich would one day have to make its choice. But Bismarck was determined to avoid that choice, whatever happened. He was anxious to seek the future of the Reich – and hence indirectly of his own domestic system – as it were between the fronts, in a position of self-sufficient independence vis-à-vis west and east alike.

Whether he believed that this would be possible in the long term and, if not, how long he thought it would be possible are matters on which he expressed himself only in very vague and inconsistent terms. But numerous remarks of his do suggest that he was far from optimistic and increasingly assigned shorter and shorter time-scales to everything. Be that as it may, for the time being he stuck to the foreign policy objectives of the Kissingen Dictate and sought to make practical political headway in that direction.

Contrary to the way in which he had seen things in 1877, however, he soon found that he could no longer confine himself to exploiting situations as they arose. He had to seize the initiative and attempt to exert a positive influence on events himself. In the last eleven years of his political career he thus increasingly practised what he had so passionately preached *against* before: he sought deliberately to create and to preserve situations of his own making rather than adapt to those he found and turn them to his advantage.

[12]

A Change of Course at Home

Nowhere is the inner connection between Bismarck's domestic policy and his foreign policy clearer than in the years after 1878. Above and beyond all matters of detail, this applies primarily to their guiding principles. In both areas of policy he now sought to exert more control over circumstances; indeed, he began to resort to increasingly artificial means of manipulating them to his advantage. In neither area, however, did those attempts meet with any real success or produce any permanent results.

In setting out to preserve the status quo by maintaining what experience had taught him to regard as favourable conditions for success, Bismarck as it were fell farther and farther behind the times. Hitherto, however much he had seemed to oppose them at first, he had in fact embodied the possibilities and prevailing tendencies of his day in his achievement and in his own person, often in surprising ways. But now it became increasingly apparent that even the greatest flexibility, a wholly power-oriented way of thinking that deliberately severed all ties and a sobriety of approach bordering on cynicism were incapable of transcending the limits within which his political career had successfully unfolded up to now and from which it had taken its bearings.

To us, looking back, provided we do not persist in subscribing to a kind of negative Bismarck worship that purports to be critical but is in fact still writing 'success story' history with altered value-judgements, the change is already detectable in the course of the grave and unexpectedly extensive economic crisis that began to affect the Reich in 1873. This quickly expanded into a political crisis and, as such, a crisis of the political system created by Bismarck.

The causes of the crisis, of this economic down-turn that in the years following 1873 ended what had been a prolonged boom throughout Europe and indeed the whole of the economically developed world, everywhere producing similar political consequences, are obvious in retrospect. It was a structural crisis of the emergent modern industrial economy that over the past twenty years had been continually infiltrating fresh territory, a kind of crisis of adjustment to new conditions. For the first time limits became visible, almost from one day to the next, that scarcely anyone had envisaged before. Markets for industrial products, even on a world scale, suddenly shrank, and competition became fiercer, with disastrous consequences for smaller firms. Profit margins dropped, and in the context of a 'quantity boom with falling prices' (Hans Rosenberg) an intensified process of selection set in.

Those who were directly involved and whose livelihoods were affected were naturally incapable of achieving this kind of calm detachment, this kind of rising above individual failure to see the whole process from the standpoint of the highly successful adjustment that the economy as a whole and society as a whole did eventually make. They saw the huge numbers of bankruptcies, the collapse of prices and profits, the worsening job situation. They saw share prices in many branches halved, often in less than a year; they saw how the banks, recently so prosperous, were in many cases able to pay out no more than a third of the – unusually high – dividends they had been paying hitherto; they saw exports and growth stagnating, and soon they saw a substantial drop in the level of returns even in the agrarian sector. And above all they saw how the drop in wages that affected many jobs was clearly contributing towards increased social insecurity and unrest among broad sections of the population, as was evident not least from the increasing number of votes attracted by the socialist parties.

All this prompted growing doubts about the future among established political groups, among the nobility and the bourgeoisie, among the intelligentsia and among broad sections of the craft-trades and industry. It gave rise, in place of a confidence in economic and social progress that had often exceeded all reasonable bounds, to increasingly pessimistic forecasts. And it fostered reactions that, viewed in retrospect, were neither appropriate nor apt to achieve the desired result.

Everywhere, not just in Germany, those who had something to lose began to cling to the existing order, to what many of them had seen only yesterday as a brief stopping-place on the way to a brilliant future. Very soon after that universally alarming series of stock exchange crises and economic collapses that started in Vienna in May 1873 and quickly spread to almost every European country as well as to the United States, people were saying, particularly in central Europe, that a 'major depression' had set in. From the standpoint of economic history the phrase is thoroughly misleading, for in soberly statistical terms the whole thing was no more than a period of stagnation coming after a period of pronounced overheating. Signs of fresh and steadily continuing economic growth soon became visible. But the fact that the phrase was coined and that it spread so swiftly shows how drastically people felt the unexpected slump and setback and how quickly the general climate of expectation changed as a result. As always in such situations, the search for culprits began immediately – culprits that only a few people were capable of identifying as belonging to the supra-personal sphere of all-embracing and ultimately inexorable conditions and trends of development.

Accordingly, in nearly every country in Europe the crisis led to a heightening of conflict in an atmosphere of increasing political bitterness. But in few places did that conflict reach greater heights than in the German

61

Reich, for example, where on the one hand the public and the political parties enjoyed a large measure of freedom of expression but where on the other hand the government was not in fact directly responsible to or dependent on the majority in parliament and the public opinion on which it rested. Here the temptation was particularly great for both sides to shuffle off the responsibility for what was felt to be an ominous development and for each to blame the other, forgetting that for long periods they had been acting in concert.

Right up until the threshold of the decisive change that occurred in 1873, Bismarck had made extensive concessions to the liberal majority not only in the Reich but in its largest member state, namely Prussia. Granted, everything remained within the limits laid down in 1866–7 and confirmed in 1871. There was no more question of a true parliamentary commitment on the part of the government than there was of a determining influence on the part of the majority in terms of policy and personnel. At the beginning of 1873 Bismarck had once again stressed to the Prussian House of Deputies: 'As soon as we get involved in party ministries, antagonisms will be sharpened. The King alone and the emanation that proceeds from him in his political capacity are above party, and it is at this level, the level of the Crown, that government in Prussia must in my view be maintained.'[1] Realising, however, that 'constitutional rule' was impossible unless a government had 'at least one party in the country' that agreed with its 'views and orientation', as the Chancellor had put it five years earlier,[2] both sides had been moving closer and closer together. This was true not only with regard to the question of relations with the Roman Catholic Church and above all the new Catholic party. It was also true of the fiercely controversial reform of Prussia's internal administration, and it was likewise true of the broad area of judicial reform as well as of the whole sphere of economic legislation.

There had been no small price to pay for that collaboration as far as Bismarck was concerned. The Prussian conservatives had increasingly turned their backs on him, including now even those groups that had stood by him after 1866. His policy had been meeting with what was in many respects an alarming increase in scepticism from this quarter. This trend had reached a peak towards the end of 1872. Only by creating a sufficient number of reliable new peers had the government finally managed to get its controversial Local Government Bill through the Upper House. The 'factious behaviour' of that house, Bismarck had said, constituted a threat to the 'monarchical order'.[3]

Impassioned protests against this step had come not only from the old conservative majority in the Upper House and from almost the entire Conservative Party; the man who for years had been their trustiest spokesman in the government, War Minister von Roon, had also opposed it, speaking of a *coup d'état* from above and warning explicitly, as he had done in the 'New Era', of the danger of moving further and further left.

Bismarck's reaction to this had taken a form that few people could make sense of at first: on 20 December 1872 he had stepped down as Prussian Minister-President in Roon's favour. His reasons for taking this sensational step are still unresolved to this day. The most likely hypothesis is that he wished to bring unmistakably home to the conservatives how swiftly, if they once opposed him, they risked finding themselves in the political wilderness. Because, as Bismarck knew only too well, Roon as their champion would be in no way equal to the office of Minister-President. He therefore believed that he could rely on his conservative critics ruefully reverting to him and his policy after the forthcoming elections to the Prussian Diet at the latest. As he told the leading conservative estate-owner Otto von Diest-Daber around this time, he had been 'abandoned' by the Conservative Party and had therefore 'put up his sword. Let the others go on building without him: the consequences would soon be apparent.'[4] Roon himself, he pointed out in another context, would 'soon come to realize that he must do as I wished if he wants to succeed'.[5]

It had become obvious yet again during this period how deeply Bismarck now depended politically on the good behaviour of the liberal majority. And just at this point – in other words, before the slump occurred – the National Liberals had publicly mounted an attack as massive as it was dramatic on the right-wing members of the government and the forces behind them.

The attack had been headed by Lasker, one of the most upright and industrious members of the parliamentary-party leadership. Despite grave misgivings among many of his party colleagues, who warned him of the political consequences of such a course,[6] at the beginning of 1873 he had exposed in the Prussian House of Deputies extensive trafficking in state concessions for the founding of railway companies. At the centre of the scandal had been the former editor-in-chief of the *Kreuzzeitung*, now a senior civil servant in the Prussian Cabinet Office, Hermann Wagener, and Count Itzenplitz, the Minister of Commerce. The immediate charge of self-enrichment in office, levelled principally against Wagener, had been coupled with the indirect but far more explosive accusation that a section of the conservative leadership in Prussia was shamelessly exploiting its connections for personal gain.

The government now headed by Roon had reacted to this sensational attack about as clumsily as it could have done. Instead of examining the charges one by one and then seeking to play them down, its spokesmen had hit back wildly and accused Lasker in turn of dubious transactions and financial irregularities. At this the latter had substantiated his accusations and dealt not only the government but also the conservatives a heavy blow that was not without effect on the ensuing elections.[7]

Although formally he had no direct responsibility at the time, Bismarck had followed the affair very uneasily. For one thing Wagener had for years been one of his closest and most important colleagues. For another he saw the whole thing as an attempt to prise apart the state and its traditional ruling class with the object of discrediting the latter and making the former more and more reliant on the new forces of middle-class liberalism.

At first the episode had had no major repercussions, even if the Chancellor did from then on number the section of the National Liberal parliamentary party and its leadership represented by Lasker among his political enemies, perhaps rather overrating its strategic plan. Both sides, namely the head of the imperial government and the National Liberal Party in the Imperial Diet, had continued to collaborate closely, that collaboration indeed reaching a kind of climax in the so-called 'May Laws' of 1873. The object of these – entirely in line with liberal policy – had been finally to 'nationalize' the church and forcibly subordinate it to the state by reorganizing the training of priests and placing it under state supervision, by giving the state supreme control over the church's internal jurisdiction and by making it easier to 'opt out' of church membership. And in this and in all further actions, up to and including the Draconian laws of 1874 and 1875, Bismarck had consistently backed his Minister of Culture, Adalbert Falk. Those laws allowed the expulsion of recalcitrant priests, the temporary administration of unoccupied bishoprics by the state, the abolition of all religious orders not involved in the care of the sick, and finally the discontinuance of all state payments to insubordinate dioceses. At most the Chancellor had occasionally criticized Falk's methods, never the substance and objectives of his policy.

Nevertheless, these years were characterized by what started out as a subliminal feeling of mistrust and detachment on both sides but grew in proportion as the economy – and with it, inevitably, the state that laid down the basic rules for the economy – got into increasingly choppy waters. Bismarck complained more and more frequently of the tendency of the liberal majority, while exploiting all the advantages of close relations with the government and a key position in parliament, always to sneak out of accepting responsibility and instead throw this wholly on the government when things did not go in the way they had hoped. And the liberals countered by saying that they saw no reason to go through thick and thin with and even answer for the mistakes of a government that persisted in confusing collaboration with subordination and insisted on reserving the final decisions to itself.

For Bismarck, however unassailable his position might appear from outside, this growing alienation between former political partners represented a not inconsiderable danger, politically speaking. His relationship with the conservatives was as bad as ever and aggravated by various private differences. And an arrangement with the Centre Party, the majority of whose members were also monarchical and conservative in their allegiance, was completely out of the question. In other words, there were no political alternatives available. On the other hand the Chancellor was well aware that, despite all the power and authority possessed by the executive in the political system he had imposed, governing without a legislative majority and without the corresponding support of public opinion would scarcely be possible in the long run. Here he had digested the experiences of the conflict period very much more soberly than many of the conservatives who had fought alongside him at that time. For that very reason, however, his bitterness at the behaviour of the liberals was particularly acute. Having always, with regard to almost all his fellow occupants of the political arena, simply used people, played them off against one another and if necessary lured them into the wilderness and sacrificed them, he suddenly found himself in the position of someone who, when he does once embark on a political partnership and become involved in genuine collaboration, has the bad luck to come up against some particularly apt pupils of his own political tactics. Whether or not the leaders of the National Liberal Party in the Imperial Diet were in fact such pupils, they were at any rate aware that Bismarck, with no parliamentary alternative at the moment, was in a position of dependence on them. At the same time they were determined not to let him simply make use of them and saddle them with embarrassing responsibilities.

It was in this situation that a decision fell due as to how the military budget was to be handled in future – a question that more than any other carried with it memories of conflict and that still, both in substance and in principle, contained plenty of explosive material. In 1867, in the context of the developing relationship between the victor of 1866 and the new National Liberal Party in the country and in parliament, an agreement had been reached to the effect that the military budget should remain fixed for the time being. At the same time it had been decided that from the end of 1871 the Diet's right to examine and approve the budget annually should be made to cover the military budget too. In 1871, because of the changed situation and the pressure of urgent business, the provisional arrangement had been extended for a further three years. Now a final decision had to be made – and in what seemed to be a more favourable parliamentary constellation than had ever obtained before as far as liberalism and specifically the National Liberal Party in the Imperial Diet were concerned.

In the election of 10 January 1874, the first 'normal' election, as it were, not held in the immediate shadow of the war and the founding of the Reich, the National Liberals had gained a further thirty seats, mainly at the expense of the conservatives, who to Bismarck's unconcealed satisfaction dropped from fifty-seven to twenty-two seats. Together with the Progressive Party, who had gained three, they now had a clear absolute majority: 204 of a total of 397 seats. Moreover, the Centre Party, with its unreservedly oppositional stance, had shot from sixty-three to ninety-one seats. Together with the Poles, the Guelfs, the Danes, the Alsace-Lorrainers and the Social Democrats, the 'protest parties' that the leaders of the Reich believed could not be included in any of their parliamentary calculations, it now constituted a bloc of 134 seats – a good third of the house, in other words.

Trying to bypass the National Liberal Party over the army question as over any other problem to be settled by legislative means would have meant risking another major conflict. On the other hand falling completely into line with the liberals would have been regarded not only in conservative circles as final proof that Bismarck was now a prisoner of his own political system. Nor was that all. There was also a risk that the man on whom, under the constitution and in the light of all developments hitherto, his position crucially depended might become totally confused by such a course, particularly since Bismarck's policy towards the Catholic Church and the Centre Party was already causing him growing anxiety. And a crisis of confidence in his relationship with William I was the last thing Bismarck could afford in the present situation.

The Chancellor therefore found himself in a very pronounced dilemma, for he could not contemplate taking on another major conflict in addition to the 'Kulturkampf' and in the light of the worsening economic situation. Nevertheless, at the beginning of February 1874 he had his new War Minister, Georg von Kameke, once again place before the Diet what was certain to be regarded by the liberals as an unacceptable maximum programme. Roon, who had introduced the relevant Bill the year before without it ever getting on the agenda, had resigned all his offices in November 1873 after only eleven months as Minister-President. Initially, of course, in reintroducing the Bill the Chancellor was probably thinking only in terms of giving himself more room to manoeuvre. Standing for all the other matters due for consideration, it was to demonstrate to the liberals that the government had no intention of capitulating before their strength in parliament.

The Roon-Kameke Bill proposed to fix the army establishment permanently – 'until the enactment of legal provisions to the contrary' – at around 400,000 men. For this a lump sum per capita was to be included in the budget, as hitherto; the previous basis had been a peacetime establishment of 1 per cent of the 1867 population. Acceptance of this proposal would in practice have removed the military budget from parliament's power of disposal for ever, creating what was called an 'Aeternat'. Predictably only a very small group of liberals led by Rudolf von Gneist, a teacher of constitutional law, was prepared to do that. The counter-programme of the liberal majority, as agreed in 1867, was annual approval. So it could be expected that, after a certain amount of poker-playing, the two sides would meet somewhere in the middle – unless of course the liberals were for their part set on a major conflict and a decisive trial of strength.

Certainly there was something of a tendency in that direction. As well as Eugen Richter of the Progressive Party, a man who was increasingly emerging as the undisputed leader of that party, it was chiefly Eduard Lasker and the Munich deputy, Baron von Stauffenberg, who argued on behalf of the National Liberal Party for a tough and uncompromising stance. They found themselves in a kind of negative coalition with the emperor and his closest advisers in the so-called Military Cabinet. They likewise rejected any thought of compromise and openly invoked the memory of the conflict period.

In the circumstances, long-drawn-out and in part very vehement discussions were unavoidable. They were further fostered by the fact that Bismarck was out of action for several weeks with a bad attack of gout and even after his return played a notably retiring role at first. Those he scornfully referred to as 'die Herren Militärs' should be left to 'see . . . how they get by with their views on their own', as he had stated months before.[8] In the end, however, the expected compromise was arrived at. Taking their cue from what had been the – unplanned – usage since 1867, both sides agreed to a so-called 'Septennat', a seven-year period of approval. This compromise, negotiated principally between Bismarck and Bennigsen, was accepted after a prolonged internal struggle by the overwhelming majority of the National Liberals in the Diet, including Lasker.

With this the understanding between the National Liberal Party and the government appeared to be largely restored. What might have been regarded as providing proof of this was the passing, on 24 April 1874, of the law allowing for the expulsion of opposition priests, a law that pushed the 'Kulturkampf' to fresh heights. Bismarck was once again fêted by the liberal majority as their champion in the secular fight for the freedom of modern civilization. When less than three months later a Roman Catholic cooper by the name of Kullmann tried to assassinate him in Bad Kissingen, the attempt was regarded as an assault on their common cause, a challenge to stick even closer together.

Bismarck immediately adopted this interpretation and sought to use the assassination attempt – in which he had been only slightly wounded – for his own purposes. It was imperative, he said over and over again, that they close ranks even more tightly than before to combat a party that was an inspiration to assassins. And to the impassioned protests of the Centre Party he replied, 'Oh, yes, gentlemen! Cast the man out to your hearts' content – he still clings to your coat-tails!'[9]

The ideal he had in mind here was one that he stated quite openly in the Prussian House of Deputies on one occasion in March 1875: the 'upshot' of the 'Kulturkampf' would, he explained, be 'that in time we will have only two main parties, one that negates and combats the state and another with the vast majority of respectable people, devoted to the state and patriotically minded . . . This party will be shaped in the school of the current struggle.'[10]

This kind of vision of the future might still be capable of impressing a broader liberal public, but the majority of National Liberals in parliament were fully aware, as was Bismarck himself, that for a long time now the real picture had looked very different. There could be no question of any true return to the relationship of bygone years. A fresh, fundamental conflict could blow up at any moment. The bitterness and increased mistrust that the dispute about the military budget had left behind it on both sides, but especially on the left wing of the National Liberal Party, in a sense acted only as an additional catalyst here; they were more symptom than cause. Of greater importance was the growing feeling that, here and in many other spheres, particularly the economic, things were pressing for a decision. A feeling often expressed was that the country was in a state of transition: new arrangements promising greater permanence were inevitable sooner or later.

This corresponded entirely to Bismarck's own view. As he said at the time, he had had enough of 'poor hare-hunting'. What he had in mind were large-scale, far-reaching solutions: 'If it were a matter of bagging a huge and powerful boar, now – an Erymanthian boar, if you will – then I'd be there, then I'd make the effort once more.'[11] In the given parliamentary and party-political situation, however, what could such large-scale, far-reaching solutions consist in – to start with, at the level of the relationship between parliament and government?

Many historians, under the influence of subsequent developments, namely the gradual elimination of the liberals through the medium of exploiting internal contradictions within their ranks, the construction – with Bismarck's active assistance – of a new conservative party taking its cue essentially from agrarian interests, and finally the attempt to come to terms with the Centrists have tended to draw a direct connection between these results and the aims of Bismarckian policy during the preceding years, for example since 1873–4. With the aid of such an interpretation it is possible to draw a very striking picture of his political achievements in the period up until the events of 1878–9. During those years, so the theory goes, the domestic affairs of the Reich were placed on an entirely fresh footing that determined the way in which the Reich developed; in effect, it underwent a second, 'internal' foundation.

In this kind of interpretation Bismarck is once again portrayed – often with a secret admiration that is only very superficially concealed – as the man who held all the strings in his hand, who mastered, marshalled and directed all relations and interrelations with a greater or lesser degree of command. But are the proofs that have been advanced for the clear consistency of his policy during those years really adequate and watertight? Is this not a case of historians succumbing yet again to the perennial temptation to colour what is often a tortuous chain of cause and effect with the intentions implicit in its ultimately dominant strand and to declare this to have been the outcome of previously articulated plans on the part of an individual or small group of people? And is this not to lose sight of precisely what exerts a very much stronger and more lasting influence on the historical process than the actions of any individual, namely the interaction of the forces, interests, aspirations and overall trends present at any one time?

The course of events from 1874 up until the decisions of 1878–9 was in fact very much more ambivalent and very much more open to potentially quite different developments than appears from the outcome. It was determined not so much by a bold, far-reaching plan as by a series of often groping attempts to achieve a sounder solution of the relationship between government and parliament or rather between the monarchical, bureaucratic state and the new middle-class society. Those attempts were made, moreover, in the context of a process of rapid social transformation during which society exhibited a swiftly changing political face as well, with constantly shifting majority ratios and constellations of opinion.

Undoubtedly Bismarck was still tempted even now by the idea of avoiding any kind of dependence in this regard, of trying instead to maintain a position above party and make use of the various forces and interests present at any one time. But had not just such a policy, guided by those objectives, recently failed to show much success? Had it not given rise to a situation in which the government was saddled with sole responsibility for anything and everything that was unpopular or turned out to be problematical, a situation in which each political group sought purely to look after its own interests and take advantage of the government while offering nothing substantial in return? And had this not landed the government in positions of even greater dependence because they defied any kind of calculation?

Against this background the concept of a more firmly grounded, more solid alliance with one or a number of the political groups in parliament, all mental reservations notwithstanding, inevitably appeared in a very much more attractive light. The most obvious candidate was the informal coalition of Free Conservatives and National Liberals that had been in existence since 1867. In it Bismarck admittedly now saw forces at work that wished to place a continuation of their collaboration on a footing that he was not prepared to accept. But by making increased concessions to the National Liberal right wing, for example by inviting representatives of it to play a direct part in government, might it not be possible to isolate those forces and even cut them off completely, thus shifting the political centre of gravity within the coalition? On the other hand, could one not at the same time attempt to give the conservative right, which because of constant defeats and growing internal differences was in the process of falling apart politically, a new lease of life – either with a view to gradually acquiring a fresh basis for closer political and parliamentary collaboration right of centre or in order to make the parties of the middle of the political spectrum, principally the right wing of the National Liberal Party, more willing to co-operate?

In the years 1873–4 Bismarck juggled constantly with such possibilities without any fundamental preferences becoming discernible at first. As in foreign policy, he concentrated entirely on the reality of existing power relations and tried to sound out what was possible and what was not. And here too, as in his review of foreign policy after the 'Is War in Sight?' crisis, he took as his starting-point a particular basic constellation of antagonisms and positions that in his view could be relied on with some certainty to remain unchanged. In foreign policy he had been thinking of France; here on the domestic policy front it was chiefly the Centre Party and the 'protest parties' that he had in mind. They constituted as it were the counter-pole of his whole calculation, the opposition that must be isolated politically, the 'enemies of the Empire', as he called them more and more often, casually equating the political programme that he personified with the Reich as such.

That was one aspect. The other was that he presupposed, as with Britain and Russia in foreign affairs, that the antagonisms between left-wing liberals and conservatives would remain permanently insurmountable. This meant, however, that he was repeatedly thrown back – as it were by the logic of circumstances – on the constellation on which in 1866–7 he had based his whole future policy and political existence, indeed that he had envisaged very much earlier, during the conflict period, as the objective worth striving for: namely, the two parties of the centre collaborating in opposition to both the staunch right and the staunch left. But – and knowledge of this fact brought with it a great temptation – the internal cohesion of those centre parties would be all the greater, the bigger the threat or in this case the stronger the political competition from right or left appeared to be.

All this was the product of a perfectly sober and wholly practical exercise in stock-taking and precise soundings and overtures embarked on accordingly. These were undertaken in the belief that he had gone as far as he could go with the system he had adopted hitherto, indeed that in the long run that system constituted a threat to his position. With them he sought to define the parameters of his future action, as it were, and through unremitting, direct involvement with the problems of the day to fathom the conditions and possibilities of that action in a form that generalized from those day-to-day problems. In this the focus was now on the left or rather on the relationship of the left-of-centre National Liberal Party to the representatives of the left.

Up to now the demarcation and consequently the internal cohesion of the informal government coalition had stemmed from the right. This was particularly true with respect to the battle now being fought with ever-increasing bitterness and passion against the Centre Party, whose leader, Windthorst, tirelessly stressed – in a way that at least some of the time Bismarck heartily welcomed – the conservative, strictly monarchical character of the party. But it was also true of the Conservative Party, particularly in Prussia. This had in practice found itself in – or rather, as its leaders said with some justification, been forced into – the role of a right-wing opposition party. As a result the centre of gravity of the parties occupying the middle of the political spectrum had – not only in Bismarck's eyes – shifted further and further towards the left. The boundaries between the left wing of the National Liberals under Lasker and the Progressive Party had become increasingly fluid as far as their respective aims and demands were concerned.

So it had to be Bismarck's most urgent objective to counter this continuing leftward trend inside the largest party in Germany and in so doing to put to the test where and with what distribution of weight it was going to be possible to draw a new, clear line of demarcation. Offering themselves as subjects for this kind of political scratch test were those who, representing the new industrial working class, advocated a thoroughgoing reorganization of the economy and society. On the one hand they constituted a challenge and a threat to the new middle-class society in an extreme form. On the other, in the eyes of many liberals at least, they forced that society to look at its vaunted tolerance and liberality, its self-confidence and capacity for integration, its power of creative development, rising above and reconciling all differences, and ask what they were really worth.

Bismarck had already worked out a very definite programme here, in direct reaction to the Paris Commune uprising: it was vital, in his opinion, to combat such elements with the greatest severity, making determined use of the power of the state and all appropriate legislation, and at the same time, by introducing social welfare measures, to cut the political ground from under their feet. This had been dictated by a highly pessimistic assessment of future developments and by his awareness of the dangers the future held as far as the maintenance of the social order was concerned and of the opportunities it held for a determined movement fighting a class war. If, after appropriate measures had been discussed in detail, particularly in the negotiations with Austria in 1871, Bismarck had let the whole matter rest for the time being, he had done so purely for reasons of expediency: he was anxious if possible to avoid a political war on more than one front. Now, in 1874, he felt that other reasons of expediency favoured tackling the question in concrete terms and introducing some initial measures in line with his programme. It cannot, however, be inferred from this that expediency was his sole guide in dealing with this whole problem or that he was not seriously persuaded of the dangers to which he referred.

In fact the exact opposite was the case. Bismarck had been waiting since 1871 for a suitable opportunity to take steps he believed to be as urgent as they were imperative. The general political situation that emerged in the shadow of the critical economic developments of 1873 and after presented him with such an opportunity. Now, he believed, the liberals would be obliged to show their true colours on this point.

The first step that offered itself in practice was a specific tightening of the Press Law currently under discussion. The appropriate legislative competence had passed to the new Reich in 1871, and after lengthy preliminary work a Bill was finally presented in the spring of 1874. Bismarck arranged for clauses to be included in the Bill threatening penalties for fundamental criticisms of the existing social order, of military service and of state institutions. By way of justification, explicit reference was made – in lurid terms in the semi-official press – to the revolutionary propaganda of a section of the socialist press and to the need to shield the broad mass of the population from such demagogic influences. The purpose of this, as Bismarck spelled it out at a meeting of the Prussian Cabinet on 30 December 1874, was 'on the one hand to transfer the responsibility for inadequate combating of the revolutionary party from the government to the Imperial Diet and on the other hand to acquaint the peace-loving population with the existence of this danger, which can be expected to produce a gradual shift of mood among the majority in the Imperial Diet'.[12]

In neither of the two liberal parties, however, with the National Liberals once again under the leadership of the Lasker group, was a majority prepared to accept Bismarck's proposals. Both parties were highly sensitive, from experience and by political conviction, to any interference with the freedom of the press, however limited. They further suspected a covert attempt, not just to silence the socialists and the anarchists, in other words revolutionary movements that they decisively rejected themselves, but to muzzle all awkward criticism and forge a weapon against the left as a whole.

A fresh and more energetic attempt launched by the government a year and a half later met with the same fate and for the same reasons. This was not a matter of the wording of individual articles of a piece of legislation that was under discussion in any case; this was a specific amendment to the criminal code passed only a few years before. Under it, a person was threatened with punishment who, 'in a manner endangering the public peace, publicly stirs up different classes of the people against one another or in a similar manner publicly attacks through the spoken or written word the institutions of marriage, the family, or property'.[13] This time the government representatives sought to dispel misgivings from the outset by arguing that the objective was surely outlined with sufficient clarity. Any further step, they said, led beyond the principle of individual responsibility into the realm of discriminatory legislation against specific groups of persons. Nevertheless, the majority of liberals fell in with the opinion of Lasker and the spokesmen of the Progressive Party that this was a prime example of an elastic clause. It simply placed the political and social status quo under taboo and threatened to make the Public Prosecutor a political tool of the government.

Initially, therefore, Bismarck had failed in his attempt to use the question of how to combat the radical left successfully in order at the same time to draw a clear line of demarcation between left and right in the liberal camp. He had failed to drive a wedge between those who favoured direct use of the power of the state and the weapon of legislation and those who, deeply mistrustful of the government, considered this an unsuitable course. On both occasions Lasker had taken the wind out of his sails by saying that it was not a matter of tougher laws but of a firm determination to fight the opponents of the existing order both politically and intellectually. And that, said Lasker, was something the liberals had in abundance.

Meanwhile, however, the situation in another sphere had become critical in a way that, given the interests to which the different political groups were committed, hastened the clarification of their relations with the government in a quite unexpected fashion. One of the basic facts from which Bismarck's policy had to and did in fact start out had been the agreement that existed between the traditional and the new, bourgeois ruling classes on the subject of economic policy. A majority in both camps had embraced the principles of economic freedom and free trade. With the appointment of Delbrück to head the new central administration in 1866–7, those principles had finally triumphed, though they had largely determined Prussian economic policy even before that date.

In a period of almost unabating boom conditions they had been in line both with the interests of the big farmers and estate-owners of East Elbia and with those of commerce, finance and at least substantial branches of a vigorously expanding industrial sector. The watchwords in both camps were expansion and the unfettered exploitation of economic possibilities and opportunities.

Since the early 1860s agriculture and industry had been enjoying an almost uninterrupted upswing, with further boosts occurring in 1867–8 and 1871. Growth-rates of over 7 per cent per annum were not unusual. Despite three wars, major territorial changes and drastically altered parameters, the area that was to become the German Reich had since 1862 shown a continuous annual growth of just under three-and-a-half per cent – an exceptionally high figure for the period.

Hidden behind that figure – for there could be no question as yet of uniform development, and industrialization and expansion claimed many victims, even on the manufacturing side – were very different growth rates and corresponding profits in the crucial branches. From the mid-1860s, with costs at first very stable, turnover and profits in heavy industry, large-scale agriculture and the textile and consumer goods industries went shooting up. Increases in yield of between 25 and 30 per cent in the space of just a few years were by no means unusual in these sectors. Railway-building in particular, with its huge and continually increasing demand for timber, steel, machinery and construction materials as well as for land, was literally a driving force powering the whole economy.

In this totally unprecedented economic boom the old and new elites, the nobility and the propertied middle class, had participated equally. As a result, beyond their political differences they had been in broad agreement with regard to principles of economic policy and in many cases also of social policy. This had furnished an important basis for the informal collaboration between conservative and liberal forces after 1866–7. Now, however, in the shadow of the economic crisis that developed in the years after 1873–4, that consensus began to disintegrate with ever-accelerating momentum. It was increasingly replaced by a difference of opinion between those who demanded protective intervention by the state in one form or another and those who, even in the teeth of the undeniable difficulties affecting many sectors of the economy, wanted to hold fast to the existing system of liberal economic policy.

The argument split practically every political group down the middle, leading almost everywhere to internal conflicts within the parties that steadily increased in intensity. But the party worst affected was that of the National Liberals. On the one hand it was committed to the liberal economy by its whole programme. On the other hand it was confronted more and more urgently each day with the growing need for protection experienced by its supporters in the middle-class economy and in certain branches of industry.

That need for protection found initial expression in the demand for the introduction or retention of protective tariffs. The first pressure group calling for tariff protection, the 'Association of German Iron and Steel Manufacturers', was founded at the end of 1873 in reaction to the removal of the last customs barriers by the government and the Imperial Diet. It was quickly followed by numerous initiatives and associations to the same purpose in various branches of the economy. The conflict of principle and interests that this sparked off very soon threatened to tear the National Liberal Party in the country and in parliament apart and to usher in entirely fresh coalitions.

However, it was far from clear at first where in the spectrum the break might occur. No one could predict whether the whole thing might not eventually lead even to a strengthening of the liberal left – for example, by way of a gradual rapprochement between the National Liberal left wing and the Progressive Party, taking in the as yet wholly undecided centre group of the former party.

In view of this, Bismarck refrained from expressing any opinion on the matter at first, although he had undoubtedly had his eye from a very early stage on the political possibilities it might contain. He looked on largely inactive as Delbrück rejected the demands put forward more and more vociferously by the steadily widening circle of protectionists with the argument that they were prompted by rank selfishness and conflicted with the interests of the community and the state. Even when Emperor William made it known on several occasions that he had a great deal of sympathy with the fears and anxieties of the branches of the economy concerned, the Chancellor continued to play a waiting game. Here too he observed the principle of letting things develop to the point where the constellation and balance of forces and the susceptibility to exploitation of the situation as a whole were firmly established. He continued to guard against the temptation to have the state intervene with a political plan developed theoretically, in other words to do what subsequent admirers and critics have so often suggested that he did.

Not until the end of 1875 did he publicly address himself to the whole question for the first time, when concern was already running very high and it was possible, above all, to tell with some degree of clarity how broadly based were the respective groups of protectionists and critics of the present direction of economic policy. And even then he expressed himself with extreme caution. He dropped hints about a possible change of course but otherwise avoided any really concrete commitment.

His prime concern, as he said in a much-noted speech in the Imperial Diet on 22 November 1875, was with fiscal reform.[14] The object of this must be to make the Reich more independent than hitherto and increase its capacity for action. In this context, he went on, the government would subsequently also have to tackle the question of a possible 'tariff reform', because in his opinion a 'system of indirect taxes' and fewer select 'revenue duties' was urgently to be preferred in future.

The message was that the government would make the direction of its economic policy dependent on how and by whom it was supported in its efforts to strengthen the authority of the Reich and increase its capacity for action. He took the opportunity to emphasize once again for the benefit of the liberal left that he intended to adhere without reserve to the 'present constitution of the office of Imperial Chancellor', in other words to the principle that that office bore sole political responsibility. Decoded, this meant that it would continue in future to be impossible to break up the government camp on the basis of possible internal differences of opinion. People must turn to him. He laid down the guidelines, and any alliances and political deals were arrived at through him alone.

Here was explicit confirmation of what his critics had long been referring to with negative connotations and emphasis as a 'dictatorship by the Chancellor'. In the case in point the reference to the realities of the constitution served in the first place as a warning against the error of believing that anyone but he – Delbrück, for instance – determined in the final analysis the principles and basic direction of the economic and financial policy of the Reich. At the same time he spelled out very clearly the conditions for eventual collaboration with parliamentary groups in terms of personnel as well. He was all for 'Imperial ministers', the Chancellor stated in his declaration of principle on 22 November 1875. 'We have them and shall, I hope and believe, have more of them . . . In a nutshell, things can develop.' But let no one count on the possibility of ministers voting together to inflict political defeat on the Chancellor. Even to reckon that participation in government would mean gaining control over at least certain areas of the administration was to reckon without one's host, as the saying goes: he would always resolutely oppose any such 'hacking up of the state into departmental states'.

The possibilities and limits of co-operation with an imperial government headed by him were thus made perfectly plain. Indeed the parties were positively invited to state their wishes and make their offers within those limits, principally as regarded the violently controversial area of future economic policy, where the Chancellor had very deliberately left all his options open.

The first to respond were not in fact representatives of the parties. They were the spokesmen of the protectionist interests of – chiefly – the iron and steel industries, that is to say of the newly emergent associations. These men were not entangled, as were the party leaders, in the often scarcely reconcilable political objectives and mutually conflicting interests of their heterogeneous followings. They were therefore in the best position to recognize the opportunities that the present situation offered of 'going straight to the Chancellor', as one of them put it.[15] And Bismarck immediately responded to their approaches, though of course it is important not to underestimate the importance of the tactical element here. In conversation with Baron von Stumm-Halberg and Wilhelm von Kardorff, both of whom were deputies and prominent members of the Free Conservative Party but figured here purely in their capacity as representatives of associations, he advised them in December 1875 to remain on the offensive and to feel free to attack the free trade policies of the government. Furthermore, he added, the chances were that they would soon begin to find increased support among agrarian interests as well; in this quarter, too, highly critical voices were already beginning to be raised against the policy of free trade.

This was a straight invitation to look beyond the organization of protectionist interests in trade and industry and include the agrarian sector. This line, which for the first time clearly aimed at the constellation of forces that crucially determined the way things developed after 1878–9, was one that Bismarck continued to follow consistently in the months to come. It began with his recognition that a change was in the offing in the agrarian sector that in extent and broad effect was entirely comparable with that which had begun to hit trade and industry in 1873–4: from the final months of 1875 onwards cereal prices, under pressure from Russian and overseas competition, began to fall faster and faster, the annual average by 1878, despite a slight rise in 1876, amounting to nearly 5 per cent, which meant a total drop of around 20 per cent within the space of a few years – and at a time when wage costs were clearly rising. As the Chancellor had prophesied to Stumm and Kardorff, the reaction of those affected was not long in coming.

Particularly in East Elbia, where agriculture was traditionally export-oriented and interested in cheap machinery, the majority had always been in favour of free trade and to that extent had supported a liberal economic system at home as well. Now, however, the East Elbian landowners were turning away from that system in increasing numbers. They too had begun

– albeit very much more mutedly and less uniformly than, say, heavy industry – to demand that the state take protective measures against foreign competition. Their mouthpiece became the 'Confederation of Fiscal and Economic Reformers', founded in Berlin on 22 February 1876, only a week after the protectionist interests in trade and industry had given themselves an umbrella organization, also based in Berlin, in the shape of the 'Central Association of German Industrialists'.

In neither case was there any question of the Chancellor being directly involved. He had indicated, however, that this kind of articulation and self-organization of economic interests without the immediate participation of the parties and without their exercising direct political control was not unwelcome as far as he was concerned. So he had encouraged them, if only indirectly. But it was always primarily the parties that he had his sights on here. A tendency to exclude these even just from certain sectors and work directly with the associations – the kind of tendency that emerged more and more clearly in the early 1880s – was not yet discernible. Bismarck's concern was by one means or another to apply pressure to the parties and force them to make their position and future policy unmistakably clear – with particular reference to their relationship to the government and to him personally.

How much this aspect of the matter dominated his thinking and how concerned he was in consequence not to commit himself prematurely as to content became obvious in a speech he made in the Imperial Diet on 9 February 1876, only days before the central lobby associations of industry and agriculture were founded.[16] The occasion was the third reading of the criminal law amendment that was to provide legal grounds for proceeding against the liberal left and above all against the Social Democrats. This was already regarded as certain to be rejected by the majority in the Diet. However, Bismarck's speech was only superficially aimed at pulling his irons out of the fire. Instead he used it to make a sensational attack on the *Kreuzzeitung* and the conservative political forces behind that paper.

The Chancellor began with a number of rambling and – with regard to their substance and truthfulness – in many ways somewhat dubious remarks about the German press, the press policy of the government and the political influence of published opinion, all under the heading of the dangers of an irresponsible press, which was what he claimed the amendment was primarily designed to combat. By way of illustration, as it were, he turned his attention towards the end of his speech to the so-called 'Era' articles that had caused such a stir when they appeared in the *Kreuzzeitung* in June of the previous year.

In five major leaders under the headline 'The Bleichröder-Delbrück-Camphausen Era' a hitherto unknown journalist by the name of Franz Perrot had sought to expose the government's economic policy as being the product of extremely one-sided interests and commitments on the part of the leading men responsible.[17] The articles, which had been carefully sub-edited by the publisher, Philipp von Nathusius-Ludom, had centred on the figure of Gerson Bleichröder, for many years the Chancellor's private banker and economic policy adviser; the lengthy and relatively insubstantial remarks about Delbrück and Camphausen could not conceal this fact. The author had portrayed Bleichröder as the embodiment of the unscrupulous profit-seeking of big capital – while the fact that Bleichröder was a Jew had in addition invoked every prejudice. At the same time he had emphasized his extremely close relationship with Bismarck, who 'to be able, on the meagre salary of a Prussian envoy and without substantial means of his own, to represent his sovereign in Petersburg, Paris and Frankfurt must indeed have had good advice in financial matters'. The suggestion had been that Bismarck himself supported the present economic policy very much for reasons of self-interest, for it was common knowledge that the Chancellor had become a wealthy man since Frankfurt and St Petersburg, quite apart from his endowments and what with all his offices was the somewhat skimpy annual salary of around 63,000 marks – the conjectures, as always, exceeding the reality many times over.

The scarcely veiled charge of corruption contained in these articles had of course made Bismarck extremely angry. It had placed an additional burden on his already very strained relations with the section of the Conservative Party concerned. Yet he had refrained from, for example, instituting legal proceedings over the matter, as he did so often over other matters. As he observed in a private letter to the secretary of state at the Imperial Ministry of Justice, Heinrich von Friedberg, they must avoid 'having the economic policy of the Empire judged in the municipal court'. That would be 'to make its indirect condemnation or acquittal depend upon the personal views and opinions that individual judges bring with them from small provincial towns'.[18] Why, then, was it not until eight months later that he gave violent expression to his anger? The reason is perfectly obvious: it now suited his political plans to do so, because he was literally looking for an excuse to throw down the gauntlet before the section of the Conservative Party responsible.

'When a paper such as the *Kreuzzeitung*', he said, 'which is regarded as the organ of a party with a large membership, is not ashamed to publish the most infamous and dishonest slanders against men in high office . . . when such a paper, having acted in this way, obstinately keeps silence for months, though it is all lies, and will not admit to being in the wrong, then that is a disgraceful scandal against which we ought all to make a stand, and no one ought by subscribing to that paper to contribute indirectly towards it.' His attack culminated in a kind of declaration of war against the publication with which his own political career had been bound up in so many ways: 'We must dissociate ourselves from such a paper if this injustice is not atoned for; anyone who takes and pays for it is indirectly contributing to the lie and to the slander purveyed therein.'

Bismarck's call for a boycott of the *Kreuzzeitung* was resolutely opposed by about a hundred representatives of the East Elbian nobility, all of them supporters of the Conservative Party. The list of signatures read like an extract from the *Almanach de Gotha*, ranging from von Auerswald to Zitzewitz by way of such resonant names as Hammerstein and Hardenberg, Schlabrendorff and Schulenberg; the last to sign, 'in great anguish', was Adolf von Thadden–Trieglaff. The signatories declared that they needed no 'lectures in honour and propriety'.[19] At the same time they publicly dissociated themselves from Bismarck and his policy and stressed that surely they at any rate could hardly be accused of not being faithful pillars of the monarchy and the traditional order.

Bismarck made a very careful note of the names of those who signed the declaration. At his instigation they were re-published as a kind of 'black list' in the official gazette, the *Reichsanzeiger*. In all future decisions about appointments he passed the list of 'Deklaranten' in review, so to speak, lest he miss a single opportunity of extracting 'atonement' for the 'injustice' done to him. 'When I lie awake at night I am often visited by memories of injustices yet unatoned for that befell me thirty years ago', he remarked two days after his speech of 9 February 1876 to the Free Conservative deputy and future Minister of Agriculture, Robert Lucius. 'I grow literally hot at the thought and in my drowsy state dream of the necessary counter-measures.'[20] He once commented humorously on this almost pathological need for revenge: 'My life is sustained and enhanced by two things: my wife and – Windthorst. The one is there for loving, the other for hating.'[21] Yet however implacably he pursued his enemies, not shrinking, in the process, from employing the pettiest means, with very few exceptions he did not allow the fact to influence either the substance or the timing of his political actions.

Nor did he in this case. The need to hit back for everyone to see was simply an additional element. The important thing was to make a political point, to destroy the illusion that anyone could do a deal with him in line with their own economic and social interests from a position of strength and with a large measure of independence, that they could put pressure on him by citing their own traditional influence and importance in society and the state.

In the case in point this meant that he and his government expected absolute allegiance even and indeed especially from the conservatives in return for any eventual concessions in the field of economic policy. They were not to imagine that he was in any way bound up by personal interests and that his decisions could therefore be counted on in advance – as many conservatives did indeed count, even though there had just been talk of a contrary commitment via Bleichröder, on Bismarck's interests as a landowner and on his understanding, acquired over many years, of the problems and fears of the agrarian sector.

This public protest notwithstanding, the political signal was received very clearly in the conservative camp. It led in a direct line through the founding of the 'Confederation of Fiscal and Economic Reformers' a mere fortnight later to what amounted to a re-foundation of the Conservative Party in July 1876. Unlike in the case of the Confederation, Bismarck significantly had a direct hand in this, even though he subsequently showed himself somewhat disappointed with the result. The programme of the new 'German Conservative Party' was drawn up by one of its leading members in direct consultation with him, and in other ways too he gave clear evidence of his approval of and political sympathy with the undertaking.

This was not, like a lobby association pure and simple, merely a potential political tool but a potential political partner with a very much broader base and very much greater mobility. Undoubtedly Bismarck was concerned in this case too to keep that potential partner's independence within bounds from the outset. But that in itself shows how broad – in contrast to the lobby associations, which under the present political system were wholly dependent on the government – he considered the scope of a political party to be and how difficult and precarious the task of binding it as closely as possible to himself and his policy.

One of the chief prerequisites for this he saw as consisting in a firm and clearly defined pressure group basis for the new party, particularly with regard to economic policy. He had long been familiar with the importance of this factor. From a different personal standpoint, his efforts in connection with the founding of the *Kreuzzeitung* party in 1848–9 had been aimed in the same direction. Since then he had repeatedly referred, in a variety of contexts and from various positions as far as his own political interests were concerned, to the importance of a party having such a basis. However, the situation was now very different. Balancing the economic interests of different social groups and classes looked like being a very much harder task in the context of an economic crisis that was now increasingly affecting agriculture as well. Moreover, the way in which such interests were specific to particular classes was emerging more and more distinctly. The consequence was that, while being more strongly rooted in economic interests could under certain circumstances bind a party more closely to the government, at the same time it made it more difficult to form a coalition. Nor did this affect only the party itself; it also affected a government that failed to find a sufficiently broad parliamentary base in that party alone.

Consequently, much as Bismarck welcomed on the one hand the fact that there was an exceptionally close connection between the 'Confederation' and the new German Conservative Party, both in substance and in terms of common membership, it was clear to him on the other hand that that connection also signified quite new problems. So for this reason too he was concerned, beyond the concrete political objectives he was pursuing here, that the new party should not see and present itself all too exclusively as the agrarian pressure group of East Elbia. In his view it ought at the same time to transcend economic interests and at least for external purposes qualify its commitment to them, conducting itself as the conservative mainstay of the Reich and its entire internal and external order. Above all, however, he was anxious to avoid for as long as possible giving the impression that with his evident sympathy for the newly founded party he had unequivocally committed himself with regard to economic policy and was now the champion of the protectionist interests that were becoming increasingly organized and of a radical change of direction in economic affairs.

For many people that impression had already deepened into certainty three months prior to the founding of the German Conservative Party. The end of April 1876 had seen the resignation of Rudolf von Delbrück, the chief exponent of liberal economic policy in the government camp and a man who had come almost to symbolize economic and, beyond that, governmental liberalism altogether. As always in such cases, Bismarck made every effort to obscure the reasons for Delbrück's step as well as his own part in the whole affair – not just so far as the current situation was concerned but also in retrospect. Now he spoke of Delbrück's being weary of office, now of the intolerable pressures exerted by conflicting economic interests. To some he insinuated that Delbrück had grown too big for his boots, that in his wranglings with other members of the government – principally with himself, Bismarck – he had placed the government's credibility and capacity for action at risk. Sometimes he laid the emphasis on material differences of opinion, specifically over questions of economic policy; in a different context he complained that the emperor had forced Delbrück out of office and 'robbed' him of his services, maintaining that there had been no question of any disagreement on policy.

One thing that does emerge clearly from his contradictory assertions is that, however much he welcomed the occurrence personally and to some extent from the standpoint of political tactics as well, its warning effect did not suit his plans at all. His guideline was and remained that individuals and parties should divide not over the attitude of the government but over questions of economic policy and the conflicts of interest sparked off thereby. The government, he reckoned, should then take its cue from the outcome of that process, from the resultant distribution of political weight, seeking in this way to gain a fresh and firmer base. Consequently any kind of hurry, any kind of hasty commitment to one side or another must be bad. This did not of course mean that one could not hold confidential talks and in each case deliberately fall in with one's partner's expectations, giving him the impression that in reality the government had already made up its mind.

Although the impression aroused by Delbrück's resignation ran diametrically counter to the line Bismarck was pursuing in this respect, it gave impetus to the debate about the future direction of economic policy in a way that was thoroughly welcome to the Chancellor. Like so much in his political career, this event too turned out to be exploitable. And, as so often, the question here too is: at what point did he deliberately start gathering and pulling the strings in this direction; at what point in the given context did a new pattern first appear?

It is no accident that we still have no sure answer to this question to this day, for basically it is wrongly posed. Formulated under the influence of the dramatic U-turn in domestic affairs that followed soon after this, it obscures the really crucial issue. The split with Delbrück was not, as such a question suggests in greater or lesser degree, even in substance a positive act. In this respect it was purely negative. It severed the ties that ran through Delbrück to a specific system of economic policy without at the time committing itself to another system, indeed without entirely ruling out a return to the old one. It sought to give the government back its freedom of decision and *not* immediately to tie its hands once more.

In other words, Bismarck still believed, at least at this time, that freedom of decision was possible in the field of economic policy. Obviously alternatives to a policy of direct state interventionism did not yet appear to him to be definitely ruled out. The quarrel over the present and future economic policy of the government was in his eyes essentially a quarrel among the interests involved and the parties and associations that they mobilized behind them. It was these that were principally affected, not the state and the government. The latter, so he believed, would eventually manage to come to terms with whichever system was adopted.

The whole thing had much in common, as the Chancellor saw it, with the situation to which the disputed Eastern Question was giving rise at the same time in the field of foreign policy. It was a conflict that affected the government of the Reich not so much in substance as in terms of its repercussions and in which the government therefore had a relatively free hand. And, as over the Eastern Question, here too a political plan eventually imposed itself on Bismarck that was based on a position of having few or no material interests at stake, a plan by means of which he sought to exploit the situation for the purposes of consolidating his own power. Here as in the sphere of foreign policy he envisaged 'an overall political situation' in which all political forces – abroad with the exception of France, at home with the exception of the Centre Party and the 'protest parties' – 'have need of us and are as far as possible kept from forming coalitions against us by their relations with one another'.

Of all Bismarck's contemporaries it was probably Eduard Lasker, his principal adversary during the 1870s, who with his intimate knowledge of developments and of many of the circumstances and the keen eye of the political opponent most clearly recognized and described that plan. Bismarck's policy during these years, he noted in retrospect after the great change of course in 1878–9, provided 'much food for thought concerning the skill with which Prince Bismarck applied the traditional methods of diplomacy to the internal affairs of the Empire and how unsuspectingly that game was regarded by those who, seemingly called upon to play a part, were drawn into highly confidential negotiations'.[22] Nor was Lasker thinking only of men from his own camp such as the leader of the National Liberal Party and of its representatives in the Imperial Diet, Rudolf von Bennigsen, who had repeatedly collaborated with Bismarck. He also had in mind many conservatives and indeed a whole series of the Chancellor's closest colleagues.

Many even of these did indeed subscribe to the notion that Bismarck was concerned about decisions of principles here. The Chancellor, they believed, was looking for firm allies for a specific policy direction. That on the contrary the individual political groups, no matter what their colour, were for him mere figures in a game of power politics aimed at maintaining and securing his own position was something that most of those concerned became aware of only in defeat, although with regard to their own group they then, like Lasker himself, often succumbed to the temptation of inconsistency and spoke of a deliberate campaign on the Chancellor's part against that group. In fact, however, such a defeat was simply the outcome of a particular constellation of circumstances in which that group's own interests and political pursuit of them had provoked counter-forces and counter-coalitions that seemed to the government and its political head to offer a more solid base for maintaining and securing their own position.

Particularly in the period immediately before the switch of 1878–9 Bismarck allowed himself to be guided in the very highest degree by circumstances and by changes in the political field of forces. These had a far greater influence on the substance of his future policy than has often been supposed. This is not to minimize unduly the personal contribution of the Chancellor and certainly not to represent him as someone who was acting with his hands tied, as it were. On the contrary, the absolute priority that he gave to maintaining and securing his own power position was in many ways what created the conditions and parameters for developments in the future. But it does mean that we must bear in mind more clearly than historians have often done hitherto the fact that those developments possessed an inner logic that was largely independent of Bismarck.

They were dominated by a process of change within society and within and between the parties for which the controversy about the tariff question, now increasingly preoccupying public opinion, was merely one symptom among others. That process found what was possibly its strongest and – in terms of its repercussions – most important expression in the continuing tendency for special interests to become more intensively organized at all levels of society, from associations of working men in a particular branch or trade, through the various professional associations and agencies and the many other middle-class bodies, right up to the associations at the highest level of the economy whose activities were becoming particularly conspicuous. All these organizations were in competition with and threatened the traditional cohesion of existing politico-social movements and parties; this was equally true with regard to the working class and the labour movement – a fact that is often overlooked. They threatened the structures of solidarity and loyalty within those movements, at least to a certain extent and in certain departments. But above all they called upon them for concerted action in support of their own interests, for a greater degree of involvement in the process of economic and social development, and for a more vigorous attitude towards what were felt to be particularly ominous tendencies.

The rapidly growing pressure of immediate expectations that accompanied the economic crisis confronted all the parties with very grave problems. For, as the tariff problem was not alone in showing, the resultant demands could in present circumstances scarcely be co-ordinated, let alone be reduced to coherent programmatic statements. Consequently there was an enormous temptation for all the parties to seek to protect their unity and preserve their traditional spectrum of politico-social integration by dodging the issue, as it were, and referring to the government's sole authority to make decisions and initiate action. All of them eventually succumbed to that temptation to a greater or lesser degree. In this way they contributed substantially towards ushering in a heyday of executive power, even though both at the time and subsequently they made repeated and verbose attempts to disguise the fact.

So the theory that as early as the mid-1870s Bismarck made a deliberate appeal to economic interests in an attempt to destroy the unity of the parties and their capacity for action is in reality a complete misrepresentation. It was the parties that sought to direct the growing pressure of economic interests and their organizations, which was a real factor in no need of being manipulated by anyone, away from themselves and against a government to which scarcely one of them felt a genuine commitment.

From their point of view this was thoroughly understandable. Moreover, in a political system that had deliberately excluded the parties from direct political responsibility and banished them to the 'forecourt of power' (Max Weber) it was only to be expected. Had the National Liberals, for example, succeeded in this way in bringing about the collapse of Bismarck's ministry and the appointment of a Cabinet of their choice, contemporaries would not have been the only ones to regard this as the triumph of a superior and quite deliberate political strategy.

Of course, such a strategy included many risks, including the one that the government might turn the tables by underlining its readiness in principle to take resolute action and to fall in with people's manifold expectations. It might try to force the parties into accepting direct political responsibility by choosing this moment to emphasize its own preparedness to accept an increased measure of parliamentary restraint.

That is exactly what Bismarck did, confronting the parties with a choice between two equally unattractive courses. They could either face up to political responsibility and to the pressure of their supporters' expectations and work closely with a government of which nearly all of them were for one reason or another extremely mistrustful. Or they could be seen – with equally alarming consequences – to be evading that responsibility and forfeiting with it any chance of directly influencing political decisions in accordance with the interests of their voters.

This was only possible, of course, in that Bismarck very largely avoided any actual policy commitments for the time being, subordinating these completely to the question of political co-operation, in other words of who would declare themselves ready to collaborate with him on a long-term basis. Everything was summed up in the sentence: the future government majority will decide. Only one thing was beyond question, namely that, whatever that majority looked like, the man in charge would be Bismarck. This was not least because virtually all the parties, albeit with quite different intentions, had focused their expectations on him and his government.

The crucial question, however, is this: did that mean that everything else was *de facto* predetermined? In concrete terms, were the actual decisions of 1878–9, that disastrous package of discriminatory legislation against the Social Democrats, an economic policy U-turn, and financial reform of the Reich, the only ones capable, in the circumstances and in their mutual interrelatedness, of creating a consensus and attracting majority support? Realistically considered rather than in the light of the observer's own wishful thinking, was there simply no alternative, in terms of policy and personnel, that might likewise have created such a consensus and received the backing of the majority?

Under the influence of an interpretation of these events that has placed ever-increasing emphasis on the alleged manipulation of the eventual outcome by the all-powerful figure of the Chancellor of the Reich and has sought to bring this out in ever more vivid and striking ways, such questions have receded farther and farther into the background. However, for a balanced assessment of future developments they are of decisive importance. They were asked very urgently by none other than Bismarck himself under the effect of developments that, as is often overlooked, in many ways failed conspicuously to come up to his expectations.

It was mainly the National Liberals that received his attention in this respect. They had been as far as any other party from providing an ideal political partner for him. But if only because of the existing majority situation it was natural that in his search for a new and more stable political base he should continue to think primarily in terms of them: he was 'ready as always', he had repeatedly told potential intermediaries even after Delbrück's resignation, 'to come to an arrangement with the National Liberals, who had provided him with his support hitherto' – not least against the forces of 'reaction', against the 'typical, extreme *Kreuzzeitung* people' who were 'jeopardizing all the great achievements of recent years'.[23] However, as he stated on various occasions in later life, his loyalty had met with no response. On the contrary, under the influence of their increasingly dominant left wing the National Liberals had withdrawn their active support and collaboration at the crucial moment. In so doing they had let slip their opportunity of exerting a positive influence on future policy. The party was therefore itself responsible for that policy, having forced him, Bismarck, to take that direction, since otherwise he would have been without any kind of political base. 'I am supposed to have disowned them, whereas they turned their backs on me because I was not able to be as liberal as they', he explained towards the end of February 1879, for example, in an interview with the journalist Moritz Busch. 'Had their leaders been true politicians they could have got a great deal out of me at the time and more as time went on. But the continued existence of the party, of the corps, was more important to them than the prospect of real success.'[24]

This was directed primarily at Rudolf von Bennigsen and his so-called ministerial candidacy. At the end of 1877 Bismarck had offered the National Liberal parliamentary leader posts in the Prussian and Reich governments. Nor had he been thinking merely of a departmental post held by the same man in both governments – the office of Minister of Finance, for example. No, Bennigsen was at the same time to have functioned as Bismarck's deputy in Prussia and the Reich, in other words to have taken over an office that had been vacant since the resignation of Delbrück and that Bismarck's ever more prolonged absences from Berlin made it seem urgently necessary to fill.

Bismarck's offer had of course carried with it a series of conditions. Above all, agreement was to be reached over the principles of 'a reform of tariffs and taxation' as well as over a reform of the internal structure of the Reich. The crucial 'remedy' here, as Bismarck put it in the letter he wrote to Bennigsen on 17 December 1877, inviting him to Varzin for talks, was probably to be found particularly in the 'extension of the system of personal union as it has existed hitherto in the Monarch, in the Chancellor, in the War Minister and in Foreign Affairs'.[25] However, Bismarck had expressly stated his readiness to negotiate all these points in detail. In other words, he had not by any means unreasonably restricted the scope of such negotiations from the outset.

Nevertheless, opponents said at the time and critics have maintained subsequently that the whole thing was a purely tactical move, the sole aim of which was to subject the National Liberal Party to additional internal stresses and if possible to split it. The right wing of the party might then indeed have been welcomed by Bismarck as a weaker and more compliant partner.

Undoubtedly Bismarck himself fuelled such a suspicion in a great many ways. For years he had been mounting ever fiercer attacks on the party's left wing, trying to play right and left off against each other. He had increasingly treated the National Liberals as a coalition that was in the process of falling apart as its common interests became fewer and its internal cohesion progressively weaker. This line seems to come through clearly even in the remarks to Moritz Busch quoted above, when he spoke of 'the continued existence of the party, of the corps', as being 'more important' to the leaders of the party 'than the prospect of real success'.

Here too, however, we must beware of representing Bismarck as the creator of circumstances of which he made use and attributing to him sole responsibility for what happened as a result. On sober consideration the ordeal through which the National Liberals had been going as a national and as a parliamentary party in many areas for a number of years now can scarcely be said to have been mainly of Bismarck's making. In fact it arose out of the steadily growing conflicts of interest amongst what was in many ways an extremely heterogeneous following. Nor is there any overlooking the fact that its left wing in particular took the lead among those who sought to preserve the unity and integrity of the party not least by dissociating themselves from the government while at the same time trying to make it solely responsible for all such developments and manifestations as the party's following or sections of that following regarded as unfavourable. In other words, there was neither wish nor readiness in this quarter to assume positive responsibility in the present situation. The obvious course, therefore, was on the one hand to raise their own conditions as high as possible and on the other to treat the sincerity of an offer of collaboration from the government with maximum scepticism from the outset.

These were precisely the tactics adopted by the National Liberal left wing under Lasker, whom Bismarck had described bitterly as early as the beginning of 1875 as 'the real disease of the state', calling him 'an even worse vine louse than Windthorst'.[26] We shall therefore get very much closer to the historical truth in our assessment of this whole episode if we see it in terms of a game of poker. In that game the stakes, the chances of success and the political intelligence of the players were by no means as unevenly distributed as those who eventually lost liked to pretend. On the contrary, at the time we are talking about, namely in the autumn of 1877, it was not out of the question that the government might find itself increasingly boxed in and perhaps even get into a hopeless situation. It had always laid great emphasis on its having sole political responsibility and ascribed every success to itself. In view of the increasingly critical turn taken by developments in many spheres, it now risked having to pay the penalty for that stance. Because nearly all the political parties and groups of any importance were now in a great hurry to dissociate themselves from it.

In addition to this, six months earlier it had once again been brought home to Bismarck that the support he enjoyed in the person of the now 80-year-old monarch, while considerable, was not unlimited. In order to have his rear, at least within the ranks of the government, completely free for all eventualities he had tried in March 1877 to get rid of the Admiralty chief, Albrecht von Stosch, who was at the same time a Prussian Minister of State and was seen as possibly the crown prince's candidate for Chancellor. He was a 'plotter and spy', Bismarck told his intimates in justification of this step, 'who never opens his mouth in the Council of Ministers but then goes blabbing to the Crown Prince and to His Majesty'.[27] To discredit Stosch in the emperor's eyes he publicly accused him, in a speech in the Imperial Diet, of allowing his political decisions to be guided not by the needs of the state but by the wishes of parliament as dictated by one-sided interests; he courted popularity, Bismarck claimed, and left to others the arduous task of finding a balance between what was desirable and what was possible.[28]

However, this attempt on Bismarck's part to scupper a rival as a precautionary measure had itself literally run aground. William thought highly of Stosch as a person and as a military expert; probably he was also looking for an opportunity to demonstrate for once that he was not prepared to bow to his Chancellor in all things. Bismarck had promptly sought, as he did so often, to stage a clarifying 'chancellorship crisis' by spreading rumours that he was about to tender his own resignation. But instead of the emphatic imperial 'Never!' mentioned on various occasions subsequently, all he had got out of this 'resignation farce', as Eugen Richter later dubbed the whole episode,[29] acted out under the gaze of an extremely attentive public, had been an extended leave of absence.

At this point, therefore, the National Liberals had every reason to take the view that the wisest course was to hold themselves in readiness and preserve their internal unity and political fighting power for future use. The party had 'time to wait', as Bennigsen himself frankly admitted; 'meanwhile the financial crisis was getting worse and the septennate was running out'.[30] Why should they invite internal stresses and subject themselves to an additional ordeal by supporting a government whose political future was somewhat uncertain and that faced decisions in many areas that must in any case inevitably kindle antagonisms?

On the other hand there was the fact that the Chancellor, now obviously dependent on stronger parliamentary support than hitherto, might after all be prepared to make substantial concessions. Moreover, a genuine participation in government might open up considerable prospects for the future both in itself and in terms of party politics. For as well as a good deal of conflict it promised to forge firmer and more permanent ties of interest both among the party's traditional following and also beyond.

After lengthy disputes, however, control of the party eventually fell into the hands of those who rejected any participation in government on the basis proposed by Bismarck and who presented deliberately excessive demands. The chief of these was that, in addition to Bennigsen, Bismarck should take two further National Liberals into his Cabinet – two, moreover, who leaned towards the left wing of the party, namely the Mayor of Breslau, Max von Forckenbeck, and the Munich deputy Baron von Stauffenberg.

It could be anticipated that the Chancellor would never accept this. The stumbling-block was not so much the question of principle regarding a possible parliamentarization of the Reich. What decided the matter was that agreeing to such a demand would have made Bismarck heavily dependent on one party without, however, giving him a majority in the Diet, even if the Progressive Party came in as well. In the recent election the National Liberals had dropped twenty-seven seats and the Progressive Party fourteen. With this the two parties had clearly lost the absolute majority that, together, they had enjoyed since 1871. And Bismarck could scarcely expect, given the new situation, to receive any additional support from the right. Lastly, it would likewise have been difficult to win the emperor's support for such a policy. According to Christoph von Tiedemann, the senior civil servant in the Prussian Cabinet Office who went on to head the Imperial Chancellory from 1878 to 1881, at the very first mention of the plan to bring Bennigsen into the Cabinet the emperor had looked at Bismarck 'as if his interlocutor had taken leave of his senses'.[31] Subsequently, too, William had expressed grave misgivings as to whether Bennigsen would ever be able to keep to 'the calm, conservative pace of my government'.[32]

So it was quite clear that, regardless of any policy questions, merely the job demands made by the National Liberals would lead to a breakdown of negotiations. Of course – and it was on this that those who had persuaded the parliamentary party to back those demands based their calculations – the person really affected, as far as anyone could anticipate, would be Bismarck. His government now appeared to be virtually paralysed in all that required implementation by legislative means, in other words not least as regarded far-reaching decisions in matters of economic and budgetary policy.

Bismarck had indeed got into a somewhat precarious situation. The liberal left had confronted him with deliberately excessive demands. The right regarded him with newly awakened mistrust. Moreover, he was once again exposed to the charge of pure opportunism, for everyone was expecting a change of monarch and everyone knew of the crown prince's sympathies for the liberal centre. There was no longer any question of the ideal 'overall political situation' in which all political groups and parties with the exception of the Centre Party and the 'protest parties' needed the government and would be 'kept from forming coalitions against us by their relations with one another'. On the contrary, it looked to many people as if the Bismarck era was drawing to a close and the Chancellor was at the end of his tether as far as domestic policy was concerned. Possibly his ever longer 'leaves of absence' were an additional sign of this: the last one had run for nearly nine months, until the collapse of the negotiations with Bennigsen. Even convinced supporters complained of a 'state of muddleheadedness' and did not think it impossible that the Chancellor really was about to throw in the towel.[33]

Faced with this situation, Bismarck decided towards the end of February 1878 to seize the bull by the horns. In what was widely regarded as an extremely dramatic speech in the Imperial Diet on 22 February he abandoned his previous public reserve with regard to matters of economic and budgetary policy on one crucial point. In so doing he gave notice, three days after his key foreign policy speech on the Eastern Question, of a fundamental change of course.[34]

The occasion was the first reading of a series of laws concerning taxation. With the aid of these the government was openly seeking not only to improve its income but also to achieve a greater degree of independence from the member states and their so-called 'Matricularbeiträge', their financial contributions to the government of the Reich. The principal measure was an increase in the tax on tobacco, which Camphausen, the Prussian Minister of Finance chiefly responsible for these legislative proposals, had discussed in advance with those concerned, following the usual practice in such matters.

All this Bismarck swept aside without even so much as informing his Finance Minister, whom he had long ago decided to 'drop',[35] of his intention to make his views public in this way. He stated that he personally saw the whole Bill simply as a 'through station', a 'preparation' for and preliminary stage in the establishment of a state tobacco monopoly, and hence a step towards what he envisaged as a 'comprehensive reform . . . that will make the Empire not poor, as it is now, but truly rich'. He went on: 'My ideal is not an Empire that must go begging for contributions at the doors of the individual states but an Empire that, holding the key to the principal source of sound finance, namely indirect taxes, would be in a position to pay out to the individual states.' He had now definitely decided, he said, in the interests of providing a sound financial basis for the Reich and hence for its power and independence vis-à-vis the individual states – and that included Prussia – not to let himself be guided any longer by dogmatic economic and budgetary principles – for of course a state monopoly in even a small sector of the economy was inevitably regarded as a mortal sin by every hard-line liberal. The only considerations that now counted for him, Bismarck declared, were those of expediency.

The same applied, so it was open to anyone to construe, to all the other questions at issue in this field – for example, to the question of protective tariffs, which could at the same time be seen as revenue duties, further improving the income of the Reich. It was therefore entirely logical that, immediately after this session of the Diet, Bennigsen should formally have announced the collapse of the negotiations regarding his joining the government. And it was equally logical that Camphausen, the Minister of Finance, and Achenbach, the Minister of Commerce, both of whom were close to the liberals and especially to liberal ideas in the field of economic and budgetary policy, should have tendered their resignations soon afterwards.

The government had now taken up a clear position for the first time. In doing so, however, it had lost any kind of adequate parliamentary base. Even assuming solid support from the two conservative parties and from a large number of dissident National Liberals voting with them, it could no longer put together a parliamentary majority.

In the present situation, however – unlike that of the early 1860s, for example – any kind of political stalemate was inevitably seen as constituting at least as much of a problem for the government as for the parties. Consequently there were even many immediate contemporaries who assumed that Bismarck, in making this thrust, was for the first time aiming at an entirely different parliamentary and party-political constellation. The Grand Duke of Baden, for example, thought he could diagnose early in April 1878 that 'the change of system is becoming more and more clearly recognizable'. Even the 'parties in the parliaments' were 'undergoing a complete transformation . . . Depending on the kind of reception the next government Bills are accorded in the Imperial Diet, we can expect that body to be dissolved.'[36]

The external impulse for such conjectures was provided not least by the death of Pope Pius IX on 7 February and the election of the former Cardinal-Archbishop of Perugia, Vincenzo Gioacchino Pecci, as the new pope on 20 February 1878. Pius IX and his Secretary of State, Cardinal Antonelli, had shown themselves wholly intransigent in the 'Kulturkampf' and the ecclesiastical controversy; in fact their position had steadily hardened. By contrast the new pope, who took the name Leo XIII, had the reputation of being concerned primarily with the concrete power base of the papacy in Italy itself and with the restoration of the Papal States. He might possibly be prepared, for the sake of this objective, to give in to the Reich and to influence the Catholic party in that country accordingly.

There was also the fact that in the mean time a very broad measure of agreement had arisen between the conservatives, who were mostly Prussian, and the Centre Party on the fundamental questions relating to the kind of course that was to be set in economic and commercial policy. This was based on the great similarity of interests between the followings of the two parties. It was open to Bismarck to calculate that, if some easing of the 'Kulturkampf' and at least some prospect of a compromise could be achieved, entirely new parliamentary combinations might enter the realms of possibility.

Now that his situation had become somewhat precarious, Bismarck undoubtedly toyed with the idea of this sort of radical reversal of the old domestic alliances. And there is a possibility that his thrust in connection with the tobacco duty question was also intended as a preliminary probe in this direction. But he was far too much of a political realist to have looked for any quick success here. Nor can there be any question of his attitude towards the Centre Party, for example, having undergone any decisive change. He had told a meeting of the Prussian Cabinet only the previous autumn that it was his intention, if he remained in office, 'to fight the battle for civilization [*Kulturkampf*] to the bitter end, to which perhaps not all those present will go with me'. He would 'rather put up with the rule of Social Democracy than with the stultifying rule of the Jesuits'.[37] Granted, this had had something to do with the situation in which it was uttered, being tailored to the hopes or rather fears of the liberals, whose standard-bearer on all these questions, Adalbert Falk, was among 'those present'. But it was also, at least in essence, in line with his own basic attitude. What came in the further course of events to be termed a 'blue-black' coalition could, in his view, offer a political alternative in a particular situation. But neither then nor later did it constitute a long-term political objective as far as he was concerned.

So we can scarcely speak of a plan to turn the Centre Party step by step from an enemy into a political ally and to re-establish his own position and that of his government on that basis. Nor would such a plan have been at all realistic. No, Bismarck's objective was of a mainly negative nature. He wanted to force the National Liberals out of their key position in the Imperial Diet, a position that in view of the absence of political alternatives up to now had been out of all proportion to their numerical strength, or at least to put them under so much pressure that a majority would eventually be prepared to say that they would enter a firm alliance with the government, rather than one that was continually being called in question, and that they would back the course it pursued.

Even at this stage, then, Bismarck clung to that basic combination that had seemed to him from very early on to be the only one that promised success in the given political and social situation. It was based on the collaboration, chiefly embodied in himself as go-between, of the traditional, overwhelmingly Prussian-Protestant ruling class with the new bourgeois one – to the extent to which the latter was prepared to co-operate and compromise and did not demand a monopoly of power for itself. In party-political terms it was based on co-operation between the conservatives – committed as deeply as possible to him – and the National Liberals up to and including the centre, as represented by Bennigsen.

For many years now this combination had provided the real basis of his success and of his unique political position, and it remained the crucial factor governing his conduct, although for understandable reasons he sought increasingly – and as far as both contemporaries and posterity were concerned very successfully – to disguise the fact. It remained his 'system', which, however, as in the field of foreign policy, he was able to maintain only by ever more complicated and eventually ever more artificial means. Moreover, in both fields he not infrequently had need of the happy accident, the special circumstance, the unexpected development that, contrary to all calculations, tipped the balance in his favour.

This was already true of the situation in the spring of 1878. Just how awkward a position the government was in at this stage was shown very clearly by the debate on the so-called 'Deputization Bill' in late February/early March. Bismarck's actual political objective was once again – as expressed repeatedly over many years now – 'to strengthen the power of the Empire', in other words in this case to anchor the political supremacy and authority of the Reich in terms of offices and men. This was to be achieved not only by having a vice-Chancellor generally deputize for the Chancellor but by creating a system of departmental deputization, so to speak. The Chancellor was to be enabled to transfer his powers as sole minister of the Reich and President of the Federal Council – temporarily, and subject to revocation at any time – to the heads of the supreme authorities of the Reich. These were to become *de facto* ministers of the Reich, though not *de jure* as far as political responsibility was concerned; on the contrary, with this the demand for a body of imperial ministers responsible to parliament was rejected anew and as it were ruled out by law. As Herbert Bismarck wrote on his father's behalf in a letter to Count Holnstein, the confidant of the King of Bavaria, 'the whole Deputization Bill' had 'nothing whatever to do with independently accountable imperial ministries'.[38] At the same time the ever present possibility, beyond any kind of regulation of competences, of a conflict of power and interests between the Reich and its most powerful member-state was to be nipped in the bud by arranging for a maximum of 'personal union', with the same man holding the two corresponding offices at Reich level and in the Prussian Cabinet.

In the present political situation, however, Bismarck had to be content with a very much watered-down implementation of his plan. It was brought emphatically home to him how severely the current atmosphere of general mistrust restricted his political scope as soon as it was no longer a matter simply of securing but one of altering existing circumstances.

He did manage to get the idea of deputization accepted in principle, but under pressure from the member-states it was limited to those areas in which the Reich had the right not only of legislation and control but also of execution. In practice it excluded all those areas that fell, even if only partially, within the traditional competence of the individual states. To get his way in this respect vis-à-vis the member-states of the Reich turned out to be beyond him in the present parliamentary and party-political constellation.

So when Eugen Richter, the leader of the Progressive Party, noted in retrospect that the Deputization Bill had served 'to ram the dictatorship of the Chancellor even more firmly home', he hit on only one aspect of the matter, namely the additional strengthening of the Chancellor's existing position.[39] The other aspect was a kind of institutional immobilization of the Reich. This was something that Bismarck, with an eye to the future, felt with some justification to be scarcely tolerable. It was inevitably seen as reducing the Reich, politically too, in an unreasonable and unwarrantable manner, to the status of a 'paying-guest of the member-states', particularly Prussia. In fact it transpired in the further course of events that the various tendencies towards greater unification and the increasingly important factor of imperial legislation were more powerful than Bismarck had originally taken them to be. But for the moment what he saw was the way in which the imperial government's effective scope for manoeuvre between the Federal Council and the Imperial Diet and within both bodies was narrowing to the point of political immobility.

This emerged as soon as it came to filling the newly created as well as the recently vacated offices in the governments of Prussia and the Reich. Instead of men who for their part committed powerful political forces to the government, as Bismarck had envisaged happening in Bennigsen's case, for the most part he could find – and in some cases it was a long search – only candidates who had yet to distinguish themselves politically and were decidedly second-string in their respective political groups.

This was true of the former mayor of Breslau, now Lord Mayor of Berlin, Arthur Hobrecht, who replaced Camphausen at the Ministry of Finance towards the end of March 1878. It was also true of Albert Maybach, who as an 'intelligent and experienced expert'[40] moved up from under secretary of state to become the new Minister of Commerce. And it was true, furthermore, of the former ambassador to Vienna, Count Otto Stolberg-Wernigerode, who now became Vice-Chancellor. The fact that Bismarck had marked him out as his potential successor two years before[41] shows only that he regarded him as a political lightweight and as such quite safe. The Chancellor was to reveal what he really thought on this question to an old Göttingen student friend in the mid-1880s: 'Why I've not yet provided for a suitable successor? . . . The answer is very simple: having done so, I might just as well be dead on my feet.'[42] Finally, as for the new Minister of the Interior, Count Botho Eulenburg, a cousin of the previous minister Friedrich Eulenburg, the man behind the local government law of 1872 who among others had blocked a final reconciliation with the conservatives, he was very soon 'ground down' between the parties and the Chancellor without having found any firm support in either camp.

This kind of ministry of second-raters may have been convenient in many respects. Bismarck's political enemies immediately started speaking in sarcastic terms of the Chancellor's increasing tendency to surround himself with men who were politically no more than puppets. At the same time, however, it made the work of government extraordinarily difficult and in addition made the government itself appear totally isolated. The 'whole history of the origins of the new ministry', said the Grand Duke of Baden, one of the most critical observers of the political scene during this period, provided 'proof' of the fact that 'there is no one else to be found who is prepared to "go on board" now that the helmsman has lost his way'.[43]

The question everyone was asking was: what will happen next? Everywhere there was speculation, particularly after Bismarck's speech in the Imperial Diet on 22 February 1878, regarding the government's intentions, plans and objectives. There was mention of a possible dissolution of so awkward a Diet, and in some quarters there was even talk of far more drastic measures in breach of the constitution. Berlin positively teemed with rumours, and the papers outdid one another in speculations as to what the Chancellor had in mind. At the same time he was reminded from many quarters of the limits to his power, now become so apparent. Many of his opponents spoke not unhopefully of the present situation as being untenable. As Bennigsen said of him around this time, it was entirely possible, given the majority situation in the Diet, the budgetary situation and the septennate question due to come up in two years' time, 'that he will leave his body in the breach if he does not come to terms with Parliament'.[44]

In view of all this it was not only Eduard Lasker, who had meanwhile become a kind of critical antipode to the Chancellor, following his every step with extreme suspicion, who found himself in retrospect strongly under the impression that Bismarck had positively yearned, in this situation, for 'some curious, striking, or stunning occurrence . . . such as would provoke a mighty and passionate mass reaction and jolt people's minds out of the rut of habit'.[45] And although no one suggested that Bismarck had anything to do with what followed, the impression grew in intensity during these weeks and months, spreading far beyond the circle of his opponents, that he would have been prepared to embrace practically any means, up to and including a *coup d'état*, in order to regain the political initiative. Nothing, it was said, reflected the basic character of his politics and his terrifying lack of scruple more clearly than the developments of the spring and summer of 1878.

The way in which he exploited the two attempts made on Emperor William's life on 11 May and 2 June 1878 – the first by a 21-year-old plumber named Hödel, who fired two shots at William without hitting anyone; the second, which was far more serious, by Karl Nobiling, an academic agronomist who had clearly allowed his psychopathic craving for attention to push him into emulating Hödel – does undoubtedly constitute one of the darkest passages in Bismarck's political career. In neither case, as very quickly emerged, was there any connection to speak of between the would-be assassin and the Social Democratic Party; even less was there any kind of direct encouragement from that quarter, to say nothing of a conspiracy to murder the emperor. But Bismarck was determined to take immediate action; he had very little interest in clarifying the background to the two attempts and finding out who was responsible. 'Ought not the assassination attempt to be taken as grounds for an immediate Bill against the Socialists and their press?' he telegraphed from Friedrichsruh on 11 May, the very day of the first attempt.[46] A mere five days later, brushing aside express warnings from several Prussian ministers against so hasty a proceeding, he had Prussia place before the Federal Council a Bill 'to guard against Social Democratic outrages'.

There was not the least indication, let alone concrete proof, of any danger ahead. Consequently it was clear immediately to almost everyone what this was all about. The liberals, and in particular the members of the National Liberal Party in the Imperial Diet, were to be forced into making a fundamental decision for or against the government. Bismarck wanted to confront them with a choice: either to continue, even now, to withhold support from energetic measures against declared enemies of the existing order or, alternatively, to abandon their misgivings with regard to any kind of exceptive or discriminatory legislation and any qualification of the constitutional principle of equality before the law.

But the Chancellor had obviously overrated the opportunity that offered here, and by his way of going about things he immediately let the National Liberals off the hook again. Even in the Federal Council Prussia found itself faced with a host of objections and criticisms that could not be reduced to simple political formulae and to the question of basic attitudes towards the government and the line it had adopted towards the Social Democrats. Simultaneously those objections received press support from various quarters and were developed further in the forum of public discussion.

All the spokesmen of the National Liberal Party needed to do in the crucial session of the Imperial Diet on 23–4 May was to collate those objections and clothe them in protestations to the effect that of course they too were in favour of determined action against all assaults on the existing order, on the state and on the rule of law. In the knowledge that a large section of public opinion and the overwhelming majority of the parties saw the government's venture as no more than a transparent political manoeuvre, the 'intention to make war on the Diet',[47] their chief spokesman, Rudolf von Bennigsen, even proceeded to a scarcely veiled counter-attack. What was at issue here, he said, was not least recognition of the principle 'that different parties representing legitimate political and material interests are necessary and justified'. That principle must on no account be abandoned, however emphatically one rejected the political methods of Social Democracy, its subversive propaganda and the practical action it advocated. Among the aims of Social Democracy was 'the betterment of the working population in terms of its economic position, including the implementation of measures to counter mass poverty – and what humane legislator will not make such aims his own?' Bennigsen's conclusion – expressed in general terms, but everyone knew whom it was aimed at – was as follows: 'We ought more than ever to avoid mounting attacks against our political opponents as if they had sinned against the common good.'[48]

Accordingly the overwhelming majority of 251 votes to 57 with which the Diet eventually threw out this first Anti-Socialist Bill was at the same time a fresh demonstration against the Bismarck government, confirming its very great isolation. The Chancellor had achieved the very opposite of what he had set out to achieve. Largely through his own fault he found himself politically exposed and – worse still – politically outmanoeuvred.

In this situation, news came on 2 June of a fresh attempt on the life of William I, who this time sustained serious injury. Bismarck's reaction has been cited a hundred times as proof of the icy ruthlessness of the man and the naked Machiavellism of his policy, impervious to any kind of human spontaneity. Breathing heavily, according to Tiedemann, who brought him the news in the park at Friedrichsruh, after a short pause he banged his stick on the ground and exclaimed, 'In that case we'll dissolve the Diet!'[49] Only then is he said to have inquired about the fate of the man with whom he had been so closely associated, politically and personally, for the past sixteen years. A different version already current among his contemporaries – Bismarck was aware of it himself and continued to protest against it in his old age[50] – was even more direct and brutal: 'Now I've got them [the National Liberals]; and I'm going to squeeze them till they yell.' Whether or not it is true, this version reflected what many people thought Bismarck was capable of as well as the viewpoint from which they regarded future developments. To that extent it is further evidence of the never-ebbing mistrust that now broke out again even more strongly, the lack of confidence in him that was like a moat around the man his whole life long.

As was the case with almost no other politician in a comparable position, it made an uninterrupted series of fresh and tangible successes a condition of his political survival.

In retrospect Bismarck himself provided indirect confirmation of this, particularly with regard to the situation after the second assassination attempt. According to him, at the crucial Cabinet meeting presided over by the crown prince on 5 June 1878 the majority of his Cabinet colleagues came out against his suggestion to dissolve the Imperial Diet, their principal argument being that that body could now be expected with certainty to approve a new Anti-Socialist Bill. As Bismarck put it in the chapter of his memoirs entitled 'Intrigues': 'The assurance evinced by my colleagues on this occasion clearly rested on a confidential understanding between them and influential parliamentarians, whereas not one of the latter had attempted so much as an exchange of views with me. It appeared that, so far as the division of my inheritance was concerned, an agreement had already been reached.'[51]

In other words, the second assassination attempt found him not in a mood of cool calculation but in an exceptional situation. He saw himself surrounded by mistrust and by political opponents who, he believed, were looking only to outmanoeuvre him once and for all. The rage the attack provoked in him, seeking an outlet, as it were, in the shape of someone to blame, fused instantaneously with the idea of doing something definite to break the ring that he claimed surrounded him and regain his freedom of action.

This kind of interpretation in no way represents an attempt to exonerate Bismarck from the moral reproaches that people have attached to this episode; those reproaches lie at a different level and remain justified at that level. What is at issue here is the nature of Bismarck's spontaneous decision to dissolve the Imperial Diet: why did he choose this course?

It is in fact possible, in defiance of the usual interpretation, to make out a good case to the effect that his doing so was really not the product of some sober, largely emotionless, purely Machiavellian power-political calculation. From everything we know today, the ministers opposing him were undoubtedly right in assuming that the majority in the Diet would now revise its recent decision and back the government. This would have given the latter a new parliamentary base without any need for the drastic step of dissolution. There might even, at this point, have been some possibility of the kind of arrangement with at least a large section of the National Liberal parliamentary group that Bismarck had relied on hitherto. On the other hand, given a realistic appraisal of the situation, it could have been predicted with some certainty that, even with full use being made of all publicistic and bureaucratic resources, a radical change in the majority situation in the Diet – a conservative landslide, for example – was simply not on the cards. Interests were too divergent and the power of social and political integration manifested by the conservatives in particular far too poorly developed for that. The outcome could only be a further splintering of the party-political spectrum, which would destroy every basis for forming a more solid, more permanent parliamentary majority.

Once we bear this in mind, the usual picture of the ruthless, coolly calculating Chancellor becomes considerably less convincing. We are tempted instead to see a politician at work here who, feeling that he was isolated and his political position in jeopardy, reacted in a thoroughly emotional manner. Bismarck simply took the bull by the horns, as it were, without looking too closely into where this course might lead him. Years later, when writing his memoirs, he gave vent to what had been his underlying mood at that time: 'It was not I who sought a deal with the National Liberals but they who conspired with my colleagues in an attempt to squeeze me out.' There had been a wide-ranging plan involving many people to replace him by a 'Gladstone ministry'. This had forced him to take prompt and decisive action.[52]

Nothing of such a 'plan' has so far come to light, if by 'plan' we mean something more than extremely general and unco-ordinated efforts and aspirations. But anyone who concludes from that that the whole passage was simply an attempt at retrospective self-justification is overestimating Bismarck's belief in the power of mere assertion and in the wholly uncritical credulity of his contemporary readership – to say nothing of that of future historians. Moreover, the motives for such an attempt remain largely obscure. A more plausible explanation is that even the retrospective evocation of such plans brought to the surface a suspicion bordering on paranoia. In that suspicion he tended to seize on and interpret individual utterances and what were in reality quite unconnected events as evidence of a political conspiracy. An instance of this was when at the end of June 1878 he told the then ambassador in Paris, Prince Chlodwig zu Hohenlohe, in all seriousness that the National Liberals had wanted to take over 'the administration of affairs' on their own and 'set [him] on the table as a show dish like a maggoty apple'.[53]

It was no accident that, looking back, he should have mentioned in this context the names of the two men whom he had regarded in former years as his most dangerous political rivals, whom he had fought with all the weapons at his disposal and with brutal ruthlessness, and whom, even after his defeat of them, he continued to persecute with undiminished hatred: Count Robert von der Goltz, his political opponent in the particularly precarious years immediately after 1862; and Count Harry von Arnim, who as the ambassador of the Reich in Paris from 1872 had, as Bismarck thought, tried to contest his political influence. Between them they stood for the almost traumatic fear that someone, some day, might tread the same sort of path as he had trodden, namely build himself up into the embodiment of a more or less vague political alternative, gain the emperor's ear and thrust him, Bismarck, aside in the next political crisis. Particularly the much-discussed 'Arnim Affair' shows how much and how constantly he was a prey to fear of this kind of 'palace intrigue', to a political-conspiracy phobia that had unmistakably pathological traits. Bismarck had not been content with virtually destroying Arnim politically by persuading the emperor to transfer him first to Constantinople and then, in reaction to a clumsy move on the ambassador's part, into retirement. He had eventually, with the aid of two dubious trials, destroyed him in civilian life as well.

Against this background we see clearly the significance of the fact that in his memoirs, looking back over the developments of the next few years, Bismarck included the newly appointed Minister of the Interior, Count Botho Eulenburg, in the ranks of alleged would-be political conspirators on a par with von der Goltz and Arnim. It illustrates the almost irrational factors that played a part in the political decisions of 1878 and in particular the decision to dissolve the Imperial Diet. With those decisions a certain destructive element entered the picture. They were dominated by Bismarck's desire to rob potential rivals of their political base as a precautionary measure – undertaken without any regard to the consequences for his own policy. In this way alternatives to that policy were to be ruled out in advance.

In the peculiar situation of the early summer of 1878, when he was deeply worried about his political future, Bismarck at the same time came closest to the political starting position of the two men with whom he has so often been compared in terms of their political tactics and their political 'systems'. Presenting themselves under the slogan 'aut Caesar, aut nihil' as the only realistic alternative to political and social chaos had been one of the recipes for success adopted by both Bonapartes, though principally by Napoleon III. That was what had kept them in power by bringing them the political allegiance of all who, for various reasons and with different ends in view, had an interest in preserving the existing order.

That political starting position, however, is as far as the parallel goes, for unlike the two Bonapartes – and this is often overlooked in assessments of his last decade in office – Bismarck was not even vouchsafed an initial success in this direction. Nor was that all. The situation in 1878 may have approximated to a Bonapartist starting position, but it had neither been brought about by deliberate calculation nor was it exploited accordingly. In fact the whole constellation of circumstances ruled out any chance of this. Because between the chaos that allegedly threatened and the one man who promised to avert it there stood in this case, unlike in France, a solidly established traditional monarchy and a now firmly reorganized conservative camp to which the army, too, felt that it belonged both intellectually and socially.

These forces were seen as the natural bulwark against all threats from the left. Bismarck could scarcely hope that the Bonapartist rallying-cry would bring him the kind of political autonomy and freedom of action in which he was primarily interested. A more likely result was a swing to the right, which threatened to increase his dependence on forces that, judging by all that had gone before, regarded him with considerable mistrust.

It was a danger of which Bismarck was very well aware. He therefore, contrary to what is widely believed, never even placed his hopes in that rallying-cry. On the contrary, the slogan – 'For a law against Socialists and for financial reform of the Empire' – that he issued for the election campaign was once again aimed unequivocally at the National Liberal vote in yet another attempt to secure that party's support for himself and his policy. The combination of repressive exclusion of the left, a change of course in economic policy and a strengthening of the power of the Reich implicit in that slogan, though certainly not to the taste of the majority that had set the tone in the party hitherto, nevertheless brought together elements of a possible compromise within its following by laying skilful emphasis on the special interests and objectives of individual groups. At the same time it steered clear of subjects that would have provoked a split or aroused the determined opposition of the party as a whole.

There could be no question of any of this with respect to the other parties, or only to a limited extent. In the case of the new German Conservative Party, in which the Prussian element still clearly predominated, it was particularly the demand for a strengthening of the central power of the Reich that, for all the party's lip-service to a powerful Reich, ran into considerable opposition, though this was not publicly expressed. Above all, however, Bismarck's election slogan was hardly likely to persuade the Centre Party to undertake even a limited change of course. Continued resistance to any kind of discriminatory legislation was as certain from this quarter as was rejection of any stronger tendencies towards centralization. In all probability not even concessions in respect of Bismarck's policy towards the church would have wrought any fundamental change here. The Chancellor was under no illusion about this: 'The forces united in the Centre [Party],' he wrote to the King of Bavaria towards the middle of August 1878, 'may currently be fighting under the Papal flag, but they are subversive *per se* and would be even if the flag of Catholicity ceased to cover them; their connection with the Progressive Party and the Socialists on the basis of hostility to the state is independent of the controversy over the church.'[54]

It is clear from this too that Bismarck was as interested as ever in restoring the informal alliance and the old relationship of practical co-operation between the conservatives and the National Liberals with some extension towards the right and a clearer line of demarcation on the left. In a statement of principle regarding the forthcoming elections that he issued to the state authorities, he wrote that the important thing was 'the test of how far the moderate members [of the National Liberal Party] who in principle favour efforts to maintain the authority of the state will go, initially in the elections, towards giving firm support to the governments, not merely in response to the needs of the moment but in order permanently to safeguard governmental authority'.[55] The strategic objective was still, above and beyond all questions of detail, the preservation of a balance in favour of the executive between the forces of old and new, tradition and modernity, and between the elites representing them on both sides. The central problem was how to offset, neutralize and politically reduce the steadily increasing weight on the one side of the scales.

To that extent the elections of the summer of 1878, coming as they did after so many fruitless political initiatives in the recent past, were at first a thoroughgoing success for Bismarck; he said himself that he 'had not expected so great an increase in strength on the right'.[56] The fact that they took place in the shadow of a major gain in prestige on the foreign policy front for the Reich and for its leading statesman undoubtedly helped. But the crucial factor was the domestic policy arguments and the interests and political and social objectives that they brought into play. It was they that caused the two conservative parties to gain an additional twenty-eight seats and 9 per cent of the votes cast. The National Liberals lost twenty-nine seats, though on a very much smaller percentage swing. The Progressive Party, too, dropped a further nine seats. The so-called 'protest parties', the 'enemies of the Reich', more or less held their own, except that the Social Democrats lost three of their twelve seats. The result was very close to a parliamentary draw between the National Liberals and the two conservative parties. With the latter enjoying a slight superiority of numbers, it now looked as if the balance was safe even against an influx of left-wing liberals.

Bismarck's calculation was that both sides, the conservatives and the National Liberals, now had the choice between collaborating with each other and cancelling each other out by bringing the Diet to a standstill. Moreover, that collaboration could be effected only through the agency of a government that was directly committed to neither side and occupied a position as it were between and above them. Only such a government would be capable, given the powerful material and personal antagonisms between the two groups, of bringing about a compromise. He spelled out that calculation in only slightly embellished terms in a directive for the semi-official press issued at the end of May 1878: 'The application of the strict parliamentary traditions of Britain to our institutions', he wrote, would 'present insuperable difficulties as long as we have no party capable of forming a parliamentary majority without a coalition with one or indeed a number of other parties'.[57]

At first his calculation appeared to be working out. Even during the election campaign, most of the members of the new National Liberal parliamentary party had not only committed themselves to voting for a fresh Anti-Socialist Bill. They had also declared their readiness in principle to collaborate with the imperial government on questions of budgetary policy and to support a further strengthening of the central authority of the Reich.

There could no longer be any question of political deals on a *quid pro quo* basis and certainly none of putting pressure on the government with any chance of success. All that was left – particularly with regard to the first item on the agenda, namely a new Anti-Socialist Bill – was to beat a halfway orderly retreat. In the process what mattered was not showing one's political opponents and rivals too many weak points and at the same time avoiding, if possible, any locking of horns within one's own party on matters of principle. Both endeavours, of course, could succeed only to a limited extent. On the contrary, despite an eventually solid vote by the National Liberals in the Imperial Diet, they heralded the end of the party's unity both at parliamentary and at national level.

Neither the Centrists nor the spokesmen of the Progressive Party lost the opportunity of telling the parliamentary National Liberal party, which had so recently been presenting itself as the spearhead of a staunchly principled liberalism and as the real political alternative, what they thought of its 'defection'. It was Bennigsen, the leader of the parliamentary party, who was the favourite target here. In his speech in May he had still been able impressively to combine political tactics with loyalty to principle. Now he had in often tortured locutions to justify his party's assent to the new Bill. 'If the genius of a statesman', Windthorst sneered, 'is to say yes in May and no in October, then I have to acknowledge that my compatriot's performance constitutes a most statesmanlike achievement.'[58]

The arguments of principle hit the majority of the parliamentary party even harder. 'What do we mean by religious, what do we mean by political freedom of belief?' the spokesman of the Progressive Party, Professor Hänel, flung at them. 'We mean, gentlemen', he pontificated amid applause from the left and embarrassed silence from the National Liberals, 'that the ruling society and the ruling state authorities are not competent to pass judgement on whether a particular doctrine is immoral, subversive, or legally reprehensible.'[59]

There was little consolation in the fact that it was the left wing of the National Liberals that managed, by exploiting the majority situation in the Diet, to put through a series of specifying and qualifying amendments and above all to attach a two-and-a-half-year time limit to the bill. The whole thing was still a piece of discriminatory legislation and as such incompatible with the principle of equality before the law and the concept of the constitutional state, in other words with the cardinal points of the liberal programme. Even the alleged 'criminal aspirations of Social Democracy' of the title of the Bill could scarcely justify the element of despotism that was here being given a legal basis. Anyone suspected of sympathizing with Social Democracy now found himself exposed to and defenceless against action by the executive power. The same applied to sympathetic associations and assemblies, to the entire Social Democratic press, and even, on proclamation of what was called a 'minor state of emergency' to whole districts. On the other hand appeals were to be channelled through a body that could hardly be expected to provide prompt and immediately effective intervention, particularly in minor disputes. This was a committee appointed by the Federal Council and consisting of four members of the council and five senior judges under a chairman nominated by the emperor. And all this was directed against a political group that, as the National Liberal leader in the Diet had emphasized back in May, had taken as its goals 'the betterment of the working population in terms of its economic position' and 'the implementation of measures to counter mass poverty', in short, alleviating the lot of the poorest of the poor – whatever objections might be made to the ways and means employed.

Just how problematical this Bill was the National Liberals knew very well. It was 'the most disgraceful law, a law that sets us back thirty years', said a man who was certainly not on the left wing of the party, namely Johannes Miquel, the future Mayor of Frankfurt and Prussian Minister of Finance, in conversation with friends. 'But if any of you present ever quote me as having said so, I shall deny it.'[60] For reasons of state but also for the party's sake, members believed they must set aside their misgivings. The division of 18 October 1878 eventually saw the conservatives and the National Liberals voting as a bloc, with 221 votes for and 149 against. But in the end the issue smashed the National Liberal Party, for in voting as it did the party destroyed the basis of shared convictions on which its internal cohesion rested.

Bismarck's hope and that of many National Liberals – that a clear demarcation vis-à-vis the left would have its own integrating effect – turned out to be an error with far-reaching political repercussions. Without a politico-social objective spanning a plurality of interests as its future goal the party was unable, for all its pragmatism, to sustain its internal and external unity. This was particularly so because it was still only in the 'forecourt of power' and was unable to justify its compromises in terms of the pressures of governmental responsibility. Johannes Miquel, while defining the expectations of the party leadership very precisely, nevertheless got the reality of the way things developed completely wrong when at the beginning of September he remarked to his National Liberal colleague Heinrich Rickert: 'The [Anti-] Socialist Bill must under no circumstances be allowed to become an object of dispute [within the parliamentary party]. If it does, our more liberal side will come off worst.' Everything must be done, he went on, 'to bring about a unanimous vote by the party. Our position vis-à-vis the government can be suitably and usefully defined in the area of fiscal and budgetary matters.'[61]

There could be no question, as very quickly emerged, of any kind of reciprocal deal – conviction against interest for the sake of the unity and political effectiveness of the party. On the contrary, once the Rubicon of abandoning jointly held principles and convictions had finally been crossed, the various interests were able to develop entirely without restraint to very destructive effect.

It has been repeatedly claimed by the successors of the liberal left of the day that this had been Bismarck's ultimate objective. In reality the vote on the Anti-Socialist Bill represented what might be called the last victory that the left wing of the National Liberal Party scored against the Chancellor – though it was a victory that did no one any good and that left a political wasteland behind it. Bismarck had obviously hoped that the Bill would provide a break-away by the left wing under Lasker such as would leave the bulk of the party unaffected; his rabble-rousing tactics at this stage, his repeated declarations that the whole thing did not go far enough for him, that the Bill was a feeble compromise, bear eloquent testimony to this. Instead, the left wing had bowed to parliamentary discipline and to considerations of party interest. In doing so it had – albeit unintentionally – shifted the conflict to a field in which the fault lines finally ran right through the middle of the party and its following in the country.

For the idea that the attitude of the party as a whole to the government could 'be suitably and usefully defined in the area of fiscal and budgetary matters', as Miquel had believed, very soon turned out to be pure illusion. When it came to deciding between abstract principles and the actual wishes of their respective followings, the individual groups within the party found that solid interests and the pressure they could exert were both getting stronger all the time. And Bismarck did everything to help this development along by bringing those interests more and more frankly into play.

On 17 October 1878, the day before the final vote on the Anti-Socialist

101

Bill, a 'National Economic Association of the Imperial Diet' had first been brought to the attention of a wider public. It openly advocated protective tariffs and with them a fundamental change of direction in economic affairs together with a redefinition of the position and influence of the state in both economic and social life. The founder members of this association included, in addition to seventy-five conservatives and Free Conservatives and eighty-seven Centrists, twenty-seven members or more than a quarter of the National Liberal Party in the Imperial Diet. And it was virtually certain that even more would join.

For Bismarck this was the signal finally to abandon all reserve and bring his economic and budgetary policy plans out into the open. On 15 December, in an official letter to the Federal Council – the so-called 'Christmas Letter' – he at last gave the go-ahead for the change of course.[62] From this point on the economic policy of the past two decades was, as far as he was concerned, simply the 'free trade interlude that in the 1860s [had] interrupted the tradition of the Customs Union' and – an absolutely untenable thing to say – 'harmed the prosperity of the nation'.[63]

For all his flexible approach to the new situation, however, it is obvious that its emergence had upset all his calculations hitherto. Granted, on the one hand there were now signs, following a long period of stagnation and internal paralysis, of some material progress in the areas that he regarded as constituting the sore spots of his political creation. Moreover, the fact that the overwhelming majority of the members of the Centre Party in the Imperial Diet had joined a non-party pressure group that was by nature dependent on the government indicated a stronger possibility than had existed hitherto of finding a way out of the 'Kulturkampf', which had become increasingly bogged down in a kind of trench warfare. On the other hand there was no mistaking the fact that the two pillars of this *ad hoc* coalition, the conservatives and above all the Centre Party, continued to hold themselves very much aloof from the government. At the same time a rapprochement between them on the basis of jointly held conservative positions leading to the formation, largely independently of the government, of a powerful bloc on the right – Bismarck's nightmare since 1871 – was a possibility not to be ruled out.

So it was not only his concern to keep a free hand at all events that made him extremely hesitant about getting involved with this new combination, even though it promised a clear majority in the Diet on the questions of economic and budgetary policy on the immediate agenda. On the contrary he, a conservative, was dominated first by misgivings about becoming even more dependent and secondly a fear that, given such a combination, everything would eventually grind to a halt. Unlike many of his contemporaries who had only recently turned conservative, he clung to the conviction that simple adherence to the status quo would endanger the existing, traditional order far more than the policy of limited co-operation with the new and with the forces of change that he had in practice – to steadily increasing criticism from the right – pursued hitherto.

Friedrich Holstein, then a 40-year-old senior civil servant at the Foreign Ministry, subsequently to become the *éminence grise* of German foreign policy, showed himself a keen-sighted observer when he diagnosed a growing scepticism as the predominant feature of the Chancellor's attitude. As to the question of a fresh dissolution of the Diet and a further polarization between right and left at the expense of the National Liberals, Holstein told Count Hatzfeld, the future secretary of state at the Foreign Ministry, in February 1879 that this was 'an eventuality that the chief contemplates without apprehension but also without enthusiasm, for the National Liberal element will take a lot of replacing as far as the imperial idea is concerned'.[64]

We do Bismarck an injustice when we represent him as having been in substance too the actual author and promoter of the tendency towards a rigid status quo policy. That tendency, which was now making increasing headway, was largely independent of him. It arose out of a growing sense of crisis, and its thrust, coming from various quarters, was towards throwing up dams against the forces of change, which were increasingly felt to imply danger and destruction. It is an open question whether any leading politician could successfully have resisted it in the long run. The reality of the majority situation in the Imperial Diet is often brushed aside far too lightly here or represented without adequate proof as having been simply manipulated. One thing we cannot say is that Bismarck was the driving force in this respect. He merely made use of the tendency. And even that he did somewhat reluctantly, not least out of very concrete considerations relating to his own position and political power. The fact was, he had a nasty suspicion that politically he was entering a blind alley, both in policy and in personal terms.

This is the only explanation of why he once again threw himself with such bitterness and with such deeply wounding passion into the struggle with the left wing of the National Liberal Party. One factor in this was the old, vague hope that he might after all be able to win the bulk of the party round. But what he was mainly giving vent to here was his indignation – which had been building up for years – at the fact that the group around Lasker had repeatedly thwarted his original intentions. It had forced him, he felt, on to a highly uncertain course in which there might possibly be no political future.

In its repercussions this event sealed the domestic policy volte-face of 1878–9 in dramatic fashion. It had been brewing up throughout the winter following the passage of the Anti-Socialist Bill and the apparent re-establishment of collaboration between the conservatives and the National Liberals. Constant soundings had been taking place during those months, all of them aimed in one form or another at the National Liberals in the Imperial Diet. They had made it steadily clearer that, given the influence of the group around Lasker and the spread of interests within the party in the country and in the Diet, there was no likelihood of that split far to the left of centre on which Bismarck was still speculating. Although Bennigsen in particular continued even now to make repeated attempts to reach the kind of compromise by which he hoped to reunite the majority of the party with the government, the general political drift of those attempts, as Bismarck clearly saw, invariably bore the hallmark of the party's left wing. Despite numerous material concessions over the question of imperial budgetary reform, they all boiled down to a strengthening of parliament's right of budgetary control and hence to increased governmental dependence on the majority in the Imperial Diet.

That was precisely what Bismarck wished at all costs to avoid. Consequently not only was it a foregone conclusion that all such attempts at compromise would fail; it was also apparent from a relatively early stage that this was going to bring about the final split. For the Chancellor once again felt that he was being put under political pressure, the Centre Party, which this question now thrust into a key position, having indicated that, while it would agree for material reasons to the package of protectionist measures and budgetary reform, it had no intention whatever of freeing Bismarck and the imperial government completely from financial dependence on the individual states and thereby further increasing the Chancellor's power.

At the beginning of May 1879 Bismarck made one final attempt to win over a majority of the National Liberals. It took the form of a speech in which he treated the Diet to a further detailed justification of his 'Bill concerning customs duty in the German customs territory', the legislative basis for the new economic policy first presented a month before.[65] His main emphasis was once again, as it had always been in the past, on the interests of the government in respect of budgetary policy, the need to put the Reich on a fresh financial footing commensurate with its growing responsibilities. 'The Empire's need for financial independence' was the 'first motive' of the Bill. And here, he said, he could find no real quarrel with the National Liberals. He was disinclined to put it so strongly, but in essence he conceded that Miquel, the party's spokesman on budgetary matters, had been absolutely right when he observed in the Constituent Diet of the North German Confederation back in 1867 that the system of levies on the member-states was 'tantamount to budgetary anarchy' in Germany. The second motive, likewise very important, was fiscal equity. Here too, he said, most experts were agreed, including those from the National Liberal camp, that fiscal equity was insufficiently provided for under the present system. Granted, opinions differed widely as to how this should be changed, and no one had the right to claim a monopoly of the truth. His personal preference was still for the system of indirect taxation. In his view this would probably offer the most effective way of reducing what had in many cases become intolerable levels of direct taxation – levels, incidentally, that represented not much more than a fifth of what the average taxpayer has to part with in present-day Germany.

Only after a lengthy dissertation on this theme, which culminated in some heartfelt complaints about the fiscal burdens on agriculture, did Bismarck come to the question that had stirred the nation more than almost any other for years past and by which public opinion was divided into two camps that were locked in an increasingly bitter struggle: the question of the change of policy with respect to foreign trade. Here he directed all his efforts towards playing the question down and representing the battle of principle between protectionism and free trade as a quarrel between opinionated dogmatists who were out of touch with any kind of reality. 'Hitherto', he asserted boldly, taking as his starting-point the present state of tariff protection rather than what had for years been the prevailing trend, 'we have all been protectionists, even the greatest free traders among us, for no one has ever wanted to go below the tariff that rightly obtains today, and that tariff continues to be moderately protectionist – and moderately protectionist', he went on to ironic applause from the left, which was intended to indicate that in that case everything could stay as it was, 'is what this Bill is that we are placing before you. A moderate degree of protection for our domestic labour is what we are asking for.' He went on: 'This is no politically biased protective tariff that we are putting to you, nothing prohibitive, not even a full return to the level of tariff protection we had in 1864.'

It was simply a matter of soberly taking stock. The great free trade movement headed in the 1860s by 'what was then the leading state in Europe', namely France, had come to a halt even before it had gained acceptance in all the major European countries, for example in Austria and Russia. By now it was everywhere on the retreat. Only Britain still clung to this 'trend towards less protection' – total free trade had never existed anywhere – 'and that won't be for long either'.

In such a situation any German government, whatever its political complexion, had a responsibility to act. Located at the heart of Europe, surrounded by protectionist neighbours, Germany had economically speaking been involved, 'ever since we set our tariffs too low – a mistake from which I . . . do not exempt myself from blame – in a process of bleeding to death that the much-disparaged payment of thousands of millions of marks [the French war indemnity] held up for a few years but that without that money would probably have reached its present stage five years ago'. He concluded almost imploringly: 'Therefore I would ask you to leave all personal feelings on these matters out of this, likewise the political aspect; the question before us is not a political but a purely economic one. Let us see how we can put the blood back into the body of Germany, how we can restore to it the strength that comes from the regular circulation of the blood, but my urgent plea is that all questions of party politics and all questions of parliamentary tactics be kept well away from what has solely to do with the general interest of Germany.'

But not even this final, movingly worded appeal to the National Liberals – for it was clear to everyone that it was addressed primarily to them – brought any return. On the contrary, the leader of the party's left wing, Eduard Lasker, took this very speech as his occasion for levelling at Bismarck a charge of extreme hypocrisy and reckless distortion of the truth. The Chancellor, Lasker stated in scarcely veiled terms, was putting himself forward as the representative of the whole nation and invoking the spirit of solidarity. In reality he was allowing himself to be guided by entirely one-sided interests that were most certainly not those of the nation and of the economy as a whole. For the Bill primarily served the economic and social interests of the East Elbian landowners as well as perhaps one or two areas of heavy industry. Everything else was window-dressing and deliberate deception.

This was an outright declaration of war. Bismarck registered it with all the passion of a man who saw his every hope, his every calculation finally and irrevocably disappointed. It goes without saying that the issue was not one of detail, although he spent a comparatively long time refuting Lasker's individual criticisms, lacing his remarks with repeated asides of a deliberately wounding nature. Nor was it so much a question of the extent of the alleged preferential treatment of agriculture. The real point so far as the Chancellor was concerned was Lasker's contention that the Bill represented the deliberate reopening of a political war 'that we believed we had fortunately already brought to a close in Prussia', the 'war of principle between agriculture on the one hand and industry and the towns on the other'.[66]

What Lasker meant was that Bismarck had unilaterally terminated the historic compromise between nobility and bourgeoisie, between the old and the new ruling classes in politics and society since 1866, which had likewise formed the basis of the new German Reich. This was a challenge to the entire middle class to set aside its divergent interests and band together. It must fight as a body for what that compromise had produced, despite all imperfections of detail, in the way of progress and a new order.

This summons to a joint defence of what had so far been achieved against a fresh attack from the right, from the party that had been the enemy in the old days of the constitutional conflict, was of course at the same time a signal to attack. Moreover, unlike many historians who have been inclined, in retrospect, to see things primarily in terms of their outcome, Bismarck took that signal very seriously indeed. For he knew very well that the distribution of weight in the economy and society was now such that, if the message got across, government in opposition to the majority representing it would be impossible. That majority, he was convinced beyond any illusion, would respond by sooner or later assuming full political power.

Consequently in his speech of reply on 8 May 1879, which possibly represents the most crucial turning-point in the internal development of the Reich during his chancellorship, Bismarck applied all his political and demagogic skill to robbing that message of its potential effect and refuting the theory behind it that the compromise of 1866–7 had been abandoned.[67] Where Lasker had stressed the differences between East Elbian agriculture and the aristocracy that represented it politically on the one hand and the middle class and the 'towns', in other words the new society, on the other, Bismarck did not shrink, in order to salvage his own political base, from the very dubious step of highlighting another difference: that between the propertied and the unpropertied. When Lasker said of him that he was pursuing 'the budgetary policy of a man of property', he could 'equally well say to Mr. Lasker that he is pursuing the budgetary policy of a man of no property. He is one of those gentlemen – and in the establishing of our laws they constitute the majority at every stage of the legislative process – of whom Scripture says "They sow not, they reap not, they spin not, and yet they are clothed."'

The one argument was as good as the other and neither was to be taken really seriously, was the superficial implication. But Bismarck would not let it go at that. On the contrary, he positively laboured the point. In the process he sought to play down the charge of a specific commitment to the agrarian interest as a transparent attempt to provoke a split. He openly appealed to the social fears of those who felt increasingly threatened by the economic and social developments of recent years. The general drift of his remarks was to the effect that it was not so much a question of what in terms of detail were the undoubtedly distinct interests of agriculture, commerce and industry. It was a question of the enormous divergence of interests between the propertied and the unpropertied. And no one with an open mind could very well fail to see who spoke for whom in this context and who could be expected to show the greater degree of firmness in the defence of the existing order of ownership. Hardly 'the gentlemen whom our sun does not warm nor our rain make wet, unless they should happen to have gone out without an umbrella, who form the majority in our legislature and who practice neither industry, nor agriculture, nor a trade, unless it be that they feel themselves fully occupied with representing the people in various directions and do this the whole year round'. On the contrary, they easily lost 'the eye and the feeling for those interests that a minister who also owns property, in other words also belongs to the *misera contribuens plebs*, who is also himself governed and feels how the laws affect the governed' never lost. To turn this round and say that that minister was pursuing 'the budgetary policy of the man of property, possibly in his own interests', was disgraceful and pure demagogy.

Decoded, this meant that he, the Chancellor, unlike many representatives of the people, paid constant attention to the interests of all sectors of the economy. Let no one be misled by slogans about a 'war between "agriculture and industry"' allegedly launched by him. 'Such a war is, I hope, a thing of the past. I hope both sides realize at last that it is in their interests to work together.' And to do so for the purpose, as he once again imploringly put it for the ears of the National Liberals, of continuing the work once again begun jointly by representatives of 'country and town'. He still stood by its basic aims: 'The struggle, which I did not launch but in which I have for years fought as hard as I have been able and as much as my work . . . and as much as my illness – illness acquired in the course of duty – has left me time for, is the struggle for reform!'

This was his old plan for a historical compromise between the old and new ruling classes. Now, however, in the light of the political challenge from the liberal left, in the light of the left's programme for a mustering of the middle class against the forces of agrarian conservatism, it was beginning to take on ever harsher features almost redolent of class warfare. In place of the idea of a balance between old and new, a reconciling of differences and a judicious measure of progress he invoked that of joint defence against what were increasingly felt to be threatening forces of change. The new concept was one of a bulwark against the process of economic, social and political change, against an allegedly imminent assault by the unpropertied masses. With it, however, he was no longer able to rally at least the left wing of the National Liberal Party, whose representatives, while they had decided in 1866–7 to compromise with the forces of the status quo in order to get things moving from a broader base, were not prepared to form part of a rigid defensive front against everything new.

The split had finally become unavoidable. When it came it was as dramatic as the weight and importance of the fundamental political alternatives invoked on either side made it. Ten days after the great confrontation between Bismarck and Lasker on the floor of the Imperial Diet a close associate of Lasker's, the president of that body and new Mayor of Berlin, Max von Forckenbeck, speaking at a banquet for the members of the *Städtetag* or Municipal Diet then meeting in Berlin, took the opportunity to make a further very public protest against the political and social objectives underlying the budgetary proposals. Like Lasker, he summoned the 'free and vigorous middle class' as a body 'into the trenches'.[68] Two days later, on 20 May, he ostentatiously resigned from his post as president of the Imperial Diet. Shortly afterwards the first vice-president, Baron von Stauffenberg, who was also a close comrade-in-arms of Lasker's, followed his example. The choice of their successors provided early evidence of the new political combination. A member of the German Conservative Party, Otto Theodor von Seydewitz, became the new president of the Imperial Diet, and a Bavarian Centre Party deputy, Baron Georg von Franckenstein, became first vice-president – for only the day after Bismarck's first major speech, on 3 May, the leaders of the Centre Party in the Diet had once again been seen, for the first time in a long time, at one of the Chancellor's regular 'parliamentary soirées', and the evening had been the occasion of a much-remarked tête-à-tête between Bismarck and Windthorst.

Not long after this the name of Baron von Franckenstein was associated with solid proof of the fact that, as Lasker and his friends had repeatedly stressed, Bismarck's budgetary proposals were not in fact concerned solely with strengthening the Reich, which was the motive he had always thrust into the foreground. In a motion brought forward by Franckenstein the Centre Party made its agreement conditional upon the Reich's passing on all revenues from the tobacco tax and customs duties in excess of 130 million marks to the member-states. In other words, the Reich was to remain bound to the member-states in budgetary terms as well – for the sum in question did not even cover current requirements, let alone the costs of the expansion of its institutions to which the Reich aspired.

The so-called 'Franckenstein Clause' made virtual nonsense of budgetary reform of the Reich as far as the concrete objectives invoked by Bismarck were concerned. This looked like a further opportunity for the man who was still looking for a compromise solution, the National Liberal leader Rudolf von Bennigsen, and for the forces behind him. But it emerged very clearly from the negotiations embarked on in this regard that Bismarck was no longer prepared to have the National Liberals dictate terms to him. He rejected Bennigsen's offer to the effect that a majority of the party in the Diet could go along with his proposals if the government for its part would give additional 'constitutional guarantees', if it would at least formally submit the duty on coffee and the tax on salt for the annual approval of the Diet as part of the imperial finance bill. Such a reinforcement – albeit minimal – of the Diet's budgetary rights obviously appeared to him to be politically more dangerous than continued financial dependence on the member-states and the key position that the Centre Party was beginning to occupy in the Diet.

Both were undoubtedly irritating, calling as they did for more and more complicated manoeuvrings and what amounted to a political hand-to-mouth existence. They did not, however, in Bismarck's view, threaten the power and independence of the government as much as could be expected if a policy of concerted middle-class action along the lines suggested by Lasker were to gain acceptance – with the crown prince in the background. There was the added fact that a rapprochement with the Centre Party, particularly after the change of pope, for the first time brought a negotiated peace in the largely stalemated 'Kulturkampf' within the realms of possibility. Not that this was the prime motive behind the fundamental political decision that Bismarck made at this point in his career; the prime motive, as always, was the securing of his own power and that of the government he led.

Indeed the securing and if possible the extension of such power as he had acquired had been the chief driving forces behind his policy throughout the foregoing years. Purely power-oriented calculations had always taken more or less absolute precedence with him and had always constituted his basic pattern of political action. But up until now a further factor had always entered into those calculations in the shape of an overall political tendency that helped him to exert a wider-ranging influence on history. It soared above his own inherent banality and, if you like, historical significance: on the back of his individual success, as it were, a supra-individual politico-social movement had asserted itself in the economy and in society in the shape of forces by which the structure of both was radically changed. By combining elements of the old and the new and bringing together the leading lights and large sections of the followings of both camps, Bismarck had not only become the creator of the German national state but had also, even more importantly, laid the foundations of modern industrial society within that state.

Only the first achievement had been at all intentional. And even here it had been the course of developments that led him to the concrete form eventually assumed by that state and crucially determining its character, though this does not diminish the historical importance attaching to Bismarck as a result. Now, however, the same power-oriented calculations led him to tread a path that, looked at in a wider perspective, meant only stagnation and an ultimately powerless inhibition of the historical process and doomed him to failure sooner or later.

Bismarck undoubtedly had a premonition of this. In no way did he feel that he was taking a step in the direction of freedom, as it were, opening up entirely new possibilities for himself and for the nation. His choice, as he saw it, was simply between two evils. And if he did come down firmly in favour of one course rather than the other, it was not through any conviction that it represented the lesser evil. He took it because the other one, the one in which there was surely more future, objectively speaking, and with which his entire political career had been associated up to now, appeared to offer him personally no real opportunity any more.

The period of a *de facto* renunciation of political power – arising out of a unique historical situation – on the part of powerful social forces in favour of an executive that was implementing some of their key objectives was about to come to an end. For the moment, admittedly, given the current economic stagnation and what in many cases looked like somewhat brittle prospects for the future, those forces had the wind against them. But their base was more solid than ever, and a fresh swing in their favour was bound to come eventually. When it did, however, the man between the political and social fronts, the mediator of compromise between them, would be superfluous. A decision would have to be made such as Britain had made decades before, at the time of Peel and the Corn Laws. It would be a question of plumping resolutely for one course or the other, for clinging to the old order, or rather to what was left of it, or for a determined transition to the new, middle-class industrial order, this time in the political sphere as well.

Soberly Bismarck bowed to this kind of realization. But he took no pleasure in doing so. Not only did it mean abandoning his whole policy hitherto; it also threatened to force him back into commitments from which that policy had once freed him. Consequently he made repeated attempts to switch positions in the years that followed and to provide himself with parliamentary and party-political alternatives. Such efforts were never really successful, however, and from now until his fall his domestic policy, regardless of the concrete advances associated with it, particularly in the field of social policy, was continually getting bogged down. It was characterized by a series of vain endeavours to regain his former political freedom of action. Its stagnation can of course be represented as the forces of the old successfully asserting themselves. But that was not the view taken by Bismarck, who had always been a believer in forward defence in politics. On the contrary, from this point on he followed the course of events with growing scepticism and increasing pessimism.

Plenty of occasion for both was provided by developments that followed immediately upon the final decision in favour of the Centre Party and against the conditions for co-operation stipulated by the National Liberals. That decision was generally taken to be a negative option, a political rebuff to the National Liberals and their objectives. Consequently its effect was in essence destructive; it created no new political base, no fresh political loyalties. The representatives of the Centre Party, in particular, saw the Chancellor's concessions in their direction merely as evidence of a desire to outmanoeuvre his former political partner. Accordingly they continued to hold themselves very much aloof. Even the resignation of their political arch-enemy, Culture Minister Adalbert Falk, on 29 June 1879 seemed to

them, although like the so-called 'Court Chaplains Party' and the majority
of Protestant conservatives they saw and celebrated it as a victory, to be
simply a by-product of the political struggle against liberalism rather than a
concession to them, let alone an offer of a new policy.

It helped considerably to foster such a view that two other Prussian
ministers resigned at the same time as Falk, namely Finance Minister
Hobrecht and Agriculture Minister Friedenthal. The resignations heightened
the appearance of a power struggle in which both sides were simply looking
for reinforcements rather than for new partners. This impression was
further enhanced by the fact that all three ministers, as had happened in the
reshuffle of the spring of 1878, were replaced by men whose names did not
give notice, as it were, of a new political combination and a corresponding
programme: Falk by the conservative deputy and former provincial
president of Silesia, Robert von Puttkamer, Friedenthal by the Free
Conservative deputy Robert Lucius and Hobrecht by a man who had
formerly been under secretary of state at the Prussian Ministry of the
Interior and before that district president of Düsseldorf, Karl Hermann
Bitter, a brother of the head of the 'Seehandlung', the Prussian national
bank.

Bismarck himself at first did little or nothing to dispel this impression.
Once again he saw himself as the focus of a 'wide-ranging plot', a
'pronunciamento' with the object of 'placing him in a deadly predicament
by means of a general strike of ministers'.[69] The resignation of his
ministers, he wrote to the emperor at the beginning of July, created the
same situation 'as if at a crucial moment of a battle the generals suddenly
went over to the enemy, leaving their comrades in the lurch'.[70] Therefore
his first concern was to be seen to be master in his own house once again and
apart from that to keep as many avenues open as possible. His first official
appearance after the ministerial crisis in Prussia had been looked forward to
with some excitement, but for the most part he used it merely for a general
settling of accounts with the liberals. In the process he once again
summarized his overall assessment of the situation and of developments
hitherto in sometimes very fundamental terms.

He told the Imperial Diet on 9 July 1879 that he had resolved to accept the
'Franckenstein Clause' – his final decision having been made a matter of
days before – 'only after I became convinced, from a general survey of the
paths that the gentlemen who are today in the opposition are following, that
they have taken paths that I can never follow and that the confederate
governments cannot follow'.[71] Behind these stood aspirations, he went on
as the left grew increasingly restive, 'with which the Reich cannot co-exist'.
They were 'subversions of the existence of the Reich just as much as the
subversions of Social Democracy that we are trying to combat with the law
passed last autumn' – 'at least', he added, qualifying his attack slightly in
response to what had meanwhile swollen to a storm of protest from the left,
they constituted 'the preliminaries thereto'.

After this bombshell, in which all his bitterness against the National
Liberal left wing once again found expression, he began by spelling out for
the party the contradiction between its claims in terms of political power

and the reality of its parliamentary strength. 'Were there', he said, 'a party in this Diet that possessed a natural majority and that did not ask of me that the drop of democratic oil that in a well-known phrase[72] was demanded for the unction of the German Emperor should become a whole bucketful, I should be able to accord to such a party quite different rights as regards exerting an influence on the government than I can at present to a party that, when it is successful and fully united, which it rarely is, still accounts for scarcely a quarter of the entire assembly.' As it was, all he could do was to 'advise' the representatives of the National Liberal Party to show 'greater modesty in future' and beyond that recommend that they did not take as their rallying-cry an allegedly imminent reaction. They ran the risk of 'possibly tempting providence' were they to do so. 'By being so suspicious of reaction and making such accusations you might under certain circumstances prompt a minister more timid than myself, precisely in order to defend himself against the hostility that being suspected of reaction brings with it, consciously or unconsciously to resort to the methods of reaction and to seek support where for the moment he finds less hostility.'

This might have appeared to constitute an accurate if somewhat tendentious description of the present situation and at the same time an indirect threat that, if opposition continued, he might take a quite different line. In the next breath, however, he added: 'I am not in a position to do that.' Nor was that all. He promptly went a step further and justified his conduct and his decisions over the past eighteen months in a way that was once again almost tantamount to wooing a National Liberal majority.

The National Liberal Party in the Diet, particularly its left wing, had wanted to overpower him politically – that had been its principal starting-point. 'A parliamentary party may perfectly well support the government and gain influence over it in the process, but when it seeks to govern the government it forces that government to react against the attempt.' What ensued was a tit-for-tat process that did not always accord with the wishes and original intentions of the side doing the reacting. 'Politics is always like visiting a country one does not know with people whom one does not know and whose reactions one cannot predict; when one person puts a hand into his pocket, the other person is already drawing a gun, and when he pulls the trigger the first one fires, and it is too late then to ask whether the requirements of Prussian common law with regard to self-defence apply, and since Prussian common law is not effective in politics people are very, very quick to adopt an aggressive defence. I have felt, if not actually under attack, nevertheless deserted and isolated; I felt it more especially on the occasion of the first Social Democratic Bill, and I hoped at the time that the disparate elements united in a large and *nominally* pro-government party would get themselves sorted out. That has not happened, and as long as it does not happen', he went on programmatically, 'you will always find any government, but especially the confederate governments, cautious about seeking support and not as trusting as was formerly the case.'

His 'formerly' was not merely a further – euphemistic – reference to his twelve-year collaboration with the National Liberals. He used it above all as a cue for drawing up, from the particular standpoint of his relationship with the 'Reichsgründungspartei', a sort of balance-sheet of his entire domestic policy up until now and pointing out what had been its guidelines. Despite a lot of deliberate self-enhancement and precisely calculated idealization of his aims and intentions, he went a very long way in the direction of disclosing the essential foundations of that policy, his basic political views and his strategy – further, possibly, than he meant to and certainly further than in any comparable context.

'Since I became a minister', he began, 'I have never belonged to a parliamentary party nor ever been able to belong to one; I have been successively hated by all and loved by a few.' At first nearly everyone had been against him, above all the entire middle class and all the forces of the new. 'I did not let it put me off, nor have I ever sought revenge for it.' His 'guiding star' from the very beginning had been: 'By what ways and means can I bring Germany to unification and, unification once achieved, how can I strengthen, foster and so organize it that it will be permanently maintained of the free will of all concerned?' If people would bear this in mind, all the apparently surprising changes and alleged about-turns would be explained, particularly the much-discussed turn of events after 1866. 'When we came back from the 1866 war, in my then position of enjoying greater influence within a smaller circle than today it would have been very easy for me to say, indeed I had difficulty in refraining from saying: "Prussia is now larger, the constitution does not allow for this, therefore we must agree on a new one" – in short, to go all out for the boldest and most radical policy of reaction, using the success that was still left over from Königgrätz. As you know, I did the opposite – and in so doing at first incurred the antipathy of a great many of my former political friends.'

His motive, he said, had not been 'love of the constitutional system' for its own sake; he had no wish to make himself out to be better than he was. 'I am no opponent of the constitutional system; on the contrary, I regard it as the only possible form of government – but had I thought that a dictatorship in Prussia, that absolutism in Prussia would have been more useful in promoting the work of German unification I should unreservedly, and without a qualm, have counselled absolutism.' However, 'after careful consideration' he had come round to the view: 'No, we must continue along the path of constitutional law.'

Although he stressed once again that this had 'furthermore' been in accordance with his 'deepest feelings' and with his 'conviction of the overall feasibility of our policy', the functional character that questions of political system, constitutionalism and constitutional policy possessed for him was brought out very clearly by these remarks. He had been guided, in other words, by considerations of pure political feasibility, by a soberly success-oriented calculation.

The same applied to his relations with the different parliamentary parties. After the 'complaisance I then showed towards enemies who had become reconciled with me' had already 'prepared the way for the future break with the Conservative Party', that break had then come about as a result of the 'conflict over church affairs'. This had arisen chiefly 'out of the connections between the church question and the Polish question', in other words as a

113

problem, once again, of national 'unification' and unity. As a result he had been 'forced closer to the Liberal group in the Diet . . . than is perhaps tenable in the long run for the Minister and Chancellor of the Empire'. For such a figure could never be the man of a particular party. He must always have an eye to 'relations with all the other circles of the Empire and of the population'; he must be above party.

Nevertheless, he had held fast all along to the combination that had emerged in this way. 'It occurred to me, and in the debate about the Socialists I developed the idea, that we would be able, counting from the right wing, to march in three battalions, perhaps separately, and fight as one. My forecast was unfortunately not confirmed.' The blame for this, as he once again stressed explicitly, had lain not with 'my will' but with 'circumstances' and with the attitude of a section of the National Liberal parliamentary party. He concluded this virtual declaration of principle within his speech by saying that the government could not 'go chasing after individual parliamentary parties'. It must 'follow its own paths, the paths it knows to be right . . . It will have those paths corrected by the decisions of the Imperial Diet; it will require the *backing* of the parliamentary parties, but it can never place itself under the *control* of one party!'

These were determined words and represented a clear-cut programme. The unity of the state, Bismarck was saying, stood for the unity of the nation. The latter must inevitably disintegrate if the state were to forfeit its position above the parties, including the strictly national parties. Only the monarchical and bureaucratic institutional state, the authoritarian state, not the party state organized along parliamentary lines, was in a position to draw and hold the nation together above and beyond all its economic, social and political differences and to give it cohesion and strength, not least vis-à-vis other countries.

The old liberal promise of a balancing of all antagonisms in the process of the self-unification of the nation in freedom was being challenged here, in the light of the actual developments of the last fifteen years, by the conservative idea of the nation. This had emerged in the wake of those developments and was now coming increasingly to dominate the field, not only in Germany, in the context of the current economic and social crisis. From being a weapon against the authoritarian state the national idea had thus become a tool of that same authoritarian state. With its help Bismarck sought to force into line with himself those who, for all their compromises and all their inconsistencies, particularly in the 'Kulturkampf', had adhered in principle to the idea of the internal self-unification and self-government of the nation following its external unification. To this end he turned to them as his 'former and also, I hope, future comrades-in-arms' and expressed his continuing readiness to collaborate in the erratic statement: 'I am too close to the end of my career to spoil my present for the sake of any future.'

Here again, though, Bismarck's intention and his impressive formulation of a programme for a concerted conservative movement headed by an authoritarian state and a powerful and independent executive have often caused commentators, looking back, to lose sight of reality. For the intention and the programme were not the whole story. And there can be absolutely no question, notwithstanding a view that is repeatedly put forward, of the programme outlined in principle – for securing the authoritarian structure of the state and hence the power of the government by means of a concerted national conservative movement – ever having shown more than a promise of success. The key group as far as that plan was concerned, namely the National Liberal middle class, could no longer, despite Bismarck's urgent appeal, be moved to make a concerted decision. On the contrary, the National Liberal Party now went into an accelerating decline with first its right wing and then its left wing splitting away. As well as problems of economic and cultural policy it was above all the question of the party's relationship to Bismarck and his political line that played a crucial role in speeding that decline. By the end of August 1880 the dissolution into two camps of approximately equal strength was complete. This tore a hole in the coalition of national conservative forces envisaged by Bismarck that, as shortly began to emerge with increasing clarity, could not really be filled, even with the help of considerable concessions towards the Centre Party, either in the short or in the medium term.

In his speech of 9 July 1879 Bismarck had said with regard to the 'Kulturkampf' that, 'if ways and means present themselves by which the severity of antagonisms can be mitigated without affecting the principles of the actual point at issue', it was 'really not my right, as minister, to block such ways and brush them aside'. In spite of their co-operation over tariff and budgetary questions, few members of the parliamentary Centre Party were under any illusion as to the context in which this peace offer – which the conservatives around Kleist-Retzow welcomed and enthusiastically supported – was being made. Even the reference to the possibility of a relationship in future in which they would come 'to know each other and through working jointly for a common, higher purpose to respect each other' made very little impression on the overwhelming majority of the 'Reichsfeinde' of yesterday, the 'enemies of the Empire' who were suddenly being allocated an entirely new function.

The same sort of reservation and scepticism greeted Bismarck in Rome. His hope that, if he wished it, agreement could be reached with the new pope in the space of six weeks soon turned out to be purely illusory. The talks with the Viennese Pronuntius, Cardinal Jacobini, initiated in Gastein shortly after this – in September 1879 – made very slow progress. Furthermore, neither at the time nor subsequently did they have anything like the effect on the attitude of the Centre Party that Bismarck had anticipated. 'The system does not change', the Chancellor observed bitterly in a directive of April 1880 to his ambassador in Vienna: 'Vigorously oppose the Emperor's government.'[73] The Centre, he noted three weeks later, always voted 'as a body against the government' and took 'every anti-imperial endeavour under its wing'.[74]

The longer it continued to do so, the less Bismarck was able to conceal from himself the fact that it was acting in complete agreement with a substantial section of public opinion. For here too the national conservative call to muster turned out to be largely ineffective, the atmosphere of economic and social crisis notwithstanding. It seemed all too obviously bound up with the power interests of the government on the one hand and with the economic and social interests of specific groups on the other. Bismarck found himself confronted by a steadily increasing mistrust that the opposition parties, including the Centre, which in this respect adhered almost completely to what had been its basic attitude hitherto, sought more and more openly to exploit for their own ends.

Initially, however, Bismarck still hoped, following his statement of principle of 9 July 1879, for a process of reorientation among the parties that would turn out to his advantage and strengthen his position. In the final vote on the new customs tariff, which in its passage through the Imperial Diet had even been tightened up, the bloc formed by the conservatives and the Centre Party had attracted a certain influx – albeit exiguous as yet – from the National Liberal camp. Consequently it seemed a not entirely unjustified hope that the whole process would unleash increased pressure from the interests involved here, pressure in particular on the National Liberal Party, and eventually start a kind of race for the government's favour between the majority of the National Liberals and the Centre Party. The rallying-cry must be not 'conservative or liberal', said an early press directive relating to the elections for the Prussian House of Deputies due in the autumn, 'but simply the protection or abandonment of the national task'. That was the way to bring about a radical realignment of the old fronts.[75]

It was in that hope that Bismarck set out in mid-July 1879 on one of those holiday trips to which people had by now become accustomed, though they never knew how long they would last nor when the Chancellor would be back at his desk in Berlin. This time the stops were Bad Kissingen, Bad Gastein and, following a state visit to Vienna at the end of September, his Varzin estate, where he stayed until the end of January 1880. Let the parties stew in their own juice for a whole and make up their minds about their future attitude towards the government; in the following session of the Prussian House of Deputies the Chancellor and head of the Prussian government took no part whatever.

Leaving aside for a moment the negotiations with Rome and their domestic repercussions, his attention during those months was concentrated chiefly on the foreign policy situation. From the point of view of the Reich this had already turned out at the Congress of Berlin to be very much more flawed and dangerous than Bismarck had originally expected. Since then it had deteriorated, if anything. Here too some fundamental decisions and a substantial change of course were called for if things were not to slip out of control. Both requirements, possibly to a greater extent than ever before, stood in immediate relation to domestic policy considerations and objectives.

[13]

Foreign Policy Reorientation, Domestic Policy Choices

Considerations relating to domestic policy were of especial and – curiously – often underrated importance in connection with a problem that became extremely acute in the summer of 1879, namely the question of a choice, now clearly becoming inescapable, between Russia and Austria-Hungary. Since the conclusion of the Congress of Berlin, the end-result of which had been a victory for Russia's rivals in the field of power politics, particularly Britain, there had been a steadily growing tendency amongst the Russian leadership to lay the blame for this and for the country's continuing foreign policy isolation primarily at the door of the Reich. The fact that, during those months, Berlin set about impeding access to the central European agricultural market, in which Russian exporters were becoming increasingly interested, had more than a little to do with this. It was no accident that the years of Russian attempts to put pressure on the Reich and force it to make a clear and binding long-term decision for or against the tsardom should have reached a climax in 15 August 1879, a month after the Imperial Diet passed the new customs tariff.

That was the date on a letter from the tsar to the German emperor that has gone down in history as the 'Ohrfeigenbrief' or 'Slap-in-the-face Letter'. In this the Russian Cabinet, using Alexander as its mouthpiece, demanded almost in the form of an ultimatum that the Reich should make a statement committing itself with regard to its future policy intentions. The tsar blamed the present confused and tense situation mainly on the German Chancellor, accusing him of allowing himself to be swayed by feelings of personal animosity against the head of the Russian government, Prince Gorchakov, and of exacerbating the differences between the two countries accordingly. 'Is it worthy of a true statesman', Alexander asked, 'to attach importance to a personal quarrel when it is a question of the interests of two great states who are destined to live in harmony and of whom one rendered the other a service in 1870 that you said yourself you wished never to forget?' And in dramatically heightened tones he went on: 'I should not have permitted myself to remind you of the fact, but the situation is becoming too serious for me to be entitled to conceal from you fears of which the consequences could be disastrous for both our countries.'[1]

117

William was deeply affected, not only by the prospect thus opened up but above all by the charge of opportunist inconstancy and personal ingratitude. His spontaneous inclination was to react in the way St Petersburg wished him to. In this his basic conservatism, which advancing age was bringing out more and more strongly, and arising out of it his affection for what was supposed to be the leading conservative power in Europe both played as great a part as did his early memory of Russia and Prussia as comrades-in-arms. His Chancellor, on the other hand, was determined from the outset not to give in but to launch a counter-move in the shape of vigorously increased collaboration with Austria-Hungary, Russia's immediate power-political rival in south-east Europe; indeed, he wanted to place that collaboration on an entirely new footing that went far beyond an alliance in the usual sense. In other words, he was determined to start by taking the reverse option.

Of crucial importance to Bismarck, as it had been in the foregoing years, was the thought that, in view of the distribution of power and power-political interests in Europe, a closer rapprochement with Russia would lead to a growing dependence on St Petersburg that would rob him of his freedom of manoeuvre on the foreign policy front. It threatened to bring about a situation in which the Reich would be made to look like no more than an instrument of Russian policy. German gratitude for the stance adopted by Russia in 1866 and 1870–1, he told William in an initial reaction to the tsar's letter, which had been sent on to him at Bad Gastein, could 'not extend so far that German policy is *permanently* subordinated to Russian policy and that we sacrifice the future of our relations with Austria for Russia's sake'.[2] He therefore advised strongly against even embarking on talks with the tsar and the Russian government at this time. As he telegraphed Bernhard Ernst von Bülow, the secretary of state at the Foreign Ministry, on 1 September, such talks could 'only alienate us from Austria and leave us alone with Russia's love. Our *total* isolation in an atmosphere of universal mistrust would then be Russia's to command.'[3] If, however, Prussia were now to cold-shoulder St Petersburg and reach an agreement with the Habsburg monarchy as quickly as possible over a 'defensive alliance', Russia would soon relent and declare itself ready to restore an association between the three eastern empires based on partnership and not on the unilateral subordination of one of the parties to it. 'The *Three* Emperors' League in the sense of a policy of peaceful conservation remains an ideal political objective', he stressed in a letter to William I on 5 September 1879.[4]

Meanwhile the emperor, acting on his own initiative, had hastily arranged a meeting with Alexander II in Alexandrovo on 3 and 4 September to try to put things right in private conversation and restore the old relationship. Bismarck had been furious. On the same day, 5 September, on which he sought to reassure William as to the ultimate objectives of his policy, he told Bülow that the Alexandrovo meeting gave him, 'if on a greatly reduced scale, the impression of an embryonic Olmütz . . . You will recall that in 1850 Count Brandenburg died broken-hearted after his

Warsaw experiences. I have no intention of doing that, but nor do I intend to take it lying down.'[5]

On the basis of this it has sometimes been claimed that the phrase about 'an ideal political objective' was coined entirely for the emperor's benefit and was not really meant in earnest. But if we look at the way things developed and at the way Bismarck commented on the process on various occasions, there is a lot of evidence to suggest that the ostentatious leaning towards Austria in which he now engaged had the simultaneous objective, right from the start, of drawing Russia closer to German policy once again – on different terms, of course, from those envisaged by the political leaders in St Petersburg.

In other words, Bismarck's attitude was still governed very clearly by the ideal of a policy of keeping as free a hand as possible, as formulated in the Kissingen Dictate. On top of that, however, there was a series of no less important motives that now prompted him to disregard the massive resistance of his emperor and head rapidly in the direction of a dual alliance with Austria–Hungary.

There was one strand of motivation with wider foreign policy implications, as it were. For years he had harboured a subliminal suspicion that the Reich, for all its military might and current influence in Europe, did perhaps possess too narrow a power base, particularly when compared with the great flanking powers of Europe, namely Britain and Russia, to be able to preserve its independence and the rank of an equal power between them for any length of time. Any enlargement of that base by means of territorial acquisitions was out of the question, threatening as it did to call a coalition of all the other European powers into being immediately, as Bismarck knew only too well. So the only way to achieve it was to form a central European bloc that in terms of duration and intensity went far beyond any ordinary kind of alliance, a bloc, moreover, that was strongly indicated not least by the historical traditions of the region.

In a direct report to the emperor dated 31 August 1879 Bismarck stated boldly: 'I already had the feeling at the peace negotiations in Nikolsburg in 1866, thinking about our thousand years of common German history, that we should sooner or later have to create a substitute for the tie that had then to be broken in order that the German constitution might be reformed.' The time had now come for them to set up a 'similar insurance pact' to the one that had 'enjoyed validity in international law for fifty years between Prussia and Austria in the shape of the former German Confederation'. To this end he had already got in touch with Andrássy, the Austrian Foreign Minister. There was of course no going back to the old German Confederation. But on everyone who recalled that 'species of mutual insurance company for peace' the question must urgently impose itself whether 'a similar peace league between the two central European empires' would not be a 'useful institution'. On this basis he had asked Andrássy straight out 'whether he believed his Emperor was amenable to such ideas'.[6]

Here and on many other occasions Bismarck insisted – and this constituted another strand of motivation, one the importance of which is often underestimated – on the popularity that such a central European 'peace league' could be expected to meet with. 'This alliance is the reconstitution of the German Confederation in a new and contemporary form', wrote the new Minister of Agriculture, Robert Lucius, summarizing Bismarck's proposals as unanimously approved by the crucial session of the Prussian Cabinet on 28 September 1879. 'A bulwark of peace for many years to come. Popular with all parties, Nihilists and Socialists excepted.'[7]

In other words, the Dual Alliance would at the same time be an instrument of concord at home. It would reconcile with the foreign policy and hence at the same time with the leadership of the Reich those persons who had hitherto, as the losers of 1866, held themselves aloof. This was aimed mainly at the Centre Party and at the very numerous body of people, particularly in southern Germany, who had once adhered to the idea of a Greater Germany including at least the German-speaking districts of Austria. Their spokesmen had repeatedly warned against too indulgent an attitude towards Russia and solemnly invoked the 'Germanic interest' that could be upheld only by standing firm with Austria in a way that to some extent went back on the separation of 1866. Windthorst had concluded his major foreign policy speech of 19 February 1878 by saying: 'May the skill of the Imperial Chancellor be equal to preserving the peace generally but also to making sure that the Germanic interest is not neglected in this whole negotiation. This *Germanic* interest, however, finds expression in the interest of *Austria*.'[8] A special kind of alliance between the German Reich and Austria-Hungary, very deliberately cast in the tradition of the German Confederation and indeed in a centuries-old German imperial tradition, may in this sense have appeared to constitute an absolutely ideal solution for urgent domestic and foreign policy problems, offering a kind of breakthrough in both spheres.

In reality, of course, Bismarck's expectations were fulfilled only to a very limited extent. The actual treaty negotiations themselves turned out to be somewhat difficult – to say nothing of the continued resistance of Emperor William to a course for which Bismarck managed to gain acceptance only by means of a massive resignation threat. Vienna was absolutely delighted by the German offer of assistance. But the Austrians were neither inclined to let themselves in for a general defensive pact, which particularly meant a commitment in the event of a Franco-German conflict, nor were they seriously prepared to go beyond the terms of a normal alliance. They were as reluctant to anchor it in a kind of legislative act of both parliaments as they were to accept an unusual duration. Subsequent attempts to couple the treaty with an agreement about the close economic ties between the two countries likewise failed to win Austrian approval.

Vienna felt too acutely that the formation of such a bloc would of necessity, even though Bismarck sought to dispel all such suspicions from the outset, be governed by the economic and power-political superiority of Berlin. That meant, however, that it not only threatened in the long run to undermine the independence of the Austrian Empire; it also threatened to wreck a recently launched endeavour to reach a settlement with the Czechs on the basis of the status quo and in defiance of the German Liberal reformers.

Just such a settlement was one of the things Vienna had constantly in mind during the Dual Alliance negotiations. By taking the external pressure off the newly formed – in August 1879 – Taaffe government, pressure that was becoming increasingly pervaded with Pan–Slav elements, the alliance was to give that government breathing-space at home as well. It was to block the claim of the German Liberals to political dominance in the Austrian half of the empire by depriving them of potential backing from the Reich.

This divergence of objectives in itself robbed the treaty – which was ratified by both monarchs in the middle of October, initially for a period of five years, with the text being kept secret – of a great deal of its value as far as Bismarck was concerned, both for domestic and for foreign policy purposes. The way things developed was likewise wholly out of tune with his original expectations. In neither policy area did the treaty constitute a truly new beginning.

On the domestic policy front there was little question of any reinforcement and internal consolidation of what from the government's point of view was a precarious *ad hoc* coalition of conservatives and Centre Party. And in foreign affairs all that was achieved at first was that, as Bismarck had predicted, Russia eventually fell into line. After protracted negotiations St Petersburg agreed to the so-called 'Three Emperors' League' in June 1881. Apart from the principle of benevolent neutrality in the event of an armed conflict between one of the three powers and a fourth party, this consisted in the main of a reciprocal commitment by the signatories 'to respect their mutual interests in the Balkan Peninsula'. This was linked to a promise that 'fresh changes in the territorial possessions of European Turkey shall be able to be effected only on the basis of a joint agreement between them'.[9]

In itself this was undoubtedly a success. However, the basic situation, which as time went on Bismarck had more and more reason to regard in moments of pessimism as permanently insecure and threatening, was left virtually unaffected. Seen in this light, the Dual Alliance of 1879 was the first in a series of foreign policy stopgaps that eventually expanded into a regular system, with the help of which the Chancellor sought to preserve the increasingly imperilled balance of power in Europe and the position of the Reich within it. The foundation of and prelude to a new policy that might have promised to maintain that balance in a more lasting fashion by forming a genuine bloc in central Europe – these it was not.

Much the same was true of Bismarck's next steps in domestic policy. Nor is the parallel the only striking thing here – how on the domestic front too he built up, with ever-increasing expenditure of effort and ever-diminishing success, a 'system of stopgaps' designed to preserve the status quo. On the contrary, what stands out above all is his endeavour to make the foreign-policy system and the domestic policy system stabilize each other.

That his first venture in this direction had met with failure was something about which Bismarck, sober as ever despite feverish attempts to find alternatives, entertained no further illusions from the very opening of the new session of the Prussian House of Deputies. 'The government will not be able to manage for long', he wrote to his new Minister of Agriculture, Robert Lucius, in a letter dated 5 November 1879, 'with a majority whose continued existence depends on the free will of the Centre [Party], for I scarcely believe it would ever be possible to win the Centre over as a sure and lasting prop for any government by any concessions whatever, even if the extent of *possible* concessions as far as our government is concerned were greater that it is.' What, then, did the future hold? He went on: 'So a majority that is no longer a majority without the Centre offers the government no security, but any other kind is possible only if the Conservative Party as a whole or more than half of it can be talked into compromising not only with the Empire Party but also with the honest section of the National Liberals.' This would be 'very difficult', however, 'as long as the present Conservative and National Liberal parliamentary parties remain undivided. To my mind the Progressives posing as National Liberals, the people of the Municipal Diet [*Städtetag*] and the "greater" liberal party, in other words the Republicans, are props as unsure and possibly even more dangerous than the Centre.' And finally: 'If the theoretical party groupings, these parliamentary limited companies, as it were, did not exist in the first place, the grouping of the majority could be better and more naturally effected along practical lines.[10]

Coming at the end of a realistic analysis, this was the purest wishful thinking. He did add immediately: 'The cure for this evil, however, does not lie with us.' But in practice he now increasingly allowed such wishful thinking to tempt him into doing things that a sober assessment of the overall political position at home and the distribution of weight and interests could have told him in advance would meet with failure.

Not that he had meanwhile become incapable of making such an assessment. But it revealed to him with increasing clarity a constellation of circumstances that threatened by degrees to dissolve away the position of power he had occupied up to now. This made him tend more and more to plan all his positive moves as it were from negative premises. He visualised those plans, right down to the details, primarily from the point of view of how they might alter what he felt to be a threatening overall situation on the domestic policy front and turn it to his advantage, even if only temporarily. In this way an element entered into his whole domestic policy that was in the highest degree destructive. For all its superficial and often bewildering vitality, that policy began to lose the initiative. The thing that over the past decade and a half had keyed it in with more general trends of development and global historical forces it now increasingly forfeited.

On the other hand it can be claimed that here too Bismarck was helping – and had been since the late 1870s, albeit with different objectives and scarcely with any awareness of the secular process – to bring to fruition a general tendency of modern historical development: the emergence of the modern interventionist state. In purely formal terms that is correct. In substance, however, what was happening here was very different from the fundamental changes in the historical constellation during the preceding years with which, albeit not in the sense of something planned and deliberately created, his name rightly remains linked, namely the formation of a national constitutional state in central Europe, its internal organization along modern lines and the establishment of modern industrialized society in that part of the continent. In this case the link with the incipient new development was very superficial – one might almost say negative. And it produced a hybrid that came to weigh very heavily on the further course of events in central Europe: the conservative interventionist state. With its help, using what were formally the most modern of means but without a genuine vision of the future or a corresponding political and social model, the status quo was defended with a sort of senile tenacity.

The process marked the transition from an extremely dynamic policy of 'conservative reform', of attempting, in the Hegelian double meaning of 'aufheben', to 'preserve' and to 'abolish' the past in the present and the future, to a policy of pure reaction, devoid of any future, in the 'après nous le déluge' spirit of Louis XV or the later Metternich. The 'white revolutionary' finally became transformed into the sorcerer's apprentice, who sought with the aid of futile spells to lay the forces of the future that he had himself helped to awaken. But what he conjured up, far from constituting any kind of order, was confusion and a general absence of orientation.

One of those 'spells' was still the idea of restoring a pro-government alliance between conservatives and National Liberals. This now became almost a kind of fetish. 'You are aware', Bismarck stressed in a letter to Christoph von Tiedemann, the new head of the Imperial Chancellery, towards the end of November 1879, 'that the most desirable majority as far as I am concerned is a right-wing National Liberal one.'[11] Anyone who said that his dream coalition was currently unrealizable or even ventured the opinion that the dissolution of the old alliance lay in the evolution of history was for Bismarck a 'doctrinarian' or was even – his worst reproach – guilty of 'Laskery' and as such tended towards the 'nihilistic parliamentary groups of Progressives and Poles'.[12] At any rate the purveyors of such views were to be counted among the 'most extreme elements' who were concerned not with the interests of their voters and with achieving practical results but purely with their own personal prestige and power within their parties. After all, the government was prepared very largely to comply with the interests of those parties and their voters. 'The government needs majorities for its Bills, so it necessarily enters into a community of interests with whoever procures them for it.' This was the nub of the matter. When, however, they made it 'tighten its belt' they obliged it – as the National Liberals had been doing 'incessantly since January 1878' – 'to look for and by its political activities establish alternative backing'.[13]

Bismarck was well aware, of course, that in talking about making the government 'tighten its belt' he was obscuring the real issue, which was one of power: who was boss? But it was precisely such tactics that made up his entire political programme. He attempted to take a fact that had its origin in an entirely specific historical situation – the fact that, in central Europe, effective possession of political power and the successful protection and implementation of interests had over a period of years parted company, at least to a certain extent – and elevate it into a kind of general principle that was, so to speak, of the essence of power and interests. Power, as he had stressed repeatedly and sought in a variety of ways to demonstrate, is primarily concerned to maintain itself. Interests, on the other hand, seek specific implementation. Consequently the two were best kept in balance in an alliance in which power maintained itself by promoting interests and interests were implemented through the medium of power. A total fusion of the two, however, could easily lead to a conflict of objectives or to a one-sided exaggeration of the interest side in the shape of pure group or class rule.

The bureaucratic, authoritarian national ideology that such a concept carried with it elsewhere was and remained deeply alien to Bismarck, however much he may occasionally have made use of it. He took his stand essentially on the basic notion that the overwhelming majority of people are chiefly concerned with their interests – specifically their material interests. That the fascination of power and the fascination of ideas were of at least equal importance for them too was something that, with his naïvely aristocratic political world view, he largely overlooked.

Precisely those men who were his fiercest critics followed his example in this, albeit setting out from quite different premises, and put forward the idea, not least in relation to Bismarck himself, that the fascination of power always arises out of a quite specific interest, remains bound up with it and can only really be understood in terms of it. It often entirely escaped their notice and at least partially escaped his that on the contrary the essence of that fascination consists in the very fact that it outstrips every precisely definable concrete interest and constitutes an end and an interest in itself. As a result, however, their basis of judgement was crucially narrowed and in Bismarck's case a mistaken assessment of the internal political situation was fostered that led to a series of failures and eventually, if we do not take too superficial a view of the course of events, to his political downfall.

Bismarck's long-term domestic policy objective, which that mistaken assessment at least sometimes deluded him into thinking was attainable, was from the early 1880s onwards more and more clear-cut: to depoliticize the parties by stressing the standpoint of material interest. In this way he hoped to bring under control the rising tide of forces and movements that questioned and threatened the existing order and to overcome 'the confusion of the parliamentary situation', as he described the attitude of the majority towards him.[14] As he had stated programmatically in a letter to Finance Minister Hobrecht back in May 1878: 'The savants with no trade, no property, no commerce, no industry, who live off earnings, fees and dividends will as the years go by have to bow to the economic demands of the manufacturing population or vacate their seats in parliament. This struggle may take longer than either of us is going to live, but I for one am determined not to give it up even if the *current* lack of success can confidently be expected to continue.'[15] And in a speech in the Imperial Diet six years later he said: 'For the rest . . . I believe that political parties and political programmes have outlived their usefulness. They will gradually, if they do not do it of their own accord, be forced to take up a position on economic questions and act more like pressure groups than they have hitherto. It is inherent in the spirit of the age, which is stronger than they will be.'[16] What he expected to happen was that the process would lead to a progressive dissolution and re-formation of the traditional parties and 'their limited companies, the parliamentary groups'.[17]

The tendency had been implicit in Bismarck's entire policy up to now. This had never recognized the parties as established powers, so to speak, to be taken into account at all events. On the contrary, in one way or another it had always aimed at altering the party spectrum to its own advantage – right down to attempting to eliminate certain parties completely, such as the Centre and subsequently the Social Democrats. But never before had this tendency been directed against all the parties simultaneously. Never before had Bismarck attempted to tamper with the traditional party structure as a whole.

This in itself indicates that Bismarck's thrust in this direction was virtually an act of desperation. And what may have looked like a prelude to success was in fact already the seal of failure. For when towards the end of August 1880 the National Liberal Party and its parliamentary group finally broke up the occurrence did not, as Bismarck so much wanted to believe and so many have repeated after him, represent the triumph of the standpoint of economic interest over the political ambitions of certain left-wing liberal leaders. It was an event that, beyond the splitting of the party, signalled the political division of the nation and ushered in a critical situation in political and social affairs such as Bismarck had successfully evaded up to now with his *de facto* policy of a mutual balance of interests on the basis of a centre-right coalition.

That alternative was blocked for ever by the definitive splitting of the National Liberal Party, which in the words of Stauffenberg had been living no more than 'a galvanic pseudo-existence'[18] since the parliamentary decisions of 1879, and there was no longer any avoiding the ever sharper accentuation of differences. The attempt to counter this by achieving a balance of interests on a fresh basis was a failure not only in its own terms. It also provoked the parties into forming a virtually united defensive front and instead of leading to their progressive dissolution resulted in an internal consolidation and consequently in a further intensification of the antagonisms that they embodied.

Bismarck initiated such an attempt almost immediately after the National Liberal Party split, of which he had high hopes. On 16 September 1880 he added to his offices as Minister-President and Foreign Minister of Prussia that of Prussian Minister of Commerce. In this his declared objective, as stated in a direct report to Emperor William on 12 October 1880, was to make possible at the highest Reich level 'a uniform collaboration over the preparation of the Bills' that the emperor – that is to say, Bismarck himself – would 'shortly . . . be placing before the other Prussian ministerial departments, the confederate governments and the Federal Council for their approval'.[19] In other words, a new control centre for economic policy was being created – for the Economic Affairs Section set up shortly afterwards at the Imperial Department of the Interior was largely staffed on a 'personal union' basis by officials of the Prussian Ministry of Commerce. From that new control centre he immediately launched what in terms of its political conception can only be called a frontal attack on the parties and their traditional place in state and society.

The attack was directed at two points that in his opinion constituted the chief sources of the inner dynamism and power of attraction of the parties and hence of their individual strength and claim to political power. It was directed at their function as representing economic interests. And it was directed at their closely associated role as representatives of immediate, unresolved social tensions and problems that the situation of the labouring population, particularly the vast army of industrial workers, was making more and more dramatic. Bismarck calculated that, if in respect of these two points he could manage as it were to shift the parties out of the centre of the hopes and expectations of those concerned, not only their function but with it their claim or title would change rapidly. And those two changes would be accompanied by a further, fundamental change in their composition hitherto, both in terms of personnel and in the distribution of weight between them.

The trend towards mediatizing the parties first emerged very clearly in this form in the autumn and winter of 1879–80 in his policy with regard to the Roman Catholic Church. Following the failure of his attempt to establish relations with the Centre Party, first in the field of economic and social affairs and subsequently in the field of foreign affairs as well, Bismarck had concentrated on bypassing the Centre and reaching an agreement directly with the Curia. His aim in this had been to drive the Catholic party into the political wilderness. What he embarked on now, however, had a quite different dimension from the start. It made his ecclesiastical policy – even as it was beginning to show signs of success – look like a comparatively minor problem.

It began with a major attempt to reduce even further the role of the parties in decision-making in the whole sphere of national economic policy and to offer those whose interests were at stake more direct ways of influencing and collaborating with the executive. On 15 October 1880, less than a month after taking over the Prussian Ministry of Commerce and in parallel to his reorganization of the whole chain of command in economic policy, he put before the Prussian Cabinet a 'draft of a decree concerning the establishment of a National Economic Council'. This body, based on French prototypes, was to comprise three sections – one for commerce, one for 'Industrie und Gewerbe', meaning industry and the manufacturing trades, and one for agriculture – and was to consist in the main of members to be presented by the relevant professional organizations – the chambers of commerce, the 'executive committees of the commercial corporations' and the agricultural associations. They were to be assisted by thirty representatives of professional interest groups appointed by the government, a condition being that 'at least fifteen belong to the artisan and labouring classes'.

The new body, which first met on 27 January 1881, was conceived from the outset as a prelude to the same sort of council at Reich level. Its function, according to Bismarck, was to be to participate directly in the preparation of Bills 'touching on the economic life of the nation' – in other words a large slice of the total national legislative programme. 'How strongly the economic groups of industry, commerce, the craft-trades and agriculture have felt the need for some greater consideration of their interests', Bismarck wrote in his letter of 15 October 1880 to the Prussian Cabinet, 'can be judged from the fact that over the last two decades, as a result of the free initiative of those concerned, three bodies have emerged – the "German Commercial Diet", the "Central Association of German Industrialists" and the "German Agricultural Council" – the functions of which consist essentially in implementing the wishes of the productive classes in legislation and in commercial and tariff policy.' The plan for a National Economic Council was an extension of that development. In fact it represented the logical conclusion of it, besides being wholly in line with the requirements of those concerned, from among whose ranks the wish had 'repeatedly been expressed' that 'a uniform central organ' should be created 'out of or alongside those three bodies'.[20]

He could not have made himself clearer. The many links already existing between the lobby associations on the one hand and the state bureaucracy and the executive on the other were finally, by becoming institutionalized, to be short-circuited and the long way round via the political parties to be declared superfluous – exactly as the 'Central Association', the 'Commercial Diet' and the 'Agricultural Council' had been demanding for years. So although, going by the letter of the constitution, no formal objection could be raised against the new institution, it was only too understandable that nearly all the parties should more or less vigorously have opposed it.

The Berlin *Vossische Zeitung* voiced the fears of many when it spoke on 30 November 1880 of an unmistakable intention 'to dissipate fledgeling constitutional life at national and imperial level in that sham constitutionalism' of which the 'essence', in the words of Prussia's leading constitutional lawyer, Ludwig Rönne, was 'that "the forms of the constitution serve only to conceal absolutist and self-seeking tendencies behind a mask of liberalism"'.[21] Although the parties could not prevent the new body from being set up they did succeed before very long in politically crippling this 'species of parallel, counter-parliament [*Neben- und Gegenparlament*]', as Ludwig Bamberger called it in an election speech,[22] and stopping it from spreading beyond Prussia. A highly effective campaign to discredit the whole thing in the eyes of the public as a fresh tool of what was becoming a more and more pronounced 'dictatorship of the Chancellor' was backed up by a no less effective threat, directed at the lobby associations, that the attempt to bypass the parties would provoke corresponding retaliatory action on their part and doom any legislation, no matter how ingenious, to failure.

The entire initiative thus very soon proved a fiasco as far as the government was concerned. Nor was that all. The parties' success in warding off what was indeed a most threatening challenge created a political climate that was extremely unfavourable to all such further plans of Bismarck's as could be even remotely suspected of aiming in a similar direction.

This came out especially in the reaction to an initiative he launched immediately after this in the field of social policy or, to be more precise, the field of social welfare, the fundamental legislative reorganization of which is still regarded as one of the most significant credit entries in the balance-sheet of Bismarckian domestic policy after 1871. That reaction has often, in retrospect, been represented in terms of a dogmatic blindness to certain crucial problems of modern society. But the parties had every reason to adopt a critical stance.

There was of course a whole series of objective motives behind Bismarck's policy in this area, including ones of an ethical and moral nature that arose out of the traditions of a Christian-conservative concept of the state and a feeling of social responsibility with patriarchal overtones. It is beyond doubt, however, that the primary political objective of Bismarck's social policy was to create a new and stronger form of direct commitment to the state; the first concern of that policy was to alienate the parties from their bases in this area too, to mediatize them, as it were, and thus to relegate them to the second rank as rivals for power. In the words of one of the greatest authorities on the subject: 'As the old parties entered a state of flux, benefits were to bind the masses to the government and remove them from the influence of agitation, creating a class of petty state pensioners.'[23]

Bismarck had had ideas of this kind already worked out back in the 1860s. As with the National Economic Council, the Napoleonic example undoubtedly played a not inconsiderable part here. During the years of collaboration with the National Liberals such considerations had related solely to the socialists and to the groups from among the 'Reichsfeinde' who were in competition with the socialists over social questions. But he had never lost his conviction that it was possible in principle, so to speak for reasons of state, to cut the ground from under the feet of the political representatives of certain social groups and interests and eliminate them by means of a combination of political repression and state benefits for their supporters.

He had had his whole 'socio-political' programme worked out along these lines as early as the autumn of 1871, mentioning 'meeting the demands of the working classes by legislative and administrative means' and 'suppressing agitation dangerous to the state by means of prohibitions and penal laws' literally in the same breath. Not only had he adhered to this but even before the Anti-Socialist Bill, in the summer of 1877, he had developed very concrete plans as to what 'meeting the demands of the working classes' should look like in detail.

Instead of individual bureaucratic interventions in the world of industrial labour by all-powerful factory inspectors, he wrote at the end of a long letter to the then Prussian Minister of Commerce, Heinrich Achenbach, on 10 August 1877, they should concentrate on the principle of 'liability for accidents' and on 'its possible extension to disablement resulting from exhaustion through work and illness contracted at work'.[24] In the further course of events the idea emerged more and more clearly, not least from detailed discussions with representatives of industry, of a general insurance scheme under the patronage of and with the participation of the state. Such a system of insurance, supported by the state and reflecting favourably on the state, was likely, as he wrote quite plainly around the middle of December 1880, 'to engender in the great mass of the unpropertied the conservative state of mind that springs from the feeling of entitlement to a pension'.[25] And as he told the writer Moritz Busch a month later: 'A man who has a pension for his old age is much happier and much easier to deal with than a man without that prospect.'[26]

It is clear from what he wrote in December 1880 that the general political idea that in the preceding decades had been channelled mainly against the socialists and related groups had now broadened out again in the wake of political developments and in particular the party-political situation. It was now showing a tendency to become a system-building principle. 'The socio-political importance of a general insurance for the unpropertied', he remarked with positive emphasis, 'would be immeasurable.' And, far from ducking the charge that many people now hurled at him, he accepted it as the central idea behind the whole thing: 'A state-socialist idea! The generality must undertake to assist the unpropertied and seek to cover itself by taxing foreign imports and luxuries'.

The 'generality' was for him the bureaucratic state with the monarch at its head and the government, appointed by the monarch, that embodied that state, not the representatives of the governed in the shape of the parties. In his eyes they represented only the particular individual interests that must take second place to the general, overall interest. 'The state must take this matter in hand', he declared over and over again, and in private conversation he added: 'State Socialism is on the move and there is no stopping it. Whoever embraces this idea will come to power'.[27]

In this way the old bureaucratic, absolutist idea of the state – of which Bismarck, albeit from various points of view, had so often been among the critics – joined forces in a quite specific domestic situation with key ideas in the fields of social reform and social welfare. That they were objectively justified seems beyond dispute. In this case, however, they undisguisedly served to force back Bismarck's political rivals and place his own dwindling power on a new and, as he hoped, more secure basis.

Parties and public had a clear sense of this, above and beyond all matters of detail. They suspected that the whole thing was aimed at an authoritarian recasting of the existing political order and a further weakening of the representative elements in the state, which were in any case not very strong in comparison with those in the western European nations, in France and particularly in Britain. And they reacted accordingly. However, their reaction has often faded into the background in the history-books while greater attention – understandably, in view of subsequent developments – has been paid to the authoritarian, manipulative factors in the history of the 1871 Reich. This has threatened – and continues to threaten – to place everything else in a false light. Because only by bearing in mind how badly Bismarck's initiatives ran aground politically can we understand the

129

underlying significance of his increasingly hectic search for fresh alternatives and possible solutions.

The point is, we are looking here not at the gradual and successful erection of a 'system' according to plan. We are looking at a kind of political struggle for survival, a desperate struggle that was of course – particularly since Bismarck the politician subsequently became a positive legend – disastrous in its consequences. Over and above the direct effect on actual circumstances, structures and modes of behaviour, the conception of the nature of politics itself threatened to become degraded in the process. It threatened to take its bearings purely from the momentarily feasible – which while it might seem to be an expression of sober *Realpolitik* was in fact merely banal, elevating a lack of any perspective to the status of a principle.

The opposition parties of 1881, the various left-wing liberal groups, the Centre Party and the Social Democrats, were of course unable to take comfort from the idea of the whole thing having no future. They saw or rather feared a very real perspective: a neo-absolutism supported by state-socialist and pseudo-plebiscitary elements. It was something that Jacob Burckhardt, the Basle historian, had foretold in a variety of ways right back in the early 1870s, speaking of the 'military state' that had of necessity to 'become a major manufacturer' and of the combination of organization of the masses and an authoritarian regime.[28] At the time he had been a voice crying in the wilderness. By 1881, however, there were many who felt moved to entertain such sombre suspicions. The memory of Imperial Rome and a policy of diversion and corruption aimed at the broad masses, not least with the object of excluding the political elites, became a veritable *topos* during those months. Even Wilhelm Wehrenpfennig, the editor of the influential *Preussische Jahrbücher* and a man whose political allegiance was with the right wing of the National Liberal Party, spoke at the beginning of June 1881 of the 'Roman grain handouts to the darling rabble in a different form' that were represented by offering 'a section of the workers chosen at random the prospect of pensions at the state's expense . . . And who is responsible for the internal chaos', he asked rhetorically, that this was intended to cure?[29] Theodor Fontane described the general mood in a letter to Count Philipp Eulenburg in the spring of 1881: 'A storm is gradually brewing against Bismarck among the people. In the upper stratum of society, as we know, it has been raging for some time. It is not his deeds that are destroying him but his suspicions. He is deceived as to the extent of his popularity. This used to be enormous but is so no longer.'[30]

Given such tendencies in public opinion and in the parties, the fate of his first major welfare proposal, the Accident Insurance Bill presented to the Federal Council on 15 January 1881, was virtually sealed in advance. In the crucial debate in the Imperial Diet at the beginning of April 1881 Bismarck found himself confronted with all the mistrust and misgivings that his political initiatives of the past few months had aroused among its members. Not even his political forward strategy, directed primarily against the left-wing liberals, brought him any return. On the contrary, it increased people's suspicions regarding his ultimate aims and intentions. 'We are

130

delighted to note', Eugen Richter, the leader of the Progressive Party, summed up triumphantly on the second day of the debate, 'that ever wider circles are becoming infused with a spirit of independent, objective criticism with regard to the proposals of the Imperial Chancellor – wider than we thought possible only a short while ago.'[31]

The debate about the government's Bill did indeed develop into a regular political ostracism of the Chancellor by the opposition parties. In this the actual problems at issue receded farther and farther into the background. There was talk of a stealthy transition not just to socialism but to communism – and of a kind worse 'than anyone has yet invented'. There was talk of class politics dressed up 'in new forms' and entirely in line with tariff and fiscal policy since 1879. 'It *looks* like a subsidy for the poor', said Eugen Richter, 'it *looks* like a subsidy for workers, but in reality it is like nothing so much as a subsidy for big industry, for the more is done for workers by the state, the less big industry needs to pay workers in competition with other sectors for those same workers.'[32]

The rising anti-Semitic movement and its alleged encouragement by the Reich authorities and use as a political instrument against the parties of the left were also brought into the argument, as was the tradition of the radical left in the French Revolution, the tradition of Jacobinism and the National Convention in the years 1793–4. According to Ludwig Bamberger: 'The only legislative power to have approached this matter in the manner in which it is being approached here was the French National Convention. That is our precursor. Moreover, it did not stop at mere accident insurance but embarked upon – though it did not complete – the project that we too are having held out to us as an idea for the future, namely the great task of old-age and disability insurance'. This was admittedly something that certain forces in France were currently engaged on, 'members of the radical opposition to Gambetta' in connection with whom every informed person knew 'what colour that party bears and that it goes far beyond what is called Republican'. The 'undauntedness' that characterized the imperial government, Bamberger jeered, was something 'it can also point to in the fact that it is not deterred by such company'.

What, however, Bamberger asked, summing up the general tone of the criticism in the most extreme terms, was the real nub of the concept behind the Bill, the underlying idea that 'as well as . . . humane, modern, Christian', could also be termed 'revolutionary'? Surely it was the idea that 'the poor man must be shown that the state does not exist just for the rich but also for him; he must be shown this positively, by gifts of money . . . Gentlemen, is that a modern idea? . . . That is the way . . . the Roman Republic thought in its decline'. Then they had built 'theatres for the darling rabble in Rome or in Athens' and tried in that way to show the people 'that the state does not exist just for the rich but also to provide pleasure and entertainment for the masses . . . This is no modern way of thinking, gentlemen, this is not the state of the categorical imperative . . . this is simply the state of the man who goes about in a white toga in order to canvass votes and shake everybody by the hand . . . but not the state that is doing its duty.'[33]

Granted, in substance there was much that did not tally here. As far as the undoubtedly pressing problem itself was concerned, the positions from which criticism was voiced were in many cases disparate as well as lacking in perspective. The spokesmen of the Centre Party, while their speeches were no less critical on many counts, proved very much more constructive in this respect. Yet the basic political trend was unequivocal. And it mustered a very clear majority in the Imperial Diet. In vain did Bismarck implore in his great speech to the plenum on 2 April 1881 that 'everything should not be approached from the point of view of party tactics, from the point of view of parliamentary tactics, out of the feeling, "Away with Bismarck" and the like'.[34] In vain did he completely exclude the Centre Party from his counter-attacks. In vain did he stress the Christian element in the Bill, insisting over and over again that in essence this was 'practical Christianity in legislative action'.[35] All his concentration on the representatives of left-wing liberalism, whose arguments he said were redolent of class warfare as well as being dictated by mere power-seeking, all his appeals for joint action on so central and momentous an issue were to no avail. In the course of the ensuing deliberations of a specially appointed twenty-eight-man committee the representatives of the Centre and the left-wing liberals together got rid of the two elements to which Bismarck attached particular importance: the projected 'Imperial Insurance Institute' and the Reich's contribution towards premiums.

In so doing they were in principle acting very much in tacit agreement with the ministerial expert responsible and Bismarck's closest colleague in matters of social policy, the under secretary of state at the Ministry of Commerce, Theodor Lohmann. With no political ulterior motive, concentrating solely on the social problems as such, Lohmann advocated the principle of self-help on the part of the individual and society and openly rejected both the Imperial Insurance Institute and contributions by the Reich. For Bismarck, however, the Bill had become virtually worthless politically after the changes made in committee and the corresponding decision of the Imperial Diet. He was firmly resolved not to accept this 'parliamentary and privy-conciliar changeling', as he later dubbed the whole thing,[36] but to wait for the imminent verdict of the electorate.

Both sides had made repeated reference to that verdict and to how they thought it would fall in the debate at the beginning of April 1881. Since then everyone had been concentrating to an unprecedented degree on the Imperial Diet elections due in the autumn. Among the things governed by that prospect was Bismarck's pointed attempt to reduce the influence of the Diet still further by introducing two-year budgetary periods and correspondingly fewer sessions. Officially the 'Confederate Governments' referred to the problem of simultaneous sessions of the Imperial Diet and the various national diets, to which many members of the former body belonged in personal union.

An initial Bill along these lines had been brought in back in 1880 but at the time had not even got on to the agenda. And it was no less certain now that the majority in the Diet would never agree to such a curtailment of its own power. In other words, the whole thing was calculated, as far as

Bismarck was concerned, to present the crippling antagonism between parliamentary majority and executive to the public and to the electorate in a favourable light for the government. The dominant concern in the government camp, it was to be generally inferred, was to do an effective, relevant, material job of work in the public interest, while the prevailing tendency in the opposite camp was towards endless sessions and debates and self-interested power struggles and intrigues. What was at issue was the claim of the mere orator – who would seldom, Bismarck said, 'make a reliable statesman'[37] – to supremacy over the experienced and expert practitioner.

This was also the substance of his last major speech in the Diet before the elections, when on 5 May 1881 he spoke in support of a proposal to amend the constitution accordingly[38] – for the principles governing budgetary rights and the length and frequency of sessions were anchored in the constitution. In decidely demagogic terms he spoke of the comforts of life as a deputy compared with the lives of those who really had to work and to perform their 'stern duty'. He stressed the danger of a man who lived and moved only in parliamentary circles, who no longer shared 'common labour, common giving and getting with the voters', losing 'all feeling for and possibility of right judgements with regard to the interests and desires of the people who elected him'. The end-result was 'simply a new species or, as I prefer to say, genus of "bureaucracy"', with all its disadvantages; 'as we have families of hereditary civil servants', so they would have 'families of hereditary parliamentarians . . . who direct their studies towards that end and say, in the colloquial phrase, "I want to learn [to be a] deputy"'. And, taking a mere assertion – which of course he knew only too well corresponded closely to a popular prejudice – as established fact, he went on: 'Extending bureaucracy further to cover parliamentary life as well, turning this too into a branch of the imperial and national civil service that has few points of contact and in particular no common interests and modes of thought with the *misera contribuens plebs*, the people who do the working and toiling and the risking and wagering and the earning and winning or losing – that I regard as a harmful development.'

The nub of this speech, which was wholly geared to the electorate and to public opinion, was that parliament, instead of being a mirror and representative of the interests and aspirations of society, had now itself become a part of the state administration. Indeed it often outdid the civil service in bureaucratism, being dominated not by practical experience and expertise but by mere theory and a know-all manner. In it the tone, as Bismarck said in even harsher terms in the *Norddeutsche Allgemeine Zeitung* towards the end of June 1881,[39] was set by 'savants' who were to 'the earning population that lives by its labour' as 'the drones are to the worker bees'. They were the 'professional deputies' who outnumbered those 'who are glad when the Imperial Diet rises'.

This was an anti-parliamentarism based on quite different premisses, and Bismarck backed it up, beyond the concrete proposal for changes, with the argument that the constitution already provided an approved antidote to this kind of undesirable development. That antidote was of course one that the left side of the House, bidding for power by any and every means, was only too keen to consign to oblivion: it consisted of the rights of the emperor as head of state and as representative of the 'monarchical principle'. 'The Emperor', Bismarck stressed in the strongest possible terms, 'has not up to now placed his personal rights before the Imperial Diet for it to discuss and vote on them'.

The old formula so endlessly repeated during the years of the constitutional conflict thus received a quite new content. The monarch as the truly individual, personal element in the life of the state and at the same time the natural representative of the whole and of the common good was also, said Bismarck, the natural counter-weight to the individual and society being overwhelmed by an ever-expanding state bureaucracy in ever new guises, to the selfishness of new classes that were alien to the people. From here it was but a step to the concept of a personal, 'charismatic' leadership that would burst out of and overcome the dependencies and abstract constraints, the 'serfdoms' of the modern world, a concept that at the time and subsequently fascinated so many very different minds and led them astray politically.

Bismarck himself did not take that step. He was too level-headed, too 'unideological' for that; above all he was too well aware of the dangers that might arise from it regarding his own position in a monarchical state. But from this point on he more and more frequently invoked perspectives and ideas of this sort. He contrasted the bureaucratic institutional state, which he alleged had already spread to parliament and would not be content to stop there, with the vision of a patriarchal monarchy. Only such a monarchy, he claimed, would be capable of reconciling present differences in new, organic forms that would preserve what time had shown to be worth preserving.

Granted, if he did not seriously believe in such things himself, neither did they constitute anything more than a threat to those whom he was directly addressing here, a warning that he might, if it came to it, act quite otherwise. Significantly he ended his speech of 5 May 1881 with a highly personal appeal to Rudolf von Bennigsen, the leader of the National Liberal Party. He referred to him as being, 'of his party colleagues, the comrade-in-arms . . . whom I have to thank for true support and to whom the German Empire is so deeply indebted for its foundation and for its consolidation'. Bennigsen, he said, ought not to become further 'alienated from the Imperial government' or let himself be drawn into a left-wing coalition that threatened to make any resumption of their association impossible. Bismarck's main objective was still to retrieve and furnish with a more solid electoral base the centre-right coalition that had constituted his support in politically more successful and happier times.

That objective, however, had long since become a mirage. By invoking it yet again, after all his attacks on the parties, Bismarck succeeded only in inspiring fresh mistrust. Indeed he sabotaged his own intention, which was to bring about an electoral decision between himself and the disunited and in fact extremely heterogeneous majority and in this way put the Diet as a whole in its place.

The opinion that was beginning to take root among the public was that what the Chancellor was offering as an alternative, personally and in terms of his policy, what he was canvasssing approval of and support for, was too diffuse, too hazy, too dubious and too unclear with regard to its ultimate objectives. All threats and pressures, all appeals and enticements, all attempts – and they were massive – to exert undue influence on voters and stress the standpoint of self-interest were of no avail: the voters decided overwhelmingly against a policy of which the chief positive features were not clearly recognisable and that therefore added to the electorate's confusion.

The parties closest to Bismarck, the Free Conservative Empire Party and those National Liberals who had remained within the old fold, both lost nearly half their votes and more than half their seats, the Free Conservatives dropping from fifty-seven to twenty-eight seats and the National Liberals, who in their heyday in the first half of the 1870s had been the largest parliamentary party by far, retaining a mere forty-seven seats, one more than the 'Secessionists' of 1880. Campaigning as the 'Liberal Union', these won a total of forty-six seats at one go. Together with the 'German Progressive Party', which almost doubled its share of the vote and by dint of clever electoral arrangements shot from twenty-six to sixty seats, they constituted a major left-wing liberal group that, though not united on every detail, was so in its bitter opposition to Bismarck and his policy. A further component of that opposition front was still the Centre Party, which with a small gain in votes had gained an additional six seats and with a total of one hundred had now reached the level of strength that it managed by and large to sustain until the collapse of the Reich.

Bismarck thus found himself up against an opposition bloc that with the help of the 'protest parties', which had also had a successful election, exceeded a two-thirds majority – a situation reminiscent of the years immediately after his taking office. With the losses suffered by the conservatives – they dropped nine of their old seats – the number of deputies who were reliably loyal to the government was down to the same as left-wing liberalism could muster.

This striking electoral defeat positively forced the Chancellor, if neither he nor the emperor was prepared to draw the political consequences, to intensify the anti-parliamentary course he had already embarked on against the majority of the existing parties. A parliamentary, party-political alternative of the kind that he had just invoked yet again with the slogan 'Against "Progress" and Free Trade'[40] was out of the question for the time being. However, this made him more dependent than ever before, in a way that was comparable only with the situation at the beginning of his career as Prussian Minister-President, on the person and favour of the King of Prussia and German emperor. As he soberly diagnosed on one occasion around this time, his party consisted 'only of the King and himself'.[41] And in view of William's age, which for a Hohenzollern was unusually advanced, and in view of the political inclinations of the crown prince this was a situation that scarcely seemed to offer serious prospects for the future.

It is understandable that with this in mind Bismarck should have indulged with ever-increasing frequency in wild speculations about potential ways of escape and begun to drop dark hints regarding possible political alternatives and an entirely fresh course. Very little of this was to be taken at all seriously. To speak of concrete plans for a *coup d'état* is undoubtedly to underestimate the man's political realism and level-headedness. Certainly the Chancellor let it be understood, shortly after the elections, that there might 'possibly . . . come a time when the German princes will have to consider whether our current parliamentarism is still compatible with the well-being of the Empire'.[42] And certainly he threatened in a speech in the Diet in June 1882 that a situation might arise in which 'the words "absolutism" and "patriotism" eventually became more closely related than is constitutionally desirable', in which 'German nationhood, German independence both without and within are honoured and protected only by the dynasties and in particular by my master, the King of Prussia'.[43] But the context was always the feverish search for solutions within the existing framework and in accordance with a policy that in one way or another would eventually attract a majority and provide him with a fresh base. Here again his tactics were as he had once described them to Roon shortly before his appointment as Prussian Minister-President: 'Especially if preceded by a certain amount of verbal sabre-rattling with expressions such as octroyation and even a gentle *coup d'état*, my old reputation for irresponsible violence comes to my aid and people think, "Now we're for it." Then all the watchers and waverers will be inclined to parley.'[44]

But what was there to 'parley' about now? What appeared likely to bring about a change in the existing distribution of political weight and the present party spectrum, now that the method of direct appeal to the various interests concerned had not even begun to produce the desired result? Undoubtedly, once his initial disappointment had been overcome, the thought suggested itself that what was needed was patience. He was on the right track; it just did not lead so quickly to his goal. And Bismarck did in fact let it be known immediately that he intended to stick to his 'state-socialist' social programme and the tax reform plans he had formulated accordingly. He chose to do this through the medium of a formal message from the emperor at the opening of the new Imperial Diet on 17 November 1881. With this accentuation and continuation of the political tactics he had employed hitherto he made the emperor 'the personal vehicle of his social and financial reform plans', as his Minister of Agriculture, Robert Lucius, expressed it.[45] In other words, he once again thrust the personal element into the foreground. On top of that he sought to push ahead with his projected Imperial Economic Council – again to no avail, of course, the relevent request for funds being refused afresh by the Diet early in December 1881.

But was that really all? Did Bismarck not contemplate other ways of escaping from the domestic policy impasse in which he now found himself? Can he have failed to recall how swiftly and fundamentally the scene had once changed in the wake of a dynamic and successful foreign policy?

It is a question that has been asked with ever-increasing emphasis in recent years and that has often been answered with a very positive 'yes'.

Indeed it has been pronounced a key question in relation to his whole policy during the 1880s. Georges Clemenceau, the leader of the French left-wing liberals during those years, once summed up his objections to his chief political opponent, the right-wing liberal French Prime Minister, Jules Ferry, in a highly effective way by saying that Ferry intended 'to bribe the poeple with his colonial policy'. This is in essence the theory on the basis of which people have also sought to account in general terms for Bismarck's policy during this period. It runs as follows: in order to preserve the status quo, the existing order in state, economy and society, Bismarck and the prevailing forces in that society made as it were deliberate use of foreign policy, particularly the policy of colonial expansion that the Reich now increasingly pursued for that very reason. A number of individual arguments are said to have come together here: the idea that only economic growth as guaranteed and stimulated by the possession of colonies was capable of ensuring the preservation of the status quo; the notion that a successful power policy as pursued in 1866 and 1871 would give a psychological boost in the same direction by making the existing order appear superior and ultimately insuperable; and finally the thought that a contest for a 'place in the sun' in overseas terms as well would enormously preoccupy and fascinate the public and push many other matters into the background. Individual interests, it is admitted, were very variously distributed here, with each group emphasizing a different aspect and to some extent pursuing very different objectives. But what all groups are supposed to have had in common, what in fact drew them together, was an 'ideological consensus' to the effect that the existing order now under threat from many quarters must be defended by every means available and that a particularly suitable means was participation in a policy of colonial expansion.

This concept of a 'social imperialism', a policy of 'joint protectionism', has all the fascination of one of those blanket explanations that promise to bring a bewildering flood of details under the control of one great idea. It also fits in with a widespread tendency to account for the march of historical progress essentially in terms of the successful doings of individual groups or outstanding individuals. At the same time, however, because it all looks so convincing right from the outset, attention is drawn away from the one thing capable of leading this whole theory out of the realm of mere speculation, namely the question of the factual reality of the alleged connection, the actual relationships between causes and effects and the inner rationale supposedly at work there. If we examine this more closely, it soon emerges that the picture is in reality a very much more complicated one and not so easily reducible to a common denominator. Above all it is very hard actually to pin down that alleged convergence on the various real interests of the different groups and forces in politics and society of which there is so much talk in the context of this kind of interpretation under the headings 'ideological consensus' and 'joint protectionism'. Eventually one is driven increasingly to suspect that what has happened here, in the tradition of interpretations confined purely to the history of thought, is that the contemporary catch-phrase about the 'ideology of self-interest' has been taken for the reality of the way things were and has consequently become invested with an importance it never in fact possessed.

Certainly a great many very varied interests were now looking to the possibility of acquiring colonial possessions. And certainly there was a great deal of thinking in terms of diverting attention from domestic conflicts and problems with the aid of wide-ranging foreign policy prospects, even though every half-way realistic observer of the situation was aware that an interest in overseas questions must first be worked up gradually among a public whose attention in foreign policy matters had for decades been focused on the European continent and its problems – indeed, had been strictly confined to that context by Bismarck's own policy. Finally it is beyond question that, even outside the circle of those with an immediate interest, an active colonial policy was encouraged in many quarters out of a belief that only a 'system' that was expanding in economic as well as power-political terms would survive in the ever harsher climate of competition now faced by individual nations and economies as well as by the different groups and forces in society. However, there were just as many dissenting voices, and the whole colonial question was the subject of fierce controversy not only in the Imperial Diet but also in leading circles of the economy, the world of finance, the civil service and the army. In view of which it seems somewhat doubtful that so sober a realist as Bismarck, however grave a predicament he was in politically, seriously believed that he could concoct from all this a relatively fast-acting patent medicine for his domestic policy ills.

Moreover, not only does the actual course of events speak against it, namely the brief duration of the whole colonial venture and the swift return to the principles and chief features of his previous foreign policy. So does Bismarck's in many instances unproven and in any case very variable and uneven interest in colonial aspirations in Germany and in the different arguments of those who entertained them. And so, above all, does his fundamental conception of the relationship between domestic and foreign policy.

As he repeatedly stressed in the 1860s in particular, when the problem became especially acute, anyone whose foreign policy was conducted essentially for the benefit of his domestic policy would never have any real success in either sphere. That remained his conviction to the very end of his political career. Harnessing foreign policy successes in the service of domestic policy was of course another matter entirely. At that he was a master. He did undoubtedly concern himself intensively, after 1881, with the possibility of exploiting for domestic purposes as well the opportunity of making colonial acquisitions that most unexpectedly cropped up around this time in the wake of developments on the foreign policy front – as in those years of acute political embarrassment he examined every last thing in terms of its potential usefulness as a political tool and put it to the test in appropriate practical initiatives. But that is the point: it was one experiment among many, and its success was scarcely such that Bismarck would have felt bound to continue with it even if, say, it had involved substantial risks in the field of foreign affairs.

So it is a good idea to look at Bismarck's colonial policy, which has occupied the minds and imaginations of posterity far more intensely than it did those of his contemporaries and which in the context of Bismarckian foreign policy constituted no more than a brief interlude, in as sober a light as possible. Most historians still agree that right up until the beginning of the 1880s Bismarck remained distinctly hostile to the idea that Germany too should start acquiring colonial possessions. This was dictated mainly by foreign policy and power-political considerations. In agreement with the bulk not only of Germany's business and financial communities but also of the public and the parties, he was inclined to rate the economic importance of colonies as almost negligible. At the beginning of 1871, for example, when it was rumoured in connection with the discussion of further war aims that he had his eye on the French colonies, specifically Pondicherry in India, he told a circle of intimates expressly that he wanted 'no colonies at all' on principle. They were 'only any use as supply posts', and particularly in Germany's case 'this colonial business' would be 'precisely the same for us as silk-lined sables in Polish noble families who own no shirts'.[46] In a similar context he told an envoy from Empress Eugénie: 'We are not yet wealthy enough to be able to afford the luxury of colonies.'[47] And ten years later, in the spring of 1881, he stressed yet again: 'As long as I am Imperial Chancellor we shall not pursue a colonial policy. We have a fleet that cannot go anywhere, and we must not have any vulnerable points in distant corners of the world that will fall into French hands as soon as anything happens'.[48]

Rejection of what was purely a prestige policy with no real interests behind it and fear of further endangering the international position of the Reich, the geography of which already made it vulnerable enough – these remained the key features governing his attitude to the colonial question for year after year. It was an attitude of which the capitals of Europe, particularly London, which represented the chief colonial power of the day, felt they could be pretty sure. All the greater were the general surprise and consternation, especially in Britain, when in late 1883 and early 1884 Bismarck very suddenly – it seemed – abandoned it and immediately announced in various quarters that the Reich wanted colonies. What, both governments and peoples asked themselves, was the reason for this abrupt change of course? Was the German Chancellor perhaps reverting to the aggressive Prussian foreign policy of the 1860s – having spent the last twelve years trying to persuade the world that Prusso-Germany was now definitely 'sated'?

Very soon, however, a calmer approach prevailed, at least among responsible politicians, an approach that bore in mind the element of continuity and that, laying aside all speculation, concentrated on the most obvious aspect, namely the question of the immediate foreign policy motive involved here and of a possible reassessment of the international situation on the part of those responsible for German policy. And this is in fact where we must still look for the real reasons behind Bismarck's surprising volte-face on the colonial question, however much he may also have been thinking, right from the outset, of the personally advantageous domestic repercussions that possible successes in this field might bring with them.

[14]

New Paths to Old Objectives:
The Foreign Policy of the 1880s

Since the crisis over the Eastern Question beginning in 1875–6 and its laborious resolution and since the crisis in German-Russian relations in 1879 and the reuniting of the three eastern powers within the admittedly insubstantial framework of the Three Emperors' League in 1881, the German Chancellor's longer-term thinking in the field of foreign affairs had been revolving increasingly round the question of a possible structural change in the traditional foundations of European foreign policy, a gradual shift in the balance of power that threatened to invalidate all the old calculations and combinations in respect of power politics. Initially, after the experiences of the Congress of Berlin, that thinking had crystallized in the highly ambitious plans and objectives of his Dual Alliance policy. In practice, however, the Dual Alliance had fallen far short of what Bismarck had envisaged at its inauguration, for there could be no question of its having produced a solid central European bloc to offset the giants of international politics now emerging more and more strongly in east and west. Consequently the Chancellor was always on the look-out, beyond the 'system of stopgaps' that the Dual Alliance and the Three Emperors' League increasingly seemed to represent, for alternatives that promised a more solid future.

This aspect has often been unduly neglected by posterity in favour of an erroneous glorification – not infrequently motivated by current political objectives – of the Bismarckian system of alliances. Yet it is this that supplies the true explanation of Bismarck's surprising about-turn not only in the matter of colonial policy but also as regards the basic direction of his foreign policy as a whole.

It was primarily a turning against Britain. Most of the areas to which the Reich now abruptly laid claim were within the British sphere of interest: Angra Pequena Bay in south-west Africa, Togo and Cameroon in West Africa and a territory in East Africa that Carl Peters occupied from Zanzibar, starting in the autumn of 1884. In the Kissingen Dictate of June 1877 Bismarck had listed as one of the key goals of future German foreign policy the 'separation of Britain from a France still hostile to us because of Egypt and the Mediterranean'.[1] Now a neat reversal of that aim was

140

becoming apparent, although in substance the effort to prevent a political rapprochement between the two western powers remained a wholly valid objective as far as he was concerned. The conflict of interests between those powers, a conflict rooted mainly in colonial affairs, was to be maintained and if necessary exacerbated, not now by deliberately favouring the British position but by according that treatment – indirectly at first but then more and more directly – to the French position.

To this end the Reich now entered the picture as being itself interested in colonizing districts to which Britain more or less openly laid claim. It began to present itself in the guise of Britain's new rival in the colonial field, which in the light of recent history and of its earlier stance on the colonial issue it had some trouble in doing: British policy and British public opinion at first showed no reaction whatever. They first had to be persuaded of the seriousness of the German thrust in this direction with a brutality that had been very rare in relations between the two powers hitherto. On this basis, by exploiting the material points of contact that flowed naturally from it, German policy sought unobtrusively to achieve a rapprochement with Paris. Not least because of the fundamental resistance of sections of the French public, that rapprochement was designed to look like the accidental outcome of quite different events and developments.

That there was most certainly a definite intention behind it is something the records have since made abundantly clear. From the early 1880s onwards the idea crops up in the most varied contexts of reaching a compromise with France by aiding and abetting that country's colonial endeavours. 'Our area of understanding with France', ran a directive to the ambassador in Paris, Prince Hohenlohe, issued at the beginning of April 1880, 'extends from Guinea right through to Belgium and covers all the Romance lands.'[2] In private conversation he said early in 1884 that he wanted to see 'French victories in Tonkin and Madagascar. It gratifies their vanity and deters them from *revanche*.'[3] And in an interview with the French ambassador to Berlin, de Courcel, towards the end of September 1884 he said that there had once been much talk of the European balance of power. Such talk belonged to the world of the eighteenth century. It was not, however, obsolete to talk of an 'oceanic balance', in other words of a global balance of power. Of course, for such a thing to be achieved Britain must be persuaded to 'get used to the idea that a Franco–German alliance falls within the realms of possibility'.[4]

Here we recognize the pivotal notion that aimed, by way of a possible rapprochement with France, at a relaxation of the overall situation. It included the prospect that Britain, reacting to this and turning away from the policy of Gladstone, would itself move closer to Germany – a prospect that is brought to light quite plainly in the letters of Herbert Bismarck, the Chancellor's elder son, who served as secretary to the Reich's London embassy up until the beginning of 1884.[5]

But it is not only subsequent knowledge of the records that brings out these connections and chains of motivation very clearly. Many contemporaries not in immediate possession of the facts were also driven increasingly to corresponding conclusions when eventually, following a prelude at the

London conference about Egypt in the spring of 1884, France and the Reich agreed in the autumn of that year on a joint course of action with regard to the Congo question: at the Congo conference that took place in Berlin from 15 November 1884 to 26 February 1885, the first colonial conference to be held on German soil, the two powers isolated and outmanoeuvred British policy to a very considerable extent. We have already seen how Georges Clemenceau said of Jules Ferry, the French Prime Minister who in the aftermath of these negotiations collaborated closely with Bismarck, that he had tried to 'bribe the [French] people with his colonial policy' and distract them from the real objective of revenge against Germany.

That charge, together with the public response that greeted it in France, at the same time showed the limits that were still set to a German–French rapprochement – almost fourteen years after the end of the war. Bismarck was fully aware of those limits. 'What the papers are saying about the German–French alliance', he wrote to William I in October 1884, 'goes beyond the present and possibly all future reality, and I would never advise your Majesty to base the future of our policy on such insecure foundations.'[6] Ferry's fall on 30 March 1885, which started a fresh wave of anti–German revanchism, very soon set the seal on the failure of this whole attempt to reach a compromise with France and possibly bring about fresh foreign policy combinations on that basis. Bismarck summed up the situation towards the end of May 1885 in a letter to the German ambassador to Paris: 'Fear of the revanchist movements and the exploitation of the same by the opposition of the day' would 'inhibit any government . . . from making a *firm* stand in our favour. We therefore should not spurn a *temporary* one, though it is not something we can rely on politically; at the crucial moment, mistrust of us will still outweigh irritation with Britain. For this reason we must continue to refrain from taking the lead against Britain and being more French than the French.'[7]

In the light of this the opinion has often been advanced that the attempted rapprochement with France was in fact no more than an exploratory probe of which Bismarck had little hope of success from the moment he launched it. The whole thing, it is said, arose more from the circumstances of the moment and the trend of current developments than from any far-reaching plan. Bismarck's real objective, disregarding for a moment the controversial question of domestic motivation, was far more direct: he wanted to force Britain into a dialogue covering the whole spectrum of foreign affairs, as it were, not just partial questions, and in so doing to induce it to make clearer choices than hitherto.

Apart from the fact that in most instances the old dream of a German–British rapprochement shines through here and colours judgements, this interpretation leaves something very important out of account, namely that one of the constants of Bismarckian policy, irrespective of its versatility and flexibility and irrespective of all changes in external circumstances, was the refusal to make an unequivocal choice in favour of one of the great flanking powers. That refusal became even more pronounced in proportion as those powers grew in international stature and so threatened to overwhelm any ally who was unilaterally committed to them. As with Russia in 1879, so with Britain now the obvious course was to try to set up counter-weights and build up counter-positions in such a way that, operating from a stronger base, one could contain the other side without falling into a position of dependence upon it. In both cases he was anxious to avoid that kind of dependence for domestic reasons as well. For both powers were at the same time seen as the champions of particular internal systems and as such had a polarizing effect, through the alliance question, on the domestic front.

From this point of view the colonial initiative of 1884 and the attempt to achieve a rapprochement with France through the medium of colonial policy appear in a very different light. The impression of an *ad hoc* undertaking embarked on with significant ulterior motives in terms of domestic policy begins to recede. Instead the whole thing presents itself as an expression of Bismarck's concern to develop his Dual Alliance policy beyond mere stopgaps and short-term solutions and arrive at completely new combinations. These were to help to take account of the insidious shifts currently affecting the balance of power and what was now emerging with increasing clarity as the imminent extension of the European system into a system of world states.

We must certainly not exaggerate here. Bismarck was not a man of far-reaching plans and long-term objectives. He was too level-headed for that, too well aware of the limits of the feasible, the calculable and the predictable, too concerned to bet on as many cards as possible. But here again we remember his dictum about the man walking in the wood who, without knowing his way exactly knows his general direction. And the general direction had to be the formation of a counter-weight to the flanking powers, which were becoming steadily more powerful – a kind of continental bloc. This ought ultimately, if at all possible, to include France as well or at least prevent it from joining forces with Britain.

Here was the key element in his foreign-policy activities since late 1883 and his colonial thrust in the following months up until the fall of the Ferry government. What he told Eugen Wolf, a well-to-do 'explorer' and colonial enthusiast, on 5 December 1888 in words that have since been quoted over and over again was no mere retrospective insight but his conviction throughout. Wolf tells us that, after he had given Bismarck a detailed account of the African situation and the current activities of the German colonialist movement, Bismarck dismayed him by saying: 'Your map of Africa is all very fine, but my map of Africa lies in Europe. Here is Russia and here – pointing to the left – is France, and we are in the middle; that is my map of Africa.'[8] In other words, colonial policy was always, for him, merely a function of the situation in Europe, and it was this that guided his every step in this field.

Five years earlier he would probably, in a comparable situation, have pointed to Britain rather than France. In the mean time, however, he had completely abandoned the idea that invoking the spectacle of power-political rivalry and danger from that quarter might have the effect of drawing France closer to the Reich and hence to the Dual Alliance and its associated system of alliances. The same was true of the idea that his own position at home might be strengthened by this means.

Developments in France since the fall of Ferry had made it increasingly clear that in the light of mounting political and social tensions the call for 'revanche' was and remained the one bond uniting the nation, indeed that as a result of those tensions it was becoming a more and more important factor on the domestic front. The man whom the left-wing forces around Clemenceau had put in as War Minister, General Boulanger, had by dint of heavy appeals to the idea of 'revanche' and by channelling a wide variety of dissatisfactions into an aggressive nationalism unleashed a movement that threatened internally to destroy the republic in favour of a neo-Bonapartist system and externally to spark off a European war.

Admittedly 'Général Revanche' had been removed from office just in time after nearly managing to provoke a conflict with Germany in reaction to the 'Schnaebele Affair': in April 1887 a customs officer of that name, suspected of espionage, had been lured on to German soil on the pretext of 'consultations' and arrested in contravention of international law. But although the republican forces finally managed to win the day, they themselves had subsequently to take increasing account of the tendencies to which the crisis had given such prominence. Even had a section of them wanted it otherwise, a rapprochement and even more an agreement with Germany would have been quite impossible from then on. In fact right up until the First World War it never again came seriously under discussion.

By the beginning of this development at the latest, that is to say by 1885–6, Bismarck had finally come to realize how disastrously, in view of the shifting global balance of power, the terms of the 1871 Treaty of Frankfurt had restricted his room for manoeuvre in foreign affairs. 'We are literally immobilized by France', Holstein wrote laconically to the ambassador in London, Count Hatzfeldt, in mid-1886.[9] The German Chancellor may have insisted to the end that France's longing for revenge was the inevitable result of its having lost its previous position of semi-hegemony; its territorial losses had been no more than a contributory factor, providing a graphic symbol. Nevertheless, there is some evidence that without that 'symbol' France would have got over its defeat very much more easily. Given a different international situation and constellation of interests, the French might perhaps have decided after all to seek a rapprochement with the Reich and undertake a reorientation of their foreign policy.

As it was, however, the situation remained as the events of 1871 had left it; indeed it was once again expressly confirmed. At the same time it was beginning to look increasingly as if the international balance of power was shifting more and more – and doing so to the disadvantage of the Reich. After the failure of his initiative of 1884–5, a fresh answer was more than Bismarck was able to come up with. On the contrary, he now fell back completely on the formula that he had worked out in the second half of the 1870s, principally in the 1877 Kissingen Dictate. And this despite the fact that, as was obvious from a sober view of the situation, a complete reversal of conditions threatened, the Reich was becoming increasingly dependent on its allies and attempts to compensate for this state of affairs led him into ever more complicated, ever more desperate actions and manoeuvres.

But what were the alternatives? The one on which against Bismarck's stubborn and ultimately successful resistance a highly heterogeneous coalition of political forces from the extreme right to the extreme left began to agree in 1886–7, namely a preventive war, in alliance with the Habsburg monarchy, against a Russia now once again pressing forward in the Balkans? Quite apart from bringing problems of its own, such a preventive war would very probably not only have prompted France to launch its own much-talked-of war of revenge and thus provoked a war on two fronts on a massive scale. If, as was to be expected, it threatened to bring about fundamental shifts in the balance of power, it would probably have drawn Britain in as well, because for all its self-restraint London would never have been prepared to accept the complete destruction of the European equilibrium. And what would that have led to? Either the establishment of a new order under British tutelage or the partition of the continent between its two flanking powers – in other words, a result that could be had merely by making a determined choice, without a war and its attendant sacrifices and incalculable risks.

The only serious alternative, then, was to make such a choice. And since by now there was scarcely a voice to be heard in Germany in favour of backing Russia, in practice this meant choosing Britain. But that meant giving up the old policy of chopping and changing between the different powers and power groups; it meant abandoning the system of alliances that had been built up and constantly added to for this purpose and making a firm and permanent commitment to the 'island state'.

This was indeed, looked at in retrospect, the only serious alternative. And it has rightly constituted the focus of debate ever since. It represents the counter-subject, as it were, for every critical discussion of Bismarckian foreign policy in its final phase.

Right up until the end, right up until his fall in the spring of 1890, whatever thrusts he may seem to have launched in this direction, Bismarck did not adopt it. His objective was and remained to preserve the greatest possible degree of independence for the Reich in foreign affairs. It was an objective he sought to achieve by means of constant chopping and changing between the powers and by a policy that amounted to making dangerous-looking forces and interests cancel one another out in a kind of general stalemate. So the only candidates for serious discussion are the dangers and consequences of that policy as weighed against what might have been achieved by making a clear choice; we cannot discuss other possibilities allegedly cut off by his fall from power. They never existed, and speculating about them serves only to distort our view of the realities of Bismarckian policy and its specific problems.

Following the interlude of 1884–5, which can also be seen as a kind of escape attempt, albeit one that left the crucial basic positions undisturbed, that policy carried straight on from the political connections and demarcations – formal and informal – that had crystallized out as a result of the eastern

145

crisis of the years after 1875 and the ensuing crisis in German–Russian relations. To start with there was the Dual Alliance of 1879, which had continued to fall far short of the aims and expectations that Bismarck had originally associated with it. As the Chancellor's son, Herbert Bismarck, who had been placed in charge of the Foreign Ministry in April 1886, summed up in the autumn of that year, a 'Jesuit Austria is after all very different from us with its Papist Slavs and the incurable, ever-growing cancer of its dual composition'. With an almost audible sigh he went on: 'If only the British were a bit less unreliable and democratized, that would be the strongest and as far as we are concerned the safest arrangement'.[10] Nevertheless, the Dual Alliance had been supplemented and extended by the Triple Alliance treaty concluded between the German Reich, Austria-Hungary and Italy towards the end of May 1882. In this the three powers had promised one another mutual assistance in the event of France's making a 'not directly provoked attack' on Italy or Germany; the same was to apply in the event of an armed conflict between one of the signatories and more than one other great power. Moreover, in almost every other event they had promised one another benevolent neutrality.[11]

The chief reason why it had been possible to draw Italy into this alliance with the two great powers of central Europe was that Rome saw its interests on the African continent across the Sicilian Channel threatened by France when the French established a protectorate over Tunisia in May 1881: Tunisia was an important target area for Italian immigration, and the Italian people saw it as a natural buffer-zone for Sicily. Bismarck had taken immediate advantage of the French action to offer Italy the prospect of the support of the Reich. As a result, Rome had eventually given up its traditionally anti-Austrian policy and with it, at least initially, the territorial claims against the Austro-Hungarian Empire that it had advanced on repeated occasions hitherto; these related primarily to South Tyrol and Trieste but also to possible compensations in the Balkans.

Not long afterwards this system of alliances had been further extended towards the south-east. After Serbia, which had in fact been a semi-vassal of the Habsburg monarchy for a long time, Romania too had become a party to the Dual Alliance – which in 1883 had been confirmed for a further five years. In a 'treaty of friendship and assistance' signed in the autumn of 1883, Vienna and Bucharest had promised each other mutual assistance in the event of an unprovoked attack by a third party. By means of an appropriate declaration the Reich had acceded to this agreement at the end of October 1883.

From the outset there was a direct connection, in the mind and intentions of the Chancellor and Foreign Minister of the Reich, between this loosely formed central European bloc and relations with Russia, that is to say with the power against whom Austria-Hungary in particular might be tempted to make use of the alliance. It was not only for tactical reasons, in order to win over his extremely reluctant emperor, that Bismarck had pointed out back in 1879 that his Dual Alliance policy was at the same time aimed at a restoration of the traditional association of the three great eastern monarchies. His entire political strategy was based on using such a double system of alliances to prevent the real emergency, a clash between the two eastern empires. 'We must be so placed that the one sword keeps the other in the scabbard', he said once in a letter to the crown prince that gave vivid expression to his objective shortly after the conclusion of the Three Emperors' Treaty of 1881.[12]

Both treaty apparatuses were designed to lock into immobility the dynamic interests and expansionist desires present on both sides. By increasing the risk they were intended to guarantee the preservation of the signatories' respective spheres of power, influence and interest as defined most recently in 1878. To that extent the whole structure was also clearly directed from the outset against Austria's covetous desires in the Balkans. But at the centre of it all was Bismarck's concern to secure for the Reich, which as he repeatedly declared had no material interest whatever here, the kind of independence and political freedom of movement for which he had pleaded in the Kissingen Dictate. It was a question, the Chancellor told Ludwig II of Bavaria at the end of July 1881, of 'getting rid' of the 'sorest point inherent in the relations of immediate concern to Germany, namely the antagonism between Austria and Russia that threatened to break out four years ago'.[13]

To this end Bismarck had tried hard in the winter and spring of 1884 to get an extension of the Three Emperors' Treaty – in other words, immediately prior to his colonial initiative and the rapprochement with France, which if it succeeded would inevitably give a substantial boost to the anti-Russian factor in the formation of the new central European bloc. In view of Alexander III's sympathies with the Russian nationalist movement, which for its part was looking for contacts with the conservative nationalists in France, an extension of the treaty had not exactly been easy to achieve even at that time. For the weakness and vulnerability of the regime at home gave constant encouragement to those who advocated seeking relief through expansion, namely the Pan-Slav war party. The more and more openly voiced desires and plans of that party had at first been offset, just as Bismarck had calculated they would be, by the high risk of a possible conflict with the central European powers, which now seemed also to be coming to terms with their western neighbour, France. This had eventually tipped the balance in favour of an extension of the treaty in March 1884.

Shortly afterwards, however, the situation had undergone a radical change. On the one hand relations between Germany and Britain had seriously deteriorated in the wake of Germany's colonial initiative. On the other hand the German-French rapprochement had not made the kind of progress that Germany hoped for but Russia feared. On the contrary, in reaction to it the revanchist party in France had become substantially more important. Its right wing had been openly seeking contact with the Russian, Pan-Slav national movement.

In view of this the representatives of the latter pressed more and more determinedly in the period that followed for Russia to seize the next available opportunity to break free of the resolutions of the Congress of Berlin with which the German Reich had robbed St Petersburg of the fruits of its victory back in 1878. Added to which there was the fact that Russian advances in Asia, notably in Afghanistan, were exacerbating the global rivalry between Britain and the tsardom. In this context St Petersburg was concerned to consolidate its European base and above all to clear the air as far as possible in south-east Europe.

The opportunity for a political initiative along these lines came sooner than expected. It plunged Europe into its most dangerous crisis since 1870–1, a crisis that very soon threatened to shake to its foundations Bismarck's system of alliances and the status quo as defined therein, so to speak. It began in September 1885 with a rebellion in Eastern Rumelia, a province that had been left with Turkey in 1878 but was principally inhabited by Bulgarians. The rebellion quickly exacted the union of the province with Bulgaria, which was the solution that had been traced out in the Treaty of San Stefano but had then been blocked by the other great powers.

For the three eastern powers this was by no means an unexpected development. They had already envisaged such an eventuality in the Three Emperors' League of 1881 and agreed on a common line. The secret supplementary protocol, likewise renewed in 1884, had contained the sentence: 'The three powers shall not oppose the eventual unification of Bulgaria and eastern Rumelia within the frontiers allotted to those countries under the Treaty of Berlin, should this question arise through force of circumstances.'

Now that the question had arisen, however, the situation was crucially complicated by two elements. For one thing the man who at the express wish of the Tsar had been elected Prince of Bulgaria in 1879, Alexander von Battenberg, had long since ceased, despite his Russian ministers and military advisers, to play the role assigned to him, which was more or less that of a vassal. Instead he was gradually turning himself into a champion of a fiercely independent Bulgarian nationalism. He did not shrink, for example, having first put out vain feelers in the direction of Berlin, from making contact with his protector's antipode on the international political scene, namely with Britain. By holding out the prospect of a greater degree of Bulgarian independence he did in fact win more and more sympathy from London. In reaction to this, Russian-Bulgarian relations became increasingly cool. An outward indication of this came when Russia recalled her ministers and advisers immediately after Eastern Rumelia became part of Bulgaria – although of course this could also be seen in terms of a belated demonstration to the effect that St Petersburg had had nothing to do with the whole affair.

The other element that complicated the situation in south-east Europe was the fact that on the Austrian side too, on the side of Russia's immediate rival in the Balkans, a client state failed to keep to the path laid down for it: King Milan of Serbia, indirectly a member of the Dual and Triple Alliance system since 1881, demanded compensation for the enlargement of Bulgaria; his demand meeting with no response, he declared war on that country in mid-November 1885.

St Petersburg refused from the outset to believe that Serbia was 'going it alone'. Its suspicions were confirmed when, following heavy Serbian defeats, Vienna intervened on behalf of its protégé against a Bulgarian army that was advancing rapidly on Belgrade. So in addition to that between Russia and Britain there now emerged a serious Russo–Austrian conflict over the Bulgarian question and consequently over the whole future of the Balkans.

Having been familiar with the problems and conflicts of the region for decades, Bismarck promptly recognized the dangers inherent in this situation. He earnestly implored the Austrian Foreign Minister, Count Kálnoky, to seek out and keep open the path of direct negotiation with the tsardom. Austria must not under any circumstances allow an apparently favourable opportunity to tempt it to disregard existing spheres of influence and interest as defined by treaty. They formed the basis of 'the whole traditional position of the three Imperial courts', he stressed in instructions for a directive to the German embassy in Vienna towards the middle of October 1884.[14] When subsequently a Serbian defeat threatened instead of the Serbian victory confidently expected in Vienna, he not only pressed the Austrians not to intervene 'without a prior treaty agreement'.[15] He emphasized strongly that the Reich would on no account allow itself to be drawn into a conflict and in the event of complications would not regard their alliance as binding in this case.

The secret objective of German policy here from a very early stage was a stronger British commitment in the Balkans. 'This whole sickness of Austrian policy', we read in a direct report of 3 November 1885, 'will be remedied as soon as there is a British Bulgaria.'[16] For, as he added a week later: 'The entire Bulgarian state has no future but conflict with Russia, and whoever wishes to speak up for its preservation must take up that struggle.'[17] Or in the rather coarser idiom of Herbert Bismarck: 'The whole thing has got to be worked in such a way that Britain and Russia end up in hard, straight antagonistic confrontation with each other.'[18]

London, of course, carefully avoided getting into such a situation. This left the Reich as the focus of its allies' expectations. And in view of their rapidly growing differences and mutual irritation it was almost inevitable that neither the one nor the other, insisting as they did on the friendly relations stipulated by treaty, would be put off with any reference to existing arrangements and agreements. There was also the fact that the Serbo–Bulgarian War was seen by both of them as a 'proxy war' in which each saw evidence of the power-political ambitions of the other. Both sides therefore pressed for clearer options. Yet that threatened to draw the Reich ever deeper into the crisis, notwithstanding the repeated protestations of its representatives that Germany had no material interests whatever at stake.

With regard to Russia there was an additional factor involved, namely that commercial relations had been going from bad to worse in the wake of increasing protectionism. This reinforced the impression in St Petersburg that an actively anti-Russian bloc was in process of formation, with the Reich playing a crucial role in which its alleged determination to preserve the status quo was simply a disguise. For it was obvious that, as a result of Bulgaria's change of attitude and the reactions of Britain and now also of

Austria to it, that status quo had been no more than formally maintained; in reality it had changed decisively. Following the restoration of relations between Serbia and Bulgaria by the Treaty of Bucharest in March 1886, the Pforte, acting under the influence of and in agreement with London and Vienna, made the Prince of Bulgaria governor-general of Eastern Rumelia for an initial period of five years. Russia inevitably feared that, rather than making progress along the lines of the Three Emperors' League, it would be forced out of the Balkans altogether.

St Petersburg did in fact succeed, in the wake of an army coup and a dramatic kidnapping episode, in forcing the hated Battenberg prince to resign in September 1886 after a successful counter-movement under the president of the country's parliament, Stambulov, had brought about his return. But under the ensuing regency of Stambulov Bulgaria continued to steer a more and more markedly anti-Russian course. In this it was encouraged by Britain and subsequently by Austria as well. In November 1886 Vienna even went so far as to announce, mainly at the urging of the Hungarians, that it would never allow Bulgaria to be placed under Russian protection – in other words, that it would resist a restoration of the *status quo ante*. This meant, however, that Austria had finally departed from the 1878 agreements as confirmed in 1881 and again in 1884.

This policy, which represented a massive provocation to Russia, culminated early in July 1887 in the election of the pro-Austrian Prince Ferdinand of Saxe-Coburg-Gotha-Koháry to the Bulgarian throne. Bismarck passionately opposed it throughout and flatly refused to go along with any aspect of it. 'The future of the Bulgars', he told the German consul-general in Sofia, might 'be of some human interest but the country of Bulgaria of no political interest' as far as the Reich was concerned.[19] He pointed out repeatedly that it was the opinion of Berlin that the old 'demarcation of spheres of interest' should be unconditionally adhered to and that Austria, if it pursued its policy, was in danger of leaving the common ground.

On the other hand, because of the widespread anti-Russian feeling in his own country and the way in which a decidedly anti-German trend was gathering strength in Russia, he was unable and unwilling to push his warnings too far. He could not risk placing a serious strain on German-Austrian relations. This meant, however, that, willy-nilly, in Russian eyes he increasingly became a party to Austria's policy

A strong feature of that policy was active containment and indeed repulsion of Russia. In Germany there were powerful forces – of varied origin and with varied aims – who sought to pursue it to the lengths of a preventive war. That was something Bismarck had no desire to get involved in. On the other hand he continued to make every effort to avoid the consequences of a clear choice. This left him with no alternative but to attempt to rebuild the old dialectically linked, antagonistic systems of alliances in a form that would take into account the growing reciprocal pressure on both sides. This meant, however – and at least as far as the question of inner inevitability is concerned this point is often overlooked – that, if Bismarck wished to commit both sides firmly to the system as a whole and avoid unilateral actions by either side that could seriously jeopardize it, he must make greater concessions to both parties than ever before. It meant, in other words, that for the sake of the 'overall situation' evoked in the Kissingen Dictate he had to accept long-term objectives that were mutually exclusive.

The tacit assumption behind this was that an emergency would not arise or that it would be possible to avoid it by the very means of this complicated system of checks and balances. But what if an unfortunate concatenation of circumstances or crass political mismanagement on the part of individuals or entire leaderships should belie that assumption? The risk then was that everyone would come down on the Reich. And that would mean not only the end of the independence and power it had enjoyed up to now; it might also mean *finis germaniae*.

At times Bismarck was thoroughly aware of treading the finest of lines with his policy. That awareness, however, did not so much alarm as enliven him. It reminded him of periods in his life when he had been able to combine calculation and risk with even greater nonchalance. Moreover he wagered, with a confidence born of an experience spanning a whole generation, that the assumption would remain valid, in other words that peace, in the form of a kind of *pax germanica*, would be preserved by the dialectic of alliances. Sustained by that conviction, he set about rebuilding 'his' system of alliances comparatively unperturbed under a lowering sky of very grave threats of war.

It became clear as early as the end of 1886 that the old system had collapsed at certain key points. St Petersburg had already pronounced the Three Emperors' League 'dead' following Austria's intervention on behalf of Serbia. Bismarck's lack of success in his efforts to restore the *status quo ante*, together with growing differences in the field of commercial policy, had also been pushing the Reich and Russia farther and farther apart. Secret negotiations had admittedly been in progress since the autumn of 1886 with the object, if all else failed, of replacing the old trilateral agreement with a bilateral one between Germany and Russia. But that progress was painfully slow, even though Bismarck seized this early opportunity of letting it be known that Germany had 'absolutely nothing against the Russians going as far as Constantinople and taking the Dardanelles' – adding characteristically, for internal consumption, that the only problem about this was 'that Russia would then be virtually unassailable as far as Britain is concerned'.[20] The Chancellor was well aware that, with the alternative of a Russo–French alliance being placed more and more vigorously before the Russian public, notably by the Pan-Slavist Katkov and his Moscow newspaper, only massive counter-pressure would persuade the tsardom actually to conclude an agreement. So when all attempts to bring Austria back into line had finally failed he concentrated his efforts initially on a precautionary containment of France; this also tied in with his domestic policy plans in the run-up to the 1887 elections to the Imperial Diet.

The prelude was the negotiation of an Anglo-Italian agreement regarding future collaboration in the Mediterranean region. In this the two powers committed themselves on the one hand to preserving the status quo in this much-disputed part of the world and on the other promised each other mutual support in looking after their respective interests – Britain's in Egypt, Italy's in North Africa – and in disputes between them and a third power, to wit France.[21]

The Mediterranean Agreement of 12 February 1887 was at the same time an important foundation for the renewal of the Triple Alliance, which was now due. However, in view of the substantially altered situation and the increased demands of Italy in particular, this proved very difficult to achieve. Simple extension, even in a modified form, was no longer a possibility. Two separate supplementary agreements were required, a German-Italian one and an Austrian-Italian one. In a final protocol these were then declared to constitute, together with the agreement about a five-year extension of the old Triple Alliance, a kind of quadripartite unity.

Of the two supplementary agreements the German-Italian was of greater current importance, the Austrian-Italian of greater long-term importance in terms of its consequences. In the German-Italian treaty concluded on 20 February 1887 the Reich promised Rome active support, beyond the defensive terms of the Triple Alliance, in the protection of its interests in North Africa and declared that in the event of a conflict with France it would regard the terms of that alliance as *ipso facto* applicable. In this way it became a sleeping partner, as it were, in the likewise potentially anti-French Mediterranean Agreement between Italy and Britain, to which Austria officially acceded on 24 March 1887. Vienna thus acquired a formal promise of British support in the eastern Mediterranean and the Balkans without, like the Reich, committing itself to anything more than indirect support for eventual offensive activities by Italy in the western Mediterranean. By way of compensation for being let off the risk of any involvement in conflicts in the west, in the separate Austrian-Italian agreement also signed on 20 February 1887 Vienna guaranteed Italy compensation in the Balkans in the event of Austria's feeling obliged, after prior consultation, to modify the status quo in the peninsula.

This whole intricate web of treaty arrangements, to which Spain too acceded in May 1887 in reaction to French policy in West Africa, was kept secret – the British government choosing the method of an exchange of notes in preference to having to place the treaty before parliament. It was sealed in mid-December 1887 in an 'Eastern Triple Alliance', also effected by exchange of notes, between Britain, Austria-Hungary and Italy. In this treaty, in the preparation of which Bismarck had once again played a very active role behind the scenes and in which the Reich once again figured clearly as a sleeping partner, the three powers explicitly re-committed themselves to preserving the status quo in the Balkans and to a policy of containment vis-à-vis Russia. To this end they reaffirmed that the continued independence of Turkey, a 'protector of important European interests', was an urgent necessity. They laid particular stress on the need to keep the Straits free and to protect Turkey's rights in respect of Bulgaria, which ought never to be allowed to be turned into a bargaining-counter, not even by Turkey itself.[22]

By the time this treaty was concluded, with the British reply to the identical Italian and Austrian notes, the German policy behind it had in fact already, in a 'top-secret supplementary protocol' to a secret treaty with Russia signed on 18 June 1887, in principle allowed the tsardom access to the Balkans and the Straits. 'In the event', the protocol said, 'that His Majesty the Emperor of Russia should find himself placed, in order to protect Russian interests, under the necessity of himself taking over the task of maintaining access to the Black Sea, Germany undertakes to offer its benevolent neutrality and to give moral and diplomatic support to such measures as His Majesty shall consider needful for the purposes of retaining possession of the keys of his Empire.'[23]

This was in conflict not only with the spirit and the letter of the 'western' treaties but also, in essence, with the Dual Alliance. Had it come to the notice of the other side it would have shattered the credibility of German policy, almost certainly brought about the collapse of Bismarck's intricate system of alliances and left Germany largely isolated. To that extent one appreciates the argument, particularly as directed against the armchair Machiavellism of the swaggering Bismarck-worshippers who became so rife in after years, that the so-called 'Reinsurance Treaty' with its top-secret supplement was not only inconsistent with that minimum measure of good faith without which lasting relations between peoples and states are impossible; it also led into an impasse that laid the Reich open to blackmail and offered no real prospects for the future.

We must immediately qualify this, however, by saying that, in the occasionally very lively and still continuing debate about the Reinsurance Treaty, both sides have often exaggerated the importance of the whole thing. In the immediate situation of 1887 Bismarck probably saw it as no more than an extreme and even in his view not unproblematic means of finding out how to obviate the currently threatening conflict.

In his characteristically straightforward manner Herbert Bismarck gave clear expression to at least one aspect of this. Immediately after the treaty had been signed he described it as 'pretty anodyne' on the one hand and on the other added that its value lay chiefly in the fact that it would 'probably, in an emergency, keep the Russians off our backs for six to eight weeks longer than without it . . . That is not to be sneezed at.'[24] His father, undoubtedly taking a longer view and envisaging other, more intricate possibilities and processes, was inclined to think more in terms of the system as a whole. For him, too, however, the first concern was that a final dissolution of the tie with Russia – and it had become precarious enough – would lead to a diplomatic and perhaps even to a military counter-move on France's part before a counter-alliance had been firmly established.

How Bismarck assessed the situation and the direction his thinking was beginning to take are revealed in a remark in the margin of a report sent by the ambassador in London, Count Hatzfeldt, towards the middle of January 1888. 'The task of Austrian policy', he noted, 'would in my view be to leave the Russians in the Turkish impasse and not load until they smell *British* powder'.[25] And as he put it even more basically in a letter to William II in August 1888, a letter he expressly requested the young Emperor to burn after receipt: 'I do not doubt the Russians' intention to push through to Constantinople . . . To my most humble way of thinking it is not within the province of *our* policy to prevent Russia from carrying out its plans with regard to Constantinople but simply to leave that to the other powers, if they see it as being in their interests . . . If Russia gets involved there it will become less of a threat to us by withdrawing from our frontiers and by virtue of the provocative relation in which it will then stand to the Mediterranean powers, particularly to Britain and in the long run also to France . . . This will make it impossible for Britain to cling to the old fiction of its role being that of a cool spectator.'[26]

Furthermore, a crucial role in the whole affair was played by structural strains currently affecting German-Russian relations. Since the 1880s Russia had been vigorously engaged, not least for reasons of internal stability and maintaining the basis of its own position as a great power, in industrializing and modernizing its economy. This was giving rise to huge financial problems. The natural solution to these, as it were – namely an increase in agricultural exports, particularly to central Europe – encountered increasing obstruction from the opposing interests of East Elbian agriculture in particular. And as far as the Reich was concerned the credit-based solution, too, met with the opposition not only of a whole series of representatives of industry who found themselves being gradually excluded from the Russian market; it met with particular opposition from the army and from all who warned explicitly against giving economic encouragement to an increasingly hostile and threatening power.

This was something Bismarck had to take into account, particularly since it was a view backed by interests and political forces that supported him on the domestic policy front. On the other hand in foreign policy terms he regarded it as an extremely risky course, in the present situation, finally to cut the 'wire to St. Petersburg' in consequence of this development. He therefore attempted to combine the apparently incompatible in the service of his own objectives.

This resolves the apparent contradiction between the Reinsurance Treaty of June 1887 and the so-called 'Lombard-Verbot' of November 1887, which largely cut Russia off from all German credit sources. The two went hand in hand. The concessions embodied in the Reinsurance Treaty were designed to avoid at least the worst effects of steadily mounting economic differences on political decisions and options and to keep an avenue open for new arrangements, if possible involving Austria-Hungary once again. And the 'Lombard-Verbot' was intended to make clear what could be expected from the Reich in the long run in the event of a definitive change of course in Russian foreign policy. As Herbert Bismarck put it the day after publication of the 'Lombard-Verbot', 'at least some attempt' must be made 'to bludgeon the Tsar into seeing where his interest lies'.[27]

However, unlike the majority of the German people, the army leaders and a large number of top Foreign Office officials, Bismarck did not believe for one moment in the possibility of effecting a 'subjugation' of Russia, whether by military, diplomatic, or economic means. In his view, putting pressure on Russia made sense and was politically justifiable only if St Petersburg was at the same time shown the possibilities and prospects of a German-Russian connection as an alliance of equal, independent partners.

In this sense the Reinsurance Treaty was no more than a stage, the expression of a future possibility. It was meant to prevent Russia from making any over-hasty decisions and commitments – just as, from the negative standpoint, as it were, the 'Lombard-Verbot' aimed to do as well.

One incontestable achievement of the treaty was that it did at least postpone a Russian option in favour of France that in the circumstances then obtaining would undoubtedly have been extremely grave. Whether it would have continued to do so, as Bismarck later claimed, is an open question. Crucial preliminary decisions were taken in the field of credit policy only a short while after this, with France giving deliberately preferential treatment to Russian state loans, and Bismarck himself remarked gloomily to the Prussian War Minister, General Bronsart von Schellendorf, at the end of 1887: 'Given the state of European politics, it is probable that in the not too distant future we shall have to face war with France and Russia simultaneously.'[28]

But what about the function of the treaty within Bismarck's foreign policy system as a whole and the prospects it sought to open up in both the narrower and the broader senses? Was it in fact ever anything more than a means of overcoming an acute crisis? Indeed was the whole, much-discussed, highly complicated 'system' of treaties in reality perhaps merely the more or less fortuitous product of what we would call 'crisis management'? Did it embody no real long-term prospects, contriving at best – which after all was surely worth something – to provide a breathing-space in which new and more stable solutions could be found? Examination of the Reinsurance Treaty at least suggested such questions. And few asked them with greater insistence than Bismarck himself. Whatever the face he put on things for the benefit of the outside world, secretly he was well aware of the fragility and precariousness of the entire structure.

Five years before this, at the beginning of 1882, he had claimed in a moment of enthusiasm that foreign policy no longer gave him a single sleepless night: 'for the last ten years' it had been 'so set up as to run by itself'.[29] It was a claim that, if he did ever advance it for more than a moment, he had now abandoned completely. Since the failure of his attempt to reach understanding with France and since the recent darkening of the European horizon by a Balkan crisis taking place against the background of years of mounting pressure from the flanking powers, he had been inclined, with his sceptical eye for history and the element of chance and of fleeting favour in it, to take an increasingly pessimistic view of the future. 'If by God's will we go under in the next war', he wrote in the so-called 'Christmas Letter' to War Minister von Schellendorf at the end of 1886, 'I consider it beyond doubt that our victorious opponent will use every means of ensuring that we never recover, or at least not for a generation, just as in 1807. The prospect of our working our way up out of our impotence at that time to the situation in 1814 would have been extremely slight without the unpredictable destruction – with which we had nothing to do – of the French Great Army by the Russian winter and without the assistance of Russia, Austria and Britain. It is hardly likely that we shall be able to count on the latter again, now that those powers have witnessed the strength of a united Germany. We shall not even be able, *after* an unsuccessful campaign, to count on the present German Empire remaining together as an entity.'[30] And in his much-quoted speech in the Imperial Diet on 11 January 1887 he publicly drew the conclusion: 'My advice will therefore never be to wage a war on the grounds that it may perhaps have to be waged later on.'[31]

Germany, in other words, was a power that had nothing to gain but everything to fear from war and must therefore strive to avoid it. It was what he referred to in the same speech as 'our peace policy',[32] admittedly in a very sober and strictly self-interested sense. It was uncoloured as yet by his later interpretation, which shed as much darkness as light, to the effect that he had been concerned for the peace of Europe for its own sake. On the contrary, we can go so far as to say that, for him, keeping the peace was just as much a tool as waging war had been before 1871. Both were harnessed in the service of his own state, to preserve and if possible to increase the power of that state. What he now emphatically called a 'peace policy' he had referred to more soberly thirteen years earlier as a 'security policy'.[33]

A year after his speech of 11 January 1887 the Chancellor told the Imperial Diet on 6 February 1888 in words that were highly acclaimed but soon became debased through over-use: 'We Germans fear God but otherwise nothing on earth', adding: 'And it is fear of God that makes us love and cherish peace.'[34] As far as he was concerned these were more than simply edifying phrases. They expressed his conviction that only blindness – 'God-forsakenness' in the pragmatic understanding of God as the Lord of History – could prompt a German politician actively to jeopardize peace. He had written to the head of the Military Cabinet, General von Albedyll, shortly before this: 'The task of our policy is, if possible, to prevent war entirely, and if that is not possible at least to postpone it. I could not have a hand in any other policy.'[35] To his way of thinking, only peace guaranteed the Reich its independence and its position of power. It owed both, as he believed he now saw with increasing clarity, to an exceptionally fortunate constellation of circumstances that had obtained from the mid-century period to the 1870s and had since, not least when seen on a world scale, been shifting steadily to its disadvantage.

As to that, many contemporaries shared his findings. As to the political consequences to be drawn from it, however, opinions differed widely. To be precise, with his view that only the maintenance of peace by any and every means, even such as were problematic and perhaps themselves dangerous, was capable of securing and preserving the position that the Reich had enjoyed hitherto, Bismarck was no longer – far from it, indeed – speaking for a majority of the German people and the political ruling class.

'We have to understand', the sociologist Max Weber wrote in 1895, 'that the unification of Germany was a youthful prank that the nation played in its old age and that, given its costliness, had better been left unplayed if it was to mark the end and not the beginning of a policy of German imperialism.'[36] To many of his contemporary readers he was saying nothing provocatively new here. On the contrary, he was echoing something that people had been saying over and over again for years, particularly since the Balkan crisis of 1885 onwards and the preventive-war movement against Russia: that German policy must seek refuge not in defence but in attack, in an active, dynamic and if necessary belligerent foreign policy.

The *Berliner Tageblatt*, for instance, asked as early as the autumn of 1886 whether a 'healthy war' were not preferable to 'so morbid a peace'. In the same vein the German military leadership compared their chances in a German-Russian war at the present time with their chances in a war against an economically and militarily strengthened tsardom. And there were many who, like the army leaders, secretly or openly advocated the formation of a resolutely anti-Russian bloc in central Europe with Britain covering its rear – a bloc that would if necessary make its demands in the form of ultimatums. As the *Kölnische Volkszeitung* put it in extravagant terms towards the end of August 1886: 'Had Germany wished to confine itself to this modest role in international affairs, the German people could have spared itself the rivers of blood and sweat that went into founding the German Empire.'[37] Early in 1888 Holstein observed in a letter to Count Hatzfeldt: 'Here everyone is for war, in fact, with almost the sole exception of His Highness, who is doing his utmost to preserve peace.'[38]

The argument that his foreign policy had no future, an argument he had to face more and more frequently during his final years in office, was one that Bismarck disputed vehemently to the last. Those who propounded it were either armchair politicians and braggarts who knew nothing of foreign affairs and allowed themselves to be guided not by sober considerations of national self-interest but by emotions, prestige-seeking day-dreams and fantasies concerning the future. Or alternatively they were unscrupulous men who would stop at nothing in their struggle against the present leadership of the Reich and who did not even shrink from the prospect of plunging Germany into hazardous adventures abroad if only they could be expected to effect a change at home. He summed up his position in almost aphoristic terms in his speech in the Diet on 6 February 1888: 'Every great power that seeks to bring pressure and influence to bear on the policies of other countries and to direct affairs outside its sphere of interest, that plays Pericles beyond the confines of the area allotted to it by God, is pursuing power politics, not the politics of self-interest, and is in the market for prestige.'[39]

Secretly, though, he had very much in mind the ultimate fate of Metternich's status quo policy, to which – and it was no accident – he more and more frequently referred. But what alternative did he have? He continued to the end to regard the Dual Alliance, particularly in its loose and not coherently controllable form, as too weak to resist eventual pressure on two fronts for any length of time. And he was far from entertaining the illusion that the other alliances more or less firmly linked to the Dual Alliance constituted any kind of bloc. In the final analysis, therefore, all he was left with was dependence on one of the two flanking powers. That meant, however, his giving up the independent and at times, in continental terms, 'semi-hegemonic' position of the Reich between the powers and power groups.

In his last years in office, after the latest Balkan crisis had been overcome and his old system of alliances built up again, Bismarck did indeed give very serious consideration to this kind of change of course, however much he was inwardly opposed to it. In the case of Russia, however, it never got beyond the realm of consideration. The anti-Russian front in Germany was too strong and Russian suspicions and the catalogue of Russian demands too substantial for such a policy actually to have been put into effect without a danger of massive upheavals. Such an option could only seriously be envisaged in the event of a war on two fronts constituting an immediate threat, as the last resort in an emergency. In such an event, as Count Hatzfeldt, the German ambassador in London and for many years a secretary of state, observed in retrospect, Bismarck had in fact been prepared if necessary to 'buy Russian neutrality at the last moment' by 'dropping Austria and so leaving the East to the Russians'.[40]

The other possibility – dependence on Britain – Bismarck did get as far as exploring in practice. However, his initiative of January 1889, which far from being improvised was carefully prepared in every detail, not only misjudged the question of Britain's interests and consequently its inclination to enter into a firm commitment on the continent, as recent research has underlined. In the final analysis it was probably not even meant to meet with any real success.[41]

This is suggested above all by the fact that the Chancellor proposed giving the prospective alliance a highly unusual form that conflicted with every British tradition. The solemn adoption of such a treaty by both parliaments was to take place after a kind of quasi-plebiscitary public acclamation in both countries had indicated that it enjoyed the support of a broad majority. This kind of long-term public fraternization was hardly a realistic proposition, given the mounting feeling of competition on both sides in economic and colonial affairs combined with the 'splendid isolation' mentality of the British and their increasing orientation towards their overseas empire and Germany's sense of itself as a continental power and nascent aspirations towards becoming a world power. Bismarck cannot possibly have been very surprised when on 22 March 1889 Lord Salisbury told Herbert Bismarck, who had been dispatched to London, that the British wished 'to leave the matter on the table for the time being . . . without saying yes or no'. That, Salisbury added, was 'unfortunately all I can do at the moment'.[42]

Bismarck's objective throughout, despite mounting scepticism regarding future developments, remained the retention of as great a degree of independence as possible between the powers and the various groups of powers. 'The security of our relations with the Austro-Hungarian state', he stressed in 1888 even with regard to the Dual Alliance, 'depends to a great extent on our being *able*, should Austria make unreasonable demands on us, to come to terms with Russia as well.'[43]

It was the ideal of a policy of keeping a free hand, a policy that permitted the Reich to intervene in a regulatory fashion in the ever precarious balance of power and thus maintain the status quo in a manner favourable to its existing position. But it must be admitted that, given the current galloping transition from a European to a global political system with new centres of gravity and a rapidly changing distribution of weight, it was not a policy that possessed any real future any more.

It was a policy that was bound up with a particular period of European history. In it Europe, with the exception of Britain, remained essentially 'turned in' in terms of its internal structure, its understanding of itself and its points of reference, notwithstanding the steadily increasing extent and importance of its external relations. Its peoples and its states still in many ways equated Europe with the world. In many respects this remained true until 1945 and the final termination of Europe's dominance in the world, and in numerous spheres its effects can still be felt today. But the particular kind of Europe-centredness that at the same time left room for the recognition of what was wholly different in kind, outside its own world, did in fact begin to disintegrate with ever-increasing speed in the 1880s with the economic and colonial permeation of the wider world. It gave way to the idea of the deliberate Europeanization of the world, the starting-point for which was taken almost as a matter of course to be a kind of linear extension of the European system into a global system. This was where, as many contemporaries saw it, their own generation was called upon to fight for a definitive 'place in the sun'.

Bismarck did take up such ideas in many respects, and at times he translated them into political tactics in what seemed a thoroughly modern manner. But in essence this was no longer his world. His world remained that of the old Europe of the powers, as reconstituted in 1815, the year of his birth; it remained that of a diplomacy schooled in that Europe and taking its bearings from it, a diplomacy of which he was himself a near-perfect exemplar; it continued to be one of political forces and political leaders who, for all their deep-seated differences, retained a certain minimum of solidarity and shared assumptions.

These were the premises on which he had implicitly based his views and actions for the past forty years. He himself had not infrequently operated on the very edge of them, particularly during the 1850s and 1860s. To such tactics he owed many of his successes, which had stemmed from a kind of 'brinkmanship' that deliberately went to extreme lengths, in terms of challenging the existing order and its rules, in order to open a door to the new thing to which he aspired. But always the principle remained precisely that the new thing, if it was to last, must fit into that existing order and obey its basic rules.

Now, however, as the 1880s drew to a close, the foundations of the whole thing threatened to shift decisively – not so must as a result of concerted attacks and calls for change, more as a result of that creeping process of economic and social transformation that even within states was beginning to invalidate the old order to an ever-increasing extent. Here too, then, he was seized towards the end by that 'sorcerer's apprentice' feeling that had dogged him for years in the field of domestic policy.

[15]

The 'Stopgap' System:

Domestic Policy after 1881

Impossible though it became towards the end of Bismarck's period in office to ignore the voices that, with regard to foreign affairs, spoke of ossification, of inflexibility, of his having fallen behind the times and the requirements of the times, the real impulse leading to his fall, which was at the same time his failure, came from the field of domestic policy. Here were the roots of those decisive shifts in the basic foreign policy situation too, in its emphases and in its inherent dynamics of idealism and self-interest, with which the Chancellor increasingly found himself confronted. Quite rightly, then, historians have inquired repeatedly in recent years, with specific reference to the 1880s, into the connection between the two spheres within the framework of his policy and into the interdependencies to which it gave rise and of which he possibly made very deliberate use.

In a kind of inversion of the exclusive concentration on foreign affairs that was the rule for decades, much has undoubtedly been exaggerated here. An example is the thesis that, from the beginning of the period of active colonial policy at the latest, all foreign policy essentially served domestic ends. On the other hand many connections have become very much clearer than they were before; one thinks of the part that all kinds of domestic factors played in the German–Russian crisis of 1886–7. The important thing is that we should carefully weigh the contribution of each individual element and above all bear constantly in mind the fact that no policy, whether in domestic or in foreign affairs, is ever in a position to create the conditions in which it shall be conducted.

This is especially true of Bismarck's policy after the 1881 election. To begin with, that election had destroyed any possible parliamentary base as far as he was concerned. In fact it had sown doubts even among his staunchest associates as to whether the Chancellor, who had once enjoyed the support of a broad parliamentary majority, would ever again find a firm political footing. Here again Max Weber was expressing a view that had been widespread in the 1880s when he remarked in the course of his inaugural lecture at Freiburg University in 1895: 'That [i.e. Bismarck's] life's work should have led . . . not only to the external but also to the internal unification of the nation, and we all know: this has not been achieved.'[1]

The remark, of course, was aimed at more than that. It was aimed at the absence of a deeper social and spiritual coherency in the nation, a uniting, binding material concept of the state, a minimum of shared ideas and beliefs. But Max Weber was just the sort of man who was inclined to account for this in strictly political terms and to trace it back to the disastrous and ultimately abortive strategy adopted by Bismarck after 1878–9, a strategy that aimed to put the parties out of the political running by mediatizing them in favour of organized interest-groups, which were supposedly easier to harness and control. As the son of a National Liberal deputy living in Berlin, the later famous sociologist and journalist had in his youth been able to observe this development at first hand. And the glaring failure of that strategy continued to haunt him throughout a career in which he eventually became an impassioned advocate of the parliamentary system of government – precisely in the interests of a vigorous and powerful state and governmental authority.

Because that was exactly what was at issue here. Anyone who tries to write the history of the late Bismarckian period as a story of achievement, whether viewing it in a positive or in a negative light, is missing the real point as well as the individual developments and processes involved. He is missing the fact that from the government's point of view it consisted of repeated, increasingly short-winded and ultimately futile attempts to regain a solid political base, attempts of which the point of departure was almost invariably the failure rather than the success of the one before. This also throws light on the concrete connection between domestic and foreign policy. In one direction at least – with a view, that is, to domestic policy – there were endless attempts at instrumentalization without any truly constructive, systematizing element asserting itself or even becoming clearly discernible in the process.

An initial thrust in this direction, following the utter failure of the 1879 attempts to bring the Dual Alliance to bear on the domestic scene and specifically on the Centre Party, was probably contemplated by Bismarck in 1883–4 when he began to explore the possibilities of a potentially fundamental reorientation of his foreign policy. It is still a matter of dispute how far and with what expectations on the domestic front Bismarck consciously and deliberately used his colonial initiative to foster anti-British and consequently nationalist tendencies; a warning against placing too much emphasis on this point is implicit in the fact that even before the election of 1884 he was once again very publicly playing down his differences with Britain. There is a great deal of evidence, however, to show that he did among other things attempt to sound the national rallying-cry and stir up ill-feeling against certain parties that evinced particular sympathies with foreign powers and their political and social systems.

Nevertheless, in the arguments about domestic policy that had been going on with scarcely flagging intensity and much belligerence on both sides since the 1881 election, this was not really a central theme. It never occurred to Bismarck seriously to regard it as an election-winning issue.

161

There was also the fact that the left-wing liberals, on whom he particularly had his sights, showed great restraint on foreign policy questions out of deference to the authority of the Chancellor and so did not present a concrete target.

The really crucial issue at this point in time was the question – posed by the opposition parties very much as a matter of principle – of the limits of the power of the state and in particular of the interventionist state in the form in which and with the specific political objectives with which it had been developed under Bismarck's leadership since 1878–9. In concrete terms it was a conflict over the attempt, which was continued even after 1881, to use direct concessions to organized or numerically significant interest-groups in order to outmanoeuvre the parties as the traditional political representatives of those groups and thus bring them permanently to heel and smash their independence.

Not that Bismarck made the slightest progress, even after 1881, in his efforts to bypass the parties by appealing directly to interest-groups – to overcome the 'domestic shambles' (*die innere Schweinerei*),[2] as he called it in moments of impotent rage. His stubborn adherence to his 'state-socialist' social policy programme, to the tax reform plans that went with it and to the always very deliberately preferential treatment accorded to the material interests of particular economic groups, notably heavy industry and large-scale farming, led on the whole to an equally stubborn resistance on the part of the majority in the Imperial Diet, even if that majority differed greatly in composition from one case to another, depending on the interests being addressed.

The real organizers of this resistance were the left-wing liberals, to wit the 1880 'Secessionists' on the one hand and the Progressive Party on the other, with Eugen Richter and above all Eduard Lasker at their head. After the autumn 1881 election Lasker believed that here was the great opportunity for liberalism to act consistently and openly raise the question of power. Henceforth he applied all his efforts and all his parliamentary and party-political experience to mustering liberals of all tendencies, irrespective of their internal differences, to form a united front against Bismarck and his policy.

As early as 8 November 1881, twelve days after what had been so successful an election for the left-wing liberals, he called upon the National Liberal Party, picking up the threads of similar pre-election initiatives, to work now towards 'the political epiphany of a Greater Liberal Party or at least a joint body comprising all parliamentary groupings'. This must 'not be precluded by differences belonging to a past that is already history . . . The election results show, much more clearly even than I had hoped, that concerted and determined action can produce a Liberal absolute majority in the Imperial Diet even in unfavourable circumstances.'

What mattered now, above all else, was unity and a joint 'repudiation of reaction'. To start with that unity might be as loose, both in programmatic and in institutional terms, as was anyhow still warrantable. The crucial thing was that it should come about: Bismarck's policy could be relied on to 'give it a boost as soon as he has to abandon his calculation that he can keep [that policy] separate from us'. Lasker concluded: 'The important thing as far as I am concerned is that the government and the parties on the other side should come to the conviction that they face what is in many respects a viable whole, capable of taking action, and not just fragments of a Liberal Party.'[3]

Such a reunion of all the liberal parties, in the interests of which Lasker at first deliberately held back a closer merger of the left-wing liberals, never did come about. The political differences between the material interests represented by the various tendencies were too great. Moreover, both political and material differences were aggravated by personal animosities and rivalries between the leading representatives of the individual groups. But although a potentially historic moment for German liberalism was in the end allowed to slip, initially the situation looked wide open. No one felt this more keenly than Bismarck, constantly aware as he was of the possibility of a change of sovereign. It was from this quarter that he anticipated the really crucial threat to his person and to his position. And it was in this quarter that his subsequent policy was quite specifically aimed.

That policy concentrated first and foremost on selective disruptive actions. Right after the 1881 election there was talk of a government reshuffle in the direction of a coalition of Free Conservatives and National Liberals, and this course was continued to the point of personal encouragement of individual members of parliament. Bismarck's chief concern here, in line with his overall strategy, was to lay particular emphasis on those elements that stood in the way of anything from the formation of a firm coalition between the individual liberal groups in the Imperial Diet to a major reunification of the party. This applied particularly to the question of state interventionism, in connection with which he tried all the time to keep open the rifts within the liberal movement that had become so apparent in 1878–9, to widen them and to prevent even a limited compromise from bridging them.

In so doing, however, he increasingly overtaxed what was in any case a scarcely promising political plan. As a result this now lost all vestige of a clear and politically appealing line. The Chancellor became entangled at more and more frequent intervals in ever murkier political manoeuvres that were in many cases dictated purely by the situation in question. He increasingly gave the impression, as he sought to put his plan into practice, that he had lost his political grip.

Even those close to Bismarck were afflicted by growing doubts about the future of his policy. After his tax reform plans, chief among them the projected tobacco monopoly, had failed yet again and his social legislation had once more run aground over the very points that were regarded as politically crucial and from which members of the government expected quite new developments, the Minister of Agriculture, Robert Lucius, noted in his diary on 10 May 1883: 'We are now reaping the fruits of our parliamentary tactics and suffering defeat after defeat . . . All Bismarck's projects', for which in addition 'the authority of the Emperor was exposed to fire', had 'miscarried'.[4]

At the same time there were overtones here of a doubt harboured in conservative circles that was not without danger as far as Bismarck was concerned. It culminated in people asking whether, in bringing the monarchical principle and the person of the emperor directly but in the final analysis unsuccessfully to bear, the Chancellor had not helped to discredit that principle and whether he did not share at least some indirect responsibility for the continued rise of the opposition movement and for jeopardizing the status quo.

Bismarck sought to defuse such reproaches, which for the time being were still of a subliminal nature, by means of increasingly vehement attacks on left-wing liberalism. But it became more and more difficult as time went on to avoid the realization that in announcing an anti-parliamentary course he had hoist himself on to the horns of a dilemma. Since he was manifestly unable to satisfy expectations within the framework of his original plan, those expectations threatened to force him not just farther and farther to the right but even, in the end, into openly unconstitutional paths, into a *coup d'état*. As in the years after 1862, however, such a course still seemed to him to offer no serious prospect of success, and the only evidence that he ever contemplated it takes the form of vague threats, the chief object of which was to force his political opponents into line.

But what did the future hold if he was even in danger of losing the support of the far right? As in the early 1870s the complaint was increasingly levelled against him, despite a rigid appointments policy favouring the right and despite a variety of measures to promote the material interests of the right, that his policy was still in essence too prone to compromise, too irresolute, for all its brave words, and that that was why it was unsuccessful. It was the policy, people on the right said, of an ageing lion that has lost most of its teeth.

Once upon a time he had contrived to make political capital out of the confrontation between right and left, between the advocates of what appeared to be mutually exclusive political and social systems and ideas of order. Indeed he had based his whole political position on his being able, both in his person and in his policy, to present a compromise – albeit always a precarious one – that avoided the extremes on either side. Now, however, he was in danger, no matter how obviously he himself leaned increasingly towards the right, of being worn down between the two camps.

The fact that he had strengthened what in the long term was the weaker side by sometimes artificial means, that since 1878–9 he had increasingly thrown his political authority and influence into the scales in its favour, now threatened to become his undoing. All the elements that he had held in check for so long in order to preserve his own power – the political influence of the military, the influence of religious and other politically non-responsible figures at court, the tendency for the bureaucracy to go its own way, this time in the direction of conservatism, the *esprit de corps* of the aristocracy with its leaning, in times of emergency, towards the spirit of the Fronde – all these began to re-exhibit increased signs of activity to the point where eventually Bismarck seemed in danger of becoming a kind of expendable figurehead. One witness who was certainly above suspicion, namely the ageing crown prince, complained early in 1882 that the youth of the country was 'reactionary through and through . . . So what possible good did the future hold?! Even if he, the crown prince, were to introduce a different kind of government, his son would change everything back again. Better, therefore, that the latter should directly succeed his grandfather, for that would ensure that continuity was preserved.'[5]

The crown prince – 'against Bismarck, let's face it, there is nothing to be done' – was assuming here, as did many contemporaries, that the Chancellor not only bore a decisive share of the responsibility for but also gained directly by this development. Many historians have made the same assumption. Bismarck himself, however, saw with increasing clarity that he might very easily fall victim to it. 'This nation cannot ride', he remarked in a mood of deep pessimism towards the end of 1883. 'I see a very black future for Germany. If the "Forchows and Wirkenbecks" [men like Forckenbeck and Virchow] take charge and are shielded from above, everything will fall apart again. They are all so petty and narrow-minded, none of them acts for the whole, each one is just stuffing his parliamentary mattress.'[6]

As early as 1878–9, after all those years as the politician between the fronts, he had felt a distinct sense of unease at what was now a very definite plumping for one side – inescapable though such a commitment appeared to him to be as far as his own position and interests were concerned, given the growing claim to power of the middle-class liberal movement. His policy had always been more than simply a one-track conservative policy of containment and concentration, however powerful and influential that element subsequently became. In his plans for tax and budgetary reform, in his attempts to institutionalize material interests in a new way and above all in his social legislation he was always at the same time concerned to create fresh positions for the government and for himself and to erect fresh bastions of independence and self-sufficiency against opposition from all quarters. His aim was not to allow anyone, even on the right, to 'throw a halter over his head', as one of his favourite sayings went.

His efforts in this regard had of course failed all along the line, as it was inevitable that they should. They were based on a fundamental misjudgement of human political and social behaviour. That misjudgement stemmed not least from the fact that the Chancellor took as absolute the behaviour of the German middle class in a quite specific historical situation and constellation of circumstances between enticement from the right and competition – even an incipient threat – from the left, between its former pretensions and present reality, between principle and self-interest, between possibility and expectation.

Bismarck's social legislation in particular, when after protracted struggles its first major components, namely the Accident and Health Insurance Bills, eventually became law in 1883–4, turned out to be a complete fiasco politically. It is not by chance that this body of legislation, which was completed in 1889 with a measure covering old-age and disability insurance and constitutes objectively the most significant legislative achievement of the Chancellor's last decade in office, does not receive a single mention in his memoirs.

The fact that the whole thing did not even begin to achieve its political objective, which was to reconcile the working class with the state in its present form or even to re-lay the foundations of the authority of the state on the mass of the working population, was due not to any 'watering-down' of the laws by the Imperial Diet, as Bismarck initially tried to pretend. It was due to his fundamental misjudgement of the relationship between political behaviour and individual self-interest among the broad mass of the people – quite apart from the fact that both contributions and benefits remained at a very low level and the actual progress made was very slight.

This became strikingly apparent when, although Bismarck largely managed to get his own way with regard to the basic political concept underlying his second Accident Insurance Bill, the whole thing never came anywhere near to achieving the objective envisaged. That underlying concept had been borrowed from the socio-political system of Albert Schäffle, a Württemberg political economist and sociologist in the tradition of Comte and Hegel who was also, having sat in the Württemberg Diet and in the Customs Parliament in the 1860s and in 1871 served briefly as the Austrian Minister of Commerce, a man with concrete political experience. It aimed at a state-ordained and state-implemented organization of the whole economy along trade co-operative lines, a sort of revival of the corporative order of the past in a form adapted to the present. According to the 'speech from the throne' at the opening of the Imperial Diet on 17 November 1871, the government was looking for 'a closer link with the real forces' of the 'life of the nation' and 'the integration of the latter in the form of corporate bodies under the patronage and promotion of the state'.[7]

It tallied with this concept and accordingly qualified as a success for the government when after two years of talks the trade co-operatives were made responsible for accident insurance instead of the 'Imperial Insurance Institute' originally projected. The same applied to the very much less controversial Health Insurance Law passed by the Diet a year before this, on 15 June 1883; that too tied in with surviving corporate institutions such as miners', guild and other provident funds and at the same time set up a new kind of corporation in the shape of the local health insurance scheme with a co-operative system of self-government in which workers predominated – unlike the purely entrepreneur-run trade co-operative associations. Of the ambitious hopes that Bismarck had placed in these measures, however, none came to fruition. On the contrary, most local health insurance schemes were immediately taken over by confirmed Social Democrats; one authority has rightly spoken of a 'Social Democratic supremacy in health insurances'.[8] The trade co-operative associations were for their part often mediatized by the parties of the right.

Among his closest intimates Bismarck spoke frankly of his original expectations. 'In itself accident insurance is of secondary importance to him, he says', Theodor Lohmann observed in a private letter written after a talk with Bismarck in October 1883. 'His primary concern is to make use of the opportunity to achieve the corporate co-operative associations he feels must gradually be implemented for all productive classes in order *to acquire a basis for a future parliament* that shall replace or complement the Imperial Diet as an essential contributory factor in the legislative process – be it even, if the worst comes to the worst, through the medium of a *coup d'état*.'[9]

It is difficult to say at what point Bismarck finally admitted to himself that his efforts had miscarried. At any rate, it was purely as a matter of routine that he attended to the Bill passed in the middle of 1889 setting up an old-age and disability insurance, a measure that even gave him contributions by the Reich. 'What we were trying to do there', he summed up towards the end of his life, 'was always a bit like the Echternach Procession: three steps forward, one step back. I wore myself out in the parliamentary sands, in the efforts I made even in the direction of legislation itself, this gum-backed law [*Klebegesetz*], as I have to call it.'[10]

What he withheld in this context was the fact that the step-by-step retreat from his plans was made substantially easier for him soon after the passage of the first piece of social legislation, the Health Insurance Bill, by shifts within the party spectrum. As a result of this development there was a marked alteration in the behaviour of the Imperial Diet before the end of the 1881–4 legislative period. Even the return of Bismarck's old dream combination of a centre-right coalition of Free Conservatives and National Liberals suddenly looked like a possibility once again.

There was a whole series of reasons for this abrupt change. It was connected with the growing concern felt by the centre parties and their voters about an increasing polarization of society and about the consequences thereof. But it also had something to do with the fact that efforts to unite the various liberal parties and form a majority on that basis were not making much headway. On the other hand the advocates of a sharp shift to the right, headed by the editor-in-chief of the *Kreuzzeitung* and leader of the 'Old Conservatives', Baron von Hammerstein-Gesmold, were working – very successfully at times – towards forming an expressly anti-liberal right-wing coalition between the Centre Party and the German Conservatives. As a result, the National Liberals and to a lesser extent the Free Conservatives began to worry that they might be crushed between right and left and ultimately swallowed up. Such fears made the memory of the advantages they had once enjoyed as junior partners of the government appear in a particularly alluring light.

There was also the fact that, for all his blunt attacks, Bismarck dropped plenty of veiled hints to the effect that he was prepared even now to consider the possibility of closer collaboration. These were not without effect on men much preoccupied by the splits and electoral losses of recent years. Members of the National Liberal group in the Diet could be heard muttering more and more frequently that the anti-Bismarck line, while it may have paid dividends for liberalism in general, had done nothing for the National Liberals.

The party was thus increasingly inclined to stress its own independence vis-à-vis the right but above all vis-à-vis the left as well by adjusting its course to some extent. Not the least of the reasons for this was that Bismarck was clearly making little political headway any more and found himself, as a result, exposed with increasing frequency to veiled reproaches from the far right accusing him of irresolution and half-heartedness. He looked weaker politically than ever before and might therefore be ready to make greater concessions, whereas on the other hand a change of Chancellor and a fundamental reorientation of policy were hardly in prospect and the crown prince was even showing increasing signs of resignation.

Bismarck did indeed regard a compromise with the National Liberals and a centre-right coalition as still representing his only chance of regaining a firm parliamentary footing. 'The government must not be allowed . . . to become parliamentarily dependent on the Centre [Party]', said a diplomatic directive of February 1882 with what was now approaching prayer-wheel repetitiveness. 'It must husband the sympathies of the moderate Liberals, particularly in view of the fact that recently the Centre has once again been looking for a weapon against the government in an unnatural alliance with progressive radicalism.'[11]

After all that had occurred, of course, Rudolf von Bennigsen, the harbinger of liberal unity at least as far as the Lasker wing, was not the right man for this kind of policy of renewed rapprochement. Whatever it was in particular, in terms of further breaking of pledges on Bismarck's part, that prompted his dramatic resignation from all his political offices on 11 June 1883, it left the way free for a change of course by the party. Logically speaking, this could lead only to a fresh rapprochement between the National Liberals and the government and Bismarck and to the abandonment of all liberal unification plans oriented more towards the left.

However, not least because of the circumstances of Bennigsen's resignation, the fact that a change of course was in the offing remained concealed from the public at large for quite some time. This made the process appear even more dramatic when it did emerge. The man who really came to champion it was the Mayor of Frankfurt, Johannes Miquel. He was a contemporary of Bennigsen's and like him a leading member of the National Union and of the National Liberal Party from the earliest days. It was he who was responsible for the basic features of the so-called 'Heidelberg Declaration' issued by the leaders of the National Liberal Party on 23 March 1884, a policy document that each of the ensuing regional party conferences endorsed by a clear majority.

With the Heidelberg Declaration, which in the words of Miquel's biographer formed 'the basis of his personal rise in national politics',[12] the radical reorientation was accomplished. With it the party took up a position behind the government on certain key issues, notably the military question, the social legislation programme, the agrarian question and even a number of once violently disputed fiscal questions such as the problem of taxing stock exchange transactions and the tax on spirits. The same was true of the colonial question. Moreover, the Declaration stressed that 'an amalgamation with other parties is . . . out of the question in present circumstances because of divergent views on crucial questions of the day'.[13]

Here was final confirmation of what by this time had long been a foregone conclusion, namely the rejection of the 'Greater Liberal Party' of which Lasker had dreamt to the last – for he had died in New York on

5 January 1884 at the age of only 54 while on a visit to America. The decision of the Progressive Party and the Secessionists on 24 February 1884, a month before the Heidelberg meeting, to amalgamate in the 'Deutsch-Freisinnige Partei', the 'German Liberal Party', had already represented an act of resignation in this respect. For the majority of the Secessionists in particular had agreed with Lasker that the merger must take place on the right, in other words that it must stem from agreements with the National Liberals.

Any such prospect had ended with Miquel's *de facto* assumption of the party leadership, and the amalgamation of the two left-wing liberal groups could be said to be the logical consequence of that. Miquel himself left no one in any doubt, within the party at least, as to the line he pursued. He was utterly convinced 'that, if the party does not this time draw a *definite line of demarcation* on the left and in the north more particularly on the right, it is lost for all time', as he wrote to Robert von Benda, a member of the executive committee of the Prussian House of Deputies and a man who had been a Prussian deputy and a member of the National Liberal group in the Imperial Diet for many years. Such a decision was dictated by the 'overall situation' and by the 'general mood of the electorate' as well, for 'every *general* alliance with the left [i.e. not confined to specific issues] *swallows us up*'. He stressed that he regarded 'the situation as *highly critical* and *crucial* for a long time to come'. As far as Bismarck and the government were concerned, there was surely no need for him to emphasize 'that all the rumours put about by the newspapers regarding my relations' with them were '*pure wind*'. He added immediately, however, that he suspected 'that we are heading for a change'.[14]

Bismarck was indeed highly delighted and inclined to fall in immediately with the combination that was beginning to emerge – and that was so close to what he himself wanted. From now on he broadly adhered to the chief features of the Heidelberg Declaration and in particular to its distribution of emphasis. Seen in this light, the passage of the Accident Insurance Bill on 27 June 1884 by a majority made up of conservatives, National Liberals and Centrists was a most remarkable event. After protracted and in part very bitter struggles, it brought to a preliminary conclusion an initiative the underlying political objective of which he was now inclined to abandon – precisely in consequence of that event, which seemed to him to point to a fresh and more promising possibility. The attempt to circumvent the parties by mediatizing them as political representatives of economic interests had – it was now only too clear – been extremely dubious as far as its effect and possible consequences were concerned. Instead, here was apparently another chance of collaborating with the Free Conservatives and the National Liberals to put together a solid parliamentary bloc.

The core of that bloc was admittedly very small to begin with; the two parties together now numbered only seventy-five out of around four hundred deputies. Bismarck hoped and believed, however, that with the aid of some clever tactics, some heavily preferential treatment during the forthcoming election and a clearly defined policy in line with the demands of both parties it might be possible to change this situation before too long.

But the main thing was that the danger that had at times overshadowed all others, that of a parliamentary bloc forming against himself and his government, appeared for the time being to have been averted. The formation of a positive majority on the liberal side and a comparatively unproblematical government-forming process in the event of a change of sovereign had now plainly receded into the remote distance.

It was characteristic of his estimate of the changed situation that in this summer of 1884 Bismarck casually swept aside all such domestic policy considerations as he might, for example, have attached to his posture of confrontation vis-à-vis Britain over colonial affairs. In his speech in the Imperial Diet on 26 June 1884, the day before the final vote on the Accident Insurance Bill, he publicly signalled for London's benefit that he was not interested in any further escalation of the conflict, at the same time indicating to German public opinion that the whole thing was not an election issue as far as he was concerned.[15] Now that the National Liberals had finally dissociated themselves from their left wing and become a potential partner in what in many material respects was a right-wing oriented government alliance, the key slogan of the forthcoming election campaign could be the preservation and further consolidation of the existing order at home and abroad.

What this meant in practice had been emerging clearly enough and with increasingly one-sided emphasis since 1878–9. It meant the greatest possible degree of protection for German industry and more especially for German agriculture. It meant the repression of revolutionary activities on the part of the far left but also on the part of those whom the historian Heinrich von Treitschke had demagogically dubbed the 'patrons' of socialism in the middle-class liberal camp. It meant the safeguarding of Germany's position as a great power at the heart of Europe by military means, by 'the maintenance of a powerful German army', as the Heidelberg Declaration put it – in other words, by a policy of strength. And finally, as was already becoming apparent, it meant the 'containment' of the advancing Slav element in Prussia's eastern provinces, which in turn implied a mobilization of nationalism in order to preserve the status quo.

A parliamentary breakthrough could not of course be achieved in so short a time – for the election took place on 28 October 1884. Despite big gains on the first ballot that seemed to confirm Miquel's course and enormously strengthened his position, with what were this time very different second ballot pacts the National Liberals did not gain many more seats than the substantially reduced number they had held on to in 1881. The Free Conservatives also stayed where they were, though with a slightly improved vote. The German Conservatives actually dropped more than 1 per cent of the vote, once again falling back behind the National Liberals, whom they had overhauled for the first time in 1881. But as the chief beneficiary of right-wing pacts they won more than half as many seats again as they had held hitherto. As a result they immediately laid claim to the leadership of a centre-right coalition. However, without the Centre Party, which held on to its previous position, this still did not constitute a majority.

170

On the other hand – and this was what really mattered as far as Bismarck was concerned – the advance of left-wing liberalism was decisively halted in this election. The new 'German Liberal Party' gained only a few more seats than the Progressive Party had won on its own in 1881. From the total of 106 seats that the Progressives and the Secessionists together had taken in 1881, the new party dropped to sixty-seven, so that in order to assemble even a negative majority with which to block the government's legislative initiatives it needed nearly all the so-called 'protest parties' as well as the whole of the Centre Party. In the circumstances a centre-left coalition was now out of the question. The danger that had threatened Bismarck from this quarter in the event of a change of sovereign seemed for the time being to have been averted. A monarch who sympathized as the crown prince did with a highly principled type of liberalism and its objectives could scarcely install a new government that in parliamentary terms was going to find itself in a minority from the start.

So it is only too understandable that Frederick William should already at this stage, before the onset of his fatal illness – a very tardily diagnosed case of cancer of the larynx – have begun to give up all hope politically. Moreover, there was a further element. As well as the decline of left-wing liberalism, the autumn 1884 election signalled a growing pressure from the far left in the shape of Social Democracy. Experience showed, however, that this kind of pressure from the left tended to produce a shift to the right on the part of the majority of the electorate and the parties of the centre. In their Heidelberg Declaration, and specifically in its uncompromising rejection of Social Democracy, the National Liberals had to some extent anticipated this.

Although banned as an organized party and subject to all kinds of persecution, the socialist candidates had increased their former vote by more than 50 per cent in the autumn of 1884. Having concentrated on certain constituencies, chiefly in highly industrialized areas, they had doubled their representation at one go – from twelve seats to twenty-four. With just over 6 per cent of the seats in the Imperial Diet and just under 10 per cent of votes cast, the figures were still relatively modest, although in terms of those votes the Social Democrats had now clearly outstripped the Free Conservatives, the so-called 'Empire Party', and attained almost two-thirds of the strength of the German Conservatives, who were so much at the focus of things politically. In contrast to these two parties the times now clearly favoured the party of the working class, the proletariat that was growing so rapidly in the wake of economic development; in the space of a few decades the number of industrial workers, who formed the true core of that proletariat, rose from just under 10 per cent to more than a third of all persons in employment. The feeling began to gain ground that in future the revolution would take place not at the barricades but at the ballot box, that the gradual economic and social upheaval would be followed by an equally gradual political upheaval.

In company with conservatives of all shades of opinion and with the majority of liberals, Bismarck loudly deplored this rapid growth of Social Democracy. Secretly, though, he was not averse to the phenomenon, given

171

the limits within which it continued to be confined, for it forced the conservatives and the National Liberals yet closer together, and even the Centre Party, which in the Ruhr and in Silesia, for example, was often canvassing the same social groups as the Social Democrats, was brought under increasing political pressure as a result.

Both effects found direct, concrete expression under the terms of the electoral law then governing the Imperial Diet. This was a straightforward majority system, which in view of the fragmentation of the party spectrum necessitated electoral pacts in favour of a joint candidate in the second ballot if not in the first, pacts that were themselves apt to have far-reaching political consequences. Since Social Democracy not infrequently – if hardly ever openly – urged support for acceptable candidates of the middle-class left where it stood no chance itself, containment for the benefit of the conservatives, the National Liberals and even the Centre Party could succeed only through the medium of centre-right coalitions. In other words, the electoral success of the Social Democrats in 1884, given the fact that the government could bring forward the date of the next election at will, gave additional impetus to the formation of the kind of majority that Bismarck favoured.

Despite the rapidly gathering clouds on the foreign policy horizon, then, after the 1884 election the Chancellor felt positively invigorated. He was now, he believed, firmly in control of things once again. Gone was the nightmare that had haunted him so often in recent years, indeed had completely dominated his thoughts at times, the nightmare of a 'Greater Liberal Party', and a monarch decisively influenced by and guided by Lasker, Forckenbeck and Stauffenberg. 'It appears', he remarked triumphantly to Moritz Busch at the end of May 1885, 'that the Crown Prince intends to keep me.' However, he went on with haughty self-assurance, 'I shall be considering whether to stay'. There was much to be said 'against and also a great deal in favour'. He was greatly tempted to think 'like Götz von Berlichingen when he threw in his lot with the peasants'. In any event he needed a 'free hand' and not 'colleagues such as Forckenbeck and Georg Bunsen and endless bother with them' after 'the old King has been letting me do what I thought fit recently, even down to choosing and replacing ministers'.[16]

The outward occasion for this self-confident and optimistic summary of the current state of affairs was provided by speculation in the British press regarding the political consequences of what by any human reckoning must be an imminent change of sovereign in Germany. Such speculation was naturally directed towards a new departure along liberal lines. Prominent among the reasons why Bismarck now felt with utter conviction that he could repudiate it and indeed deny that it had any realistic foundation was his belief that he already had several irons in the fire once again.

The attempt if not to eliminate at least to mediatize the parties to a great extent by making a direct appeal to economic interests and fostering their increasing institutionalization had turned out, as we have seen, to be a complete impasse. But it did have one side-effect that Bismarck now took to representing to those around him as having constituted his primary objective from the outset. This was that the parties of the centre and the right began to show a willingness to collaborate the moment the Chancellor more or less abandoned his previous policy of seeking to undermine their existence. In this way there was even a chance for him, or so at least he believed, once again to chop and change between the parties of the centre and the right, between the National Liberals, the Centre Party and the conservatives. Once again he could encourage that tendency among the German Conservatives that voted with Baron von Hammerstein for close collaboration with the Centre Party – and then again give his backing to the formation of a Conservative/National Liberal axis. Again it was the ideal expressed in the Kissingen Dictate with regard to foreign policy that shone through here, the ideal of an 'overall situation' in which all parties needed the government 'and are as far as possible kept from forming coalitions against us by their relations with one another'.

Accordingly his policy after the 1884 election focused on three points. It was that ideal that gave them their special significance, irrespective of the concrete impulses and objective pressures that of course individually played a vital role in each case. The three points were: the extension of economic protectionism, particularly in the agrarian sphere; the final settlement of the 'Kulturkampf'; and the deliberate cultivation of the national idea whenever opportunity offered.

By stepping up agrarian protectionism the Chancellor was serving primarily the interests of the conservatives and of the social groups represented or canvassed by them but also those of the Centre Party, though he was concerned to provide suitable compensations for the industrial clientele of the National Liberal Party. In mobilizing national feeling he had his eye chiefly on the National Liberals, who under Miquel's leadership were once again seeking to present themselves as the party of national integration. With this return to direct and even closer collaboration with the parties concerned, Bismarck not only hoped to create the relations of dependence that he considered so important; he was also concerned to enhance the appeal of the political groups now co-operating with him, particularly the conservatives and the National Liberals, in order that the next election should provide him with a solid base once again.

Unlike his policy in the years immediately after 1878–9, which had repeatedly got bogged down and, judged by its original objectives, had been largely unsuccessful, this plan of Bismarck's made a good deal of progress at first, both in substance and in terms of the intentions he used it to pursue. This even applied, despite many appearances to the contrary, to his policy towards the Roman Catholic Church and the Catholic party, that is to say to the final settlement of the 'Kulturkampf' represented by the two so-called 'Peace Laws' of May 1886 and April 1887.

Since the change of course in domestic policy in 1878–9 Bismarck had in fact made several attempts to hit upon a *modus vivendi* that would make possible a gradual reconciliation with Catholic interests. They had met with little success. On the one hand the political indigence of the Chancellor had been too plain to a Curia kept well informed by the Centre Party leadership. And on the other his efforts to outmanoeuvre the Centre Party and cut the political ground from under it had been too transparent. Consequently the Vatican had seen little reason to drop its demands for a complete return to the legislative position before 1872 and the conclusion of a concordat.

A similar lack of success had greeted a series of legislative initiatives by the Prussian government in the period 1881–3 aimed at qualifying or allowing for a more elastic interpretation of the anti-Catholic 'Kampfgesetze', the chief of those initiatives having been the restoration of the church's 'cure of souls', so badly affected in many places by bans and expulsions. Not even these moves led to any substantial change of attitude at first, either on the part of the Centre Party, which once a majority was assured even voted against the first of these qualifying measures, or on the part of the Curia. Nor had the resumption of diplomatic relations with the Holy See had any great practical effect, particularly since both Emperor William and Bismarck himself refused to reciprocate by agreeing to the establishment of a papal nunciature in Berlin – for Bismarck feared that this would create a unified Catholic control centre in the Reich that would finally block the separation of Catholic Church from Catholic party that he still had hopes of achieving. Only as the Chancellor increasingly moved away in general terms from the idea of suppressing and mediatizing the parties did developments begin to look like taking a more promising turn.

The process began on 9 May 1884, the day the Imperial Diet voted on a further renewal of the Anti-Socialist Law. On that day the parliamentary Centre Party very obviously split into two wings: a conservative wing that helped the Renewal Bill to win a narrow majority and a more centrally oriented wing under the leader of the parliamentary group, Ludwig Windthorst. There had been a prelude to this on the occasion of the first renewal of the Anti-Socialist Law at the end of May 1880. However, not only had the majority relations been very different then; the whole issue had been very much less contentious. Bismarck had not even taken part in what was a comparatively brief debate. The divided vote of the parliamentary group – not unusual for the Centre Party – had been noted on that occasion but quickly forgotten. Now, however, in the run-up to the election and in the context of vigorous efforts on the Chancellor's part to mobilize people against the 'left', it was a political affair of the very first importance, particularly since the National Liberals took this opportunity to make their first unambiguous profession of renewed support for the imperial government.

While Windthorst and a section of his party once again sided with the opposition, another section let it be known that, when what was at issue was the preservation of the existing order, it was prepared to see things differently and to rally to the support of the government. This meant, however, that under certain circumstances the Centre Party could by means of a skilfully contrived policy be subjected to internal stresses and strains that might in future make it more tractable and less independent. Possibly one might even bring the Curia into play here by drawing its attention to the problems inherent in having a wing of a Catholic party oriented towards the left and stating those problems in the context of trends towards democratization and liberalization within the church itself.

This was in fact the course that Bismarck increasingly pursued. Not long after the autumn 1884 election, the trend of which had been so gratifying to himself, he delivered a major speech in the Imperial Diet on 3 December 1884 outlining the basic features of his future policy towards the Roman Catholic Church and consequently towards the Catholic party. In it he made abundantly clear, at least to observers enjoying the benefit of hindsight, what path he intended to take here.

The occasion was a Bill introduced by Windthorst to abolish the so-called 'Expatriation Law', a measure passed in May 1874 that allowed the state to prohibit priests who performed ecclesiastical functions without state approval from residing in specific localities and regions or even to expel them from Reich territory. Windthorst had presented such a Bill in the Imperial Diet twice already: in January 1882 and in the spring of 1884. On both occasions, however, despite overwhelming majorities in the Diet, it had failed to receive the assent of the Federal Council.

In itself the Bill was entirely in line with the qualifying laws of 1880, 1882 and 1883. But since it stemmed from the opposition and implied a tacit claim to exert an influence on the course of policy in general by way of the right to present Bills to the Imperial Diet, Bismarck was determined from the outset not to accept it. 'We must above all take steps to counter the mistaken belief of the Curia and the Centre Party', the Chancellor had laid down as his guideline at the beginning of 1884, 'that "attacks" could dispose the government to make concessions.'[17] A further factor was that Windthorst and the Centre Party leadership had made virtually no attempt to contact him on this issue; in other words they had made no political counter-offer. But whereas he had hitherto confined himself to mere refusal, in his speech of 3 December 1884 he openly counter-attacked. Windthorst, he accused, had by reintroducing his Bill within a matter of weeks of the Federal Council resolution not only shown a complete disregard for the latter; what was worse, his doing so had constituted a renewed attempt to overthrow the existing constitutional system and upset the existing balance of power within the Reich.

What, the Chancellor asked, was this 'petitionary assault on the Federal Council' if not 'that they are holding up, in the name of the majority in the Imperial Diet, the equivalent of Gessler's hat for the Council to salute? The Bill can have no other effect and no other purpose than to insult the confederate governments.' They and the imperial government were forced to draw a twofold conclusion: first, that everyone must now finally say goodbye to what he, Bismarck, had also seen as being, in principle, the highly acceptable idea of a coalition of conservatives, Centre Party and National Liberals; secondly, that an internal German peace settlement in matters of cultural and ecclesiastical policy was now postponed indefinitely. Because such a settlement, he went on, clearly emphasizing not only his strategy with regard to ecclesiastical policy but also his future domestic policy strategy as a whole, presupposed national solidarity and reliability as well as conservative trustworthiness on the part of the Centre Party. Both qualities seemed to him to be lacking in sections of the party at least, as Windthorst's Bill made clear. On the contrary, those sections were pursuing a policy as to the consequences of which he could only warn the

Catholic Church, to wit the Curia, on the one hand and the German nation on the other. The Curia because that policy rested on the illusion entertained by its advocates that they could force the imperial and Prussian governments into making further unilateral concessions and eventually into complete surrender simply by 'applying strong pressure, making themselves absolutely indispensable in Parliament . . . winning votes at elections and supporting the opposition parties against the government'. And the nation because that policy continued to rely on an alliance with the oppositional Polish populations in the eastern parts of Prussia and the Reich and hence ultimately tended to foster the destruction of the unity of the Reich and with it of the whole existing order.

Furthermore, he said in a retrospective gloss on his conduct thirteen years earlier, this had been the chief reason for his allowing himself to become involved in the 'Kulturkampf' in the first place, for hostilities had been initiated on the other side. 'It was only the Polish aspect of the affair that drew me into the whole struggle.' And in view of that aspect he was as determined as ever to retain the anti-Catholic laws that were still in force. At stake were the preservation of the existing order at home and abroad and the power and integrity of the German nation – for him and for his policy these were the crucial points of reference, the decisive values. On this basis he was open to any kind of negotiation and prepared to make many concessions.[18]

This was exceptionally shrewd tactics. From various points of departure it brought the different tendencies among conservatives and National Liberals into close proximity. In the ranks of the Centre Party it nourished many a secret doubt about Windthorst's confrontation and coalition policy, even with regard to the Polish groups. And to the Curia it indicated that a 'diplomatic' solution that took account of the respective interests of both sides, not just in detail but in a general sense, was probably the one most likely to guarantee both sides the greatest degree of independence and freedom of movement, each within its own sphere. It was a fundamental error, he informed the ecclesiastical negotiators in a directive to the Minister of Culture, von Gossler, six weeks later, 'that the Centre [Party] adjusted its behaviour in precise accordance with the state of the ecclesiastical negotiations . . . For as long as Mr. Windthorst holds the reins the Centre will always be an opposition party, and the state of negotiations with Rome governs at most the form of its attacks on the government.'[19]

Windthorst immediately recognized the dangers that this implied for himself and for his policy. He stood solidly by his demand, but at the same time he announced that if the government would make concessions over the Expatriation Law, in other words if it would give a sign here and now of its continuing goodwill, the representatives of the Centre Party would in future support it on all crucial political and economic questions – not, of course, as he was careful to add immediately, 'as mere lackeys of the government's will' but 'as independent men standing on their own two feet'.[20]

Bismarck, however, would have none of it. 'I have no faith in the possibility of our improving our parliamentary circumstances by making concessions to Rome', he remarked laconically not long after this.[21] On the contrary, convinced that the Centre Party was going to have to come round to collaborating sooner or later, he again drew attention to the new keystones of his policy. This was now openly directed towards the unqualified preservation of the existing political, economic and social order. It coupled its appeal to people's fear of change and of a radical transformation of conditions generally with an invitation to the parties of the centre and the right to collaborate with the government accordingly. The crucial integrating factor here was to be the idea of the nation – now no longer, as in previous decades, a formula for change but a symbol of what was to be preseved.

In other words, it was a sort of policy of national consolidation with a strongly conservative flavour. In accordance with it he sought to play off the more conservative elements in the Centre Party – and with them the Curia – against the elements backing Windthorst who, though their basic stance was indubitably conservative, were concerned to keep open for themselves an avenue into a changed future and into fresh political combinations. As he declared in his reply to Windthorst's speech, he could 'no longer face the parliamentary [Centre] party with the same confidence as before now that it has its hands on this miniature Pandora's box and is in a position to release all kinds of evils from it to right and left, possibly even in other than denominational directions. People familiar with this activity', he went on in an allusion to a portentous remark, which he had quoted several times already, made by the man who had been the pope's nuncio in Munich in the late 1860s and early 1870s, 'might regard as correct what Nuncio Meglia is supposed to have said, namely that "only revolution can save us" and that supporting every purely political and secular opposition party was the first step in that programme.'[22]

But what he chiefly invoked on this occasion, in line with the new policy, was the so-called 'Polish menace'. It was on this that he sought very deliberately from now on to concentrate the attention of the German people. Here again we must probably beware of thrusting the purely manipulative element too exclusively into the foreground. Fear of a revolutionary uprising on the part of Prussia's Polish population had been with him since the early years. The alarming brutality of many of his comments on the Polish 'problem' at the same time reflects his deeply felt misgivings about its explosive potential in terms of both domestic and foreign affairs. Nevertheless, there is no mistaking the way in which, here too, he took advantage of a given situation for quite different purposes and with quite different ends in view. This was true of the years 1848–9 as it was of 1863 and of the critical period of the 'Kulturkampf'. And it is equally true of Prussia's rightly notorious Polish policy in the years after 1885.

The situation was certainly explosive enough. Polish hopes for a state of their own were still intact, and nationalism was rife among them. Added to which, many Polish historians had drawn on remote historical epochs to nourish far-reaching expectations regarding the territorial extent of that future state, expectations that did not stop at regions that had belonged to Prussia for centuries past. In the light of all this it was to some extent understandable that the Germans should have looked with growing concern and unease on the activities of the Polish national movement and on the continuing advances of the Polish element in consequence of increased migration from Prussia's eastern provinces.

But even if judicious allowance is made for the actual situation and the problems arising from it, Bismarck's Polish policy has to be called calamitous as well as – in relation to the future – irresponsible. Because Bismarck had a very clear idea of the intrinsic importance of the problems and formed a very accurate estimate of their specific explosive force. By choosing nevertheless to exploit them for other purposes he further encumbered them with other problems and drew them into the centre of conflicts of political principle. As a result the situation eventually became almost hopeless.

This was already foreshadowed in the dispute with Windthorst. On that occasion the Chancellor, who really knew better, sought to attribute the Polish problem not just to the demands of the Polish nobility but above all to the subversive activities of 'Polish-nationalist priests'. He would not, he declared, allow the Centre Party and an opposition majority in the Imperial Diet to strike from his hand the weapon he needed to prevent 'this backing of the upper classes by the prelacy'. In the 'interests of maintaining public order and internal peace' the Reich had no choice but 'to take a Polish nationalist fanatic who wears the robes of a priest away from the locality in which he has his roots and pursues his activities and intern him somewhere'.[23]

This problem too, in other words, could be solved by discriminatory legislation and by a policy of repression and precautionary containment; anyone who maintained the contrary was a secret accessory to and partisan of revolution. In this way the Polish problem, like the denominational question and the question of Social Democracy before it, was so to speak placed under a taboo. Attitudes to it and to the government's policy in regard to it took on something of the character of fundamental political avowals. Again, the crucial opposites from now on, constituting the friend/enemy yardstick, were: nationally reliable or revolutionary.

Accordingly a full-scale policy of Germanization was launched soon after this in the eastern provinces of the Reich. It was also, at least in original intention, a policy very distinctly in the interests of the large East Elbian landowners as well as of the state. Expulsion of those Poles not possessing Prussian nationality from the autumn of 1885 onwards was followed, after prolonged and at times very heated debate in the Prussian House of Deputies, by the so-called 'Settlement Law' of 26 April 1886. This placed at the government's disposal a fund containing what was then the enormous sum of 100 million marks with which to acquire Polish possessions in Posen and West Prussia and generally to ensure 'the strengthening and augmentation of the German element in the face of pro-Polish endeavours'. At the same time a 'Settlement Commission' was charged with the administration and distribution of the fund.

The discussions of the relevant Bill in January and February 1886 found the Prussian House of Deputies once again forming the same fronts as had characterized the political scene both in Prussia and in the Reich since the spring of 1884. These were the very groupings at which Bismarck's overall political strategy was aimed with a view to altering the numerical balance between them to his advantage at the next available opportunity: on the one hand the two conservative parties and the National Liberals, with a section of the Centre Party secretly sympathizing with them, and on the other the German Liberals, the 'protest parties' and the bulk of the Centre Party under Windthorst.

So the direction of his thrust was already determined when on 28 January 1886 Bismarck took the floor of the Prussian House of Deputies for a declaration of principle. His survey of the development of the Polish question and of Prussia's Polish policy since the partititions, with its highly characteristic emphases and peremptory bias, quickly culminated in a frontal attack on the left-wing liberals and a section of the Centre Party. Both groups were similarly responsible for the fact that Prussia and the Reich were now – as he stressed dramatically – having to fight for their lives. For decades they had fostered and encouraged the Poles and from purely ideological or even narrowly party-political motives repeatedly kept the state from taking preventive action. Worse, they had not infrequently forced the state to adopt the wrong course. Even now they were once again withholding their support, placing party before country and before the national interest. It might be, therefore, he went on to threaten obscurely, 'that our domestic entanglements will place the confederate governments under the necessity of seeking for their part – with Prussia first among them – *ne quid detrimenti res publica capiat*, as far as possible to increase the strength of each and every one of them and of the confederation in which they are joined and to make themselves, as far as they legally and constitutionally can, independent of the policy of obstruction pursued by the majority in the Imperial Diet'. He, Bismarck, was 'not among the advocates, not *yet*' – he qualified immediately – 'among the advocates of such a policy, and it stands in fundamental contradiction to my endeavours over recent decades'. However, he concluded on a note of pathos, 'before I allowed the national interest to falter and fall into jeopardy I should give His Majesty the Emperor and the confederate princes the appropriate advice and I should stand by that advice. I regard as a miserable coward any minister who will not, when it comes to it, stake his life and his honour on saving his country, be it in defiance of the will of majorities.'

It was a further example – this time on a huge and public scale – of the kind of 'verbal sabre-rattling' with which he sought to make 'all the watchers and waverers . . . inclined to parley'. The Settlement Bill was simply the outward occasion. The majority for that Bill was virtually assured in advance, even if the government did have to make a substantial concession to the National Liberals, who managed to get peasant settlements favoured rather than large landholdings and government estates. The real objectives were to unsettle the Centre Party and to put the government in a favourable starting-position for the next election. This was to be dominated by the national rallying-cry, which was at the same time to be regarded as betokening loyalty to the government.

Notwithstanding the inner dynamics and the besetting urgency of the Polish question, however, Bismarck himself was in some doubt as to whether it would develop sufficient appeal on its own, particularly as far as the electorally crucial southern and western regions of the Reich were concerned. The Chancellor therefore went on in the same speech to invoke a much greater danger, one that potentially threatened the very existence of the Reich and of the nation. For the moment, admittedly, he saw 'no disturbance of the external peace as likely'. But it was not impossible 'that, after the way in which we have received and made use of the extraordinary good fortune that has fallen to our lot over the last twenty years, Providence might find it useful to expose German patriotism to yet another fire of European coalitions of major anti-German neighbour nations, yet another tempering and refining fire'. What made it even less possible to rule out such a danger was the fact that potential enemies 'continue even now to derive a certain encouragement from our internal dissensions – for folk are not familiar with our domestic circumstances or aware that the people do not think in the way the majorities in our parliaments vote'. The message was that anyone who on questions of national principle took up a position hostile to the government was potentially unleashing a deadly danger upon a Reich that, because of its position at the heart of Europe, was under constant threat. For every such stand gave other nations the impression that the Reich 'is falling apart, that it is weak, that it won't last'.[24]

At this stage Bismarck was content to leave it at a vague hint. He did not name an 'object' around which these fears might crystallize; he was confident that he would hit one at the crucial moment, namely in the run-up to the election. All he was interested in for the present was marking out the starting-positions in his favour. On the one hand this involved not just a general emphasis on the national idea but also some deliberate fostering of the interlocking ideological and above all material interests of the National Liberals and of conservatives of all persuasions. And on the other hand it involved further unsettling the Centre Party with regard to the political line it ought to take.

This was what Bismarck chiefly had in mind when on 29 January 1886, the day after his major speech on the Polish question, he again intervened in the general debate on the Settlement Bill in reaction to the comments of Windthorst. Windthorst, he claimed, had once again made the real situation very clear. It was not in essence a question of the rights of this or that group of people, whether Catholic or Polish. It was a question of the existing domestic order of the Reich as a whole and consequently of defining what were the Reich's principal national interests. 'Wholly intransigent' as far as any kind of genuine collaboration with the government was concerned, even over questions affecting the fate of the nation, 'encased in the triple armour of the Guelf, of the leader in the battle for civilization [*Kulturkampf*] and of his progressive sympathies', Windthorst repeatedly showed himself to be a benevolent spectator of 'the efforts of a powerful parliamentary group legally to undermine our constitution'. He accordingly defended 'the rights of the Poles *more energetically* than those of the Germans'. Bismarck concluded: 'Did he not sit with the Centre [Party], the honourable gentleman would in my opinion belong not at all to the Conservative Party but to the Progressives.'[25]

This was aimed not only at the right wing of the parliamentary Centre Party and at the not inconsiderable number of its voters who were becoming increasingly uneasy about the actual or alleged leftward orientation of the party leadership on matters of general policy. It was aimed above all at the Curia and at that mainly conservative group of German bishops that was seeking to steer a compromise course and to bring about a reconciliation between state and church. Here was the true background to the speech.

Windthorst was perfectly aware of this. Moreover, he knew full well that he was walking a tightrope with his policy and that there was a not inconsiderable risk of his falling off it. If the current negotiations for a final settlement of the 'Kulturkampf' were to fail, others besides Bismarck, for whom as he quite rightly assumed the whole thing was in any case subordinate to considerations of general political expediency, would lay the blame for that failure on him and on the tendency he represented. If, however, in the interests of the success of those negotiations he were to entertain compromises not only in matters of substance but also in matters of principle, he would be abandoning not only his own strict position but with it all claim to political independence on the part of the Centre Party. And that applied not only to its relationship vis-à-vis the government but also to its relationship vis-à-vis the Curia and the bishops. Windthorst's speech of 28 January left very clear glimpses of this dilemma, as when he stressed repeatedly: 'We find ourselves on the defensive; we are not to blame for this question coming up today, and it would be wrong to reproach us with having occasioned this very delicate . . . discussion – at a time when talks are supposedly being held with Rome that might possibly be interfered with.'[26]

Although it meant supplying Bismarck with additional ammunition against him and positively inviting the charge that he was playing a purely tactical game, on the issue itself he took what from the point of view of the party was the only right course in the long run: he stuck to his guns and resigned himself to letting his political adversary take a temporary advantage. Anything else would probably have deprived the party of its base and its credibility for a long time to come.

For the moment Bismarck did indeed take a very clear advantage. Just as he had once imagined it as doing, the compromise between church and state very largely bypassed the Centre Party and came about through direct negotiations with the Curia and with those bishops who were prepared to co-operate, chief among them being Bishop Kopp of Fulda, whom William I had made a member of the Prussian Upper House before the Poland debate.

The prelude had come in September 1885, when the Reich asked the pope to mediate in a not particularly important colonial dispute with Spain over the ownership of the Caroline and Palau Islands in Micronesia. As Bismarck quite openly told the Vatican envoy, von Schlözer, this was an act of 'courtesy towards the Pope' from which he expected 'in connection with our dispute with the Church' that it would 'have the effect of making the Pope less susceptible to the impact of Catholic democracy as headed by Windthorst'.[27] Leo XIII did indeed feel extraordinarily flattered at being thus elevated to the position of an arbiter in international affairs by one of the great powers of Europe, particularly since Bismarck subsequently went out of his way to lay proper emphasis on the carefully prepared success of the papal arbiter's decree. 'Our objective', he noted triumphantly in a direct report to the emperor on 18 December 1885, 'of showing the Catholics and the Pope that the denominational dispute involves no personal hostility towards the Pope has been attained to the extent that the opposition in the Imperial Diet and in the press has misgivings on the subject and is dissatisfied with the Pope.'[28]

It had been possible on this basis to take an important step forward in respect of the principal appointments in dispute. In December 1885 the archiepiscopal see of Cologne and in March 1886 that of Gnesen-Posen were filled with candidates acceptable to the government, to wit Philipp Krementz, Bishop of Ermland, and the Provost of Königsberg and army chaplain Julius Dinder respectively; the highly controversial previous incumbents, Cardinals Melchers and Ledochowski, were summoned to Rome to sit on the Curia. Furthermore, the rapprochement between Berlin and the Curia constituted an important prerequisite for the emergence of the first so-called 'Peace Law' in the spring of 1886. This abolished the 'Kulturexamen', the examination in German history and literature that Catholic ordinands had to take, recognized the pope's disciplinary authority over the clergy, did away with the Royal Court for Ecclesiastical Affairs that had been set up in 1873 and re-permitted the study of theology at episcopal schools and the establishment of episcopal seminaries.

Contrary to parliamentary custom, the relevant Bill had been debated and passed by the Upper House first, with a newly appointed member, Bishop Kopp of Fulda, playing a prominent part. This too was a pointed accentuation of the peculiar nature of this whole business. It was to be made clear to everyone that this was an act of supreme political significance in which the parties – and that included the Centre Party – had only a very limited say. Windthorst and his colleagues had nothing with which to counter this. Because of course they could not withhold their assent when it came to a division in the House of Deputies, especially since the National Liberals, for all their flexibility, in the end decided not to play ball and the bill threatened to fail if the Centre Party did not vote for it. This had the effect, however, of strengthening the impression – so dear to Bismarck – that the Centre Party was here confined to a purely supernumerary function, indeed that it had been forced back into the role of a mere agent of the Curia and the Prussian government.

The Chancellor promptly pushed on in this direction. The pope had responded by instructing the German bishops to comply with the law of 1873 in future in giving the government prior notice of new ecclesiastical appointments, in other words to accept, at least in principle, its right to object. Whereupon Bismarck offered the Curia a settlement of the last remaining questions – the extent of the church's internal sovereignty and the readmission of monastic orders – in the same spirit of generous compromise, which would bring the 'Kulturkampf' to an end at last. In doing so he again stressed the personal element, appealing to Leo XIII not to let himself be deprived of the magnificent role of peacemaker both at home and abroad and not to allow anyone, not even the leader of the German parliamentary Centre Party, to contest his right to the 'renown' attaching to that role. The whole business must, he said, be negotiated and sealed at the highest level. Naturally he, Bismarck, expected the Centre Party not only to acquiesce in the relevant bilateral decisions, which after all were very much in its own interest, but positively to adopt a more co-operative attitude towards the government on other matters as well.

So completely did Leo XIII swallow this that eventually he urged the Centre Party several times in the strongest terms to fall in with the government over a crucial issue of domestic policy that emerged in the course of 1886, thus plunging the party into very serious conflict. The issue in question was the renewal of and simultaneous increase in the long-term military budget, the so-called 'Septennate'. This was put forward by the government in the context of an allegedly serious threat of foreign conflict. There was talk of a possibly imminent war on two fronts with a France that General Boulanger had whipped into a frenzy of revanchism and a Russia in which Pan-Slav, pro-Polish forces had finally gained the upper hand.

Granted, Bismarck was by no means free of apprehensions on either count. There can be no question, in other words, of his having simply sought to instil them in others. In the case of Russia, faced with a growing clamour among ever broader sections of the population for a preventive war, he even took pains in his public utterances to play down the dangers. And if in so doing he shifted the emphasis on to France and insisted on the far greater danger ostensibly threatening from that quarter, this was partly with a view to providing a counter-weight. On the other hand he did contrive, as many a clear-sighted contemporary realized and as the sources have subsequently confirmed, very purposefully to harness real dangers on the foreign policy front in the service of his domestic strategy. The purpose was to help shift the distribution of weight between the domestic fronts in favour of a centre-right coalition committed to himself.

Once again, but this time very much more impressively and insistently than over the Polish question, the message was this: anyone who in this situation of national peril seeks to juggle with legal niceties, raises objections on grounds of principle and fails to give unreserved and unconditional support to the demands of the political and military leadership, no matter what justification he may advance, is nationally unreliable, a revolutionary in disguise, in short an enemy of the Reich. This was the most important dividing-line of all. Anyone operating on this side of the line would find that a national government could work closely with him and meet him half-way over many questions. Anyone operating beyond it that government would fight with every weapon at its disposal.

The whole thing was of course calculated to allow real freedom of choice only to the individual voter. As far as the parties were concerned Bismarck deliberately set the threshold so high that only those that were welcome to him as partners could cross it without incurring a crucial loss of face. This was particularly true with regard to the Centre Party. Although he persuaded the Curia to bring massive pressure to bear on the party, whether that pressure was actually successful or not mattered very much less to him than its effects on the party's membership and on the appeal of the party generally. Indeed, the fact that it was unsuccessful ultimately suited him very much better. The question of the expansion of the army and the military budget and above and beyond it the national question were not intended to throw the battle order of the parties into disarray. The object was to bring about a decisive change in their parliamentary ranks through the medium of a fresh election.

In this way Bismarck for the first time committed himself quite unequivocally to a particular combination of parties – one, moreover, that was itself anything but united in its approach to such key questions as, for example, its relationship to the Centre Party. In other words, in the hope of making a major breakthrough to a new and more solid parliamentary base in the Reich he very largely abandoned his old policy of deliberately chopping and changing.

In this he was extremely successful at first, or so at least it seemed. The development of a protectionist tariff and trade policy was not only drawing a stronger and stronger belt of common interests around the conservatives and the National Liberals: as early as May 1885 German agricultural tariff rates were tripled on average, and in December 1887 they were again almost doubled, while industrial tariffs increased likewise, if less dramatically. It also enhanced the attractiveness of the two groups in the eyes of those with a direct interest in that policy, who were now once again expressly referred to them. In addition there was the systematic emphasis placed on the national reliability of those parties and the insistence on the dangers that threatened on the foreign and domestic policy fronts. The connection between the two – in relation to the Polish question, for example, or the ecclesiastical question – was as firmly underlined by the government as was the allegedly ambivalent role of the other parties when it came to combating those dangers.

All these things came to a head in the army question, which Bismarck had been increasingly drawing into the centre of his policy since the beginning of 1886. Past experience showed that on this issue differences could be focused more effectively than on almost any other. And with its help emotions could be aroused that looked as if they might successfully obscure the fact that the situation was now radically different. Here, if anywhere, is where we can speak of deliberate manipulation on the part of the Chancellor, who in reviving the old formulation of the problem sought to resuscitate the old parliamentary constellation too.

His starting-point was the very markedly privileged position that the army occupied in the state. This was something that Bismarck, despite his claim to unrestricted political leadership in this sphere as well, had repeatedly and energetically underlined and defended. Hardly a year had passed since the resolution of the constitutional conflict over the army question and the eventual compromise over the military budget in which he had not demonstratively and often spectacularly and dramatically drawn attention to the fact that the army constituted the core of the state, the bulwark against every attempt to overthrow the existing order – not only from without but also from within. Again and again he had referred to the role of the army in the conflicts of 1848–9, when only 'Prussian militarism' had been capable of 'damming' the activities of the left.[29] Again and again he had stressed that a man's attitude to the army was symptomatic of his attitude to the state; consequently all discussion of this issue, even where it concerned questions of apparently minor importance, was a matter of principle. And again and again he had sought to label his political opponents as anti-army and consequently anti-authority in general in the eyes of a public of whom the majority succumbed on every conceivable occasion to the intoxication of past military successes and fêted the successors of those responsible for them. This was the spirit in which, though he had never been a regular officer and though his knowledge of and taste for military affairs were both extremely limited, he appeared more and more frequently in the uniform of a general, for as chief of the 1st Magdeburg Landwehr Regiment he had meanwhile been promoted to the rank of cavalry general. This was the purpose of his suggesting that the basic attitude to be adopted vis-à-vis the Imperial Diet in the 'representation of the interests of the army in Prussia and in the Empire' should be one of a 'reserved, dry unapproachability little open to discussion';[30] it was a question 'not of getting the Army Bill through but of asserting our position', according to the plainer version given in a directive to the War Minister.[31] And it was to this end that he eventually used the army question to re-establish an exaggerated 'friend or foe' situation on the domestic front.

The external occasions for this were on the one hand the fresh deterioration in German-French relations that followed the fall of Ferry and on the other hand developments in the Balkans. The fears and anxieties that Bismarck associated with these events chiefly found expression in the so-called 'Christmas Letter' that he wrote to the Prussian War Minister, Bronsart von Schellendorf, towards the end of 1886[32] There is no doubt, however, that he also made use of those fears and anxieties – depicting them in dramatically heightened terms – in order to advance his domestic policy. No less a figure than the quartermaster-general of the German army, Count Waldersee, noted in mid-March 1886, at a time when Bismarck was becoming more and more vociferous about the risk of armed conflicts, that it was 'all play-acting'. They were not real but merely putative dangers 'that the Chancellor sees fit to trot out just now'.[33]

Waldersee was confirmed in his opinion by Bismarck's flagrant attempts to establish a connection between alleged external threats and the dangers of opposition at home. The Chancellor warned repeatedly that an imminent military conflict might finally rupture the ties of national solidarity and make way for the much-invoked solidarity of class and of shared revolutionary aims and beliefs.[34]

Such doom-laden predictions also caused many representatives of the anti-government majority in the Imperial Diet to see the whole thing simply as a transparent manoeuvre designed to arouse bad feeling against the left in general and in particular to pave the way for the renewal of the military budget, due in April 1888. However, in so doing they not only underestimated the effectiveness of this line of argument among broad sections of the public. More than anything they underestimated Bismarck's determination not to parley on this occasion but to seek a clear decision, convinced that both the time and the topic were in his favour.

Just how determined he was became increasingly clear in the months following his clash with the opposition and above all with Windthorst and the main body of the Centre Party under his leadership in January and February 1886. What additionally goaded the Chancellor here was the fact that, as in the foregoing years, the opposition majority consistently blocked every attempt to place the Reich on a firmer financial footing – by means of a monopoly on spirits, for example – and so strengthen the executive. Behind this he sensed with some justification a renewed attempt to force the government into a commitment to parliament. By now there was sympathy for such an attempt even among those sections of the Conservative Party that favoured a merger with the Centre Party to form a 'blue-black' bloc. They saw it as a means of harnessing the Chancellor even more firmly to their own interests and objectives.

Not least with the object of countering such tendencies, Bismarck now began quite frankly to steer a collision course. He was ready 'if need be', he told the Prussian ministers as early as 7 March 1886, 'to violate the constitution', and he expected their 'unanimous support'.[35] And a fortnight later he was saying that the time for negotiating with representatives of the opposition was now past. 'Any hope of persuading the gentlemen' was 'non-existent', and there was 'a possibility of the dignity of the state being dragged down in discussions with them'; in most cases the person concerned would simply 'use' the answer 'to forge a weapon against the government'.[36] It was a question, now, of forcing relations between government and parliament into a new mould by bringing forward a Bill asking for the military budget to be extended and demanding an increase in that budget, in other words a major augmentation of the army's strength.

Not that he put it in so many words. But his intention is clear from the fact that at a meeting of the Prussian Cabinet in the middle of February 1886 he brought down a 'lesser' Army Bill that confined itself initially to a limited increase in military strength with the remark that such a Bill scarcely lent itself to striking a decisive 'blow against the majority in the Imperial Diet'.[37]

It was with the object of striking that decisive blow that, after a particularly long summer recess, the 'greater' Army Bill was presented to the Diet at the end of November 1886. This provided for an increase of around 10 per cent – more than 40,000 men – in the army's peacetime strength. The deadline for this was put at 1 April 1887, one year before the current budget was due to expire. Moreover, the new budget was also to remain in force for seven years.

Given the tense international situation and the fact that a peacetime strength of around 10 per cent of the population had always been the norm, there was scarcely anyone, even deep in the ranks of the opposition, who objected to an increase in the size of the army. The objections were directed primarily at a fresh 'septennate' and the concomitant further reduction in the influence of parliament on the eve of a change of sovereign.

In other words, agreement on the concrete question of increasing the size of the army – allegedly the government's chief concern – would not have been difficult to achieve. Just such an agreement, however, was the very last thing Bismarck wanted. He therefore went all out to obstruct it in order to be able, following a premature dissolution of the Diet, to present the opposition to the electorate as being anti-army and nationally unreliable.

He could not of course put it quite so openly, even among his intimates, with a change of sovereign now expected almost daily and in the context of the attendant clandestine jockeying for position; he stressed repeatedly that it was not, in his opinion, 'compatible with conscientious politics' that anyone should 'work for the rejection of our Bill'. But those were mere words, escape clauses for the benefit of more scrupulous natures. Nor, he wrote to War Minister Bronsart von Schellendorf, would he wish 'to advise that we bow to the natural inclination of honest folk to "accomplish" something any farther than decency requires. *We* have nothing to fear from the practical consequences of a rejection; Windthorst and Richter do, though.'[38] And in a private letter he came straight out with it: 'As regards our overall position, the most useful outcome would be the opposition's persisting in its initial antagonism and the dissolution that would result . . . Shifting the decision into the field of the *time* question of either five or seven years makes our position more difficult but does not alter it.'[39]

His candour reached its height when a manoeuvre of his that had meant to fail threatened to become an unwelcome success. This was the initiative – apparently so urgently requested – taken by the Curia in favour of the Army Bill. It culminated in a note sent by the papal Secretary of State, Cardinal Jacobini, to the Nuncio in Munich, di Pietro, on 3 January 1887 and saying in essence that it was the Holy Father's wish 'that the Centre [Party] back the septennate in every way possible'.[40]

The contents of this note were as yet unknown when on 2 January, the day on which the Prussian Cabinet discussed the concluding 'Peace Bill', which again was to be negotiated direct with the Curia, Bismarck sent a telegram to Kurd von Schlözer, the Prussian envoy at the Vatican, saying that Rome clearly 'overrated' the value 'that we put upon the Centre's assent to the Army Bill . . . Rejection of the latter would place the government on an admittedly different but possibly very much more favourable operational footing. Only honest conscientiousness', he went on, 'makes us do everything we can to get it accepted.' His asking Schlözer to use his influence to bring about a papal intervention had been 'inspired purely by the desire to give the Pope a fine role, not to pull off an ugly piece of barter. In the latter event, Windthorst would reap the glory for the deal, not the Pope.' And then, taking brutal frankness to the extreme: 'We shall strengthen the army even without the Centre and if necessary even without the Diet.'[41] The septennate was in any case something he clung to only for tradition's sake and not 'out of any conviction of the usefulness of this provision', he told the Prussian Cabinet shortly afterwards.[42] The constitution, he said, made it quite clear that fixing the peacetime strength of the army was the business of the emperor alone; any right on the part of the Imperial Diet to have a say in the budget was simply something that liberal constitutional lawyers had read into it.

This was his position when he appeared before the Imperial Diet on 11 January 1887. He was firmly resolved to use the general debate at the beginning of the second reading of the Army Bill principally to thwart any conceivable compromise with arguments as convincing as possible and to get the election campaign off to a good start as far as he was concerned. With the emperor's dissolution decree in his pocket, after dealing with the foreign policy aspects and giving repeated assurances, chiefly for Russia's benefit, to the effect that the projected increase in the size of the army was in no way an offensive but purely a defensive act, he immediately got down to the question of political principle. With this he hoped to be able to mobilize voters for the parties of the centre and the right and provoke and expose the opposition parties, including the Centre Party. It was a question, the Chancellor declared, not of details, of individual concrete issues and considerations of expediency. It was a question of making the security of the empire and the continuance of its internal and external order independent of 'the changing majorities in the Imperial Diet'. It was a question of 'the principle of whether the German Empire is to be defended by an Imperial army or by a parliamentary army'.[43]

As he explained in a series of interventions, this was a question of principle not for any dogmatic reasons. It was a question of principle because the Diet comprised, among others, Centre, Liberal and Social Democratic parties whose representatives really, despite all statements to the contrary, particularly from the Centre Party, wanted a different sort of empire and an entirely different internal order. Not only the liberals and the Centre Party but also the Social Democrats and the Centre Party had now adopted a common line. 'The whole Windthorst group, including the Social Democrats, marches in serried ranks. For the policy pursued by its leader is such that the Social Democrats are delighted to go along with it; it is calculated to unsettle, to breach and generally to cast doubt on the existing order; and that is something the Social Democrats will always go along with.' This, he said, was the tie that united what was admittedly, in other respects, often a negative coalition and therefore one that would never be capable of governing. That tie was reinforced by an 'aversion to the persons that make up the present government . . . *Une haine commune vous unit*; as soon as this ceases, as soon as you are required to do something more positive, you are totally disunited, you are no majority at all.'[44]

The quintessence of his speech and its direct appeal to the electorate was this: anyone who did not want chaos and the dissolution of all order in consequence of mere negation must make a stand against this negative coalition and the parties that made it up; he must rally round those political groups that, despite all their differences of opinion over details, were determined to defend the state and the rule of law embodied in it. 'In the end', he shouted confidently at the opposition, 'we shall convince the voters where true patriotism and concern for the security and prosperity of the

German Empire and for its unity are to be found. Of that I have no doubt.'[45]

After that the adoption by the opposition majority of a compromise motion, put forward by the progressive German Liberal Party, limiting the life of the budget to three years instead of seven and the proclamation of the imperial decree of dissolution on 14 January 1887 were little more than formalities. Everyone knew by then that the Chancellor was no longer interested in compromise but only in seeing a decision by the electorate. And he was very much concerned to dress that decision up as being one of momentous principle.

Notwithstanding his positively belligerent remarks in the run-up to that decision, it is idle to speculate as to how Bismarck might have acted had the election of late February 1887 produced a negative outcome from his point of view. It is idle not only because of the difficulty of proving anything that did not actually happen, purely on the basis of assumptions; here again expressions of determination to stage a *coup d'état* are cancelled out by others of a quite different tone. It is above all a futile exercise because in that event quite other factors would have come into play: the attitudes of the confederate governments and their respective monarchs, that of the 'government' parties and not least the person of the emperor. It is hard to imagine a *coup d'état* being staged on behalf of a man nearly 90 years old and in defiance of the express wish of the heir to the throne.

Nevertheless, Bismarck quite deliberately located this election on the very brink of a full-scale national crisis. Nor did he shrink from linking people's fears of such a crisis with the bogy of armed conflicts of unprecedented proportions and unprecedented, ideologically exacerbated intensity. Outwardly this was the old Bismarck, recklessly playing with fire. Inwardly, though, judged in terms of content and objectives and in terms of relevance to the major motive forces of the period, there was little of any consequence left – just a stubborn, senile clinging to the status quo, indeed to the past pure and simple. It was precisely what he reproached his opponents with: pure negation. It was the rejection of any kind of movement and change, politics no longer as creative action but as mere reaction.

Even here the nation seems once again to have followed his lead. Yet hardly was the battle over and the opposition numerically defeated before it became obvious that the new majority in the Imperial Diet had very little positive to unite it. It was certainly not in any position to unite the nation. And that, in the long run, was Bismarck's political death sentence. The Chancellor was rightly seen as the creator and moving spirit of the new majority. He had identified himself with it as with no other parliamentary grouping or coalition since the late 1860s and early 1870s, still chasing after the constellation that had obtained at that time. So it was in obedience to a logic not merely of the moment, the logic of an increasingly backward-looking political 'progress', that he eventually went under in the whirlpool of the paralysing disunity of that new majority.

The majority in question was a centre-right coalition of German Conservatives, Free Conservatives and National Liberals who, immediately after the dissolution of the Diet, encouraged by Bismarck in a variety of ways, had joined together in the so-called 'Cartel'. The material basis for this was provided in essence by the National Liberal Party's 'Heidelberg Declaration' of 1884. But what brought the Cartel together was above all the promises of the government, in the light of which the parties concerned agreed on an election strategy: in each constituency, where the victorious candidate at the last election had been one of theirs, the Cartel parties this time gave him their joint support, and where the victor had been from the ranks of the opposition they put up a joint candidate.

Thus the result of the election of 21 and (second ballot) 28 February 1887, which gave the Cartel parties a clear absolute majority of 220 out of 397 seats, though generally regarded as sensational, had if you like been manipulated in advance. Magnifying the one-sided effects of the system of absolute majority suffrage and of highly problematical constituency boundaries, it in no way reflected the actual pattern of votes cast. In terms of these the Cartel parties, apparently so clearly triumphant, in reality mustered a mere 36·3 per cent compared with more than 50 per cent falling to the opposition parties.

An additional factor was that before the election Bismarck had irresponsibly had the atmosphere of crisis heightened not only at home but also with respect to foreign policy. Twelve years previously, at the time of the 'Is War in Sight?' crisis, the connections had been less clear. Now, with a fresh incendiary article by Constantin Rössler appearing in the Berlin *Post* on 31 January 1887 under the title 'Auf des Messers Schneide' ('The Razor's Edge'), they were quite unequivocal. The call-up of 72,000 reservists for exercises with a new repeating gun in Alsace-Lorraine at the beginning of February, the orchestrated rumours about a projected war loan bill in the sum of no less than 300 million marks, which sowed panic on both the Paris and the Berlin stock exchanges – all these things served to conjure up, to the advantage of the 'parties of order', a danger in which Bismarck did not seriously believe or that at any rate he regarded as far inferior to that of an entanglement in the east; unless Boulanger came to power, he told friends around this time, war was 'completely out of the question'.[46]

In the short-term interests of winning an election, in other words, the German Chancellor and Foreign Minister allowed the conviction to take root unchallenged that a 'second war with France over Alsace-Lorraine' was and remained 'a historical necessity . . . Only after it has been fought and won will the German state be permanently secure.' The words were Bennigsen's, penned in a private letter the day after his return from a long campaigning trip during which he had repeatedly expressed himself to this effect.[47] Ludwig Bamberger observed resignedly after the election that Germany, 'in so far as it is not dictated to by the squire or the priest', was now 'led by the Philistine', who was 'so foolish' as to believe that 'without a septennate the French would invade tomorrow'.[48] However, on his wing of liberalism they had their own obsession – with Russia and with the danger from that quarter. That, they said, was the one that needed countering as a precaution. But with that the potential common denominator was already

190

widely visible, at least in embryo. It ran: encirclement of Germany – a world of enemies.

The theory that peace and unity at home – a *Burgfriede* – were the country's only hope in such a situation is one that was already drummed into the Germans by Bismarck, culminating in the election campaign of 1887. Yet however far, particularly in this instance, he took the domestic instrumentalization of alleged or actual dangers on the foreign policy front, he never let himself be carried away by the temptation actively to tailor his foreign policy to domestic policy requirements and allow the latter to guide his hand in the field of foreign affairs; developments during the rest of 1887 leave no doubt on this score. Nevertheless, he did in this final phase evolve the model of which less scrupulous and at the same time less far-sighted natures were later to make use.

Closer examination of the course of events after the 1887 election might in fact have put anyone on his guard. For neither did the hysterical mood of crisis so violently whipped up over both domestic and foreign issues succeed in inwardly uniting the nation, nor did it provide the government with even a passably stable base. Admittedly there were many, particularly among the vanquished, who felt after the election victory of the Cartel that there was henceforth 'no alternative to Bismarck . . . He has built himself a solid position now.'[49] Yet, as the following weeks and months already showed, the government's room for political manoeuvre remained limited even now; the changes within the pro-government coalition had given rise to fresh problems.

Whereas the German Conservatives had gained only two seats and virtually no additional votes, the National Liberals had shot to almost twice their previous number of seats and were once again the strongest party in the Imperial Diet. The right was immediately worried that it would be outmanoeuvred politically, especially since most of the Free Conservatives, who had also recorded major gains, traditionally leaned towards the National Liberals. Even the Chancellor himself was still suspected by the right of continuing to cherish secret leanings towards the party with which the memory of his most successful years in terms of domestic policy was associated. There was also the obvious consideration that close co-operation with the Liberal right wing would recommend itself to the head of the government if only in the light of the coming change of sovereign. And in that case would the Cartel not soon start to drift leftward once again? 'The Conservatives have already got the wind up', Herbert Bismarck observed early in March 1887, only days after the second ballot, 'lest Bennigsen's silly ideas about "constitutional guarantees" once again become rife' among National Liberals.[50] Consequently the eyes of many German Conservatives were soon on the Centre Party once more, the right wing of which they had in fact long regarded as their ideal partner.

So there was a rift in the Cartel virtually from the outset. And for all its ostensible unity over questions of principle, the rift was driven deeper in the future course of events by the divergent interests of farmers on the one hand and groups representing trade and industry on the other. In view of this the army question continued to be of crucial importance as far as domestic policy was concerned even after the prompt approval of the septennate by the new Cartel majority. It was and remained the tie that held the Cartel parties together, the formula for a policy of strength both abroad and at home.

It was not least with this in mind that the government brought a fresh Army Bill before the Imperial Diet as early as the autumn of 1887 together with a related Loan Bill for a sum of 278 million marks. In addition to extending the period for which a conscript had to serve in the reserve, the new Bill was designed to reincorporate the Landwehr in the wartime army. In other words, it sought to rescind that separation of the two bodies that had been one of the most controverial points of the Prussian army reform programme of the early 1860s – a clear indication that, all prophecies of doom notwithstanding, the military and political leadership had long since ceased to believe in the danger of subversive infiltration of the army.

As it happened, the Bill got through even without the Cartel majority being required to vote as a solid bloc. At the very beginning of 1888 the Centre Party and the German Liberal Party unanimously declared that a careful distinction must be drawn between the question of increasing the size of the army in order to strengthen the defences of the Reich and the question of fixing the term of the military budget. True to this principle, on 6 February the Centrists and the German Liberals cast their votes in favour of the Landwehr and Loan Bill. Thus in the context of this crucial question the common enemy, whose appearance might have preserved the unity of the Cartel, failed to materialize, and the new coalition's internal contradictions and the secret leanings of certain elements towards other coalitions began to manifest themselves more and more openly.

How pronounced these were had already been seen back in the spring of 1887 when the Prussian House of Deputies debated the second and final 'Peace Bill' to end the dispute with the Roman Catholic Church, a measure that, like its predecessor, had been presented to the Upper House first. Bismarck had done his best to dispel the impression of a compromise with or even a capitulation to the Centre Party and gone to a great deal of trouble to create the impression that the newly discovered *modus vivendi* between the Curia and the government upheld the crucial rights of the state and tended to diminish the prospects of those who sought to undermine the state's authority, the rule of law and the foundations of modern civilization. Despite this, however, the majority of the National Liberals had been unable, with their former comrades-in-arms on the left wing of the liberal movement looking on, to bring themselves to vote for the government's Bill and so confirm the unity of the Cartel and its political dependability even in controversial areas. At the same time the right wing of the German Conservative Party had taken the opportunity to plead the cause of ecclesiastical orthodoxy by demanding a greater degree of independence for the Protestant Church as well.

Bismarck's former Young Conservative colleague, von Kleist-Retzow, had brought two Bills to this effect before the Upper House on 9 March. With these the German conservative right, not least with an eye to corresponding sections of the Centre Party, had openly sounded the call to reaction in church policy too. This had constituted a challenge both to the National Liberals and to many Free Conservatives. As a result, Bismarck had not only felt compelled sharply to reject the initiative in question; he eventually had to ask for what almost amounted to a vote of confidence in order to secure for the 'Peace Bill' a somewhat heterogeneous majority of Centrists, German Conservatives and Free Conservatives. 'My political honour is at stake here', he had told the Prussian House of Deputies on 21 April 1887. 'I can no longer be associated with a body politic that compromises me in this direction, if only because a large part of the influence I wield in Europe rests on people's faith in my political uprightness and reliability.'

This was heavy artillery to bring out in support of a Bill whose contents were relatively undramatic: it limited the church's obligation to notify the authorities to permanent appointments of parish priests, abolished the 1873 law restricting the church's right to administer its own punishments and readmitted virtually all ecclesiastical orders with the exception of the Jesuits, who were banned under imperial law. But its passage gave rise to conflicts and confrontations that were by no means easy to iron out. Thus the Chancellor had felt obliged to go even further than the question of confidence and to appeal to all the social fears and anxieties about the future that had been so instrumental in bringing the Cartel and its voters together. It was a question, he had declared, of securing their rear for the really decisive battles of the future. 'We may face grievous ordeals in the shape of conflicts abroad and conflicts at home against a variety of revolutionary parties. My desire has been to deal with all the internal squabbles that we can really do without before we are exposed to those ordeals. And one I feel we can do without is the ecclesiastical dispute, provided that it can be settled in this fashion.'[51]

However, even this appeal to revolution phobia and the national fear of encirclement had borne only limited fruit. The majority of the National Liberals had let him down. The rift running through the Cartel had become plain for all to see. Nor could the internal lines of communication and secret leanings between sections of the German Conservative and Centre parties be overlooked any longer. The government did manage to patch up the split shortly after this with the aid of a legislative manoeuvre aimed with extraordinary skill at the common interests of both sides. But it was clear by the autumn of 1887 that not even this community of material interests provided an adequate foundation any more.

The manoeuvre in question was a fresh government initiative in the matter of reforming the finances of the Reich. This time it was a new law regulating the tax on sugar and spirits, it too designed primarily to improve the imperial income. What made the Bill – to which the Cartel parties had already committed themselves in principle – so attractive as far as they were concerned was the tax relief it provided for medium-sized and small distilleries: below a certain level of output no tax was payable at all. This so-called 'Liebesgabe' (a 'gift of charity') benefited both the conservatives' clientele in the east and that of the National Liberals in southern and western

Germany. At the same time, however, it provided the opposition parties with additional arguments to present to a public that was still highly sensitive on the question of direct state subsidies and tax concessions to individual social groups.

Initially, however, the whole thing acted as a powerful clasp, not only drawing the Cartel parties together but more especially bringing them closer to not inconsiderable sections of their following, who saw this as vigorous confirmation of their electoral decision. But the government's very next step, taken in the autumn of 1887, promptly wrecked the first of those effects and indeed drove a deep wedge between the Cartel parties.

This took the form of a further massive increase in the duty on imported grain, bringing with it a sharp rise in the cost of living for non-agrarian sections of the population in particular; the import duties on wheat, rye and barley were in future to be almost five times what they had been set at in 1879, which meant that domestic prices, which for years had been falling, would have been fixed at a correspondingly inflated level. This immediately raised the question of where the coalition's basic interests lay and of whether it was in fact possible to achieve a genuine and mutually satisfactory balance between agrarian interests on the one hand and those of industry and trade on the other.

It was a question to which the National Liberals, for all their post-1884 reorientation, could no longer give a uniformly positive answer; the mood of the non-agrarian public and the election results since the 1879 change of direction in economic policy were too plain for that. 'It seems to us', the *Nationalzeitung* warned towards the middle of September, 'that the agrarian politicians are well on the way to driving sections of the population that do not as yet show a proper understanding of Social Democratic agitation, with the aid of a very much simpler train of thought, indeed by simply offending their natural feelings, into the camp of those opposed to the existing system of ownership.'[52] In the end the Cartel and National Liberal unity could be salvaged only by the old expedient of declaring a free vote.

In practice this meant that the Tariff Bills attracted a majority only because the Centre Party voted for them. It had become clear in the process that, in terms of concrete, material interests and ideas of order, the rather artificial coalition of National Liberals and German Conservatives, hinged together, as it were, by Free Conservatives, was opposed by an almost natural one comprising the German Conservatives and the Centre Party.

Bismarck could not fail to see this himself, of course. But to stake his political future on a 'black-blue' coalition of Centrists and German Conservatives was a practical impossibility for him – and not simply because of his whole political record; the attitude of the forces and personalities concerned, starting with Windthorst, also stood in the way of such a switch. If he did not wish voluntarily to resign his offices, Bismarck remained tied to a coalition whose community of interests was largely a thing of the past and which was bound by its very nature to evade all the really basic social and political issues currently outstanding. Its principle, for all the government's superficial activity, was a total opposition to progress. In the atmosphere thus engendered the Reich was in danger of suffocating.

This was the situation at the end of 1887, a year that with the formation of the Cartel and the so-called 'Cartel Election' had looked like promising yet another political new beginning under the leadership of the now nearly 73-year-old Chancellor – whatever one's view of that 'new beginning' in terms of its substance and underlying political tendency. At an earlier point in time those who saw it as being disastrously backward-looking would have found new hope. In fact they would have seen it as a real opportunity for a particularly swift and thoroughgoing change of direction following the crown prince's accession to the throne. In the mean time, however, virtually everyone in a position of political influence had come to realize that such a succession would at best usher in a brief political interlude: Frederick William, on whom so many had pinned their hopes, was incurably ill with cancer – Virchow's diagnosis to the contrary in May 1887 having by now been finally proved wrong. Prince William, the 90-year-old emperor's 28-year-old grandson, already stood on the steps of the throne.

He was a man the public knew little about as yet. But even that little was not such that those who had pinned their hopes and expectations on the father could now simply have transferred them to the son. This much was clear: the prince took his cue entirely from his grandfather, who for his part more and more openly placed his faith in the prince. Beyond that he was largely a product of the Prussian officers' mess and an arch-conservative social and political environment. The secret escapism of its younger members, with whom he was particularly intimate, Count Philipp Eulenburg at their head, merged with a variety of romantic fancies that reinforced a sense of monarchical mission already much in evidence from an early age.

He was further confirmed in this by the circle presided over by the court chaplain, Adolf Stoecker, who also directed his attention to the social responsibilities of the monarchy, to the task of reconciling the new masses with the state and with the crown. Such a reconciliation, according to Stoecker and his group, could be successfully accomplished only in close alliance with the forces of a religiously orthodox and politically arch-conservative Christianity and in unambiguous opposition to the abuses of modern capitalism and its representatives, the Jews. In party-political terms this amounted to a massive vote of confidence in a coalition of conservatives and Centrists and a blunt rejection of Bismarck's Cartel policy.

Here was the root of an initial conflict between the Chancellor and the cocky young prince who already saw himself wholly in the role of emperor and was beginning to count the days till his succession to the throne. In the late autumn of 1887 young William had taken part, as the public noted with interest, in a meeting held at the house of Count Waldersee on behalf of Stoecker's Berlin City Mission. Around the same time he had sent Bismarck a draft 'Proclamation Addressed to the Confederate Princes' on which he was already working and had asked for the Chancellor's comments. The two events prompted Bismarck to write the prince a long letter early in 1888, strongly urging a greater measure of political restraint.

Precisely in order that he might retain 'the requisite free hand' when he came to the throne it was necessary, the Chancellor told him, 'to prevent

195

Your Royal Highness from being regarded by the public as entertaining, while still heir to the throne, a particular party allegiance'. There would always be 'periods of liberalism and periods of reaction, even' – he slipped in – 'of despotism'. For this changing state of affairs the ruler, if he did not wish to place the monarchy in jeopardy one day, must always keep his hands free. Above all, however, the principle must be preserved that it was not parties and associations but the state alone that was the positive, organizing force in the life of society. And that state, as he stressed once again, must remain a state above party: 'In our case it is *only* the King as head of the authority of the State who, proceeding by *legislative* means, is qualified positively to initiate and uphold viable reforms.'

What he meant by all this in concrete terms, what his remarks were essentially aimed at he summed up at the end, apologizing for their length, in a sentence that rather devalued his ostensibly very high-minded point of view. 'I have suffered too much', he burst out, 'for the last twenty years from the venomous concoctions of the gentlemen of the *Kreuzzeitung* and the Protestant Windthorsts to be able to talk about them *in brief.*'[53]

Small wonder that the prince, who in the person of his grandfather's Chancellor had above all admired and continued to admire the 'Machtmensch', the resolute man of power, who was in other words himself under the spell of the emergent legend of the 'Iron Chancellor', should therefore have set all other considerations aside. Posing as the pupil who already knows more than his master, he in turn promptly put everything in the letter down to the Chancellor's personal power interests. And among his intimates – Eulenburg, Douglas, Helldorf, Hahnke, Waldersee – he was already making no secret of the fact that he was determined to disregard these. He even told Scholz, the Prussian Minister of Finance, as early as December 1887 that 'Prince Bismarck would of course be needed very urgently for a few years yet; later on his functions would be divided up, and the sovereign would have to shoulder more of them himself'.[54] 'I'll wind the old man for six months, then I'll govern myself' – so went the far more drastic version put about by Stoecker in the now famous 'Scheiterhaufenbrief' of 14 August 1888.[55] The conflict was as good as marked out in advance.

[16]

The End

'Looking back now', Bismarck summed up in the second volume of his memoirs, written in 1891 but not published until after his death, 'I take the view that, during the twenty-one months when I was his Chancellor, the Emperor stifled his inclination to be rid of an inherited mentor only with difficulty until it exploded.' That was indeed the situation; everything else arose out of it with inner logic. However, Bismarck's claim that it was only with hindsight that he became fully cognisant of the fact carries no more credibility than his comment that – 'had I been aware of the Emperor's wish' – he would spontaneously 'have instituted a separation with careful regard to all outward impressions'.[1]

For years already, almost for decades Bismarck had borne constantly in mind, in all his deliberations, the possibility of a change of sovereign. His concern the whole time had been to survive this, all desires for policy and personnel changes notwithstanding, by making himself politically indispensable. He had opposed every move to 'be rid of' him with a grim determination to remain in office for as long as possible. Among the possibilities he had always allowed for was even that of a power-political confrontation. The time was long gone when he had flung at the crown prince, the future Emperor Frederick, that he could wish for him only that he should 'find such loyal servants as I am to your father. I do *not* intend to be one of them.'[2] He had long since adjusted to the idea of remaining in office even under him. And what had been true with regard to the previous heir to the throne was naturally true with regard to the new one. As he declared at the beginning of June 1888, already with Prince William in mind: 'One ought not to console oneself in such situations by saying: never mind if everything goes wrong, why were we treated so badly and ordered out of office!' He would 'cling fast to his chair and not go even if they tried to throw him out'. Nor would he go 'even if they sent his dismissal to his home address because he had not counter-signed it'. He had 'had too many fierce battles with his late master to go lightly'.[3] And two months later, in a letter to Finance Minister Scholz, he wrote: 'In my long service as a minister I have always found that the hardest tasks of diplomacy lie in relations with one's own court.' One must 'get used to the young master' too.[4]

Once again, speculation as to how far Bismarck would if necessary have been prepared to take this confrontation leads us away from the concrete problems. What matters is not what Bismarck was prepared to do but what it was actually possible for him to do. From this standpoint the confrontation and the course it took become a mirror-image of the circumstances actually obtaining, the distribution of forces, the various coalitions and fronts, and not least the views and expectations entertained by the different forces and camps. It is in this perspective that the personal power conflict assumes its supra-personal substance and its supra-personal significance and the purely individual element becomes fused, in that conflict, with something that reached far beyond it. In other words, it is only by refusing to adopt the point of view and personal bias of either the young emperor or Bismarck and by bearing in mind that the conflict acted as a nucleus of crystallization for very much deeper-seated antagonisms and forces that we shall do justice to the true dimensions of this whole episode.

William I died on 9 March 1888 at the age of nearly 91. Many people had been asking themselves the macabre question whether they would ever in fact see the crown prince on the throne or whether the father would outlive his son. Everybody's thoughts were already centred on the grandson. The tragic and embarrassing aspects of the situation became almost unbearably interwoven. Already virtually incapacitated for all practical purposes, cut off from any earthly future, Frederick III seemed, when he finally acceded, no more than a symbol of hopes and expectations that had been disappointed for so long. As if to underline this, his one independent act as head of government consisted in the mainly demonstrative dismissal of the arch-conservative Prussian Minister of the Interior, Robert von Puttkamer – the implication being that this was the way things would have gone had fate left him the time.

This act, together with corresponding remarks and expressions of intent dating from his days as crown prince, became the basis of a legend that grew up rapidly after his death on 15 June 1888. With Frederick, it was believed, everything would have taken a quite different course. With him Germany would have followed the British path of national and constitutional development and the Reich would yet have been granted that era of liberalism whose non-appearance had had such disastrous consequences.

None of which, of course, is susceptible of proof. Moreover, it undoubtedly rests on a colossal overestimate of one individual's chances against the given conditions and the pronounced trends of development of his time. Yet in the way in which it focused and gave expression to certain expectations and polarized opinion it developed a force of its own.

That force was something with which the political *dramatis personae* of the day had to grapple, foremost among them Bismarck on the one hand and the new emperor, William II, on the other. For the latter this involved a kind of self-affirmation in a tragically heightened generation conflict. For Bismarck, however, it was a far more serious question of a polarization that made his own position look wholly anachronistic and lacking in any future, thus providing the young emperor with additional weapons to use against him.

In league with a monarch born in the last century, it was argued on the one hand, Bismarck had for all his indubitable merits in many respects attempted to halt the wheel of time. When at last an opportunity had presented itself of breaking through, on the initiative of the head of state, into a liberal future in line with the modern trend, Frederick's fatal illness had put paid to everything. And on the other hand it was argued that, rather than be guided by such long-obsolete alternatives as Emperor Frederick had embodied, the nation must seek new avenues to the future. The future belonged neither to liberalism nor to other movements of that ilk but to those who on the basis of a tried and tested status quo were facing the real problems. For this, of course, the present Chancellor, whatever his achievements in the past, was too old, too tired and too deeply involved in struggles and problems that had long belonged to that past.

Over and above mere claims to power and transparent party-political calculations this gave rise, in a pronounced break with the alternatives of the past, to a new dynamic, an attitude of expectation, albeit one that was somewhat vague as to concrete objectives and therefore capable of being mobilized in a number of different directions. Increasingly it became focused on the figure of the new emperor and looked to him for the hoped-for fundamental 'fresh start'. This tendency was not associated with any firmly established plans or clear-cut party positions. Furthermore, its illusive and indeed irrational character rapidly became apparent and eventually spilled over into some very dubious channels. For these reasons it has often been underestimated by historians. But the man whom it really affected, the over 70-year-old Chancellor whom the death of Frederick III seemed to have delivered from the really acute danger, had a very clear awareness of the threat that this sense of a new departure held for himself. The two factors associated with the death of Emperor Frederick, the resignation on the one hand and the emergent legend on the other, might all too easily bring about a sudden change and lead to the formation of a common front – albeit from a variety of motives – against him, the Chancellor. This might then make the emperor look like someone who was freeing the nation from the burden of the past.

Only on this basis is it possible to understand why, with Frederick III barely in his grave, Bismarck embarked on some thoroughly petty, not to say pitiful manoeuvres in an attempt to keep the two fronts apart and deepen the gulf between them. He began by stepping up his long-running campaign to exacerbate the existing differences between the new emperor and his mother. He missed no opportunity of dressing these up as questions of fundamental political principle to which the son's filial obligations had to give way. Things reached an initial climax when Bismarck caused legal proceedings to be instituted to prevent the publication of extracts from the diary of Emperor Frederick III dating from the period of the Franco-Prussian War, extracts of whose authenticity even he was in no doubt. His official argument was that the material had been forged in an attempt to misuse the high regard in which the late emperor was held in order to further the efforts of forces hostile to the Reich.

Bismarck had obtained the young emperor's consent to this course by hinting at allegedly threatened national interests and above all by discreetly suggesting that this placing of his father on a pedestal of liberal legend did his own position no good, nor did it favour the requisite focusing of present expectations on himself. William II changed his mind, however, as soon as it became clear that public reaction to the whole affair was extremely negative. What impressed him particularly was the consideration – voiced even in conservative circles – that Bismarck's scarcely veiled attacks on the late emperor were likely to do general harm to the monarchical idea. So he quickly dissociated himself from his Chancellor's action.

In the end the episode back-fired as far as Bismarck was concerned. It united a number of very diverse forces against him and made him look petty to a degree that repelled the very people whose admiration for his ruthless use of power was in principle so great. For the justification had always been that such ruthlessness served great ends. In this case, however, there could be no question of any such thing. The almost universal view of the situation was that here was a man clinging to power by any and every means and seeking to exploit an undoubtedly inexperienced but also less power-obsessed, more idealistically minded young monarch.

There was also the fact that, following the domestic and foreign policy crises of 1887 and the two changes of sovereign in 1888 with their attendant atmosphere of unease, something like a climate of stagnation, indeed an almost total freeze had set in both at home and in foreign affairs. A numbing and at the same time alarming silence dominated the political scene. In it the conflicts associated with the dispute about the dead emperor's diary had a positively eerie quality. They heightened the impression that, as Ludwig Bamberger put it dramatically around this time, the Reich and its people were now politically, intellectually and above all from the human point of view 'living in a dog-kennel'.[5]

This was the situation in which the conflict proper between emperor and Chancellor began to unfold. From the outset it clearly favoured the position of the young monarch. But if Bismarck had an instinctive feeling for anything it was for the character of particular constellations, for the lie of the political land, above all for the distribution of views and opinions. Accordingly he very deliberately selected, in the context of what was available, the arena in which the decision was eventually to be reached. That is to say, there can be no question of his having been surprised by circumstances or by the skill of his immediate adversary, the young emperor.

Bismarck owed his whole political position, his unique position of power in the Prussian and subsequently in the German state to a situation in which the existing political order, the primacy of the monarchical authority but also of the traditional elites in state, army and society, had been massively endangered. With his policy he had successfully averted those dangers. At the same time, however, he had always taken great care not to appear too successful, be it in the eyes of the outside world or, more particularly, in those of the emperor and the latter's other advisers. Consequently at almost no time in his nearly twenty-seven years in office as Minister-President of Prussia and subsequently Chancellor of the Reich had there been no talk of deadly dangers threatening the continued existence of state and society.

It is often hard to say, in a given case, when he did not believe in such dangers at all himself but was merely exploiting corresponding fears and anxieties entertained by others. But there is no mistaking the fact that he managed over and over again to convey and to confirm the impression that state and society were teetering on the brink of an abyss and that the chief task of all politics was to throw up dams and take every sort of precaution in order at least to postpone their fall. At times he managed it very successfully, at others less so. The law of diminishing returns led to many of his political opponents no longer taking seriously what were undoubtedly genuine fears on his part. But, as the events of the 'Cartel election' had made clear, this was still and would always remain a central and – despite many disappointments – favourite political principle of his. In this situation too, the thought that immediately suggested itself to him was that he should use that principle to make himself indispensable.

Foreign policy offered no opportunities here. Bismarck had his hands full, trying with his ultimately unsuccessful offer of an alliance to Britain in January 1889 and by emphasizing the provisional character of the Reinsurance Treaty to undermine the arguments of the critics in his own camp and answer the charge that he was inflexible and allowed himself to be guided solely by the past. Moreover, since the dismissal of General Boulanger and the sorry end of his movement the French card had become virtually worthless. There was also the fact that, since Bismarck's manoeuvres in 1887, the top military leadership around the emperor, headed by the new chief of staff, Count Waldersee, regarded him with more than scepticism in this respect.

As things stood, therefore, any exploitation of foreign policy for domestic purposes was largely ruled out. Nor did Bismarck seriously contemplate even now forcing a change in the basic foreign policy situation with the object of exploiting the new circumstances accordingly. This left only the field of home affairs and only one corner of that field in which his own indispensability could be demonstrated with any hope of success by dropping hints about a possible collapse of all order. That corner was the social question, or to be more precise the mounting tension between the propertied classes of whatever kind on the one hand and the growing army of the unpropertied on the other – in all more than two-thirds of the population, who even when they had jobs and food were often living at subsistence level, having to make do with an average yearly wage of 650 marks, little more than a tenth of the salary of a Prussian *Regierungsrat*, or one-fiftieth of that of a minister.

It must remain an open question whether Bismarck regarded an explosion as ultimately unavoidable, whether he seriously believed in a secret antagonism between leaders and led in the unpropertied camp, which was to say primarily the working class, or whether he even shared the optimists' assumption that the whole problem, at least in its acute form, would as it were solve itself in the wake of increasing economic prosperity. On the other hand recent research in particular has made abundantly clear the extent to which he exploited circumstances in the field of home affairs in order to rescue his position, consolidate it once more and render himself indispensable.

201

He was aware that not only the young emperor and his circle but also a majority among the public and no doubt among the parties too started out from the need for some sort of settlement, if only limited in extent, with the working class and the forces representing it. The prevailing opinion in many quarters was that simple repression must be replaced by a policy of cautious co-operation and carefully measured compromises if the governing classes did not wish to call down the catastrophe of political and social upheaval on themselves. 'Not only justice and equity' favoured a new course, according to the *Frankfurter Zeitung*, but also 'calculation and good sense'.[6]

Resistance to this from the right, principally from those with an immediate interest, was admittedly as strong and politically influential as ever. Nor can it have seemed entirely out of the question that a broader base might once again be found for it in parliamentary terms as well. However, Bismarck doubtless took the possible failure of such endeavours soberly into account from the outset, promptly setting up a kind of second front behind the first and evolving an alternative plan of action for it. The first plan aimed to mobilize revolution phobia; it was directed at people's fear of social upheaval and at their desire to avert the dangers thereof by taking direct action to suppress threatening elements. The Progressive Party, he warned at a meeting of the Crown Council in mid-March 1889, was 'well on the way towards amalgamating' with the Social Democrats, and 'even the democrats within the Centre [Party] belonged with them'; everything now depended on the government's determination to act.[7] The second plan consisted in blocking alternatives by depriving them of any conceivable parliamentary base. In other words, Bismarck did not shrink from deliberately provoking chaos on the domestic front with the object of subsequently figuring as the nation's saviour in time of need.

His efforts to maintain his position at the head of a defensive front against an allegedly imminent revolution found a most welcome pretext in the shape of a miners' strike that broke out in Gelsenkirchen early in May 1889. The strike swept right through the Ruhr district and quickly spread to all the German coalfields, leading in many places to bloody clashes. Bismarck immediately argued in favour of leaving it to the participants to settle the conflict and against having the state intervene in support of either side. He would regard it as 'politically useful', he explained to a meeting of the Prussian Cabinet held on 12 May 1889 and presided over by the emperor, who promptly took a very strong line, if 'a settlement of this dispute and its deplorable consequences were not effected too smoothly and swiftly but rather that the latter should make themselves more keenly felt among the liberal bourgeoisie', who 'always assume that the government suffers more from Social Democracy than the citizens do and that if the movement becomes serious the government suppresses it by force if need be, in other words preventive legislation is not even particularly necessary'.[8]

With regard to the material question of the justice of the miners' wage demands, Bismarck appeared to place himself entirely on the side of the emperor, who strongly favoured the miners' standpoint and advocated putting ostentatious pressure on the employers. It looked on the face of it as if the Chancellor was arguing in favour of restraint for purely tactical reasons in order eventually to kill two birds with one stone: to make the employers give in and to point out to them and to the entire middle-class public how necessary it was, in their own interests, to take preventive measures lest such a strike should one day, exploited by Social Democratic agitators, get completely out of hand.

In reality Bismarck, confident of the power of the state, was all for the strike movement 'getting out of hand' to some extent. Before long he was noting with great satisfaction how the emperor, who at first had so strongly advocated intervening in favour of the employees, began to back-track and to suggest suppressing the strike by force. As he repeated with an unmistakable note of triumph at a meeting of the Cabinet a fortnight later, he thought it 'best, for the common good and in the interests of preventing repetitions and promoting a proper understanding of the futility and universally calamitous consequences of such withdrawals of labour, if one lets the fire burn itself out, as it were, rather than quenches it by force. In the latter event', he went on, not without a certain secret irony in the face of the vacillations of the young emperor, 'one arouses in the workers a feeling that they have been prevented from doing better for themselves only by unlawful repression on the part of the state. By allowing things as far as possible to take their course one earns laurels for having acted in strict accordance with the law, without resorting to discriminatory measures, and stands the best chance of showing the troublemakers up as absurd.' However, he was careful to add, he had 'no objections whatever' to using the most powerful weapons at the state's disposal – including, if necessary, declaring a state of siege. He was ready at any time personally to assume responsibility for this – '*provided* such a measure proves appropriate'.[9]

Granted, in the further course of events William II succeeded in gaining some personal prestige through his support for certain of the strikers' demands, a fact that at the same time gave a boost to a policy of social compromise. But politically Bismarck could feel for the time being that he had won. Fear of the consequences of such a policy had been aroused along a broad front. And the emperor himself had received a first-hand impression of how hard it was to hold the ship of state firmly on course in a heavy sea.

That impression would have quenched his thirst for action for a while and qualified his desire to get rid of an experienced helmsman as soon as possible. Bismarck observed sarcastically at the time that 'the young master' shared the 'views of Frederick William I with regard to his powers' and that it was 'very necessary' to protect him 'against precipitate actions in this respect'.[10] Certainly William stuck consistently to his line of a policy of social compromise: backed up by his social policy advisers, chief among them his former tutor, Georg Hinzpeter, and the president of the Rhine province, Baron von Berlepsch, he concentrated most of his efforts in the ensuing months on planning an initiative in the field of legislation for the protection of labour. As far as the period immediately following the miners' strike is concerned, however, it is only to a very limited degree that we can speak of a deliberate collision course vis-à-vis his Chancellor. Moves in that direction came much more from Bismarck himself during these months. Increasing his stake, so to speak, the Chancellor sought for his part to commit the new monarch, who had become noticeably unsure of himself at times, to himself and to his policy.

The climax came on 25 October 1889 when Bismarck presented to the Imperial Diet, whose legislative period expired in a matter of months, a Bill for an unlimited extension of the Anti-Socialist Law. The implication was that the continued suppression of the socialist movement must have absolute priority over all attempts to take up a mediatory position in labour relations and improve the material situation of workers generally by legislative means. Only the state – strong, above any kind of extortion and legally endowed with the means required to enforce its will – was truly able to mediate and at the same time to command the allegiance of all political and social groups.

If under the influence of the miners' strike the majority in the Diet were to accept this line of argument, that would knock the bottom out of any policy of genuine social compromise. It would mean that the state was now permanently a repressive instrument in the hands of a single class. If it did not accept it, that would be the end not only of the current government majority but also of any potential government majority that did not include the liberal left and with it the followers of Emperor Frederick.

Bismarck knew full well that William II was not prepared to accept such a coalition. He calculated accordingly that the emperor would be left with no alternative but a resolutely right-wing course over the heads of the parties. This must, however, embrace at least a readiness, should the need arise, not only to ignore the opposition of the Diet but even to set aside the constitution. In other words, either outcome – an unlimited extension of the Anti-Socialist Law or the consequences of a rejection of the government's Bill – would commit the emperor firmly to him. In any event it would become impossible for him, in so critical a situation, to repudiate his Chancellor.

Apart from its many other weaknesses, such as its author's increasing tendency to see everyone around him as mere marionettes, that calculation was marred by one absolutely crucial flaw: in spite of the Chancellor's knowledge of human nature and his scepticism with regard to the character of the young emperor, it underestimated William's will to power and yearning for recognition as well as his totally self-centred lack of any wider concern. These qualities prevented William from paying any serious attention to the question of the inner homogeneity and political viability of the forces and tendencies that for a time, chiefly in opposition to the Chancellor, mustered behind him and placed their hopes in him. He enjoyed the expectations that became focused on himself without worrying about their mutually contradictory nature. And he fancied himself in the role of the man of the future without wasting too much concrete thought on what form that future might take. He thus eluded virtually every reasoned conjecture and left Bismarck making his ever riskier manoeuvres on his own. Without William's noticing it, the Chancellor started to become more and more entangled in his own net, a net whose meshes no longer found a purchase, as it were, on a counter-position of any kind.

At the same time this points to the truly fateful aspect of the whole affair. When Bismarck fell, the real concern of those who toppled him was not at all with the future or with any sort of forward-looking alternative but almost exclusively with what the ageing Chancellor himself so stubbornly clung to, namely power as such, and not least the outward appearances and trappings of power. Everything that, beyond the circle of the principal protagonists, was invested in the conflict in terms of concrete interests and broader expectations, far-reaching hopes and fears, and ideas regarding certain immensely important decisions of principle that were involved here – all that was swiftly disappointed almost *in toto*. The cynicism of power and the conceited stupidity of most of those who wielded it became increasingly apparent as people made less and less effort to conceal them. And against this distasteful background attitudes towards the first Chancellor of the Reich changed very fast – especially among the very people who had greeted his fall with a sigh of relief. In his case, so it now appeared, power had at least been harnessed for much of the time to a plan, a conception, clear ideas of order and of what was to be aimed at, even if all or some of these were things one had passionately opposed. With him all had not been mere show, blind selfishness, an end in itself. With him power had in spite of everything been subject to a certain control by elements existing in a higher plane.

This was the basis of the Bismarck legend that began to emerge very soon after the Chancellor's dismissal. It weighed on subsequent developments no less than did the young Emperor and his associates with their zigzag course and roving search for recognition. Systematically promoted by Bismarck, it increasingly concealed the fact that in the end the Chancellor, a spent force with no serious prospects, had likewise been concerned solely with self-preservation, that is to say with maintaining his office and his position as such. It concealed the fact that here too William II was conducting himself as his faithful pupil. 'Had the Emperor put up with him in office for only a short while longer', wrote Gustav Freytag five years after Bismarck's fall, describing the actual situation as clear-sightedly as the subsequent change in people's evaluation of it, 'he would have worn himself out on Prussian aristocrats, Ultramontanes and Socialists and his departure, when it came, would have been a lasting bitterness. Now, however, the very thing that seemed to him the greatest smart and to the rest of us his undoing has become the exaltation of his old age. A popularity and a mobilization of universal gratitude such as no German has ever enjoyed before. His dismissal has turned out to have been his last great stroke of luck, his atonement.'[11]

Freytag's words reflect the outcome, following the bitter experiences and disenchantment of a large part of the nation, of a total reversal of the situation in 1889–90. At that time Bismarck's intriguing and his senile clinging to power had constituted as it were the dark background that threw into radiant relief the figure of the young emperor and the expectations he aroused. Now, five years on, his own figure gilded what many had already forgotten had been a past without any kind of future. In this way his fall eventually became a richly embroidered legend persisting right into our own day.

And yet to the sober observer the course and character of the entire episode are plain to see, even without the additional sources and details that have come to light subsequently. In presenting his Bill for an unlimited extension of the Anti-Socialist Law towards the end of October 1889 Bismarck had seized the initiative and opened the decisive battle. This was true with regard not only to his relationship with the emperor but also, very much bound up with that, to his relations with the Cartel parties that had constituted his support since 1887 but that were becoming more and more difficult to hold together as a coalition. In marked contrast to his political practice over many years he now, clearly encouraged by the emperor's vacillating approach to the miners' strike, flew a very definite flag. In this he was guided by the expectation that doing so would enable him to open up various avenues for himself while blocking all those available to his opponents.

Either, he reckoned, the Cartel would follow him, in which case every political alternative that was not oriented towards the left would in practice be ruled out. Or his National Liberal wing would let him down, in which case the forthcoming election could be fought under a slogan to the effect that the existing order was seriously threatened. If the slogan worked, his election victory would put him in a virtually unassailable position as far as the right was concerned. If it did not, then a man of his experience and authority would appear doubly indispensable in the eyes of the intimidated right and the young emperor.

Because no matter how popular William's advocacy of a policy of social compromise with the state mediating between the conflicting interests and no matter how controversial Bismarck's own line on social policy, forming anything like a politically homogeneous majority behind a compromise programme was not even a remote possibility. Therefore to advocate such a policy, as Bismarck now more and more openly gave William to understand, was to betray crass political inexperience. It reflected a futile striving for popularity that was bound to be followed swiftly by disillusionment and a backlash in public opinion against the imperial advocate of that policy. After all, among his intimates the emperor left no one in any doubt that a radical, sweeping change of political course was certainly not his aim.

The flash-point – and probably the 'irreparable breach', as Robert Lucius noted at the time[12] – came when at the Crown Council meeting of 24 January 1890 Bismarck brushed aside as mere suggestions the emperor's plans for a labour protection programme, which William set forth on this occasion as his own ideas. Instead the Chancellor insisted on absolute priority for a policy of harsh repression directed against the Social Democrats.

The Imperial Diet had to decide next day about a continuation of that policy in the shape of an unlimited extension of the Anti-Socialist Law.

Following protracted negotiations among the coalition partners, negotiations that centred on the very principle of the coalition, it now appeared that if the government gave in on one detail, namely the question of the expulsion of socialist 'agitators', a Cartel majority was assured, despite some determined resistance within the ranks of the Cartel parties. Bismarck, however, in opposition not only to the emperor but also to most of his ministerial colleagues, rejected any kind of compromise. He was neither prepared to agree to the repeal of the expulsion clause, as demanded by the majority of the National Liberals, nor would he have any part in a confidential government declaration to the effect that, should the Diet carry such a repeal on its own initiative, this should not be allowed to wreck the Bill.

Such a declaration had been demanded by the conservatives, and William II expressly endorsed it. Nevertheless, at the Crown Council meeting of 24 January 1890 Bismarck told him in the strongest possible terms that that kind of 'softness' would have 'fateful consequences'. If the emperor was 'of a different opinion over a matter of such importance', he went on, then he, Bismarck, was 'doubtless no longer in the right place'. Were the Bill not adopted in the form proposed by the government, they must – he absolutely insisted – 'do without it and let the waves get up higher'. In that event, however, a 'collision' could not be ruled out.[13]

William was of course well aware of the way in which his Chancellor was trying to manoeuvre him into a corner. His reaction was correspondingly heated. As Lucius noted down his reply, he wished 'to steer clear of such an extreme emergency and forestall such catastrophes as far as possible by preventive measures rather than stain the first years of his reign with his subjects' blood'. However, his attempt to win the support of a majority in the Cabinet for his position and so isolate Bismarck was foiled by the obvious reluctance of most ministers to commit themselves before the dice seemed finally cast. The emperor was obliged to look on in impotent rage while the Chancellor's inflexible stance in practice carried the day. For he could not and would not risk bringing about Bismarck's fall in defiance of the right, which as far as the principle of the matter was concerned did in fact support the Chancellor over this issue.

Predictably, the absence of the government declaration demanded by the conservatives led the following day to the Bill to make the Anti-Socialist Law permanent being thrown out by an extremely heterogeneous majority composed of German Conservatives, Centrists, German Liberals and Social Democrats. It was the death-blow for the Cartel. Forming a parliamentary majority from the right had clearly become an impossibility, and the state and the social order appeared to be at the mercy of the threat from the far left. Worse than that, there was no practicable watchword with which a new government majority might have been mobilized and won over in the forthcoming election. For neither a permanent Anti-Socialist Law nor a policy of limited material concessions on the social question without politically involving any forces left of centre could draw on an adequate reservoir of voters. The inevitable impression was that Bismarck and his policy of total intransigence had plunged the country into chaos by placing it in a situation in which it could well become ungovernable by parliamentary methods in the context of the present constitution. A serious constitutional crisis could no longer be ruled out.

The suspicion did rather suggest itself that the Chancellor had quite deliberately risked such a crisis in order subsequently to appear as the only possible saviour in time of need and to make himself virtually indispensable. As the envoy from Baden and later secretary of state von Marschall wrote at the height of the crisis in a letter to Philipp Eulenberg, the emperor's closest confidant, Bismarck was seeking 'to conduct domestic policy not along the lines of reform but in the direction of scandal, provocation and confusion'. As a result – and this was perhaps his true objective – a moment might come 'when the propertied classes see the Imperial Chancellor as their one friend in need'.[14]

In fact such an estimate of the situation positively obtruded itself, and this of course at the same time threatened the success of the whole manoeuvre. Only if Bismarck managed, in the run-up to this crucial election, to convince at least the emperor and his immediate circle that he had himself been surprised and upset by the turn events had taken was that kind of success conceivable. In the light of which there is a perfectly simple explanation for his apparent surrender after the vote in the Diet on 25 January, a move that bewildered so many at the time as it has continued to do subsequently. It was intended purely and simply to demonstrate his goodwill. It was meant to parry any suspicion of deliberate control of and manipulation of a development that he almost certainly foresaw and secretly encouraged.

The very next day, on 26 January, he told the Prussian Cabinet, in an abrupt reversal of his inflexible stance in the Crown Council two days previously, that he was after all willing to go along with the social policy being promulgated by the emperor. Perhaps there really was something in it, and in any case one must 'adjust oneself to the monarch as to the weather', which one was likewise powerless to do anything about.[15] And to remove all doubts about his change of mind he stood down from the Ministry of Commerce in favour of Baron von Berlepsch, the emperor's most experienced social policy adviser in terms of practical politics. On top of which he surprised his ministerial colleagues with the announcement that he intended before long to concentrate entirely on the Foreign Office, in other words on the management of foreign policy, and to give up all his Prussian offices; he had in mind 20 February, the day of the election. He spent the next few days working enthusiastically on his contribution to two imperial edicts in which William meant to announce the new social policy in bold and attractive terms.

When it came to it, however, he used some thoroughly threadbare pretexts to back out of counter-signing those edicts, which were published on 5 February. Moreover, in his diplomatic dealings not only with German but also with foreign envoys he made no secret of his criticisms of certain details of the labour protection programme. The whole thing should really be termed 'labour coercion laws' ('Arbeiterzwangsgesetze' instead of 'Arbeiterschutzgesetze'), for they prevented the worker from using his labour as he wished, he told the Saxon envoy, Count Hohenthal. In any case the social question was 'not to be solved with rose water but called for blood and iron'.[16]

The emperor and his circle, however, were able to construe these as mere side-effects of acquiescence and submission and as attempts to save face. For Bismarck continued to stress his readiness to retire from the field of domestic affairs. He even went as far as to broach the subject of a possible successor, actually mentioning General Caprivi. It was a colossal exaggeration – and one which, quoted repeatedly, often in a truncated form, puts the situation at the time in a wholly false light – when the French ambassador, Jules Herbette, concluded after a conversation with the Chancellor on 10 February in which the latter had expressed his scepticism with regard to a plan elaborated by William II for an international conference on labour protection to take place in Berlin: 'The Chancellor showed unequivocal opposition to his sovereign's views.'[17] The suggestion that preference be given to a long-standing Swiss proposal for a conference on the same subject in Bern could equally well be interpreted as an attempt to protect his monarch by diplomatic means from the incalculable domestic and foreign policy problems to which such a conference might have given rise.

Bismarck was most certainly neither so intemperate nor so short-sighted as to take into his confidence the diplomatic representative of France, of all countries. Nor is it clear for what purpose he may have been trying to use him. It was one thing to ensure, by skilfully exploiting the situation, that the emperor had no choice but to retain him as Chancellor. It was quite another to seek a direct clash and a trial of strength with him. Such a clash, given the traditional as well as the constitutional power of the Prusso-German monarch, would have been a wholly senseless enterprise. Its ultimate and quite unthinkable consequence must inevitably have been the collapse of the Hohenzollern dynasty. The only policy that made sense was to show William II that – for all his Chancellor's readiness to pursue the imperial proposals as far as was possible – sheer force of circumstances and an uncontrollable trend left only one viable course: that of open confrontation and a trial of strength with the Imperial Diet, including a readiness to resort to a *coup d'état*.

In the run-up to the crucial election of 20 February Bismarck consistently pursued such a policy to the point where, again contrary to his original stance, he declared himself ready to back a fresh major Army Bill abandoning the septennate. It was to be expected that such a Bill would in any case meet with massive resistance in the Diet. In other words, it would even further aggravate the difficulties the government could anticipate having with that body, whatever its composition. But Bismarck was not concerned with the question of practicability and the foreseeable consequences. All he was concerned with was convincing the emperor of his good intentions in the confident expectation that, given the real constellation of forces and the internal contradictions in the emperor's programme, things would turn out very differently in practice, making him master of the situation once again.

Consequently he saw the outcome of the election of 20 February 1890 not as the beginning of the end but as positively welcome proof of what a confused and self-contradictory policy threatened to lead to, namely the dissolution of any conceivable parliamentary base and hence the blocking of every political possibility – unless it was decided to pursue a strong-arm policy that stretched the constitution to the limit if not beyond.

Reassembling the Cartel, with whatever distribution of political weight within it, was now out of the question. Its two main pillars, the Free Conservatives and the National Liberals, had virtually collapsed. Retaining fewer than half their previous number of seats each, the two parties recorded their worst results ever. They dropped back, as in 1881, below the total of seats won by the left-wing liberal groups now united in the German Liberal Party. These recovered completely from their slump of 1887 to regain their 1884 total of sixty-six seats. But the big upset was the Social Democrats' shooting from eleven seats to thirty-five. Moreover, it was common knowledge that only the increasingly unjust constituency boundaries, the conditions of absolute majority suffrage and the coalitions that virtually all other political groups formed against them had prevented a parliamentary landslide in their favour. With nearly 20 per cent of the vote the Social Democrats were the best-supported party in the Reich. They had attracted even more votes than the Centre Party, which with 106 seats was celebrating the greatest electoral victory of its existence and had now become politically indispensable.

This last Bismarck had foreseen with a fair degree of certainty. His real worry was that the Centrists and the German Conservatives, particularly given the enormously increased pressure from the left, might reach an understanding that bypassed himself. It was with this in mind that he drew the attention of William II, in a direct report written on the very day of the election, to an electoral battle that Centrists and conservatives had been fighting with particular vehemence in a constituency in Westphalia. The 'phenomenon', he remarked, was 'of especial interest politically' because 'it brings to light the desire of the democratic, Guelfic elements in the Centre [Party], as led by Windthorst, to force the conservative Catholics out of the Centre and democratize the parliamentary party'. In this they had not shrunk from 'discrediting' the conservative candidate and previous deputy for the constituency with the accusation that he had 'voted for the septennate, the [Anti-] Socialist Law, the Disability Bill and the army and navy appropriations'.[18]

The conclusion that the emperor was meant to draw from this was that a government coalition with the Centre Party would mean opening the door to a gradual process of political and social upheaval. The sole alternative – such was the substance of all Bismarck's utterances in the days that followed – was a policy of containment pursued to a large extent independently of the Imperial Diet and the parties and directed not only against the current powerful thrust of Social Democracy but against all forces that did not profess clear and unreserved support for the government and the programme it must now reformulate.

Bismarck agreed the broad lines of that programme only a matter of days later with an emperor who on the one hand was stunned by the outcome of the election and on the other was handled by his Chancellor with consummate skill. In addition to the labour protection programme, which Bismarck promised to back with all his strength, there was to be an even stricter Anti–Socialist Law making it possible to ban 'socialist agitators' not only from their place of residence but also from the country, formally depriving them of their citizenship. Furthermore, the Army Bill was deliberately to be made a touchstone of the parties' loyalty to the Reich and readiness to co-operate with the government.

With this the new emperor too appeared, under pressure from a parliamentary situation that had clearly got quite out of hand, once again to have placed himself unequivocally behind his Chancellor. The latter for his part did his best to make it look as if he, the Chancellor, had now finally bowed to the imperial will, particularly over the question of labour protection, so dear to the emperor's heart. Granted, he almost simultaneously – on 24 February – drew the attention of the man chiefly responsible for the labour protection programme, the new Minister of Commerce, von Berlepsch, to a Cabinet order of Frederick William IV whereby the Prussian Minister-President was to be involved in all direct official contacts between the monarch and his ministers, with the exception of those between the Crown and the War Minister. But he gave the whole thing a thoroughly innocuous and indeed, from the emperor's point of view, positive justification. It was purely and simply a question of safeguarding the close understanding and uninterrupted co-operation between emperor and Chancellor that were so indispensable in the present situation and of guaranteeing the consistent implementation of the imperial will.

It was possible, of course, to put a very different interpretation on it. It was possible to see it as an attempt on the part of the politically very much more experienced and resourceful Chancellor to tie the young emperor down to a predetermined programme and to a Cabinet majority committed to its chief, so preventing him from launching any effective political initiatives of his own. This was the interpretation quickly adopted by William II. After Bismarck had brought the order to the attention of the remaining ministers at a Cabinet meeting on 2 March and had a copy of it circulated to them on 4 March, William increasingly inflated the whole thing into an assault on his royal and imperial rights and indeed on the monarchical principle itself. 'Those who . . . oppose me', he declared belligerently in a speech given at a banquet of the Provincial Diet of Brandenburg on 5 March, 'I shall smash to pieces.'[19] In the end he issued an ultimatum demanding Bismarck's agreement to an abrogation of the order and in this way, since it could be predicted that the Chancellor would refuse, at last compelled him to tender his resignation.

The clash over the Cabinet order was not, however, the cause but an effect or outward manifestation of the ever more rapid disintegration, both in substance and personally, of the understanding apparently reached on 25 February. From the emperor's point of view that understanding had been based on his assumption that Bismarck had clearly been correct in his predictions and in his assessments of the situation and that the state threatened to become ungovernable without him. A separation from him could thus turn out to be a fiasco of enormous embarrassment to the monarch himself. However, in the course of a great many conversations in the days that followed and in the light of reactions in the press that assumption had progressively broken down. The country threatened to become ungovernable not without Bismarck but because of him – that was the impression that emerged not least from the remarks of the various party leaders.

In reaction to the election result a kind of negative coalition formed both in the public mind and within and among the parties, drawing together all those who felt threatened in one way or another by the Chancellor's bewildering manoeuvres and unscrupulous Machiavellism. What that coalition urgently desired was to escape at last from the total unpredictability of developments and political relationships. At the same time it placed more and more faith in the emperor, who for his part was only too ready to be swept along by it. It was one of the great ironies of history that, of all the party-political forces, the leadership of the parliamentary Centre Party under Windthorst was the only one to speak up, behind the scenes, in favour of Bismarck's remaining in office. Of course, when the Chancellor tried to take advantage of this and opened negotiations with Windthorst, it only hastened his fall.

Bismarck can hardly have been in any doubt as to the risk involved in his taking so extremely unusual a step. His attempt to make the Centre Party the nucleus of crystallization for a new centre-right coalition under his leadership was therefore little more than an act of desperation. Windthorst saw the situation very clearly when after an interview with Bismarck arranged by Bleichröder on 12 March he said: 'I come from the political death-bed of a great man.'[20]

It had taken a surprisingly long time, though, for Bismarck to recognize what was brewing behind his back. There is every indication that after the discussion with William II on 25 February he was still very optimistic. He clearly believed that for the time being he was in some respects over the worst, if not in terms of the problem in hand – here the situation was indeed one of extreme confusion – at least with regard to himself and the threat to his position.

At the meeting of the Prussian Cabinet on 2 March, clearly buoyed up by the belief that he had the total support of the emperor, he set forth a kind of step-by-step plan for dealing with the Imperial Diet and the hostile forces on the party-political front. 'To begin with' the labour protection legislation should be proposed, 'then the Army Bills', and 'only later on', following clarification of the fronts on these matters, the Anti-Socialist Bill – 'the latter in a more stringent form'. As well as the 'power to banish' it must contain 'more stringent penalties for workers seeking to compel others to strike'. In the event of the Diet's showing 'continued opposition' – the writer of the minutes put 'unruliness' (*Renitenz*) originally, which is undoubtedly what Bismarck said, but the Chancellor later amended the record in his own hand – a whole series of measures could be contemplated. A start could be made by paralysing the Diet politically with a boycott of the government bench; theoretically quite low-ranking civil servants could sit there as authorized representatives of the Federal Council. If this and other measures did not work, they could consider as a final step loosening the existing federal relationship or indeed dissolving and re-founding the Reich. This, he said, insisting that the emperor 'shares this opinion', was a confederation of the 'princes and senates' of the free cities rather than of the 'states' and as such could, if it came to it, be dissolved by them.[21]

This was very much a theoretical speculation about extreme possibilities. Moreover, the ministers understood it as such. But it did reveal the full extent of Bismarck's determination to fight. There was no trace of resignation here. Rather his demeanour radiated an unimpaired sense of power and an awareness of having once again found a solid support in the emperor. Accordingly the ministers unreservedly approved at least the practical programme.

Yet a mere two days later Bismarck's conviction that the emperor now had no choice but to back him up proved to be pure illusion. On 4 March William II ordered him to drop his Bill for a more stringent Anti-Socialist Law. The whole enterprise, he said, echoing the arguments of Bismarck's opponents, who even included men on the right, was a 'quite futile provocation of the electorate' and threatened in addition to jeopardize the labour protection legislation.[22]

With this the whole programme of a judicious blend of repression and severely restricted material concessions to the working class became null and void, a programme that regardless of certain differences of detail was in principle entirely in line with Bismarckian policy hitherto. The state, so it inevitably appeared to Bismarck, was at the behest of the monarch not simply to give in but positively to capitulate by renouncing what had been its whole policy up until now – and to do so under the impact of the Social Democrats' dramatic success at the polls.

But instead of countering with an impassioned protest, as the emperor undoubtedly expected him to, and at least holding out the prospect of resignation, as he had done at the Crown Council meeting of 24 January, Bismarck assented even to this. Undoubtedly what he thought was that, given the existing balance of forces and the basic positions in the new Diet, a clash with that body was going to be inevitable in the long run, so he could go along even with this fresh change of course on the emperor's part.

But it was precisely this piece of flagrant calculation that finally – and degradingly – cost him his position. William was undoubtedly hesitant, unsure of himself, in need of someone to lean on and at the same time vain. But he was not as yet entirely cynical about power. Consequently he now felt as it were morally justified in taking resolute action. The impression literally thrust itself upon him that this man possessed no principles whatever, that he was no longer pursuing any kind of clear political line but was guided only by his own power interests. He was a danger – to the state, to any kind of future development and possibly also to him personally. From this point on, if not before, William II was determined to force Bismarck to resign. Now he could tell himself that he was prompted not by his own hunger for power and thirst for recognition but by his concern for the state and for the future of the Reich.

The Chancellor, now approaching his seventy-fifth birthday, was of course reluctant to concede that the game was up, that he was no longer shielded by people's asking themselves how they would ever manage without him. 'Away with this man!' was now the almost universal cry. His attempt to come to some arrangement with the Centre Party only increased this feeling among the other parties.

In retrospect Bismarck spoke of there having been a kind of Catilinan conspiracy against him, particularly among those whom he had trusted and on whom he had bestowed many favours. Along with a growing number of his contemporaries, many historians too have taken his lead here and have sought to provide detailed proofs. In reality, however, what was involved in most instances was a kind of political euthanasia. The end-result was a foregone conclusion, accepted by almost everyone. In practical terms it was simply a matter of facilitating and accelerating the process, drawing a line under what many people now regarded simply as 'a national calamity', as the leading conservative politician Otto von Helldorf is said to have told the emperor.[23]

The same was true of the advice that Helldorf and the liberal-minded Grand Duke of Baden, Frederick I, gave the emperor with regard to the projected Army Bill. Of course the proposal to agree the contents of the Bill with the parties in advance and secure a majority for it by an extensive readiness to make concessions was directed against the Chancellor's collision course. And of course it was calculated to make Bismarck's position wholly untenable and to compel him to resign. But when William II put the proposal to Bismarck on 15 March as representing his own wish, it was not as the outcome of an initiative embarked on for its own sake; it was a case of the emperor availing himself of a means to an end. Moreover, at least as far as the grand duke was concerned it was already directed at the post-Bismarck period in its endeavour to pin the emperor down politically through the way in which the Chancellor's fall was effected.

That was in fact the crucial element in this final act. Essentially the only question at issue here, even before the curtain had fallen, was the new play to be acted on this stage. Accordingly the critics of Bismarck's foreign policy too, particularly his Russian policy, began increasingly to make themselves heard, now that, with the extension of the Reinsurance Treaty pending, a decision needed to be made as to the direction that policy was to take in future. Here again, all that was really at issue now was setting course for the future by way of the Chancellor's fall, not actually occasioning that fall. Bismarck's dismissal was actually a *fait accompli* when the chief of staff, Count Waldersee, sounded the alarm on the basis of consular reports from Kiev regarding troop movements on Russia's south-west frontier. It was the purest bluster on William's part, particularly since Bismarck had himself forwarded the reports to him, when on 17 March he accused the Chancellor in an open letter of having failed to draw his attention 'long ago' to the 'dreadful impending danger', adding: 'It is high time we warned the Austrians and proceeded to counter-measures.'[24]

In fact the Russian ambassador, Count Shuvalov, had called on Bismarck that very day and produced an authorization to negotiate an extension of the

Reinsurance Treaty, so that the Chancellor was able to offer quite convincing proof of the baselessness of the charges. The only effect of this, however, was the reactive one of confirming William II still further in his opposition to the old policy towards Russia.

Actually, his final decision in this regard had probably been taken on 15 March, when at the end of their dramatic clash Bismarck handed him secret reports from London to read in which there was mention of some highly disparaging comments by the tsar on the subject of his imperial nephew: 'C'est un garçon mal élevé et de mauvaise foi', Alexander III was said to have remarked.[25] That had been Bismarck's somewhat small-minded response to a scene in which William had in his most imperatorial style forbidden him to conduct independent negotiations with party leaders, demanded his consent to an abrogation of the Cabinet order of 1852 and informed him that he was thinking of coming to terms with the new Imperial Diet over the army proposals as well. With that the emperor had finally severed relations, and resignation was the only course remaining; Bismarck's spontaneous reaction in handing over the secret reports had as it were symbolized the irreparable nature of the breach.

Bismarck's immediate inclination may have been to take his leave without a word. But that would have been to cast irrevocable suspicion on his tenacious struggle for power, a struggle in which he had spared himself neither humiliations nor a great many compromises that had long since become incomprehensible. The important thing now was to dress the whole thing up and in this way perhaps even lay the foundations for an eventual return to power, however remote such an idea may have seemed at the time. He would not let himself be rushed by the impatience of the emperor, who underlined the humiliating nature of this dismissal by twice reminding Bismarck that his letter of resignation was expected. Instead he applied to this last great document of his almost forty years of service to the Prussian and subsequently also to the German state all the political flair and tactical skill, all the concentration and feeling for form at his command.

Boldly abstracting from all points of material contention with respect to home affairs, in the letter he finally sent off to William II at 8 p.m. on 18 March 1890 he at first concentrated entirely on the formal question of the Cabinet order of 1852. One was dealing here – thus Bismarck, who had recently been toying with the idea of a *coup d'état* against the Imperial Diet – with crucially fundamental prerequisites of the constitutional state. 'Under the absolute monarchy a provision such as that contained in the 1852 order was superfluous, as it would be today if we were to return to absolutism, without ministerial responsibility.' If on the other hand ministerial responsibility – 'as constituting the essence of constitutional life' – was to be retained, the order could under no circumstances be dispensed with. It alone guaranteed, 'in the Ministry of State [the Cabinet] and in its relations with the Monarch, the unity and continuity' without which ordered co-operation in the context of the constitutional state was utterly impossible.

In other words, the emperor, as his demand for the abrogation of the order made clear, was not concerned with any material differences of opinion. He was looking for a return to a neo-absolutist system to which

215

he, Bismarck, as guarantor of the existing order rooted in the constitution, represented an obstacle. As he clearly also represented an obstacle, the Chancellor went on, in the field of foreign policy – to be precise, in the field of Germany's policy towards the tsardom. Here he was being asked to place in jeopardy 'all the important successes for the German Empire that our foreign policy of recent decades, as pursued by Their Majesties, Your two late predecessors, has achieved in our relations with Russia despite unfavourable circumstances and the unexpectedly great significance of which for the present and for the future Count Shuvalov recently confirmed to me on his return from Petersburg'.[26]

The tacit rebuke was that here too a hazardous policy was in the process of being launched for which he – and after all the writer was the most experienced and successful practitioner of foreign policy that the last two generations had produced – likewise could not assume the responsibility. Any reader must inevitably conclude that the two things, the trend towards neo-absolutism and a foreign policy involving incalculable risks, were intimately connected. They reflected the rejection of everything that, notwithstanding all the impassioned disputes, had distinguished the period of history now drawing to an end: continuity, moderation, a holding on to what had been tried and tested, extensive safeguarding of existing institutions and legal relations, and security within the limits of the possible.

All this scarcely accorded with the reality of the moment. However, it contained within it the kernel of a legend that, cultivated by Bismarck in every conceivable way right up until his death, grew more and more luxuriant as the policy of the emperor and his changing governments came increasingly under the cross-fire of very diverse and conflicting aims and interests. Just as the emperor had placed himself at the head of a negative coalition in order to topple his Chancellor, Bismarck now sought to mobilize a negative coalition for his own purposes.

In this he was unsuccessful as far as he himself was concerned. But he encumbered the Reich – his 'creation', as he now proclaimed with ever-decreasing reserve – with a burden from which it never really managed to free itself, right up until the end. It was the burden of a legend that bathed the past in a rosy glow in which the realities disappeared and people were able to abandon themselves to their very disparate dreams.

Bismarck's immediate successors, of course – with William II himself foremost among them – contributed in full measure towards the development of that legend. It was they who made it possible for the fallen Chancellor to emerge from the shadows of his own policy, which in his final decade in office had been growing ever longer. It was they who made possible his ever-renewed attempts to dress up his policy and accomplishments in the style that he had already launched in his letter of resignation on 18 March 1890.

Much of what he said in retrospect and in implacable criticism of his heirs contains enduring insights as far as the interpretation and evaluation of his own achievement are concerned. But on the whole it was the subterranean aspect of his existence that surfaced here as never before: the imperative will

216

to power and self-affirmation that was never able to see his achievement as something separate from himself – that as it were never granted it its independence.

The greatness of true resignation – to relinquish but also to become reconciled – was wholly lacking in Bismarck. And he for his part did everything – if only, as in Caprivi's case, in terms of resistance and self-dissociating disagreement – to hold his successors to the old, outmoded paths and to block the Reich's way into the future. When in the late afternoon of 29 March 1890, having been created Duke of Lauenburg and promoted Colonel General of Cavalry with the rank of Field Marshal, he left Berlin with enormous ceremony – 'a first-class funeral', as he sarcastically called it[27] – to settle finally in Friedrichsruh, it was not the end of an era. On the contrary, it was in many respects the beginning of an existence in its shadow, a long and agonizing argument about where Germany was committed to the legacy of that era and where it must determinedly step over it and go on, what positive traditions it did after all contain and at what points a decisive break offered the only hope for the future.

The argument was carried on for decades under varying auspices, and for all its apparent remoteness it is in many respects still in progress today. The nation's self-awareness still seems to be determined by the external configuration of the Reich as founded in 1871. Modes of behaviour, institutions, the way in which parties and groups see themselves and the terms in which social relations of all kinds are conceived still seem to be largely influenced by the traditions of Bismarck's Reich, albeit in various refractions. Academic history is still focused primarily on this period – even, in many instances today, in a peculiarly impassioned manner. Despite its often vigorous attempts at detachment, it is only rarely able, after a prolonged struggle, to bring itself to declare the period historically closed.

In this way Bismarck as a political figure has at the same time remained the man who, in the eyes of the Germans as in those of the world, and even given the critical detachment that undoubtedly prevails today, stands for the nation in the period in which it acquired its historical identity. It was for this kind of identification with the nation that Bismarck himself, aiming for a lasting retrospective coupling of his achievement with himself and his will, worked so hard and so purposefully in the final years of his life. And his succeeding in it can be said to have been his last and perhaps his greatest triumph.

But it was undoubtedly at the same time his most disastrous one. It forced the nation farther into continuities of thought, behaviour, ideas, battle-lines and prejudices, into continuities of historical self-appraisal and appraisal of the world that, the longer they persisted, placed greater and greater obstacles in the way of a sober fixing of its present position and taking of bearings for the future. As the ancient historian Theodor Mommsen, speaking as a contemporary, summed up resignedly at the end of his long life, the 'harm' done by the Bismarck era was 'infinitely greater than the good'. He went on: 'The gains in power were assets that were lost again in the next great storm of history; but the subjugation of the German personality, the German spirit, was a disaster that can never be made good.'[28]

In other words, the Reich as created by Bismarck had not only narrowed the historical possibilities for the German nation; it had deformed the nation itself and in so doing had as it were perpetuated itself in its negative consequences. In the same strain Ludwig Bamberger once wrote of the 'ravages wrought by the Bismarckian system in the spirit and in the laws of the country'.[29] There is undoubtedly much in what they said. Yet Mommsen's verdict, delivered under the influence of the turn-of-the-century preoccupation with historical continuity, rather underestimated the power of recent radical changes in Germany's historical circumstances. To put it in more concrete terms, how completely the 'gains in power' would be 'lost again in the next storm of history' was something of which not even Mommsen could conceive. Nor, consequently, could he imagine the effect it must have in the long run.

True, that effect has been slow in manifesting itself, not least because its causes, of painful memory, were predominantly negative in character, consisting as they did in losses of all kinds, including that of national unity. It has been accompanied by deep-seated crises of orientation of which no one knows whether they have been finally overcome as yet. But that it will eventually prevail cannot be in any doubt, given the wholly altered realities obtaining in every sphere of life. It is only from this vantage-point, in terms of a conscious leave-taking from an era, that a definitive verdict is possible in respect of the person and achievement of a man who in the last years of his life once again tried with all his might and with all his passion to make such a leave-taking impossible.

[17]

The Shadow of the Past

Bismarck survived his fall by eight years – and 'survived' is the word for it. Once upon a time he had feared nothing so much as the modern phenomenon that Max Weber was to dub *Berufsmenchentum*, the occupational disease of the modern professional man whereby his life is wholly taken up by his function and the man lives entirely for his job and its responsibilities – even given such a job and such responsibilities as his. Now, however, he admitted that it had manifested itself in him too. One's drives, one's passions were like trout in a pool: 'One eats the other until there is only one fat old trout left. In my case a passion for politics has in the course of time consumed all other passions.'[1]

Kanzler ohne Amt – 'Chancellor without Office' – is the title of a recent study of the final years of Bismarck's life.[2] The author meant it positively, and his book puts forward the thesis that even after his dismissal Bismarck remained one of the key figures in German politics. But quite apart from anything else it affords a very precise description of the situation and self-appraisal of the fallen Chancellor and beyond that of his endeavour to hold on to as much influence and actual power as he possibly could. This was more than many people supposed after his death. But it was not only very much less than he himself aspired to; it was also less than his opponents feared and those around him would have had him believe.

The very discrepancy between this unbroken, indeed if anything intensified desire for power and the reality, a discrepancy that the great realist was never truly able to conceal from himself, marked not only the inner tragedy of his final years but also the character of all he undertook in them. 'Never has anyone so "raged" against his own fame as this man', the Basel historian Jacob Burckhardt pronounced with this in mind as early as the end of September 1890. 'The purely historical view of his nature', he went on, 'has thus been dispensed from all reverence by the man himself'.[3] And three years later Theodor Fontane echoed: 'The perpetual playing the part of the novice and the honest fellow is awful, and one has constantly to remind oneself of all the colossal achievements that he so brilliantly fiddled together in order not to be disgusted by the fiddling, supported as it was by the crassest contradictions. He is the most interesting character imaginable. I know of no one more interesting; but this permanent addiction to out-smarting people I find actually repellent.'[4]

219

Bending the past into a shape that suited his own immediate objectives had always been Bismarck's approach. Moreover, it was one he imputed to everyone else, including historians, which was why he was thoroughly scornful of their science. Now, however, it came out in quite another way and became, in the absence of any other expedients, a weapon pure and simple. The past and the great mass of factors that had crucially shaped and conditioned it – that was the weapon he employed against his present, which had wrenched itself from him and threatened to wrench itself farther from him, rendering him powerless and robbing him of a future. With it he smote his successors, great and small. They were represented virtually without exception as both incompetent and scheming, from ministers of long standing such as Boetticher and once trusted colleagues such as Holstein to the new secretary of state at the Foreign Office, Marschall, and the Cabinet chief, von Lucanus, and including all the men of whom he had hoped in vain that they would sacrifice their careers to repay an alleged debt of gratitude to himself. And with that weapon he threatened and persecuted everyone who had the audacity to be of a different opinion politically from the 'Reichsgründer', the 'founder of the empire'.

An empire can only ever be maintained by the same means as were used to found it – Tacitus had written that. Bismarck may have guarded against quoting the passage, the context of which was hardly such as would show his creation in a very positive light; in fact it made the future of that creation look somewhat gloomy. But the general insight contained therein was entirely in line with his own special objectives. Only he had the appropriate knowlege at his command. Only he knew the 'secrets of empire', the means by which the Reich could be preserved and guided to fresh successes. Politics, he now emphasized repeatedly, was not an exact science; it was not in fact predictable, nor was it learnable, and it could certainly not be reduced to simple formulae. Politics was an art and as such was bound up, at the level of true greatness, with specifically personal elements, with the great individual. But where was such a one to be found among the pygmy race of his heirs and successors? 'I am the big shadow that stands between him and the sun of fame', he sneered of William II.[5] And of the new Cabinet he said: 'So insubstantial are the personalities of the present ministers . . . that the figure of the monarch always shines through.'[6]

Everything that emerged after 1890 in terms of the glorification of the great man and of his genius and uniqueness and that in many instances soon assumed grotesque forms, degenerating into a veritable Bismarck cult, we now know to have been very largely the work of Bismarck himself. Very early in his career he had recognized the ever-increasing importance of public opinion and the press and had learned to play this instrument with masterly skill. Immediately following his dismissal, having lost a large proportion of his old press outlets – those that went with his office – he built up a veritable propaganda network centred on the *Hamburger Nachrichten* and its chief political editor, Hermann Hofmann. With the aid of the utterly devoted Rudolf Chrysander, who as his private secretary worked himself almost to death during these years, and of a series of journalist associates with Moritz Busch, Heinrich von Poschinger and Horst Kohl chief among them, he fed the public an uninterrupted supply of political statements, historical surveys and above all a kind of regular court circular. The latter furnished a constant supply of details, anecdotes and aphorisms designed not only to maintain interest in 'the grand old man of the Forest of Saxony' but to bring the uniqueness of his existence to the attention of one and all.

His success was evident not only in a steady stream of visitors, in addresses of homage, in the huge crowds that gathered every time he left Friedrichsruh and in an increasing idolization of the man and his achievement even among serious and not directly dependent journalists and historians. It was evident above all in a growing fear among his opponents and successors that Bismarck might seek to translate the public esteem and influence now accruing to him into tangible political power by, for example, placing himself at the head of a new kind of plebiscitary movement with himself and what he declared to be the obligations arising out of his achievement as its programme.

That fear haunted not only government circles and the emperor's immediate entourage: from time to time William II gave serious consideration to having Bismarck tried for 'high treason' and stated repeatedly that if the former Chancellor went on in this way he really would 'end up in Spandau one day'.[7] It also haunted the established parties and their respective leaderships. When after some initial hesitation Bismarck decided in March 1891 to accept the invitation of the local National Liberal election committee to stand in a by-election for the Imperial Diet in the constituency of Hanover-Lehe, many people believed they were already seeing the prelude to such a development.

Whether Bismarck toyed with such ideas himself is an open question. Here too potential success was probably his lodestone as regarded further decisions. And that success failed to materialize. In the first ballot, with a low poll, he won only 43 per cent of the vote, and in the requisite second ballot of 30 April 1891 his Social Democratic opponent still held on to more than a third of the votes cast – and this was in Rudolf Bennigsen's old constituency, which he and his successors had always won with comfortable majorities.

Bismarck never in fact took his seat, and he turned down all further invitations to stand as a candidate. But for the time being he was an elected member of the Imperial Diet. And no one knew whether he might not suddenly, given a parliamentary conflict situation, appear in Berlin 'like the ghost of Banquo at Macbeth's table' and seek to make the Diet his political forum.[8] This lent an extra significance to everything that appeared in the Friedrichsruh-inspired press, particularly in the *Hamburger Nachrichten*, on contentious domestic and foreign policy issues. It confirmed both supporters and opponents in the impression that Bismarck, even out of office, was and remained a political power factor of the first importance.

This is the only explanation for the almost hysterical reaction of the imperial government and of the emperor himself when it became known that the former Chancellor was planning a trip to Vienna for the belated marriage of his eldest son Herbert to the Hungarian Countess Marguerite Hoyos and that he intended to visit Dresden on the way there and Munich on the way back. There was talk of a 'political demonstration by the Bismarck dynasty'[9] and of a 'tangled web of intrigue'.[10] An audience at the Austrian court, William II warned Francis Joseph, was planned as the 'main attraction' of a 'swindle' aimed at the sensation-seeking curiosity of the imbecile masses.[11]

Of course Bismarck was anxious to know what sort of reception he would encounter at his various destinations. And of course he meant to ask for audiences at all three courts. What could be more natural in a man who had headed the government of the German Reich for almost twenty years and had always cultivated first-hand contacts with its various princely houses? We may also assume without hesitation that at the same time he saw the whole thing as a kind of test of his popularity. Yet it seems equally clear, from everything we know today, that he was not, in making this journey, pursuing any immediate, concrete political plans.

That was very much what people suspected, though, particularly the ever mistrustful Friedrich von Holstein, who on the strength of seniority had in practice headed the political department of the Foreign Office since 1886 and who had for years been one of the key figures behind Germany's foreign policy. He was in many ways an able and unscrupulous pupil of the former Chancellor. Yet for all his critical detachment he was still wholly under the spell of Bismarck's personality as well as of his retrospective embellishments of his image as a man always in full command of his intentions and actions. Inclined to see him as a kind of super-Machiavellian, he took it for granted that the former Chancellor's journey presaged a major coup. According to Holstein, this was Bismarck's way of forcing the emperor to give in and seek a reconciliation – by showing him how eagerly everyone awaited such a step, including the head of Germany's closest ally and the leading princes in Germany itself. Possibly, in view of mounting criticism of the policy of the 'New Line', the process was already under way that would eventually put the ex-Chancellor back into office.

This was a far cry from the reality of the situation. Holstein's constant nagging had its effect, however, especially since it chimed with the fears of William II and the head of his government that Bismarck, received and treated almost in the manner of royalty, would seek wherever he went to undermine the authority and prestige of the young emperor and his new government still further. On 9 June 1892 Caprivi instructed Prince Reuss, the German ambassador in Vienna, in what soon became known as the 'Uriasbrief' – a reference to the treacherous letter that sealed the fate of Uriah the Hittite – that the embassy was ostentatiously to cold-shoulder Bismarck on the occasion of his visit and to refuse any invitation to the wedding.[12] And on 12 June William himself wrote to Francis Joseph, asking him 'not to make the situation at home more difficult for me by receiving this disobedient subject of mine before he has come to me and cried *peccavi*'.[13] Similar requests and instructions were dispatched to Dresden and Munich. Superficially they may have achieved their purpose, but their deeper effect was to invoke precisely what their authors had sought to preclude.

The journey now began to take the form of a massive demonstration of sympathy for Bismarck and of criticism of the petty behaviour of the emperor and his government. In many quarters that criticism was directed at the policy and at the political pretensions of the new regime as a whole – in Munich, for example, where not a year before this William II had entered his name in the visitor's book of the city together with the pithy adage: *Suprema lex regis voluntas*, 'the will of the King is the highest law'. There was a special piquancy about his having done this in a country where the king was mentally ill and had to be represented by a prince regent.

Bismarck himself took up the gauntlet at once. In an interview that he granted to the *Neue Freie Presse* on the last day of his stay in Vienna and that immediately received general circulation he expressed his gratitude for the exceptionally friendly welcome given him by the people of Vienna.[14] They had clearly taken the rumours of his allegedly anti-Austrian stance put about by certain German interests as seriously as they deserved to be taken. Of course he had always been concerned to protect German interests; that was the basis of his criticism of the Caprivi government's German-Austrian commercial treaty, which did not do that. He had also tried constantly to maintain close relations not only with Austria but also with Russia. But this was precisely where German interests were largely identical with Austrian. This was something the present German government failed to recognize with its ostensibly so pro-Austrian policy towards Russia. The gist of the whole interview was that he was able to say this in public. For he had 'no further personal obligations whatsoever to today's leading figures and to my successors. All the bridges are down.' He was concerned, in other words, only with safeguarding his legacy, which was in danger of being gambled away.

In the same interview he had admittedly ruled out the possibility of a return to office as 'quite hopeless' but had left open the question of whether he might not put in an appearance in the Imperial Diet sooner or later and there 'take the government in my sights, so to speak as head of the opposition'. He might, in other words, yet make a come-back, this time not from above as confidant, adviser and resolute defender of the Crown but from below, as a successful leader of the parliamentary opposition.

Even to his most anxious opponents, of course, this came to seem less and less serious a danger as time went on. The hysteria of Holstein's initial reaction to the prospect of an enforced reconciliation between the emperor and the ex-Chancellor was matched by the sobriety of his and others' estimates, in the further course of events, of Bismarck's chances of acquiring a leading position in the Diet. And the attitude of most of the established parties and their leaders was not the only reason for this.

The question people were asking more and more insistently was this: what, in concrete terms, did Bismarck have to offer? What was his programme, apart from criticism that was based primarily on the past? What did he have, beyond the ultimately unpolitical, almost religious veneration in which he was widely held by votaries celebrating their own past and their own youth, that was capable of positively sweeping people along? His foreign policy objectives? Here it was always the same things he advocated: moderation, restraint, being content with what had been achieved, which was sufficiently under threat, holding fast to the old allies, especially Russia, on whose attitude to the Reich the whole future depended. The first and foremost concern was the security of 'what we have laboriously salvaged under the threat of . . . armed assault from the rest of Europe'.[15] Nothing was more dangerous than to play the part of a man 'who has suddenly come into money and, bragging about the cash in his purse, proceeds to make a general nuisance of himself'.[16] What about domestic policy? Did he exude a more powerful dynamism in this sphere? Was he capable of attracting and mobilizing people's expectations and creative visions and giving some positive substance to his criticisms – shared by many – of the established parties and of the sheer waste of energy involved in the 'to-do' of politics? Not a bit of it. Here too the predominant element was a rigid adherence to positions that during his time in office he had not by any means regarded as taboo.

This was seen above all in his attitude to the economic problems of the day. Here he now became a totally biased advocate of the material interests of agriculture, that is to say primarily of the land-owning aristocracy, which in his view were guaranteed only by an extended system of protective tariffs and maximum elimination of competition. Structural changes in the economy in a context of rapid industrial growth, the need, clearly recognized by his successor, Caprivi, to open up new markets and to make appropriate concessions to that end – these were things for which he showed little understanding any more. All that was no longer his world, and as he deliberately turned his back on it he became increasingly incapable of apprehending it in sober and impartial terms.

This is particularly clear from the view he took of the political changes that announced themselves in the wake of these developments. He continued to see the Social Democrats as a host of 'enemies bent on pillage and murder', their only object being 'to slit the throat of bourgeois society'.[17] Their success at the polls was based mainly on protest voters, people who wished 'to use their vote simply to show that they are dissatisfied'.[18] Indeed in their uninhibited brutality his remarks on this subject outdid everything that has come down to us from his period in office. 'They are the country's rats and should be exterminated', he told an American journalist in the summer of 1893.[19] And in a letter – corrected in Bismarck's hand as an authentic expression of his own opinion – that Chrysander wrote towards the end of 1894 to Maximilian Harden, possibly the most influential journalist of his day, we read: 'His Highness sees the state and the human race as an aggregate of many individuals . . . some of whom are healthy, others a public nuisance in that they are contagiously infected. These latter it will be the duty and the concern of the defender of governmental order to destroy; if necessary this is to be achieved by eliminating the principal carriers of the infection, of whom there are not a great many.'[20]

According to Bismarck, anyone who regarded Social Democracy as a normal, albeit extremist political party representing specific interests was dragging a Trojan horse into the beleaguered citadel of bourgeois society. And anyone who believed in a process of inner transformation affecting at least sections of the party was doing the same thing. It was all simply a 'contrived piece of play-acting with allotted roles and all the escapades agreed on in advance'.[21] And in August 1897, eleven months before his death, the 82-year-old ex-Chancellor went so far as to write: 'The social question could at one time have been solved by using the police; now it will be necessary to use the army.'[22] Hatred and incomprehension of those who opposed the existing order had finally burst all bounds and swept away any possibility of even a half-way realistic view of the future.

It was not, however, only the representatives of Social Democracy but also the left-wing liberals and the great majority of the Centre Party that remained, in his eyes, *Reichsfeinde* – enemies of the state. He continued to see them as potential destroyers of everything that, boldly disregarding all the dramatic changes of the last thirty years, he now claimed always to have fought for. They allegedly threatened something to which he referred reverentially as the 'internal order' of the Reich – and which was in fact little more than the simple status quo.

In other words, everything was to stay as it was. Because the way it was, or rather had been when he was in office, was good – or at any rate very much better than what the 'New Line' was aiming at. It was therefore essential, he pontificated, to strengthen all such forces as were capable of opposing the omnipotence of the central government and of an ever-spreading bureaucracy bent on change with a reckless emperor hungry for power and prestige at their head – one of those forces being the Imperial Diet. 'I fought the Imperial Diet fiercely for decades', he said in a speech in Kissingen in July 1892, explaining this change in his views, 'but I perceive that that institution was weakened in this very struggle with William I and myself . . . When I became minister the Crown was under pressure and the King, disheartened because the ministers had refused him their support, wished to abdicate. I therefore endeavoured to strengthen the Crown as against parliament. Possibly I went too far in this. We need a counter-balance, and I regard freedom of criticism as indispensable in a monarchical system of government; otherwise it falls victim to the absolutism of civil servants. Nowadays it is not monarchs that govern absolutely but bureaucrats.'[23] In private conversation, too, he stressed repeatedly that he had always 'simply advocated a balance between the two constitutional powers, Crown and parliament. Formerly that balance was disturbed to the disadvantage of the monarchy; now the same is the case to the disadvantage of parliament.'[24] And finally, as he wrote in very general terms in his memoirs: 'The ideal I have always had in mind is a monarchical power that is controlled by an independent and in my view corporative or trade-cooperative national representative body to the extent that neither monarch nor parliament can alter the existing legal state of affairs *unilaterally* but only by common consent in a climate of openness and public criticism of all governmental processes by press and Diet.'[25]

It was a classic expression of his cardinal political principle, the principle that over long periods had helped him to so overriding and – in many people's eyes – semi-dictatorial a position of power: the exploitation of a socio-political equilibrium between the forces of old and new, between the aristocracy and the bourgeoisie, between 'monarchy and the sovereignty of the people' in a specific, transitory historical situation and constellation of political circumstances. As such it also held good in other, wider contexts. But for the immediate contemporary who set most store by current political consistency and purpose, what such utterances revealed above all was how completely the ex-Chancellor was fixated on the past in the domestic sphere as well. They indicated a rigid, anti-reformist insistence on the 'existing legal state of affairs'. For all his level-headedness in other respects, this became increasingly idealized – at least in comparison with the present and when set against the future of the 'New Line', both of which he repeatedly referred to and commented on in the gloomiest terms. And although this view of things was widely and increasingly applauded – by very diverse groups and forces, be it said, who were scarcely capable of acting in concert – the purely backward-looking character of such concentration on the status quo and its lack of any practical future were in fact coming home to more and more people.

Even in 1891 the young Count Harry Kessler, an ardent Bismarck fan like many students of his day, remarked after one of the many 'group audiences' for students, this one in Kissingen: 'The longer one listened, the more one was forced to recognize that what he was saying was addressed to a generation that belonged to the past . . . To us, the young, he clearly had nothing to say . . . What he was offering us young Germans as our goal in life was the political equivalent of an old-age pensioner's existence, hanging on to and enjoying what we have got; our creative urge went unsatisfied . . . It was painfully obvious that he was not a beginning; he was an end, a magnificent final chord – a fulfiller rather than a prophet!'[26] And in his Freiburg inaugural lecture in 1895 Max Weber observed: 'When in the winter of last year, wreathed in his monarch's good graces, he made his entry into the decorated imperial capital, there were many – as I know full well – who felt as if the Forest of Saxony were unlocking its depths like a modern Kyffhaüser. Only not everybody shared that feeling. For it was as if one could feel in the air of that January day the cold breath of historical ephemerality. A strangely oppressive feeling came over us – as if a spirit had come down from a mighty past and were strolling among a new generation through a world grown unfamiliar to him.' According to Weber the 'tragedy' inherent in 'his career as a statesman, alongside its incomparable greatness' – a tragedy, he noted, that 'still escapes the attention of many people today' – was one that 'the future may well find in the fact that under him the work of his hands, the nation to which he gave unity, slowly and ineluctably changed its economic structure and became something different, a people that was obliged to call for other forms of organization than those he was able to give it and to which his imperious nature was able to adapt itself.'[27]

That was the crucial point. Even if the emperor and the majority of his advisers were far from sharing the insights of the young economist and sociologist and the bulk of the middle class tended to be sceptical with regard to the conclusions Weber drew from those insights in terms of a domestic policy fostering a parliamentary democracy organized along party lines – a 'Back to Bismarck' movement no longer constituted a serious political alternative; that was now clear to nearly everyone, even to members of the inner circle of his most ardent supporters and admirers.

Consequently the superficial reconciliation between the emperor and the former Chancellor that took place at the beginning of 1894 – the occasion to which Weber was referring – was not in any real sense a political event from which a change of direction or even a change of government might have been expected. On the contrary, the 'reconciliation', at which politics either present or past was not mentioned once, by declaring that Bismarck was now 'harmless' finally set the seal on his political retirement. As Count Philipp Eulenburg remarked over a year later in a letter to Count Cuno Moltke, the emperor's aide-de-camp: 'It was not a surrender but a victory over the adversary, and the adversary felt it as such.'[28] And William himself said: 'Now they can build triumphal arches for him in Vienna and Munich – I'll always be a length ahead of him.'[29]

Bismarck, however, failed to reciprocate with the good behaviour expected of him. 'Hercules is swinging his clubs again' became a common saying among the emperor's associates. Right up until the end people in Berlin and elsewhere remained on the alert for broadsides from Friedrichsruh. Yet in comparison with the first few years things did now quieten down considerably around the former Chancellor. His advancing age had a good deal to do with this, of course, but there was another contributory factor as well. Bismarck saw very clearly that many of those who pretended to be ardent supporters and admirers of his were simply making use of him: the big agriculturalists with their newly founded 'League of Farmers', representatives of heavy industry headed by Krupp and Stumm-Halberg, the Pan-Germans and the colonial enthusiasts, critics of centralization in the Reich and of Prussia and the Prussian emperor's claims to power. All these and many more had no intention whatsoever of allowing themselves to be drawn together by Friedrichsruh and launched into common action.

In this way the ex-Chancellor became a mere figurehead even in his lifetime. Even he could not escape the bitter realization that he was being used as a kind of historical justification for forces and interests to which he was admittedly more or less close in substance and that he had once taken into account in varying degrees in his policy but that could not, any of them, really claim that they and they alone embodied the basic tendency of his political thinking. It was chiefly these 'inheritance squabbles', particularly on the right of the political spectrum, in which Bismarck himself occasionally intervened, usually with the effect of compounding the confusion, that led in 1895 to the decision of the Imperial Diet – a decision that was widely criticized both at home and abroad and was certainly not exactly far-sighted, politically speaking – to deny the former Chancellor the official eightieth birthday congratulations that had been proposed by its president. The majority of Centrists, German Liberals, Social Democrats and members of the so-called 'protest parties' that was responsible for this decision wished to make a demonstration against a particular policy and its self-styled heirs. What they failed to appreciate was that by their very action such thoroughly controversial claims as those of the Pan-Germans, for example, or the colonial enthusiasts were most effectively bolstered and as it were confirmed.

Petty as this behaviour appeared even to many contemporary critics of Bismarck, it very soon back-fired. Moreover, it bestowed an aura of preserving and enhancing the increasingly transfigured legacy of the past upon forces that Bismarck himself had once regarded with very great scepticism and to some extent still did. Taking advantage of the mood of the moment, William II now joined their ranks. In a telegram to Friedrichsruh he said that he had learned of the Diet's decision with 'the most profound indignation'. That decision was 'utterly contrary to the feelings of all the German princes and peoples'.[30] It was evidence – so ran the conclusion to which all this was leading up – of the deep gulf that existed between the nation and the majority of its representatives, the inmates of the 'Imperial monkey house', as William once scornfully called the Imperial Diet around this time.[31]

On only one further occasion did Bismarck emerge from the gathering twilight of a conflict over his legacy in which the aims and realities of his policy became increasingly blurred. This was on 24 October 1896, when he had the *Hamburger Nachrichten* reveal the secret of the Reinsurance Treaty, the 'wire to St. Petersburg' at whose existence he had so often hinted since his resignation. The revelation unleashed a violent controversy both at home and abroad, with reactions ranging from assertions that the former Chancellor had taken emergency action to safeguard his achievement and secure the future of Germany – thus his unconditional supporters, who of course were rather embarrassed by the whole episode – to outright accusations of 'high treason' and of a 'crime against the state' punishable in the courts. In Austria, a country that was particularly concerned, Foreign Minister Count Goluchowski spoke according to Eulenburg of additional proof 'that Bismarck is a scoundrel', as indeed 'all of us here' had known 'for a long time',[32] and Francis Joseph himself talked of the 'onset of senility' in the 'wicked old man of Friedrichsruh'. The pro-government *Welt am Montag*, published in Berlin, allowed its gutter-press style of attack to culminate in the remark that this latest contribution to a series of 'persistent moral perversions' could be accounted for only by Bismarck's 'ravaged nerves' and his 'senile wreck of a brain'.

All this reflected people's deep sense of shock at the extent to which this act had brought German foreign policy under suspicion. And all the retrospective attempts at justification have been able to set only one plea against the obvious arguments of the critics: Bismarck's allegedly overriding concern for the foreign policy future of the Reich – as if this reckless exposure of the deeper problems of German foreign policy in the second half of the 1880s and the revelation of the balancing-act that the Chancellor had felt compelled to perform would have been capable of clarifying circumstances to Germany's advantage and enhancing confidence in the Reich and in its dependability as an ally.

As far as Bismarck was concerned, however, it seems on present evidence that there was never any question of this kind of rather dubious weighing up of pros and cons. A recent study shows that he had obviously become very confused in his mind regarding the details of his own treaty policy vis-à-vis Russia; when the row blew up, his son Herbert had to set him straight, in writing, as to the course that policy had taken and the different stages it had been through. But above all there is every indication that he was incapable of forming a proper estimate of the continuing explosiveness of the Reinsurance Treaty. In conversation he spoke of his sincere astonishment at the general fury that had been provoked by his attempt to counter the 'two-faced calumny', and 'incessant falsification of history . . . practised by the clerical-Liberal press, not without the assistance of certain semi-official organs'.[33] In other words, Francis Joseph and the *Welt am Montag* were very much closer to the truth than they themselves suspected: age, as the euphemistic saying goes, was taking its toll of the 81-year-old ex-Chancellor.

As so often in such cases, physical decline went hand in hand with a growing weariness of life without it being possible to weigh up the relative contributions of the two factors. The sharpest turning-point came with the death of Johanna on 27 November 1894. Her undiscriminating partisanship and the apparent banality of her whole existence have earned her an often embarrassingly heavy sentence of condescending disparagement from most Bismarck biographers. This even shows through – indeed it can be particularly obtrusive – in the work of those who seek to pay tribute to her as the great man's 'life companion'. The list of the reproaches that have been levelled against her, whether directly or indirectly, is a long one. She has been blamed for the paucity of Bismarck's contacts with art, literature, music and the general intellectual life of his day, and she has been held responsible for the prevailing style of the Bismarck household having been one of a brutish masculinity that in its immoderate indulgence in food and drink and the coarseness of its amusements not infrequently verged on the barbaric. Many authors have also laid at her door the fact that the brutality of what were often inhuman opinions and a wholly unjustified, bragging self-righteousness were able to develop so uninhibitedly in her sons, notably in Herbert. And the same applies, at a more superficial level, to the fact that the family's taste and life-style were governed almost exclusively by considerations of practicality and the accidents of availability and circumstance: the old room-numbers were left hanging above the doors of the former 'Woodpecker Hotel' in Friedrichsruh for years after the family took up residence there in the late 1870s.

There is much in these reproaches that is undoubtedly justified. In essence, however, they are based on largely unreal assumptions and in particular on a romantically idealized concept of women being pronounced viable in a wholly patriarchal environment. Johanna would not only have had to be a thoroughly exceptional personality, towering above Bismarck himself in many respects. Even in the position in which her husband's rise in the world of politics placed her, she would have had to throw off all the limitations that the age placed upon virtually every woman. In the nineteenth century not only politics but also culture and science, life-style and taste, and indeed not least women's understanding of themselves, right down to the propagation of the romantically indealized view of them so much in favour as a model – all these were in fact male preserves to a degree that we can scarcely conceive of today. And if Johanna shared one quality with her husband it was his sober, practical realism, the ability to bow to circumstances and to adapt to and cope with them – not of course for their own sake, out of mere opportunism, but with a view to a specific objective. In Bismarck's case that objective was power and the use of power, his own and that of the state he served. And in Johanna's? The answer is as plain as the tradition of bourgeois sobriety is reluctant to spell it out, preferring as it does to consign great passion and the bonds that dominate human existence either to the realm of artistic and literary exaltation or alternatively to the darker side of human nature. Nevertheless, that answer is simply: Bismarck. Not in terms of service, devotion, subordination, although of course elements of those were present, in accordance with her own education and the spirit of the age. Rather in terms of a love that saw and conceived of the other as part of the self. Only on that basis will we be able to understand what governed Johanna's actions and filled her life with meaning.

Nor is this true only of Johanna. If Bismarck stressed repeatedly that it was his marriage that gave his life its firm foundation, we should take him as seriously as he meant to be taken, as seriously as his children took him, as for example when Herbert wrote once in 1887, at a time when his mother was ill, that her death would leave 'Papa's life . . . completely shattered'.[34] Visitors often heard him say: 'When she passes on, I'll not want to stay.'[35] Johanna was in a very real sense the soil in which his whole life – public as well as private – was rooted. And anyone who under the influence of a highly bourgeois, not to say petty-bourgeois view of things as it were reduces that marriage to the external framework that it created for both is missing the relationship between the two as well as misunderstanding the nature of the marriage.

Johanna's death constituted a far more important turning-point in his life than March 1890, we read in a letter to Johannes Miquel written in November 1894. The tone is that of a man quite soberly striking a balance. But someone who knew him as Miquel did and who appreciated what the dismissal had meant to him and how free he was of any trace of sentimentality will have sensed what was meant by 'turning-point' here and by the 'emptiness of the future' towards which Bismarck must now direct his gaze. 'Life is a perpetual process of combustion, and my stock of material for keeping the flame going is nearly used up.'[36] The words reveal more than any complaint would have done. 'What I was left with was Johanna', he wrote three weeks later in a letter to 'Malle', his sister Malwine, 'my dealings with her, the daily question of one's comforts, the practice of the gratitude with which I look back over forty-eight years. And today all is dreary and hollow . . . I chide myself for my ingratitude in the face of all the love and recognition shown me by the nation, in excess of my deserts; for four years I rejoiced over them because *she* rejoiced too, if with a feeling of anger towards my opponents, high and low. Today, however, this ember too has ceased to glow within me.'[37]

'Not for ever, I hope, if God should grant me life', he added. But even if the old eagerness for a fight did occasionally flare up, the dominant elements from now on were resignation, a feeling of increasing isolation and finally a growing weariness of life. Serious circulatory disturbances – aggravated by increasing immobility, they became concentrated in one leg and gradually caused it to go numb – sometimes gave rise to unbearable pain. With no acute clinical condition beyond that, he laboured on towards the end. Ernst Schweninger, his doctor of long standing who had for many years been very successful in his psychological treatment of his patient as well, left Friedrichsruh shortly before Bismarck's death, believing there was no immediate danger. '*Gib, dass ich meine Johanna wiedersehe*' – 'Let me see my Johanna again' – is how Herbert's wife recorded her father-in-law's last prayer.[38] The end came a little before eleven o'clock in the evening of 30 July 1898.

The end, that is, of his life, his personal existence. But not of the controversy surrounding the man and his policy, his historical legacy and the era that he had so materially influenced and represented. That now flared up anew, more violent than ever. And it must have looked very much as if the 'old man of the Forest of Saxony', upon whose mortal remains the emperor immediately and ostentatiously bestowed the highest honours, had very deliberately prepared for this and planned and arranged everything to this end. On the very day on which his death was announced Moritz Busch had the *Berliner Lokalanzeiger* publish his 1890 letter of resignation, which had been destined for public consumption from the outset. And at the end of November the first two volumes of his memoirs appeared under the title – surely passed by Bismarck himself – *Gedanken und Erinnerungen*, 'Thoughts and Reminiscences'. They became one of the greatest publishing successes of the century, with over 300,000 copies sold in the first few days of December alone. The third volume, which focused on William II and the dismissal, had been separated from the others. It was eventually published, after a protracted tug-of-war, at the end of September 1921, by which time the overthrow of the monarchy and the generally altered circumstances had created a totally new situation. But even without it the memoirs contained political dynamite in plenty. And it seemed quite obvious that the work had been conceived as a political last will and testament – one that, given the way things were, was of course addressed not to the ex-Chancellor's formal heirs but to his potential heirs, summoning them to action.

As indeed it had been. *Thoughts and Reminiscences* is essentially a polemical treatise, a work of undimmed political passion aimed entirely at the present. Lothar Bucher, Bismarck's colleague for many years and the man largely responsible for the realization of this project between October 1890 and December 1891 – after his death ten months later, on 12 October 1892, not so much as a line was written of the further volumes originally planned – had had his work cut out for him, trying to make an author locked in combat with his present and with his successors conform at least partially to the requirements of historical truth. Even so, in terms of many details but above all in terms of its structure, in the way in which it stressed connections, in what it said and what it left unsaid, and in its opinions and

231

allusions the whole work was anything but an attempt to draw up a historically accurate balance-sheet of a political career, anything but a self-critical review of his public life and his achievement.

It was concerned at all points, before anything else, with the present and with the way things were to go from there – that is to say, with the future. The last thing Bismarck was interested in doing was defining his own place in history and giving future generations a lead in this regard. That would have meant closing the books, standing back, saying a retrospective farewell, renouncing all involvement. No – every line of the work was to desmonstrate how decisively history and political good sense were still on his side and to make clear that he still stood for the future, just as he had done before, the future that was always at the same time, *mutatis mutandis*, a keeping faith with the past.

The strength and liveliness of the whole work and the fascination that it is still capable of exerting today stem from the fact that Bismarck did not stick rigidly to these leading ideas. He repeatedly slipped into narrative and in so doing deployed a range of nuances of characterization of persons and situations such as virtually no other politician, indeed virtually no other writer of the nineteenth century could command. A master of the seemingly unintentional emphasis, the carefully administered ambiguity and the malicious subordinate clause, he wrested new life and fresh perspectives as much from the forgotten and supposedly over and done with as from what had been long known and endlessly described – to say nothing of the insights and experiences of a long life, which often came out almost incidentally, simply in the way in which he tackled certain questions and problems.

Although it was these things that very substantially accounted for the success and abiding influence of the work as well as for the special place it occupies in the literature of political memoirs, from the standpoint of the author himself they were all more or less trimmings, digressions, historical entertainment designed to 'sell' the part that mattered, namely the political interpretation and the opinions and the programme put forward. Everything was governed by his analysis of the current political parallelogram of forces, which Bismarck still hoped to use for his own purposes and which he therefore endeavoured to influence.

'Pseudo-politics', Herbert once scornfully but not altogether inappropriately dubbed his father's activities in this regard.[39] And that was how the memoirs were widely misunderstood as to their content, their tacit allusions and their real objectives when they appeared in November 1898 in what was once again a substantially altered situation – and how since that time they have repeatedly given rise to fresh misunderstandings and misinterpretations. Beyond his own intention, Bismarck thus contributed towards his becoming chief witness for the most diverse political forces without those forces, in collaboration with and in conflict with one another, falling into line as he had envisaged them doing in the interests of his own objectives and expectations. To put it another way: the memoirs had an effect, not only at the time but for decades to come, that was politically and historically in the highest degree misleading. They were and are in no way apt to provide access to a historically correct judgement. They rest on the proposition that only a quite specific past has a future and that it is therefore important, in the interests of the future, to bind the present to that past.

Both parts of the proposition were undoubtedly false and missed the special place that that specific past occupied in the historical process, a place that Bismarck was elsewhere, under the pressure of particular historical forces and crucial situations, thoroughly capable of determining, albeit never in more than the implicit and fragmentary manner peculiar to the historical agent. He belonged, as he glimpsed at key moments, to an age of transition characterized by a major political and social upheaval, an upheaval that was shaking all the old systems to their foundations, making them appear useless without revealing any new systems that were really viable as yet or that above all enjoyed general acceptance. This opened up hitherto undreamt-of possibilities for bold improvization, surprising links between old and new, the involvement of what in themselves were highly antagonistic economic, social and political forces in a fresh overall context dictated essentially by one's own power interests – especially if one promised security and a future to the forces of the existing order, which though still dominant in many places were nevertheless already under serious threat. But the whole structure that arose on this foundation was at the same time extremely unstable. It was itself threatened, almost as soon as it had been erected, by the very forces of change to which, through having exploited some and resisted others, it owed its emergence. For those forces would not in reality allow themselves to be bewitched in a new order that, having been established with their help by more or less arbitrary means, now sought all of a sudden to halt their movement. The creator of that new order inevitably became a sorcerer's apprentice who had to pay for the magnitude of his success with the magnitude of his defeat, not in personal but in historical terms.

Nothing, not one jot remains of what Bismarck wrung, whether by resisting them or by making concessions to them, from the forces of upheaval in the shape of the revolutionary changes of his day: the Lesser German national state, the perpetuation of the power of the Prussian Crown in a wholly new political and institutional setting, the securing of the position of the traditional elites together with its material basis, the position of power occupied by the new Reich in the circle of the European powers. On the contrary, the seemingly so successful alloy of old and new elements turned out to be an illusory patina. It merely concealed the process of corrosion and led to self-delusions of all kinds, particularly among those to whom it had seemed to lend fresh strength. What initially looked so stable, so permanent, so independent historically, so closely in tune with a particular historical development, was swept aside in the space of a few decades. Today we see the Reich of 1871, if we consider it soberly and eschew all wishful thinking, as a highly unstable and short-lived historical entity.

Of course, just this kind of apparently illusion-free sobriety of approach can, in fixating on a sort of counter-image as a defence against the illusions of the past, itself become misleading. We must ask ourselves whether such

233

an interpretation does not in the end simply lead back – albeit from the opposite direction – to what with the active assistance of the ageing Bismarck had already become a cliché at the time, namely the notion that the Reich enjoyed a quite specific, genuine domestic order and was anchored in a quite specific foreign policy 'system'. On the contrary, was not every aspect of both domestic and foreign policy, far from being tied to any system or order, in fact in a state of flux during the greater part of Bismarck's time in office? In other words, does not this version of events, whether expressed affirmatively or critically, tend rather to obscure the true nature of this whole phenomenon and the real historical significance of the man and his achievement?

Unquestionably that significance did not at any time, not even in Bismarck's old age, lie in what he allegedly or actually intended. The objectives he consciously pursued were often somewhat short-windedly as well as short-sightedly conceived, the only purposes they served being the acquisition and the preservation of power. They radiated – this was one of the great weaknesses of the 1871 Reich – virtually no force of appeal or integration; there was nothing stirring about them. Bismarck himself never possessed a 'Reichsidee', an imperial ideal as an inspiring model for and vision of the future. Consequently he and the rulers of the Reich were unable to communicate such an ideal. Bismarck's significance lies rather in the fact that for long periods of time, while paying lip-service to the past, he in fact, in the way he practised politics, played the future card, in effect helping to usher in the future to an extent that those who called themselves the partisans of that future would probably never have dared to do. As Maximilian Harden once put it, in a verdict as pithy as it was keen-sighted: 'He did not know where he was going, which is why he got farthest.'[40] What it is nowadays fashionable to refer to as the process of modernization of a society, a state, a nation is, on close examination, crucially bound up with Bismarck and with his concrete policy and its actual historical consequences: national unity, which was at the same time economic, cultural, legal, political and – admittedly in a very much more restricted sense – also social unity and above all unification, standardization, a bridge to new, more modern patterns; the rise and ever-expanding development of the modern industrial economy, for which his policy steadily created fresh room legally, territorially, and in terms of the domestic and foreign policy context in which it operated; the construction of the modern bureaucratic, interventionist state, which by the end of his time in office was further developed than anywhere else in the world and which in the field of social and economic policy was taking more and more forceful and determinative action affecting everybody's living conditions; and finally the evolution of a rationally based, in other words largely ideology-free international system as a factor of the first importance in making for and maintaining order, a factor in the creation of which he played an outstanding part.

Granted, all these were secular processes and trends that were beginning to make themselves felt throughout European civilization, albeit at varying speeds. But what Bismarck did with his policy, for all that he spoke continually of digging in and of throwing up dams, was to give them a decisive boost over broad areas and for an extended period. It was this, beyond all tactics and diplomacy and beyond all his skill and years of experience, that constituted the basis of his success. For many years he, Bismarck, to a far greater extent than many other seemingly more progressive spirits, was the man of his time – not in the sense of opportunistic self-adaptation but in the heightened, almost breath-taking matter-of-factness and feeling for reality of a man who sought to wrest from the age and from the historical moment a freedom of action that is in actual fact only very rarely – in periods of transition, during truly major historical upheavals – theirs to give. As he explained on one occasion in later years, he did not say with Louis XIV, 'L'État c'est moi!' but 'Moi je suis l'État'.[41]

For that very reason, however, his success also had its sharply defined limits – not only in what he did and did not find possible and in the concrete shaping of circumstances, in which he was far less free and far less in full command than he is often represented as having been and much more often obliged to make sweeping concessions and to sacrifice the ideas he had originally entertained, but also in the time allotted to him for active achievement along these lines.

This was very much briefer than his twenty-seven-and-a-half years in office, first as Minister-President and Foreign Minister of Prussia and subsequently as Chancellor of the Reich as well, might lead one to believe. It did not really begin until 1866, after a number of extremely laborious years spent in establishing himself in power, not without many set-backs. And it was in many respects over by the late 1870s, however heavily his claim to power weighed on all circumstances until his fall and however powerfully it continued to shape those circumstances individually. From that time onwards he concentrated entirely on clinging doggedly to what had been achieved, sometimes doing so with a very clear awareness that any further change would be detrimental to this threefold objective – the preservation of his own power, that of the Prussian Crown and the monarchical state, and that of the Reich, which encompassed the other two. In this he displayed all his skill and political experience and for years, despite many obvious failures, deployed them with success. And although the tendency simply to preserve the status quo and reject any radical change now came clearly to the fore, given the gradual extension of the interventionist state that went on in that context his policy was once again, even in these years, allied to a secular process.

Yet in terms of the peculiar historical importance that this subsequently attained it was a mere by-product, an ultimately unintentional side-effect. Moreover, it came into effect historically only when the interventionist state abandoned its purely reactionary stance and began actively to influence political and above all socio-economic conditions – a development that, significantly, Bismarck himself criticized vehemently after his dismissal.

His sole concern was to freeze a position that had once been so extremely favourable to himself and his immediate political objectives. In the final analysis, however, this was not possible. In simply damming up the thrusting forces and trends of development, it threatened in the long run to sweep away all those elements of the old that Bismarck had contrived to preserve by himself setting sail on the river of change.

Once upon a time he had been perceptive enough to recognize that policies of mere reaction usually accelerate the destruction of what they seek to preserve. And he had adapted his whole policy to that recognition. Yet here he was, himself reverting to that kind of approach – not because he now saw things differently but because he saw no future for himself, nor indeed could he have seen a future for himself in any other approach. The age of the statesman who commuted between different political and social worlds, sometimes uniting them, sometimes dividing them, seeking always to maintain them in a somewhat artifical symbiosis – that age was no more. Those worlds now demanded more direct, one might say more partial representation. They no longer wanted a mediator, whose triumph was always a personal one; they wanted a man to represent their own class, their own ideology and philosophy of life, their own power interest. It was a demand to which Bismarck yielded, albeit with deep reluctance: the 1880s showed an unmistakable trend towards class politics.

Of course, given his constitutional position and his personal authority Bismarck did not need to go as far in this direction as a genuine party leader and representer of interests. That very fact, however, linked the trend towards class politics in a quite disastrous way with the claim, insisted on for reasons of power, that the government was the natural mediator between interests and parties. It emphasized what Gustav Radbruch, the great jurist of the Weimar Republic, was to call the 'vital lie of the authoritarian state'. And in so doing it further impeded the kind of transition to new forms of politico-social compromise that, as the example of western Europe and particularly Britain showed, was capable of evolving precisely from the practice of the undisguised representation of interests. For it identified specific interests with the existing legal and administrative order as such and sought in consequence to paralyse all change and suspend all historical movement. Paralysis, ossification, rigid adherence to the status quo – taken all in all, this was the end. Many people felt that, beyond the immediate point at issue, the young emperor initially had as it were the right of history, the right of the future, on his side.

To admit this even to a limited extent, cautiously to detach himself, in retrospect, from the narrowness and rigidity into which he had eventually fallen and to set his own political career and his own achievement in the perspective of their original dynamic – that was something of which Bismarck, with his unbroken will to power and his total fixation on present conflicts, remained incapable until the time of his death, whether in composing his memoirs or in his incessant commenting on the past. It would of course have been tantamount to an admission that he had outlived his political usefulness, that his policy had in many respects led to a stalemate, an admission, too, of the relativity of his own already historical existence.

Yet it is only in that relativity that the peculiar nature of what may be called historical greatness and above all what historical significance means is revealed: the specific part played by an individual in history. For the really crucial component of this is not the arbitrary element, the supposed freedom of the successful agent, but the bond attaching him to the past and to the future. It is this that enables him, in a specific historical situation, to combine together, at least temporarily and transitionally, hitherto unconnected and indeed mutually hostile constituents in surprising turns of events and entirely new forms.

In this sense nearly every great historical agent has been, like Bismarck, a conservative revolutionary who paid tribute to the past without becoming a slave to it and used the future to invoke the element of his own power and freedom. Here nothing could be calculated, and like their rivals who failed and are today forgotten they were all to a greater or lesser extent gamblers by nature. What lifts them above their time, however, what in a deeper sense constitutes the significance of their success, is not the way in which that success was achieved in detail. It is the generic fact that they very often used as a means what was regarded by most of their contemporaries as an end and proved historically to be a determinative force. This was the case with Bismarck. What he wanted belonged wholly to the past. Yet for a time, at the height of his career, the means he employed had the effect of enormously accelerating the historical process and ushering in at a rapid rate what for the sake of brevity we call the modern world. Largely against his will he came to play a decisive part in helping to create that world – therein lie both his historical greatness and his great limitation.

Notes

Chapter 10: New Constellations, New Conflicts

1   Letter to Catherine Orlov, 25 December 1871: Fürst Nikolai Orloff, *Bismarck und die Fürstin Orloff, Ein Idyll in der hohen Politik* (Munich, 1936), p. 129.
2   Letter to Johanna, 28 August 1863: GW, Vol. 14, p. 652.
3   J. von Eckardt, *Lebenerinnerungen*, Vol. 1 (1910), p. 124.
4   R. Vierhaus (ed.), *Das Tagebuch der Baronin Spitzemberg*, 4th edn (Göttingen, 1976), p. 238.
5   Letter to Karoline von Bismarck-Bohlen, September 1838: GW, Vol. 14, p. 15.
6   F. Stern, *Gold and Iron: Bismarck, Bleichröder, and the Building of the German Empire* (London, 1977), particularly pp. 280 ff.
7   Letter to Catherine Orlov, 25 December 1871 (see above, note 1).
8   Letter of 19 April 1859: GW, Vol. 14, p. 513.
9   Letter of 30 June 1850: GW, Vol. 14, pp. 159 f.
10 Quoted in Lucius, *Bismarck-Erinnerungen*, p. 48.
11 In a letter to Roon, 20 November 1873: GW, Vol. 14, p. 857.
12 GW, Vol. 15, p. 352.
13 Heyderhoff, *Liberalismus*, Vol. 1, p. 494.
14 Quoted in L. Gall, *Der Liberalismus als regierende Partei* (Wiesbaden, 1968), p. 485.
15 Letter to Friedrich Kiefer, 13 December 1870: 'Aus Eduard Laskers Nachlass', in *Deutsche Revue*, Vol. 17, no. 4 (1892), pp. 67 f.
16 H. Kohl (ed.), *Bismarck-Regesten*, Vol. 1 (1891), pp. 418 f.
17 Directive of 12 April 1868: GW, Vol. 6a, p. 348.
18 Quoted in M. Stürmer, *Regierung und Reichstag im Bismarckstaat 1871–1880* (Düsseldorf, 1974), pp. 74 f.
19 Directive to the Bavarian envoy in Rome, von Tauffkirchen, 30 June 1871: GW, Vol. 6c, p. 9.
20 Reply to an address from German students, 1 April 1895: GW, Vol. 13, p. 558.
21 Lucius, *Bismarck-Erinnerungen*, p. 10.
22 Letter of 21 July 1869: GW, Vol. 14, p. 752.
23 H. Schnatz (ed.), *Päpstliche Verlautbarungen zu Staat und Gesellschaft* (1973), p. 5.
24 Directive to Schweinitz/Vienna, 27 January 1873: GW, Vol. 6c, p. 32.
25 In a speech in the Prussian House of Deputies on 16 April 1875: Kohl, *Reden*, Vol. 6, p. 270.
26 N. Siegfried, *Aktenstücke betreffend den preussischen Kulturkampf* (1882), p. 93.
27 E. L. von Gerlach, *Kaiser und Papst* (1873), p. 72.
28 Quoted in Lucius, *Bismarck-Erinnerungen*, p. 47.
29 In a letter to von Gossler, 25 November 1881: GW, Vol. 6c, p. 234. Robert

239

von Mohl, a celebrated liberal authority on constitutional law, served as *Reichsjustizminister* in 1848.

30 E. Förster, *Adalbert Falk* (Gotha, 1927), p. 75.
31 Kohl, *Reden*, Vol. 5, pp. 228 ff.
32 *Stenographische Berichte des Deutschen Reichstags*, 1871–2, pp. 541 ff.
33 Kohl, *Reden*, Vol. 5, pp. 242 ff.
34 Roon, *Denkwürdigkeiten*, Vol. 3, p. 372.
35 Letter to Roon, 13 December 1872: GW, Vol. 14, p. 845.
36 Letter to Roon, 20 November 1873: GW, Vol. 14, p. 857.
37 In a letter to Minister of the Interior Eulenburg, 21 December 1873: GW, Vol. 6c, p. 48.
38 Dated 5 February 1874: GW, Vol. 6c, p. 53.
39 Kohl, *Reden*, Vol. 5, p. 338.
40 *Stenographische Berichte des Deutschen Reichstags*, 1871, Vol. 2, p. 921.
41 Kohl, *Reden*, Vol. 7, p. 267.
42 Dated 7 June 1871: GW, Vol. 6c, p. 8.
43 GW, Vol. 6c, p. 10.
44 Letter of 17 November 1871: Poschinger, *Wirtschaftspolitik*, Vol. 1 (1890), p. 165.
45 T. Schieder, 'Das Problem der Revolution im 19. Jahrhundert', in *Staat und Gesellschaft im Wandel unserer Zeit* (1958), p. 40.
46 In a letter to Itzenplitz, 17 November 1871: Poschinger, *Wirtschaftspolitik*, Vol. 1 (1890), p. 166.

Chapter 11: The Reich and Europe

1 Letter of 23 July 1870: GW, Vol. 6b, p. 417.
2 Letter to his daughter Marie, 23 June 1862: GW, Vol. 14, p. 834.
3 W. F. Monypenny and G. E. Buckle, *The Life of Benjamin Disraeli*, Vol. 2 (1929), pp. 473 f.
4 Quoted in H. Lutz, *Österreich-Ungarn und die Gründung des Deutschen Reiches* (Berlin, 1979), p. 365, and GW, Vol. 6b, p. 596.
5 Directive to Schweinitz/Vienna, 7 February 1871: GW, Vol. 6b, p. 690.
6 Speech on 19 February 1878: Kohl, *Reden*, Vol. 7, pp. 105 f.
7 Quoted in Schoeps, *Bismarck über Zeitgenossen*, p. 84.
8 GW, Vol. 8, p. 45.
9 Lucius, *Bismarck-Erinnerungen*, p. 27.
10 Directive to Reuss/St Petersburg, 21 January 1869: GW, Vol. 6a, p. 526.
11 Reuss/St Petersburg to William I, 16 July 1872: *Grosse Politik*, Vol. 1, p. 198.
12 ibid., Vol. 1, pp. 206 f.
13 Said in conversation with the Hungarian writer Maurus Jókai, 27 February 1874: GW, Vol. 8, p. 107.
14 Lucius, *Bismarck-Erinnerungen*, p. 72.
15 Said to von Oettingen at the end of May 1873 in the light of the possibility of a fresh conflict: GW, Vol. 8, p. 87.
16 GW, Vol. 15, p. 364. He had already expressed himself in very similar terms in August 1878: Hermann Freiherr von Mittnacht, *Erinnerungen an Bismarck, Neue Folge (1877–1889)*, 5th edn (Stuttgart/Berlin, 1905), pp. 10 f.
17 Letter of 5 December 1872: W. Frank, *Nationalismus und Demokratie im Frankreich der Dritten Republik* (1933), p. 26.
18 Letter to Reuss/Paris, 29 November 1862: GW, Vol. 14, p. 630.

19 Speech in the Imperial Diet on 5 December 1876: Kohl, *Reden*, Vol. 6, p. 461.
20 Dictate of 14 October 1876: *Grosse Politik*, Vol. 2, p. 647.
21 Speech in the Imperial Diet on 19 February 1878: Kohl, *Reden*, Vol. 7, p. 92.
22 Letter of 2 September 1876: *Grosse Politik*, Vol. 2, p. 38.
23 ibid., Vol. 2, p. 37.
24 ibid., p. 55.
25 Letter from Bülow to Schweinitz/St Petersburg, 23 October 1876: ibid., p. 251.
26 Dictate of 2 October 1876: ibid., p. 55.
27 The 'Kissingen Dictate': ibid., pp. 153 f.
28 Lucius, *Bismarck-Erinnerungen*, p. 112.
29 Speech in the Imperial Diet on 19 February 1878: Kohl, *Reden*, Vol. 7, pp. 80 f.
30 On 30 November 1876: *Hatzfeld-Papiere*, Vol. 1, p. 307.
31 *Stenographische Berichte*, Vol. 1, 19 February 1878, p. 114.
32 Quoted in R. Seton-Watson, *Disraeli, Gladstone, and the Eastern Question*, 2nd edn (1926), p. 423.
33 Letter to Drummond Wolff, 4 November 1880: W. F. Monypenny and G. E. Buckle, *The Life of Benjamin Disraeli*, Vol. 2 (1929), p. 1239.

Chapter 12: A Change of Course at Home

1 On 25 January 1873: Kohl, *Reden*, Vol. 5, p. 378.
2 Speech in the Prussian House of Deputies, 5 February 1868: Kohl, *Reden*, Vol. 3, p. 456.
3 Note of 2 November 1872: GW, Vol. 6c, p. 25.
4 O. von Diest-Daber, *Lebensbild eines mutigen Patrioten* (1901), p. 37.
5 L. E. von Schulte, *Lebenserinnerungen*, Vol. 1 (1908), p. 322.
6 Note by Rudolf Delbrück concerning a conversation with Johannes Miquel, 9 February 1873: Nachlass Bismarck, B 34, 17.
7 The reference is to Lasker's speeches of 14 January and especially 7 February 1873: *Stenographische Berichte*, Vol. 1, pp. 536 ff., Vol. 2, pp. 934 ff.
8 Frederick I of Baden to Charles Alexander of Sachsen-Weimar, 12 April 1873: *Grossherzog Friedrich I. und die Reichspolitik*, Vol. 1, p. 114.
9 Speech in the Imperial Diet on 4 December 1874: Kohl, *Reden*, Vol. 6, p. 222.
10 Speech on 18 March 1875: Kohl, *Reden*, Vol. 6, p. 256.
11 Quoted in H. von Poschinger, *Fürst Bismarck und die Parlamentarier*, 2nd edn, Vol. 1 (1894), p. 87.
12 Quoted in M. Stürmer, *Regierung und Reichstag im Bismarckstaat 1871–1880* (Düsseldorf, 1974), p. 142.
13 *Stenographische Berichte*, Vol. 3, Anlage 54, p. 157 (§ 130).
14 Kohl, *Reden*, Vol. 6, pp. 292 ff.
15 The industrialist August Servaes to the General Secretary of the Association of German Iron and Steel Manufacturers, Dr Rentzsch on 6 November 1875: H. Böhme, *Deutschlands Weg zur Grossmacht*, 2nd edn (Cologne, 1972), p. 388.
16 Kohl, *Reden*, Vol. 6, pp. 333 ff.
17 Reproduced in L. Feldmüller-Perrot, *Bismarck und die Juden, 'Papierpest' und 'Aera-Artikel von 1875'* (1931), pp. 271 ff.
18 Letter of 18 July 1875: GW, Vol. 6c, pp. 61 f.
19 In the *Kreuzzeitung*, 26 February 1876.
20 Lucius, *Bismarck-Erinnerungen*, p. 85.

21 Quoted in Tiedemann, *Aus sieben Jahrzehnten*, Vol. 2, p. 15.
22 Wilhelm Cahn (ed.), *Aus Eduard Laskers Nachlass* (Berlin, 1902), p. 107.
23 Said in conversation with the National Liberal deputy von Benda in Kissingen, mid-July 1876: quoted in H. von Poschinger, *Bismarck und die Parlamentarier*, 2nd edn, Vol. 2 (1894), p. 209. He expressed himself in similar terms to the Free Conservative deputy Lucius at the end of September 1876: Lucius, *Bismarck-Erinnerungen*, p. 94.
24 Busch, *Tagebuchblätter*, Vol. 2, pp. 548 f.
25 GW, Vol. 14, pp. 890 f.
26 Quoted in Tiedemann, *Aus sieben Jahrzehnten*, Vol. 2, p. 16.
27 Lucius, *Bismarck-Erinnerungen*, p. 105.
28 Speech on 10 March 1877: Kohl, *Reden*, Vol. 7, pp. 17 ff.
29 E. Richter, *Im alten Reichstag*, Vol. 2 (Berlin, 1896), p.13.
30 Lucius, *Bismarck-Erinnerungen*, p. 127.
31 Tiedemann, *Aus sieben Jahrzehnten*, Vol. 2, p. 129.
32 Letter to Bismarck, 30 December 1877: appended to *Gedanken und Erinnerungen* (1901), p. 278.
33 Letter from Lucius to Tiedemann, 9 February 1878: Tiedemann, *Aus sieben Jahrzehnten* Vol. 2, p. 226.
34 Kohl, *Reden*, Vol. 7, pp. 109 ff.
35 H. von Mittnacht, *Erinnerungen an Bismarck*, 3rd edn (Stuttgart/Berlin, 1904), pp. 61 ff.
36 Letter to Heinrich Gelzer, 3 April 1878: *Grossherzog Friedrich I. von Baden und die Reichspolitik*, Vol. 1, p. 280.
37 Said on 6 October 1877: quoted in E. Förster, *Adalbert Falk* (Gotha, 1927), pp. 384 ff.
38 Letter of 22 February 1878: appended to *Gedanken und Erinnerungen*, Vol. 2 (1901), p. 511.
39 E. Richter, *Im alten Reichstag*, Vol. 2. (Berlin, 1896), p. 54.
40 Bismarck's words to von Benda: quoted in H. von Poschinger, *Bismarck und die Parlamentarier*, 2nd edn, Vol. 2 (1894), p. 208.
41 Lucius, *Bismarck-Erinnerungen*, p. 86.
42 To August Firks-Samiten in 1885: GW, Vol. 8, p. 518.
43 Letter to Heinrich Gelzer, 4 April 1878: *Grossherzog Friedrich I. von Baden und die Reichspolitik*, Vol. 1, p. 281.
44 Lucius, *Bismarck-Erinnerungen*, p. 125.
45 W. Cahn (ed.), *Aus Eduard Laskers Nachlass* (Berlin, 1902), p. 110.
46 GW, Vol. 6c, p. 109.
47 Letter from Hobrecht to Bismarck, 18 May 1878: M. Stürmer, *Regierung und Reichstag im Bismarckstaat 1871–1880* (Düsseldorf, 1974), p. 220.
48 *Stenographische Berichte*, Vol. 2, p. 1508; for the whole debate, pp. 1495 ff.
49 Tiedemann, *Aus sieben Jahrzehnten*, Vol. 2, p. 263.
50 Address to a deputation of National Liberal agents from the nineteenth Hanoverian constituency, 2 May 1891: GW, Vol. 13, p. 423.
51 GW, Vol. 15, p. 372.
52 ibid., pp. 372 f.
53 Friedrich Curtius (ed.), *Denkwürdigkeiten des Fürsten Chlodwig zu Hohenlohe-Schillingsfürst*, Vol. 2 (Stuttgart/Leipzig, 1907), p. 243.
54 Letter of 12 August 1878: GW, Vol. 14, p. 894.
55 *Bismarck-Jahrbuch*, Vol. 1, p. 118.
56 Quoted in H. von Mittnacht, *Erinnerungen an Bismarck, Neue Folge*, 5th edn (Stuttgart/Berlin, 1905), p. 9.

57   Dated 29 May 1878: GW, Vol. 6c, p. 114.
58   *Stenographische Berichte*, p. 201. Bennigsen's speech of the previous day, 10 October 1878: ibid., pp. 165 ff.
59   *Stenographische Berichte*, p. 62.
60   Quoted in F. C. Sell, *Die Tragödie des deutschen Liberalismus* (Stuttgart, 1953), p. 266.
61   Said on 3 September 1878: Heyderhoff, *Liberalismus*, Vol. 2, p. 223.
62   The 'Weihnachtsbrief': H. von Poschinger, *Fürst Bismarck als Volkswirth* Vol. 1 (Berlin, 1889), pp. 170 ff.
63   GW, Vol. 6c, p. 184.
64   15 February 1879: *Hatzfield-Papiere*, Vol. 1, p. 330.
65   Speech on 2 May 1879: Kohl, *Reden*, Vol. 8, pp. 11 ff.
66   *Stenographische Berichte*, Vol. 2, p. 1048.
67   Kohl, *Reden*, Vol. 8, pp. 33 ff.
68   Schultess, *Europäischer Geschichtskalender 1879*, pp. 164 f.
69   Said to Tiedemann on 30 June 1879: Tiedemann, *Aus sieben Jahrzehnten*, Vol. 2, p. 243.
70   Direct report of 3 July 1879: GW, Vol. 6c, p. 155.
71   Kohl, *Reden*, Vol. 8, pp. 137 ff.
72   The reference is to Ludwig Uhland's speech in the Paulskirche in Frankfurt on 22 January 1849: *Stenographische Berichte über die Verhandlungen der deutschen konstituierenden Nationalversammlung*, Vol. 7, p. 4819.
73   Directive to Reuss/Vienna, 20 April 1880: GW, Vol. 6c, p. 178.
74   Directive to Reuss/Vienna, 14 May 1880: GW, Vol. 6c, p. 186.
75   Letter from Herbert von Bismarck to Count Rantzau, 27 July 1879: H. von Bismarck, *Privatkorrespondenz*, p. 90.

Chapter 13: *Foreign Policy Reorientation, Domestic Policy Choices*

1   *Grosse Politik*, Vol. 3, p. 14.
2   ibid., pp. 16 ff.
3   ibid., p. 25.
4   ibid., pp. 41 f.
5   Rothfels, *Briefe*, pp. 397 f.
6   *Grosse Politik*, Vol. 3, pp. 27 ff.
7   Lucius, *Bismarck-Erinnerungen*, p. 176.
8   *Stenographische Berichte*, Vol. 1, p. 104.
9   *Grosse Politik*, Vol. 3, pp. 178 f.
10   GW, Vol. 14, p. 910.
11   Letter of 22 November 1879: GW, Vol. 6c, p. 165.
12   Letter to Lucius, 5 November 1879: GW, Vol. 14, p. 910.
13   Letter to Tiedemann, 22 November 1879: GW, Vol. 6c, p. 165.
14   In a letter to Ludwig II of Bavaria, 1 June 1880: GW, Vol. 14, p. 917.
15   Letter of 25 May 1878: GW, Vol. 6c, pp. 111 f.
16   Speech on 15 March 1884: Kohl, *Reden*, Vol. 10, p. 56.
17   Busch, *Tagebuchblätter*, Vol. 3, p. 89.
18   Letter to Eduard Lasker, 28 January 1880: Heyderhoff, *Liberalismus*, Vol. 2, p. 290.
19   *Werke in Auswahl*, Vol. 6, p. 469.
20   Poschinger, *Wirtschaftspolitik*, Vol. 2, pp. 10 ff.

21 Quoted in V. Dorsch, 'Die Handelskammern der Rheinprovinz in der zweiten Hälfte des 19. Jahrhunderts', thesis (Frankfurt, 1979), V, 1, 1.
22 In Bingen on 4 March 1882, published in the *Mainzer Tagblatt*, 12 March 1882. I am grateful for this information to Frau M.-L. Weber, who is writing a monograph on Bamberger.
23 Hans Rothfels, 'Prinzipienfragen der Bismarckschen Sozialpolitik', in H. Rothfels, *Bismarck, der Osten und das Reich*, 2nd edn (Stuttgart, 1960), p. 171.
24 Poschinger, *Wirtschaftspolitik*, Vol. 1, pp. 258 ff.
25 GW, Vol. 6c, p. 230.
26 Busch, *Tagebuchblätter*, Vol. 3, p. 10.
27 Said in late June 1881: ibid., p. 45.
28 Letter to Friedrich von Preen, 26 April 1872: F. Kaphahn (ed.), *Jacob Burckhardt, Briefe* (undated), p. 364.
29 Letter to Treitschke, 2 June 1881: Heyderhoff, *Liberalismus*, Vol. 2, p. 380.
30 Letter of 23 April 1881: O. Pniower and P. Schlenther (eds), *Briefe Theodor Fontanes, Zweite Sammlung* (1910), p. 42.
31 Speech on 2 April 1881: *Stenographische Berichte*, Vol. 1, p. 710.
32 ibid., p. 709.
33 ibid., pp. 678 f.
34 Kohl, *Reden*, Vol. 9, p. 31.
35 ibid., p. 29.
36 H.-P. Ullmann, 'Industrielle Interessen und die Entstehung der deutschen Sozialversicherung', in HZ, Vol. 229 (1979), p. 608.
37 Speech on 29 April 1881: Kohl, *Reden*, Vol. 9, p. 56.
38 ibid., pp. 63 ff.
39 Issue of 20 June 1881.
40 Letter from Herbert von Bismarck to Tiedemann, 6 July 1881: M. Stürmer (ed.), *Bismarck und die preussisch-deutsche Politik 1871–1890* (Munich, 1970), p. 174.
41 Said to his private physician Dr Cohen: GW, Vol. 8, p. 394.
42 Said to Mittnacht, Minister-President of Württemberg: H. von Mittnacht, *Erinnerungen an Bismarck*, 3rd edn (Stuttgart/Berlin, 1904), pp. 29 f.
43 Speech on 14 June 1882: Kohl, *Reden*, Vol. 9, pp. 420 f.
44 GW, Vol. 14, p. 601.
45 Lucius, *Bismarck-Erinnerungen*, p. 217.
46 Busch, *Tagebuchblätter*, Vol. 2, p. 157.
47 Théophile Gauthier, Jr, on 24 October 1870: GW, Vol. 7, p. 382.
48 Said to the Conservative deputy Count Frankenberg: H. von Poschinger, *Fürst Bismarck und die Parlamentarier*, Vol. 3 (1896), p. 54.

Chapter 14: New Paths to Old Objectives: the Foreign Policy of the 1880s

1 *Grosse Politik*, Vol. 2, p. 153.
2 Dated 8 April 1880: *Grosse Politik*, Vol. 3, p. 395.
3 Said to his private physician, Dr Cohen, 8 January 1884: GW, Vol. 8, p. 499.
4 Courcel's report of 23 September 1884 in *Documents diplomatiques français (1871–1914)*, Series 1 (1871–1900), Vol. 5 (Paris, 1929–59), p. 424.
5 H. von Bismarck, *Privatkorrespondenz*, pp. 239 ff.
6 Letter of 9 October 1884: GW, Vol. 6c, p. 308.
7 Letter of 25 May 1885: *Grosse Politik*, Vol. 3, pp. 445 f.
8 E. Wolf, *Vom Fürsten Bismarck und seinem Haus* (1904), p. 13.

9 Letter of 26 July 1886: *Hatzfeld-Papiere*, Vol. 1, p. 513.
10 Letter to Rantzau, 24 September 1886: H. von Bismarck, *Privatkorrespondenz*, p. 379.
11 *Grosse Politik*, Vol. 3, pp. 245 ff.
12 Letter of 23 August 1881: GW, Vol. 6c, p. 223.
13 Letter of 31 July 1881: GW, Vol. 14, p. 928.
14 Letter from Rantzau to Herbert von Bismarck, 14 October 1884: H. von Bismarck, *Privatkorrespondenz*, p. 320.
15 Directive to Reuss/Vienna, 6 December 1885: *Grosse Politik*, Vol. 5, p. 27.
16 *Hatzfeld-Papiere*, Vol. 1, p. 459.
17 Nachlass Bismarck, B 128 (copy).
18 Letter to Bülow, 31 October 1885: H. von Bismarck, *Privatkorrespondenz*, p. 332.
19 Note by Rantzau, 6 October 1886: *Grosse Politik*, Vol. 5, p. 137.
20 Rantzau to Herbert von Bismarck, 15 October 1886: H. von Bismarck, *Privatkorrespondenz*, p. 396.
21 *Grosse Politik*, Vol. 4, pp. 311 ff.
22 ibid., pp. 393 f.
23 ibid., Vol. 5, pp. 253 ff.
24 Letter to his brother Bill, 19 June 1887: H. von Bismarck, *Privatkorrespondenz*, pp. 457 f.
25 *Hatzfeld-Papiere*, Vol. 1, p. 658, n. 9.
26 Letter of 19 August 1888: *Grosse Politik*, Vol. 6, p. 342.
27 Letter to his brother Bill, 11 November 1887: H. von Bismarck, *Privatkorrespondenz*, p. 479.
28 On 30 December 1887: GW, Vol. 6c, p. 378.
29 Said to his private physician, Dr Cohen, on 11 April 1882: GW, Vol. 8, p. 446.
30 Letter of 24 December 1886: GW, Vol. 6c, p. 350.
31 Kohl, *Reden*, Vol. 12, p. 186.
32 ibid., p. 178.
33 Directive to Reuss/St Petersburg, 28 February 1874: *Grosse Politik*, Vol. 1, p. 241.
34 Kohl, *Reden*, Vol. 12, p. 477.
35 Letter of 19 December 1887: *Grosse Politik*, Vol. 6, p. 58.
36 Max Weber, 'Der Nationalstaat und die Volkswirtschaftspolitik', in *Gesammelte politische Schriften*, 3rd edn (1971), p. 23.
37 K.-E. Jeismann, *Das Problem des Präventivkriegs im Europäischen Staatensystem* (1957), p. 135. The *Berliner Tageblatt* quotation is taken from the same source.
38 Letter of 14 January 1888: *Hatzfeld-Papiere*, Vol. 1, p. 657.
39 Kohl, *Reden*, Vol. 12, p. 447.
40 Letter from Hatzfeld to Holstein, 18 June 1885: *Grosse Politik*, Vol. 9, p. 353.
41 Letter from Holstein to Hatzfeld, 13 January 1889: *Hatzfeld-Papiere*, Vol. 1, p. 411.
42 *Grosse Politik*, Vol. 4, p. 405.
43 Letter to Crown Prince William, 9 May 1888: *Grosse Politik*, Vol. 6, p. 305.

Chapter 15: The 'Stopgap' System: Domestic Policy after 1881

1 Max Weber, 'Der Nationalstaat und die Volkswirtschaftspolitik', in *Gesammelte politische Schriften*, 3rd edn (1971), p. 20.
2 Said to his private physician, Dr Cohen, 12 May 1882: GW, Vol. 8, p. 448.

3 Letter to Bennigsen or Miquel (the name of the addressee is missing from the draft, which is all that has survived): Heyderhoff, *Liberalismus*, Vol. 2, pp. 386 f.
4 Lucius, *Bismarck-Erinnerungen*, pp. 264 f.
5 Letter from Karl von Normann to Gustav Freytag, 20 January 1882: Heyderhoff, *Liberalismus*, Vol. 2, p. 391.
6 Said on 2 December 1883: *Tagebuch der Baronin Spitzemberg*, p. 202.
7 H. von Poschinger, *Fürst Bismarck als Volkswirth*, Vol. 2 (Berlin, 1890), p. 82.
8 F. Tennstedt, *Sozialgeschichte der Sozialversicherung, Handbuch der Sozialmedizin*, Vol. 3 (1976), p. 390.
9 H. Rothfels, *Theodor Lohmann und die Kampfjahre der staatlichen Sozialpolitik (1871–1905)* (Berlin, 1927), pp. 63 f.
10 Address to the representatives of German corporations, 17 April 1895: GW, Vol. 13, p. 574.
11 Directive to Schlözer/Rome, 17 February 1882: GW, Vol. 6c, p. 246.
12 H. Herzfeld, *Johannes von Miquel*, Vol. 2 (1938), p. 14.
13 Heidelberg Declaration of 23 March 1884: W. Mommsen, *Deutsche Parteiprogramme* (1960), pp. 158 ff.
14 Heyderhoff, *Liberalismus*, Vol. 2, pp. 404 f.
15 Kohl, *Reden*, Vol. 10, pp. 186 ff.
16 Busch, *Tagebuchblätter*, Vol. 3, pp. 191 f.
17 Letter to von Gossler, 14 January 1884: *Werke in Auswahl*, Vol. 7, p. 73.
18 Kohl, *Reden*, Vol. 10, pp. 281 ff. Gessler was the brutal Landvogt of the William Tell legend, who forced Tell to shoot an apple from his son's head.
19 Letter of 23 January 1885: *Werke in Auswahl*, Vol. 7, pp. 245 f.
20 *Stenographische Berichte*, p. 164.
21 Letter to Gossler, 23 January 1885: *Werke in Auswahl*, Vol. 7, p. 245.
22 Kohl, *Reden*, Vol. 10, p. 311.
23 ibid., pp. 309 f.
24 ibid., Vol. 11, pp. 410 ff.
25 ibid., pp. 453 ff.
26 *Stenographische Berichte*, p. 175.
27 Telegram of 21 September 1885: GW, Vol. 6c, p. 324.
28 GW, Vol. 6c, p. 325.
29 Speech in the Imperial Diet on 29 November 1881: Kohl, *Reden*, Vol. 9, p. 153.
30 Direct report of 24 February 1883: GW, Vol. 6c, p. 276.
31 Letter from Rantzau to Herbert von Bismarck, 11 December 1885: H. von Bismarck, *Privatkorrespondenz*, p. 353.
32 GW, Vol. 6c, pp. 349 ff.
33 H. O. Meisner (ed.), *Denkwürdigkeiten des Generalfeldmarschalls Alfred Grafen von Waldersee*, Vol. 1 (Stuttgart/Berlin, 1923), p. 281.
34 One such warning was contained in his speech on 26 March 1886: Kohl, *Reden*, see particularly p. 365.
35 Lucius, *Bismarck-Erinnerungen*, p. 335.
36 Said at a meeting of the Prussian Cabinet, 21 March 1886: *Werke in Auswahl*, Vol. 7, p. 383.
37 Said on 14 February 1886: quoted in M. Stürmer, *Bismarck und die preussisch-deutsche Politik 1871–1890* (Munich, 1970), p. 230.
38 Letter of 14 December 1886: GW, Vol. 6c, p. 347.
39 Letter to Bronsart von Schellendorf, 13 December 1886: GW, Vol. 14, p. 971. Similar sentiments were expressed by Herbert von Bismarck in a letter to Rantzau, 12 December 1886: H. von Bismarck, *Privatkorrespondenz*, p. 412.

40 E. Soderini, *Leo XIII. und der Kulturkampf* (1935), p. 204.
41 GW, Vol. 6c, p. 352.
42 At a meeting on 11 January 1887: *Werke in Auswahl*, Vol. 7, p. 431.
43 Kohl, *Reden*, Vol. 12, pp. 175 ff.
44 Speech on 12 January 1887: Kohl, *Reden*, Vol. 12, pp. 238, 229.
45 Speech on 13 January 1887: Kohl, *Reden*, Vol. 12, p. 276.
46 Letter from Bleichröder to Hatzfeld, 15 February 1887: *Hatzfeld-Papiere*, Vol. 1, p. 563.
47 H. Oncken, *Rudolph von Bennigsen*, Vol. 2 (1910), p. 535.
48 Letter to Franz von Stauffenberg, 3 March 1887: Heyderhoff, *Liberalismus*, Vol. 2, p. 432.
49 Letter from Karl Schrader to Frank von Stauffenberg, 9 April 1887: Heyderhoff, *Liberalismus*, Vol. 2, p. 434.
50 Letter to his brother Bill, 4 March 1887: H. von Bismarck, *Privatkorrespondenz*, p. 430.
51 Kohl, *Reden*, Vol. 12, p. 381.
52 Issue of 14 September 1887: G. Seeber *et al.*, *Bismarcks Sturz* (Berlin, 1977), p. 130.
53 GW, Vol. 6c, pp. 382 ff.
54 Lucius, *Bismarck-Erinnerungen*, p. 413.
55 Letter to Wilhelm von Hammerstein: W. Frank, *Hofprediger Adolf Stöcker und die christlich-soziale Bewegung* (1928), p. 318. The letter acquired its name from Stoecker's reference in it to the 'piles of faggots' that must be lit around the Cartel in order to put Bismarck under pressure politically and so bring about his fall.

Chapter 16: The End

1 GW, Vol. 15, p. 471.
2 Noted on a letter from Frederick William of 3 September 1863, clearly in preparation for his subsequent audience with the crown prince: Nachlass Bismarck, B 43.
3 Lucius, *Bismarck-Erinnerungen*, p. 457.
4 Letter of 2 August 1888: GW, Vol. 14, p. 987.
5 Letter to Franz von Stauffenberg, 13 May 1888: Heyderhoff, *Liberalismus*, Vol. 2, p. 441.
6 Issue of 21 October 1888: G. Seeber *et al.*, *Bismarcks Sturz* (Berlin, 1977), p. 247.
7 Meeting on 18 March 1889: *Werke in Auswahl*, Vol. 7, p. 694.
8 M. Stürmer, *Bismarck und die preussisch-deutsche Politik 1871–1890* (Munich, 1970), p. 276.
9 Meeting on 25 May 1889: *Werke in Auswahl*, Vol. 7, pp. 716 f.
10 Lucius, *Bismarck-Erinnerungen*, p. 497.
11 Letter to Stosch, 30 March 1895: *Gustav Freytags Briefe an Albrecht von Stosch* (1913), p. 189.
12 Lucius, *Bismarck-Erinnerungen*, p. 509.
13 Georg von Eppstein (ed.), *Fürst Bismarcks Entlassung* (Berlin, 1920), pp. 157 ff. See also Lucius, *Bismarck-Erinnerungen*, pp. 506 ff.
14 Letter of 12 March 1890: J. C. G. Röhl (ed.), *Philipp Eulenburgs politische Korrespondenz*, Vol. 1 (Boppard, 1976), pp. 493 ff.
15 Lucius, *Bismarck-Erinnerungen*, p. 512.

16 Letter of 30 January 1890: GW, Vol. 8, p. 680.
17 'Le Chancelier a pris nettement position contre les vues de son souverain', Herbette's report of 10 February 1890: *Documents diplomatiques français (1871–1914)*, Series 1 (1871–1900), Vol. 7 (Paris, 1929–59), p. 604.
18 GW, Vol. 6c, p. 431.
19 J. Penzler, *Die Reden Kaiser Wilhelms II. in den Jahren 1888–1895* (1897), p. 97.
20 E. Hüsgen, *Ludwig Windthorst* (1907), p. 340.
21 E. Zechlin, *Staatsstreichpläne Bismarcks und Wilhelms II. 1890–1894* (Stuttgart, 1929), pp. 179 ff.
22 Telegram from Marschall to Frederick I of Baden, 4 March 1890 (concerning a conversation between Helldorf and the Emperor): *Grossherzog Friedrich I. von Baden und die Reichspolitik 1871–1907*, Vol. 2, p. 741.
23 Quoted in S. von Kardorff, *Bismarck im Kampf um sein Werk* (Berlin, 1943), p. 114.
24 GW, Vol. 15, p. 517.
25 H. O. Meisner (ed.), *Denkwürdigkeiten des Generalfeldmarschalls Alfred Grafen von Waldersee*, Vol. 2 (Stuttgart, 1922), pp. 115 f.
26 GW, Vol. 6c, pp. 435 ff.
27 GW, Vol. 15, p. 531.
28 Quoted in E. Gagliardi, *Bismarcks Entlassung*, Vol. 2 (Tübingen, 1941), p. 238.
29 P. Nathan (ed.), *Ludwig Bamberger, Erinnerungen* (Berlin, 1899), p. 501.

Chapter 17: The Shadow of the Past

1 H. von Poschinger (ed.), *Fürst Bismarck, Neue Tischgespräche und Interviews*, Vol. 1 (Stuttgart/Leipzig/Berlin/Vienna, 1895), p. 173.
2 M. Hank, *Kanzler ohne Amt, Fürst Bismarck nach seiner Entlassung 1890–1898* (Munich, 1977).
3 Letter to Friedrich von Preen, 26 September 1890: F. Kaphahn (ed.), *Jacob Burckhardt, Briefe* (undated), p. 536.
4 Letter to A. von Heyden, 5 August 1893: O. Pniower and P. Schlenther (eds), *Briefe Theodor Fontanes, Zweite Sammlung*, Vol. 2 (1910), p. 304.
5 *Tagebuch der Baronin Spitzemberg*, pp. 289 f.
6 In conversation with Maximilian Harden, 29 October 1892: GW, Vol. 9, p. 267.
7 As William said to his generals in June 1891: *Zwischen Kaiser und Kanzler, Aufzeichnungen des Generaladjutanten Grafen Carl von Wedel aus den Jahren 1890–1894* (1943), pp. 182 f.
8 Said to Maximilian Harden, February 1891: GW, Vol. 9, p. 118.
9 Letter from Kiderlen-Wächter to Philipp Eulenburg, 4 June 1892: J. C. G. Röhl, *Philipp Eulenburgs politische Korrespondenz*, Vol. 2 (Boppard, 1979), pp. 884.
10 Letter from Holstein to Philipp Eulenburg, 10 June 1892: ibid., p. 889.
11 Letter of 12 June 1892: Hank, *Kanzler ohne Amt*, p. 334.
12 O. Grandenwitz (ed.), *Akten über Bismarcks grossdeutsche Rundfahrt vom Jahre 1892* (1922), p. 5.
13 Hank, *Kanzler ohne Amt*, p. 334.
14 Issue of 23 June 1892: GW, Vol. 9, pp. 214 ff.
15 GW, Vol. 13, p. 559.
16 J. Penzler, *Fürst Bismarck nach seiner Entlassung*, Vol. 2 (1897), p. 245.
17 Hank, *Kanzler ohne Amt*, p. 548.

18 GW, Vol. 9, p. 220.
19 ibid., p. 355.
20 Hank, *Kanzler ohne Amt*, p. 549, n. 1.
21 J. Penzler, *Fürst Bismarck nach seiner Entlassung*, Vol. 2 (1897), p. 297.
22 GW, Vol. 9, p. 481.
23 GW, Vol. 13, p. 464.
24 H. Hofmann, *Fürst Bismarck 1890–1898*, Vol. 1 (Stuttgart, 1913), p. 128.
25 GW, Vol. 15, p. 15.
26 *Gesichter und Zeiten*, 2nd edn (1962), pp. 257, 265 f.
27 Max Weber, 'Die Nationalstaat und die Volkswirtschaftspolitik', in *Gesammelte politische Schriften*, 3rd edn (1971), pp. 19 f. The Kyffhäuser, in Thuringia, is the mountain beneath which, according to an ancient legend, there slept an emperor who would one day emerge to restore the nation's past glories.
28 Letter of 6 June 1895: Hank, *Kanzler ohne Amt*, p. 413.
29 Quoted in Hank, *Kanzler ohne Amt*, p. 412.
30 *Bismarck-Jahrbuch*, Vol. 2, p. 397.
31 Letter to Philipp Eulenburg, 9 December 1894: J. C. G. Röhl, *Philipp Eulenburgs politische Korrespondenz*, Vol. 2 (Boppard, 1979), p. 1424.
32 Philipp Eulenburg's report to William II, 14 and 26 November 1896: Hank, *Kanzler ohne Amt*, p. 602. The remaining quotations in this paragraph are from the same source.
33 J. Penzler, *Fürst Bismarck nach seiner Entlassung*, Vol. 7 (1898), pp. 129 f.
34 Letter to his brother-in-law, Count Rantzau, 2 July 1887: H. von Bismarck, *Privatkorrespondenz*, p. 458.
35 Said in conversation with the writer Sidney Whitman in mid-October 1891: GW, Vol. 9, p. 150.
36 Letter to Johannes Miquel, 28 November 1894: Nachlass Bismarck, B 78 (draft). The word *Einschnitt*, here translated as 'turning-point', literally means 'cut' or 'incision' (Tr.).
37 Letter of 19 December 1894: GW, Vol. 14, p. 1017.
38 Nachlass Bismarck, A 37c.
39 Letter to Alexander von Keyserling, 9 July 1890: Nachlass Bismarck, B 61.
40 M. Harden, *Apostata, Neue Folge* (1892), pp. 20 f.
41 Said in June 1884: W. von Schweinitz (ed.), *Denkwürdigkeiten des Botschafters General von Schweinitz*, Vol. 2 (Berlin, 1927), p. 270.

Sources and Literature

Bibliographical Aids

Born, Karl Erich (ed.), *Bismarck-Bibliographie, Quellen und Literatur zur Geschichte Bismarcks und seiner Zeit* (Cologne–Berlin, 1966).
Bullock, A. and Taylor, A. J. P., *A Select List of Books on European History, 1815–1914* (Oxford, 1948).
Gall, Lothar (ed.), *Das Bismarck-Problem in der Geschichtsschreibung nach 1945* (Cologne/Berlin, 1971), pp. 427–45.
Hamerow, T. S. (ed.), *Otto von Bismarck, A Historical Assessment*, 2nd edn (Lexington, Mass./London, 1972).
Stolberg-Wernigerode, Albrecht Graf zu, *Bismarck-Lexikon, Quellenverzeichnis zu den in seinen Akten, Briefen, Gesprächen und Reden enthaltenen Äusserungen Bismarcks* (Stuttgart/Berlin, 1936).

Printed Sources

BISMARCK'S WRITINGS AND LETTERS

Kohl, Horst (ed.), *Die politischen Reden des Fürsten Bismarck 1847–1897, historisch-kritische Gesamtausgabe*, 14 vols (Stuttgart, 1892–1905).
Bismarck, Otto von, *Die gesammelten Werke (the 'Friedrichsruh Edition')*, 15 in 19 vols (Berlin, 1924–35).
Bismarck, Otto von, *Werke in Auswahl, Jahrhundert-Ausgabe zum 23 September 1862*, 4 parts in 8 vols, ed. Gustav Adolf Rein *et al.* (Darmstadt, 1962–80).
Poschinger, Heinrich von (ed.), *Fürst Bismarck als Volkswirth*, 3 vols (Berlin, 1889–91).
Poschinger, Heinrich von (ed.), *Aktenstücke zur Wirtschaftspolitik des Fürsten Bismarck*, 2 vols (Berlin, 1890–1).
Kohl, Horst (ed.), *Fürst Bismarck. Regesten zu einer wissenschaftlichen Biographie des ersten deutschen Reichskanzlers*, 2 vols (Leipzig, 1891–2).
Poschinger, Heinrich Ritter von (ed.), *Fürst Bismarck und die Parlamentarier*, 3 vols (Breslau, 1894–6).
Bismarck-Jahrbuch, ed. Horst Kohl, 6 vols (Berlin, 1894–9).
Poschinger, Heinrich Ritter von (ed.), *Fürst Bismarck, Neue Tischgespräche und Interviews*, 2 vols (Stuttgart/Leipzig/Berlin/Vienna, 1895–9). English edn, *Conversations with Prince Bismarck*, edited with an introduction by Sidney Whitman (London/New York, 1900).

Bismarcks Briefe an General Leopold von Gerlach, new edn by Horst Kohl (Berlin/Stuttgart, 1896).

Poschinger, Heinrich Ritter von (ed.), *Fürst Bismarck und der Bundesrat*, 5 vols (Stuttgart/Leipzig, 1897–1901).

Poschinger, Heinrich Ritter von (ed.), *Bismarck-Portefeuille*, 5 vols (Stuttgart/Leipzig, 1898–1900).

Bismarck, Otto von, *Bismarck, the Man and the Statesman, being the reflections and reminiscences of Otto Prince von Bismarck*, 2 vols, trans. A. J. Butler (London, 1898).

Poschinger, Heinrich Ritter von (ed.), *Fürst Bismarck und die Diplomaten 1852–90* (Hamburg, 1900).

Kaiser- und Kanzler-Briefe, Briefwechsel zwischen Kaiser Wilhelm I und Fürst Bismarck, collected and annotated by Johannes Penzler (Leipzig, 1900). English edn, *Correspondence of William I and Bismarck with other letters*, 2 vols, trans. A. J. Ford (London, 1903).

Anhang zu den Gedanken und Erinnerungen von Otto Fürst von Bismarck, ed. Horst Kohl, 2 vols (Stuttgart, 1901).

Littlefield, W. (ed.), *Bismarck's Letters to his Wife from the Seat of War, 1870–71* (London, 1903).

Bismarcks Briefwechsel mit dem Minister Freiherrn von Schleinitz 1858–1861 (Stuttgart/Berlin, 1905).

Bismarck, Herbert Fürst von (ed.), *Fürst Bismarcks Briefe an seine Braut und Gattin*, 4th edn (Stuttgart, 1914). English edn, *The Love Letters of Prince Bismarck*, 2 vols (London, 1901). *Prince Bismarck's Letters to his Wife, his Sister and other letters from 1844 to 1870*, trans. F. Maxse (London, 1878).

Kohl, Horst (ed.), *Briefe Otto von Bismarcks an Schwester und Schwager Malwine von Arnim, geb. v. Bismarck und Oskar von Arnim-Kröchlendorff 1843–1897* (Leipzig, 1915).

Petersdorff, Hermann von (ed.), *Bismarcks Briefwechsel mit Hans Hugo von Kleist-Retzow* (Stuttgart, 1919).

Die politischen Berichte des Fürsten Bismarck aus Petersburg und Paris (1859–1862), ed. Ludwig Raschdau, 2 vols (Berlin, 1920).

Neue Bismarck-Gespräche, vier unveröffentlichte politische Gesprache des Kanzlers mit österreichisch-ungarischen Staatsmannern sowie ein Gesprach Kaiser Wilhelms II, ed. Helmut Krausnick (Hamburg, 1940).

Bismarck, Otto von, *Briefe*, selected and introduced by Hans Rothfels (Göttingen, 1955).

Rothfels, Hans, *Bismarck und der Staat*, 3rd edn (Stuttgart, 1958).

Stolberg-Wernigerode, Otto Graf zu, 'Ein unbekanntes Bismarckgespräch aus dem Jahre 1865', in *Historische Zeitschrift*, Vol. 194 (1962), pp. 357–62.

Bismarck, Otto von, *Gespräche*, ed. Willy Andreas and Karl Franz Reinking, 3 vols (Bremen, 1963–5).

Sempell, Charlotte, 'Unbekannte Briefstellen Bismarcks', *Historische Zeitschrift*, Vol. 207 (1968), pp. 609–16.

Bismarck, Otto von, *Aus seinen Schriften, Reden und Gesprächen*, selected and postfaced by Hanno Helbling (Zurich, 1976).

SOURCE COLLECTIONS, LETTERS, MEMOIRS

Abeken, Heinrich, *Ein schlichtes Leben in Bewegter Zeit, aus Briefen zusammengestellt*, ed. Hedwig Abeken (Berlin, 1898).

Die auswärtige Politik Preussens 1858–1871, diplomatische Aktenstücke, ed. Historische Reichskommission, 10 vols (Oldenburg, 1933–41).

Bamberger, Ludwig, *Gesammelte Schriften*, 5 vols (Berlin, 1894–8).

Bamberger, Ludwig, *Erinnerungen*, ed. Paul Nathan (Berlin, 1899).

Bamberger, Ludwig, *Bismarcks grosses Spiel. Die geheimen Tagebücher Ludwig Bambergers*, ed. and introduced by Ernst Feder (Frankfurt, 1932).

Bebel's Reminiscences (New York, 1911).

Bennigsen, Rudolf von, *Reden*, ed. Walther Schultze and Friedrich Thimme, Vol. 1 (Halle, 1911).

Bernhardi, Theodor von, *Aus dem Leben Theodor von Bernhardis*, 9 vols (Leipzig, 1898–1906).

Im Kampfe für Preussens Ehre. Aus dem Nachlasse des Grafen Albrecht von Bernstorff und seiner Gemahlin Anna. geb. Freiin von Koenneritz, ed. Karl Ringhoffer (Berlin, 1906).

Beust, Friedrich-Ferdinand Graf von, *Aus drei Vierteljahrhunderten, Erinnerungen und Aufzeichnungen*, 2 vols (Stuttgart, 1887).

Bismarck, Herbert Graf von, *Graf Herbert Bismarck. Aus seiner politischen Privatkorrespondenz*, ed. and introduced by Walter Bussmann and Klaus Peter Hoepke (Göttingen, 1964).

The Bismarck Calendar. A quotation from the writings and sayings of Prince Bismarck for every day of the year (London 1913).

Bismarck in Time. By a fellow student, trans. H. Hayward (London, 1890).

Böhme, Helmut (ed.), *Die Reichsgründung* (Munich, 1967).

Buckle, G. E. (ed.), *The Letters of Queen Victoria*, First Series, 3 vols, A. C. Benson and Viscount Esher (eds) (London, 1907). Second and Third Series, 6 vols, G. E. Buckle (ed.) (London, 1926–30).

Busch, Moritz, *Tagebuchblätter*, 3 vols (Leipzig, 1899).

Dalwigk zu Lichtenfels, Reinhard Freiherr von, *Die Tagebücher des Freiherrn Reinhard von Dalwigk zu Lichtenfels aus den Jahren 1860–1871*, ed. Wilhelm Schüssler (Stuttgart/Berlin, 1920).

Delbrück, Rudolf von, *Lebenserinnerungen von Rudolf von Delbrück 1817–1867*, 2 vols (Leipzig, 1905).

Documents diplomatiques français (1871–1914), Ser. 1 (1871–1900), 16 vols (Paris, 1929–59).

Dunker, Max, *Politischer Briefwechsel aus seinem Nachlasse*, ed. Johannes Schultze (Stuttgart, 1923).

Eckardstein, Hermann Freiherr von, *Lebenserinnerungen und politische Denkwürdigkeiten*, 3 vols (Leipzig, 1919–21).

Ernst II, Herzog von Sachsen-Coburg-Gotha, *Aus meinem Leben und aus meiner Zeit*, 3 vols (Berlin, 1888–9).

Eulenburg-Hertefeld, Philipp Fürst zu, *Philipp Eulenburgs politische Korrespondenz*, ed. John C. G. Röhl, 2 vols (Boppard, 1976–9).

Faber, Karl-Georg, *Die nationalpolitische Publizistik Deutschlands von 1866–1871. Eine kritische Bibliographie*, 2 vols (Düsseldorf, 1963).

Fenske, Hans (ed.), *Der Weg zur Reichsgründung 1850–1870* (Darmstadt, 1977).

Fenske, Hans (ed.), *Im Bismarckschen Reich 1871–1890* (Darmstadt, 1978).

Grossherzog Friedrich I. von Baden und die deutsche Politik von 1854 bis 1871, Briefwechsel, Denkschriften, Tagebücher, ed. Hermann Oncken, 2 vols (Stuttgart, 1927).

Grossherzog Friedrich I. von Baden und die Reichspolitik 1871–1907, ed. Walter Peter Fuchs, 2 vols to date (Stuttgart, 1968/75).

Kaiser Friedrich III, *Das Kriegstagebuch von 1870/71*, ed. Heinrich Otto Meisner (Berlin/Leipzig, 1926).

Kaiser Friedrich III, *Tagebücher von 1848 bis 1866*, ed. and introduced by Heinrich Otto Meisner (Leipzig, 1929).

253

Geiss, Immanuel (ed.), *Der Berliner Kongress 1878, Protokolle und Materialien* (Boppard, 1978).

Gerlach, Ernst Ludwig von, *Aufzeichnungen aus seinem Leben und Wirken 1795–1877*, ed. Jakob von Gerlach, 2 vols (Schwerin, 1903).

Gerlach, Ernst Ludwig von, *Von der Revolution zum Norddeutschen Bund, Politik und Ideengut der preussischen Hochkonservativen 1848–1866*, ed. and introduced by Hellmut Diwald, 2 parts (Göttingen, 1970).

Gerlach, Leopold von, *Denkwürdigkeiten aus dem Leben Leopold von Gerlachs*, 2 vols (Berlin, 1891/2).

German Diplomatic Documents, Bismarck's Relations with England, 1871–1914, Vol. 1, trans. E.T.S. Dugdale (London, 1926).

Hamerow, T. S. (ed.), *The Age of Bismarck, Documents and Interpretations* (New York, 1973).

Hatzfeldt, Paul Graf von, *Botschafter Paul Graf von Hatzfeldt. Nachgelassene Papiere 1838–1901*, ed. and introduced by Gerhard Ebel in association with Michael Behnen, 2 vols (Boppard, 1976).

Hohenlohe-Schillingsfürst, Chlodwig Fürst zu, *Denkwürdigkeiten*, ed. Friedrich Curtius (Stuttgart/Leipzig, 1906). English edn, *Memoirs of Prince Chlodwig of Hohenlohe-Schillingsfürst*, 2 vols (New York, 1906).

Holstein, Friedrich von, *Die geheimen Papiere Friedrich von Holsteins*, ed. Norman Rich and M. H. Fisher. German edn by Werner Frauendienst, 4 vols (Göttingen/Berlin/Frankfurt, 1956–63). English edn, *The Holstein Papers*, 4 vols (Cambridge, 1955–63).

Huber, Ernst Rudolf (ed.), *Dokumente zur deutschen Verfassungsgeschichte*, Vols 1 and 2 (Stuttgart, 1961/4).

Keudell, Robert von, *Fürst und Fürstin Bismarck, Erinnerungen von 1846 bis 1872* (Berlin/Stuttgart, 1901).

Knaplund, P. (ed.), *Letters from the Berlin Embassy, 1871–74* (Washington, 1944).

Lasker, Eduard, *Aus Eduard Laskers Nachlass*, pt 1: *Fünfzehn Jahre parlamentarischer Geschichte (1866–1880)*, ed. Wilhelm Cahn (Berlin, 1902).

Lassalle, Ferdinand, *Gesammelte Reden und Schriften*, ed. Eduard Bernstein, 12 vols (Berlin, 1919).

Loftus, Lord Augustus, *Diplomatic Reminiscences*, 4 vols (London, 1894).

Lucius von Ballhausen, Robert Freiherr, *Bismarck-Erinnerungen* (Stuttgart/ Berlin, 1920).

Manteuffel, Otto Freiherr von, *Unter Friedrich Wilhelm IV, Denkwürdigkeiten des Ministers Otto Freiherr von Manteuffel*, ed. Heinrich von Poschinger, 3 vols (Berlin, 1901).

Medlicott, W. N. and Coveney, D. K. (eds), *Bismarck and Europe* (London, 1971).

Miquel, Johannes von, *Reden*, ed. Walther Schultze and Friedrich Thimme, 4 vols (Halle, 1911–14).

Mittnacht, Hermann Freiherr von, *Erinnerungen an Bismarck*, 3rd edn (Stuttgart/ Berlin, 1904).

Mittnacht, Hermann Freiherr von, *Erinnerungen an Bismarck, Neue Folge (1877–1889)*, 5th edn (Stuttgart/Berlin, 1905).

Moltke, Helmuth Graf von, *Gesammelte Schriften und Denkwürdigkeiten*, 8 vols (Berlin, 1891–3).

Mommsen, Wilhelm (ed.), *Deutsche Parteiprogramme* (Munich, 1960).

Oldenburg, Karl, *Aus Bismarcks Bundesrat, Aufzeichnungen des Mecklenburg-Schwerinschen 2. Bundesratsbevollmächtigten Karl Oldenburg aus den Jahren 1878–1885*, ed. Wilhelm Schüssler (Berlin, 1929).

Oncken, Hermann (ed.), *Die Rheinpolitik Kaiser Napoleons III. 1863–1870 und der*

Ursprung des Krieges von 1870/71. Nach den Staatsakten von Österreich, Preussen und den süddeutschen Mittelstaaten, 3 vols (Stuttgart/ Berlin/Leipzig, 1926).

Les Origines diplomatiques de la guerre de 1870–1871, Recueil de documents publié par le Ministère des Affaires étrangères, 6 vols (Paris, 1910–12).

Orloff, Nikolai Fürst, *Bismarck und die Fürstin Orloff, ein Idyll in der hohen Politik, mit unveröffentlichten Briefen Bismarcks und der Fürstin Orloff* (Munich, 1936).

Die grosse Politik der europäischen Kabinette von 1871–1914. Sammlung der diplomatischen Akten des Auswärtigen Amtes, ed. Johannes Lepsius, Albrecht Mendelssohn-Bartholdy and Friedrich Thimme, 40 vols (Berlin, 1922–7).

Poschinger, Heinrich von (ed.), *Preussen im Bundestag 1851–1859. Dokumente der Königlich Preussischen Bundestagsgesandtschaft*, 4 vols (Leipzig, 1882–5).

Poschinger, Heinrich von, *Aus grosser Zeit, Erinnerungen an den Fürsten Bismarck* (Berlin, 1905).

Poschinger, Heinrich von, *Stunden bei Bismarck* (Vienna, 1910).

Quellen zur deutschen Politik Österreichs 1859–1866, ed. Heinrich Ritter von Srbik, 5 vols (Oldenburg, 1934–8).

Radowitz, Josef Maria von, *Aufzeichnungen und Erinnerungen aus dem Leben des Botschafters 1839–1890*, ed. Hajo Holborn, 2 vols (Stuttgart, 1925).

Raschdau, Ludwig, *Unter Bismarck und Caprivi, Erinnerungen eines deutschen Diplomaten aus den Jahren 1885–1894* (Berlin, 1928).

Richter, Eugen, *Im alten Reichstag*, 2 vols (Berlin, 1894/6).

Roehl, J. C. (ed.), *From Bismarck to Hitler. The Problem of Continuity in German History* (London, 1970).

Roon, Albrecht Graf von, *Denkwürdigkeiten aus dem Leben des Generalfeldmarschalls Kreigsministers Grafen von Roon. Sammlung von Briefen, Schriftstücken und Erinnerungen*, 3 vols, 4th edn (Breslau, 1897).

Rosenberg, Hans, *Die nationalpolitische Publizistik Deutschlands, vom Eintritt der neuen Ära in Preussen bis zum Ausbruch des deutschen Krieges, eine kritische Bibliographie*, 2 vols (Munich/Berlin, 1935).

Schloezer, Kurd von, *Petersburger Briefe, 1857–1862, nebst einem Anhang: Briefe aus Berlin/Kopenhagen, 1862–1864*, ed. Leopold von Schloezer (Stuttgart/Berlin, 1922).

Schloezer, Kurd von, *Letzte römische Briefe, 1882–1894*, ed. Leopold von Schloezer (Berlin/Leipzig, 1924).

Scholz, Adolf von, *Erlebnisse und Gespräche mit Bismarck*, ed. W. von Scholz (Stuttgart, 1922).

Schweinitz, Hans Lothar von, *Denkwürdigkeiten des Botschafters General von Schweinitz*, ed. Wilhelm von Schweinitz, 2 vols (Berlin, 1927).

Schweinitz, Hans Lothar von, *Briefwechsel des Botschafters General von Schweinitz*, ed. Wilhelm von Schweinitz (Berlin, 1928).

Simon, W. M. (ed.), *Germany in the Age of Bismarck* (London, 1971).

Snyder, L. L. (ed.), *Documents of German History* (Connecticut, 1958).

Das Tagebuch der Baronin Spitzemberg geb. Freiin von Varnbüler, Aufzeichnungen aus der Hofgesellschaft des Hohenzollernreiches, selected and ed. Rudolf Vierhaus, 4th edn (Göttingen, 1976).

Stosch, Albrecht von, *Denkwürdigkeiten des Generals und Admirals Albrecht von Stosch, ersten Chefs der Admiralität, Briefe und Tagebuchblatter*, ed. Ulrich von Stosch (Stuttgart/Leipzig, 1904).

Sturmer, Michael (ed.), *Bismarck und die preussisch-deutsche Politik 1871–1890* (Munich, 1970).

Tiedemann, Christoph von, *Aus sieben Jahrzehnten, Erinnerungen von Christoph von Tiedemann*, 2 vols (Leipzig, 1905/9).

Tirpitz, Alfred von, *Erinnerungen* (Leipzig, 1919). English edn, *My Memoirs* (London, 1922).

Unruh, Hans Victor von, *Erinnerungen*, ed. Heinrich von Poschinger (Stuttgart, 1895).

Waldersee, Alfred Graf von, *Denkwürdigkeiten des Generalfeldmarschalls Alfred Grafen von Waldersee*, ed. Heinrich Otto Meisner, 3 vols (Stuttgart/Berlin, 1923–5).

Waldersee, Alfred Graf von, *Aus dem Briefwechsel des Generalfeldmarschalls Alfred Graf von Waldersee*, ed. Heinrich Otto Meisner (Stuttgart, 1928).

Wentzcke, Paul, and Julius Heyderhoff, *Deutscher Liberalismus im Zeitalter Bismarcks, eine politische Briefsammlung*, 2 vols (Bonn, 1925–6), repr. Osnabruck, 1967.

Wilhelm II, *Ereignisse und Gestalten aus den Jahren 1878–1918* (Berlin, 1922). English edn., *My Memoirs* (London, 1922).

Wilmowski, Gustav von, *Meine Erinnerungen an Bismarck. Aus dem Nachlass*, ed. Marcell von Wilmowski (Breslau, 1900).

GENERAL ACCOUNTS AND INDIVIDUAL PROBLEM AREAS

Abel, Wilhelm, *Agrarkrisen und Agrarkonjunktur. Eine Geschichte der Land- und Ernährungswirtschaft Mitteleuropas seit dem hohen Mittelalter*, 3rd edn (Hamburg/Berlin, 1978).

Anderson, M. S., *The Eastern Question, 1774–1923* (London, 1966).

Aubin, Hermann, and Wolfgang Zorn (eds), *Handbuch der deutschen Wirtschafts- und Sozialgeschichte*, vol. 2 (Stuttgart, 1976).

Bachem, Karl, *Vorgeschichte, Geschichte und Politik der deutschen Zentrumspartei, Zugleich ein Beitrag zur Geschichte der katholischen Bewegung, sowie zur allgemeinen Geschichte des neueren und neuesten Deutschland 1815–1914*, 9 vols (Cologne, 1927–32).

Bartel, Horst (ed.), *Arbeiterbewegung und Reichsgründung* (Berlin, 1971).

Bergsträsser, Ludwig, *Geschichte der politischen Parteien in Deutschland*, 10th edn (Munich, 1960).

Böhme, Helmut (ed.), *Problem der Reichsgründungszeit, 1848–1879* (Cologne/Berlin, 1968).

Böhme, Helmut, *Deutschlands Weg zur Grossmacht, Studien zum Verhältnis von Wirtschaft und Staat während der Reichsgründungszeit 1848–1881*, 2nd edn (Cologne, 1972).

Bondi, Gerhard, *Deutschlands Aussenhandel 1815–1870* (Berlin, 1958).

Born, Karl-Erich, 'Von der Reichsgründung bis zum I. Weltkrieg', in B. Gebhardt, *Handbuch der Deutschen Geschichte*, ed. Herbert Grundmann, 9th edn, Vol. 3 (Stuttgart, 1970), pp. 221–375.

Brandenburg, Erich, *Die Reichsgründung*, 2 vols, 2nd edn (Leipzig, 1922) with an appendix volume *Untersuchungen und Aktenstücke zur Geschichte der Reichsgründung* (Leipzig, 1916).

Brandenburg, Erich, *From Bismarck to the World War*, trans. A. E. Adams (Oxford, 1927).

Bussmann, Walter, *Das Zeitalter Bismarcks*, 4th edn (Constance, 1968).

The Cambridge Economic History of Europe, Vols 6 and 7 (Cambridge, 1965–78).

The New Cambridge Modern History, Vols 10 and 11 (Cambridge, 1960/1).

Carr, W., *A History of Germany, 1815–1945* (London, 1969).

Clapham, J. H., *Economic Development of France and Germany, 1815–1914* (Cambridge, 1921).

Conze, Werner, and Dieter Groh, *Die Arbeiterbewegung in der nationalen Bewegung, die deutsche Sozialdemokratie vor, während und nach der Reichsgründung* (Stuttgart, 1966).

Craig, Gordon A., *Germany 1866–1945* (Oxford, 1978).

Craig, G., *From Bismarck to Adenauer: Aspects of German Statecraft* (New York, 1965).

Dawson, William H., *The German Empire 1867–1914 and the Unity Movement*, 2 vols (London, 1966).

Engelberg, Ernst, *Deutschland von 1849 bis 1871* (Berlin, 1959).

Engels, E. F., *The Role of Force in History. A Study of Bismarck's Policy of Blood and Iron*, trans. J. Cohen. Edited with an Introduction by E. Wangermann (London, 1968).

Farr, I., 'From Anti-Catholicism to Anticlericalism: Catholic Politics and the Peasantry in Bavaria, 1860–1900,' *European Studies Review*, Vol. 13(2), pp. 249–69.

The Fontana Economic History of Europe, Vol. 4: *The Emergence of Industrial Societies*. ed. Carlo M. Cipolla (London, 1973).

Gagli, Walter, *Die Wahlrechtsfrage in der Geschichte der deutschen liberalen Parteien, 1848–1918* (Düsseldorf, 1958).

Gladen, Albin, *Geschichte der Sozialpolitik in Deutschland. Eine Analyse ihrer Bedingungen. Formen, Zielsetzungen und Auswirkungen* (Wiesbaden, 1974).

Grebing, Helga, *Geschichte der deutschen Parteien* (Wiesbaden, 1962).

Grebing, Helga, *Geschichte der deutschen Arbeiterbewegung. Ein Überblick* (Munich, 1966). English edn, *History of the German Labour Movement from 1848 to the Present* (Leamington Spa, 1985).

Hamerow, Theodore S., *Restoration, Revolution, Reaction: Economics and Politics in Germany 1815–1871* (Princeton, N. J., 1958).

Hamerow, Theodore S., *The Social Foundations of German Unification*, 2 vols (Princeton, N. J., 1969/72).

Henderson, William O., *The Zollverein*, 3rd edn (London, 1968).

Henning, Hansjoachim, *Das westdeutsche Bürgertum in der Epoche der Hochindustrialisierung 1860–1914, soziales Verhalten und soziale Strukturen*, pt 1 (Wiesbaden, 1972).

Herzfeld, Hans, *Die moderne Welt 1789–1945*, pt 1: *Die Epoche der bürgerlichen Nationalstaaten*, 4th edn (Brunswick, 1964).

Hillgruber, Andreas, *Bismarcks Aussenpolitik* (Freiburg, 1972).

Hoffmann, Walther G. u.a., *Das Wachstum der deutschen Wirtschaft seit der Mitte des 19. Jahrhunderts* (Berlin/Heidelberg/New York, 1965).

Holborn, H., *A History of Modern Germany, 1840–1945* (London, 1969).

Huber, Ernst Rudolf, *Deutsche Verfassungsgeschichte seit 1789*, Vols 2 and 3 (Stuttgart, 1960/3).

Hunt, J. C., 'Peasants, Grain Traffic and Meat Quotas: Imperial German protectionism reexamined', *Central European History*, Vol. VII(4) (1974), pp. 311–31.

Kehr, E., *Economic Interest, Militarism and Foreign Policy*, trans. and edited by G. Craig (Berkeley, 1977).

Kent, G. O., *Bismarck and His Times* (Carbondale/Edwardsville, Ill., 1978).

Koch, H. W., *A History of Prussia* (London, 1978).

Lambi, Ivo N., *Free Trade and Protection in Germany, 1868–1879* (Wiesbaden, 1963).

Landes, David S., *The Unbound Prometheus. Technological Change and Industrial Development in Western Europe from 1750 to the Present* (London, 1960).

Mann, Golo, *Deutsche Geschichte des neunzehnten und zwanzigsten Jahrhunderts* (Frankfurt a.M., 1958). English edn, *The History of Germany since 1789* (London, 1968).

Marcks, Erich, *Der Aufstieg des Reiches, Deutsche Geschichte von 1807–1878*, 2 vols (Stuttgart, 1936/43).

Martin, Günther, *Die bürgerlichen Exzellenzen, Zur Sozialgeschichte der preussischen Generalität 1812–1918* (Düsseldorf, 1979).

Messerschmidt, Manfred, *Militär und Politik in der Bismarck zeit und im Wilhelminischen Deutschland* (Darmstadt, 1975).

Nipperdey, Thomas, *Die Organisation der deutschen Parteien vor 1918* (Düsseldorf, 1961).

Passant, E. J., *A Short History of Germany, 1815–1945* (Cambridge, 1962).

Pinson, K., *Modern Germany – Its History and Civilization* (New York, 1954).

Ramm, A., *Germany, 1789–1919. A Political History* (London, 1967).

Rosenberg, H., 'Political and Social Consequences of the Great Depression of 1873–96 in Central Europe', *Economic History Review*, Vol. 13 (1943), pp. 58–73.

Rosenberg, Hans, *Grosse Depression und Bismarckzeit: Wirtschaftsablauf, Gesellschaft und Politik in Mitteleuropa* (Berlin, 1967).

Schieder, Theodor (ed.), *Handbuch der Europäischen Geschichte*, Vol. 6 (Stuttgart, 1968).

Schieder, Theodor, 'Vom Deutschen Bund zum Deutschen Reich', in B. Gebhardt, *Handbuch der Deutschen Geschichte*, ed. Herbert Grundmann, 9th edn, Vol. 3 (Stuttgart, 1970), pp. 99–220.

Schieder, Theodor, *Staatensystem als Vormacht der Welt, 1848–1918* (Frankfurt/Berlin/Vienna, 1977).

Sell, Friedrich C., *Die Tragödie des deutschen Liberalismus* (Stuttgart, 1953).

Sheehan, James J., *German Liberalism in the Nineteenth Century* (Chicago/London, 1978).

Spree, Reinhard, *Die Wachstumszyklen der deutschen Wirtschaft von 1840 bis 1880, mit einem konjunkturstatistischen Anhang* (Berlin, 1977).

Srbik, Heinrich Ritter von, *Deutsche Einheit: Idee und Wirklichkeit vom Heiligen Reich bis Königgrätz*, Vols 3 and 4 (Munich, 1942).

Stern, Alfred, *Geschichte Europas seit den Verträgen von 1815 bis zum Frankfurter Frieden von 1871*, 10 vols (Stuttgart, 1899–1924).

Sybel, Heinrich von, *Die Begründung des Deutschen Reiches durch Wilhelm I*, 7 vols (Munich, 1889–94).

Taylor, Alan John Percivale, *The Struggle for Mastery in Europe 1848–1919* (Oxford, 1954).

Tormin, Walter, *Geschichte der deutschen Parteien seit 1848* (Stuttgart/Berlin/Cologne/Mainz, 1966).

Wachenheim, Hedwig, *Die deutsche Arbeiterbewegung 1844 bis 1914* (Cologne/Opladen, 1967).

Wehler, Hans-Ulrich, *Bismarck und der Imperialismus* (Cologne, 1969).

Wehler, Hans-Ulrich, *Krisenherde des Kaiserreichs 1871–1918, Studien zur deutschen Sozial- und Verfassungsgeschichte*, 2nd edn (Göttingen, 1979).

Wehler, Hans-Ulrich, *Das deutsche Kaiserreich 1871–1918*, 4th edn (Göttingen, 1980). English edn, *The German Empire, 1871–1918* (Leamington Spa, 1984).

Williamson, D. G., *Bismarck and Germany, 1862–90* (London, 1986).

Zechlin, Egmont, *Bismarck und die Grundlegung der deutschen Grossmacht*, 2nd edn (Stuttgart, 1960).

Zechlin, Egmont, *Die Reichsgründung*, 2nd edn (Frankfurt/Berlin/Vienna, 1974).

Ziekursch, Johannes, *Politische Geschichte des neuen deutschen Kaiserreiches*, 3 vols (Frankfurt a.M., 1925–30).

Zunkel, Friedrich, *Der rheinisch-westfälische Unternehmer 1834–1879, ein Beitrag zur Geschichte des deutschen Burgertums im 19. Jahrhundert* (Cologne/Opladen, 1962).

LIFE AND POLITICS OF BISMARCK

Bismarck as a problem of historiography

Dorpalen, A., 'The German Historians and Bismarck', *Review of Politics*, Vol. XV (1953), pp. 53–67.

Eyck, E., 'Bismarck after Fifty Years', in *Historical Association General Series* (London, 1948).

Gall, Lothar (ed.), *Das Bismarck-Problem in der Geschichtsschreibung nach 1945* (Cologne/Berlin, 1971).

Gall, Lothar, 'Bismarck in der Geschichtsschreibung nach 1945', in Karl Otmar Freiherr von Aretin (ed.), *Bismarcks Aussenpolitik und der Berliner Kongress* (Wiesbaden, 1978), pp. 131–58.

Gooch, G. P., 'The Study of Bismarck', *Studies in German History* (London, 1948), pp. 300–41.

Hallmann, Hans (ed.), *Revision des Bismarckbildes, die Diskussion der deutschen Fachhistoriker, 1945–1955* (Darmstadt, 1972).

Kohn, H. (ed.), *German History: Some New German Views* (London, 1954).

Pflanze, O., 'Bismarck and German Nationalism', *American Historical Review*. Vol. 60 (1955), pp. 548–66.

Schmitt, H. A., 'Bismarck as seen from the nearest church steeple: a comment on Michael Stürmer', *Central European History*, Vol. XI(4) (1973) pp. 362–72.

Steefel, L. D., 'Bismarck', *Journal of Modern History*, Vol. 2 (1930), pp. 74–95.

Stürmer, M., 'Bismarck in Perspective', *Central European History*, Vol. IV(4) (1971), pp. 291–331.

Williamson, D. G., 'The Bismarck Debate', *History Today*, Vol. 34 (Sept. 1984), pp. 47–9.

Zmarzeik, Hans-Günther, *Das Bismarckbild der Deutschen – gestern und heute* (Freiburg, 1967).

Bismarck biographies

Apsler, Alfred, *Iron Chancellor, Otto von Bismarck* (Folkestone, 1972).

Crankshaw, Edward, *Bismarck* (New York/London, 1981).

Darmstädter, F., *Bismarck and the Creation of the Second Reich* (London, 1948).

Eyck, Erich, *Bismarck, Leben und Werk*, 3 vols (Erlenbach/Zurich, 1941–4). English edn, *Bismarck and the German Empire* (London, 1950).

Grant Robertson, C., *Bismarck and the Foundation of the German Empire* (London, 1918).

Headlam, J., *Bismarck and the Foundation of the German Empire* (New York, 1899).

Hillgruber, Andreas, *Otto von Bismarck, Gründer der europäischen Grossmacht Deutsches Reich* (Göttingen/Zurich/Frankfurt, 1978).

Jerusalimski, Arkadij S., *Bismarck, Diplomatie und Militarismus* (Frankfurt a.M., 1970).

Kent, George O., *Bismarck and his Times* (Carbondale/Edwardsville, Ill., 1978).

Lehmann, Max, *Bismarck, Eine Charakteristik* (Berlin, 1948).

Lenz, Max, *Geschichte Bismarcks*, 2nd edn (Leipzig, 1902).

Ludwig, Emil, *Bismarck, Geschichte eines Kämpfers* (Berlin, 1926). English edn, *The Story of a Fighter* (London, 1927).

Marcks, Erich, *Bismarck. Eine Biographie 1815–1851*, 21st edn including the posthumous vol., *Bismarck und die deutsche Revolution 1848–1851*, with a foreword and postscript by Willy Andreas (Stuttgart, 1951).

Meyer, Arnold Oskar, *Bismarck, Der Mensch und Staatsmann*, with an introduction by Hans Rothfels, 2nd edn (Stuttgart, 1949).

Mommsen, Wilhelm, *Bismarck, ein politisches Lebensbild* (Munich, 1959).

Palmer, Alan, *Bismarck* (London/New York, 1976).

Pflanze, Otto, *Bismarck and the Development of Germany, the Period of Unification 1815–1871* (Princeton, N.J., 1963).

Reiners, Ludwig, *Bismarck*, 2 vols (Munich, 1956/7).

Richter, Werner, *Bismarck*, 2nd edn (Frankfurt a.M., 1971). English edn, *Bismarck* (London, 1964).

Sempell, Charlotte, *Otto von Bismarck* (New York, 1972).

Snyder, L. L., *The Blood and Iron Chancellor. A Documentary Biography of Otto von Bismarck* (New York, 1967).

Taylor, Alan John Percivale, *Bismarck. The Man and the Statesman* (London, 1960).

Vallotton, Henry, *Bismarck* (Paris, 1962).

Verchau, Ekhard, *Otto von Bismarck, eine Kurzbiographie* (Berlin, 1969).

Waller, B., *Bismarck* (Oxford, 1985).

Individual problems and monographs

Augst, Richard, *Bismarcks Stellung zum parlamentarischen Wahlrecht* (Leipzig, 1913).

Baumgarten, Otto, *Bismarcks Glaube* (Tübingen, 1915).

Baumgarten, Otto, *Bismarcks Religion* (Göttingen, 1922).

Becker, Josef, 'Bismarck et l'empire libéral', *Francia*, Vol. 2 (1974), pp. 327–46.

Berdahl, M., 'Conservative Politics and Aristocratic Landholders in Bismarckian Germany', *Journal of Modern History*, Vol. 44(1) (1972), pp. 1–20.

Bussmann, Walter, *Otto von Bismarck, Geschichte – Staat – Politik* (Wiesbaden, 1966).

Bussmann, Walter, 'Wandel und Kontinuität der Bismarck-Wertung', in Hans Hallmann (ed.), *Revision des Bismarckbildes, die Diskussion der deutschen Fachhistoriker, 1945–1955* (Darmstadt, 1972), pp. 472–89.

Engelberg, Ernst, 'Zur Entstehung und historischen Stellung des preussisch-deutschen Bonapartismus', in Fritz Klein and Joachim Streisand (eds), *Beiträge zum neuen Geschichtsbild* (Berlin, 1956), pp. 236–51.

Engelberg, Ernst, 'Die politische Strategie und Taktik Bismarcks von 1851 bis 1866', in Horst Barthel and Ernst Engelberg, *Die grosspreussisch-militaristische Reichsgründung 1871, Voraussetzungen und Folgen*, Vol. 1 (Berlin, 1971), pp. 73–117.

Fischer-Frauendienst, Irene, *Bismarcks Pressepolitik* (Münster, 1963).

Franz, Günter, *Bismarcks Nationalgefühl* (Leipzig, 1926).

Gall, Lothar, 'Bismarck und der Bonapartismus', *Historische Zeitschrift*, Vol. 223 (1976), pp. 618–37.

Gall, Lothar, 'Bismarck und England', in *Aspekte der deutsch-britischen Beziehungen im Laufe der Jahrhunderte* (Stuttgart, 1978), pp. 46–59.

Geuss, Herbert, *Bismarck und Napoleon III, ein Beitrag zur Geschichte der preussisch-französischen Beziehungen 1851–1871* (Cologne/Graz, 1959).

Gollwitzer, Heinz, 'Der Cäsarismus Napoleons III im Widerhall der öffentlichen Meinung Deutschlands', *Historische Zeitschrift*, Vol. 173 (1952), pp. 23–75.

Gooch, George Peabody, 'Bismarck's legacy', in idem, *Catherine the Great and Other Studies* (London/New York/Toronto, 1954), pp. 275–89.

Griewank, Karl, *Das Problem des christlichen Staatsmannes bei Bismarck* (Berlin, 1953).

Hagen, Karl Heinz, 'Bismarcks Auffassung von der Stellung des Parlaments im Staat', doctoral thesis (Marburg, 1950).

Hammer, Karl, and Peter Claus Hartmann (eds), *Der Bonapartismus, Historisches Phänomen und politischer Mythos* (Zurich/Munich, 1977).

Heuss, Theodor, 'Das Bismarck-Bild im Wandel, Ein Versuch', in Otto von Bismarck, *Gedanken und Erinnerungen: Reden und Briefe* (Berlin, 1951), pp. 7–27.

Holborn, Hajo, 'Bismarck's Realpolitik', *Journal of the History of Ideas*, Vol. 21 (1960), pp. 84–98.

Kaehler, Siegfried A., 'Zur Deutung von Bismarcks "Bekehrung"', in idem, *Studien zur deutschen Geschichte des 19. und 20. Jahrhunderts, Aufsatze und Vorträge*, ed. Walter Bussmann (Göttingen, 1961), pp. 90–104.

Kardorff, Siegfried von, *Bismarck im Kampf um sein Werk* (Berlin, 1943).

Kissinger, Henry A., 'The white revolutionary: reflections on Bismarck', *Daedalus. Journal of the American Academy of Arts and Science*, 1968, pp. 888–924.

Kober, Heinz, *Studien zur Rechtsanschauung Bismarcks* (Tübingen, 1961).

Lenz, Max, 'Bismarcks Religion', in idem, *Kleine Historische Schriften*, Vol. 1, 2nd edn (Munich/Berlin, 1922), pp. 360–82.

Lösener, Albrecht, *Grundzüge von Bismarcks Staatsauffassung* (Bonn, 1962).

Mann, Golo, 'Bismarck', *Die Neue Rundschau*, 1961, pp. 431–48.

Martin, Alfred von, 'Bismarck und wir, Zur Zerstörung einer politischen Legende', *Der Monat*, Vol. 2 (1950), pp. 215–18.

Mayer, Gustav, *Bismarck und Lassalle, ihr Briefwechsel und ihre Gespräche* (Berlin, 1928).

Meyer, Arnold Oskar, *Bismarcks Glaube im Spiegel der "Losungen und Lehrtexte"* (Munich, 1933).

Mitchell, A., 'Bonapartism as a model for Bismarckian Politics', in *Journal of Modern History*, Vol. 49(2) (1977), pp. 181–209.

Mommsen, Wilhelm, 'Der Kampf um das Bismarck-Bild', *Universitas*, Vol. 5 (1950), pp. 273–80.

Muralt, Leonhard von, *Bismarcks Verantwortlichkeit* (Göttingen, 1955).

Muralt, Leonhard von, 'Die Voraussetzungen des geschichtlichen Verstandnisses Bismarcks', in idem, *Der Historiker und die Geschichte, Ausgewählte Aufsätze und Vorträge, Festgabe zum 60. Geburtstag*, ed. Fritz Büsser, Hanno Helbling and Peter Stadler (Zurich, 1960), pp. 277–94.

Noack, Ulrich, *Das Werk Friedrichs des Grossen und Bismarcks als Problem der deutschen Geschichte* (Wurzburg, 1948).

Noell von der Nahmer, Robert, *Bismarcks Reptilienfonds, aus den Geheimakten Preussens und des Deutschen Reiches* (Mainz, 1968).

Pflanze, Otto, 'Bismarck's Realpolitik', *Review of Politics*, Vol. 20 (1958), pp. 492–514.

Rein, Gustav Adolf, *Die Revolution in der Politik Bismarcks* (Göttingen, 1957).

Ritter, Gerhard, *Die preussischen Konservativen und Bismarcks deutsche Politik 1858–1876* (Heidelberg, 1913).

Ritter, Gerhard, 'Das Bismarckproblem', *Merkur*, Vol. 4 (1950), pp. 657–76.

Rothfels, Hans, 'Bismarck und das 19. Jahrhundert', *Schicksalswege deutscher Vergangenheit. Festschrift für Siegfried A. Kaehler* (Düsseldorf, 1950), pp. 233–48.

Rothfels, Hans, *Bismarck, Vorträge und Abhandlungen* (Stuttgart, 1970).

Rothfels, Hans, 'Probleme einer Bismarck-Biographie', in Lothar Gall (ed.), *Das Bismarck-Problem in der Geschichtsschreibung nach 1945* (Cologne/Berlin, 1971), pp. 65–83.

Saitschik, Robert, *Bismarck und das Schicksal des deutschen Volkes, zur Psychologie und Geschichte der deutschen Frage* (Basel, 1949).

Schieder, Theodor, *Das Deutsche Kaiserreich von 1871 als Nationalstaat* (Cologne, 1961).

Schieder, Theodor, 'Bismarck – gestern und heute', in Lothar Gall (ed.), *Das Bismarck-Problem in der Geschichtsschreibung nach 1945* (Cologne/Berlin, 1971), pp. 342–74.

Schieder, Theodor, 'Bismarck und Europa. Ein Beitrag zum Bismarck-Problem', in

Hans Hallmann (ed.), *Revision des Bismarckbildes, die Diskussion der deutschen Fachhistoriker 1945–1955* (Darmstadt, 1972), pp. 255–86.

Schmoller, Gustav, 'Vier Briefe über Bismarcks sozialpolitische und volkswirtchaftliche Stellung und Bedeutung', in idem, *Charakterbilder* (Munich/Leipzig, 1913), pp. 27–76.

Schnabel, Franz, 'Das Problem Bismarck', *Hochland*, Vol. 42 (1949), pp. 1–27.

Schoeps, Hans-Joachim, *Bismarck über Zeitgenossen, Zeitgenossen über Bismarck* (Frankfurt/Berlin/Vienna, 1972).

Schüssler, Wilhelm, 'Der geschichtliche Standort Bismarcks', in idem, *Um das Geschichtsbild* (Gladbeck, 1953), pp. 99–141.

Seeberg, Reinhold, *Das Christentum Bismarcks* (Berlin, 1915).

Silverman, D. P., *Reluctant Union – Alsace-Lorraine and Imperial Germany* (University Park, Penn./London, 1972).

Snyder, Louis L., and Ida M. Brown, *Bismarck and German Unification* (London, 1971).

Srbik, Heinrich Ritter von, 'Die Bismarck-Kontroverse, zur Revision des deutschen Geschichtsbildes', *Wort und Wahrheit, Monatsschrift für Religion und Kultur*, Vol. 5 (1950), pp. 918–31.

Stehlin, S., *Bismarck and the Guelph Problem* (Amsterdam, 1973).

Stern, Fritz, *Gold and Iron. Bismarck, Bleichröder and the Building of the German Empire* (New York/London, 1977).

Thadden-Trieglaff, Reinhold von, *Der junge Bismarck. Eine Antwort auf die Frage: War Bismarck Christ?* (Hamburg/Berlin, 1950).

Vierhaus, Rudolf, 'Otto von Bismarck', in Lothar Gall (ed.), *Das Bismarck-Problem in der Geschichtsschreibung nach 1945* (Cologne/Berlin, 1971), pp. 375–91.

Vossler, Otto, 'Bismarcks Ethos', *Historische Zeitschrift*, Vol. 171 (1951), pp. 263–92.

Wendt, Hans, *Bismarck und die polnische Frage* (Halle, 1922).

Windell, G. G., 'Bismarckian Empire: Chronicle of Failure, 1866–1880', *Central European History*, Vol. 2(4) (1969), pp. 291–311.

Wolff, Helmut, *Geschichtsauffassung und Politik in Bismarcks Bewusstsein* (Munich/Berlin, 1926).

Origins, childhood, youth and entry into politics

Becker, Gerhard, 'Die Beschlüsse des preussischen Junkerparlaments von 1848', *Zeitschrift für Geschichtswissenschaft*, Vol. 24 (1976), pp. 889–918.

Engelberg, Ernst, *Über mittelalterliches Städtebürgertum. Die Stendaler Bismarcks im 14. Jahrhundert* (Berlin, 1979).

Lenz, Max, *Bismarcks Plan einer Gegenrevolution im Marz 1848* (Berlin, 1930).

Marcks, Erich, *Bismarck, eine Biographie*, Vol. 1: *Bismarcks Jugend 1815–1851* (Stuttgart/Berlin, 1909).

Marcks, Erich, *Bismarck und die deutsche Revolution 1818–1851*, ed. Willy Andreas (Stuttgart, 1939).

Rein, Gustav Adolf, 'Bismarcks gegenrevolutionäre Aktion in den Märztagen 1848', *Die Welt als Geschichte*, Vol. 13 (1953), pp. 246–62.

Valentin, Veit, *Geschichte der deutschen Revolution von 1848/49*, 2 vols (Berlin, 1930/1), repr. Aalen, 1968.

Up to his appointment as Minister-President of Prussia

Augst, Richard, *Bismarck und Leopold v. Gerlach, ihre persönliche Beziehungen und deren Zusammenhang mit ihren politischen Anschauungen* (Leipzig, 1913).

Bigler, Kurt, *Bismarck und das Legitimitätsprinzip bis 1862* (Winterthur, 1955).

Dahlmann, Ingeborg, 'Bismarck in Frankfurt', doctoral thesis (Erlangen, 1949).

Kronenberg, Wilhelm, 'Bismarcks Bundesreformprojekte 1848–1866', doctoral thesis (Cologne, 1953).

Lange, Friedrich Wilhelm, 'Bismarck und die öffentliche meinung Süddeutschlands während der Zollvereinskrise 1850–1853', doctoral thesis (Giessen, 1922).

Meyer, Arnold Oskar, *Bismarcks Kampf mit Österreich am Bundestag zu Frankfurt (1851–1859)* (Berlin, 1927).

Mittelstädt, Annie, *Der Krieg von 1859, Bismarck und die öffentliche Meinung in Deutschland* (Stuttgart, 1904).

Mombauer, Hans, *Bismarcks Realpolitik als Ausdruck seiner Weltanschauung, Die Auseinandersetzung mit Leopold v. Gerlach 1851–1859* (Berlin, 1936), repr. Vaduz, 1965.

Nolde, Boris, *Die Petersburger Mission Bismarcks 1859–1862, Russland und Europa zu Beginn der Regierung Alexanders II* (Leipzig, 1936).

Wertheimer, Eduard von, *Bismarck im politischen Kampf* (Berlin, 1929).

The conflict period

Anderson, Eugene N., *The Social and Political Conflict in Prussia 1858–1864* (Lincoln, Nebr., 1954).

Börner, Karl Heinz, *Die Krise der preussischen Monarchie von 1858–1862* (Berlin, 1976).

Craig, Gordon A., *The Politics of the Prussian Army 1640–1945* (Oxford, 1955).

Dehio, Ludwig, 'Bismarck und die Herresvorlagen der Konfliktszeit', *Historische Zeitschrift*, Vol. 144 (1931), pp. 31–47.

Gugel, Michael, *Industrieller Aufstieg und bürgerliche Herrschaft, Sozioökonomische Interessen und politische Ziele des liberalen Bürgertums in Preussen zur Zeit des Verfassungskonfliktes 1857–1867* (Cologne, 1975).

Hess, Adalbert, *Das Parlament, das Bismarck widerstrebte. Zur Politik und sozialen Zusammensetzung des preussischen Abgeordnetenhauses der Konfliktszeit (1862–1866)* (Cologne/Opladen, 1964).

Howard, M., 'William I and the Reform of the Prussian Army' in Gilbert, M. (ed.) *A Century of Conflict: Essays for A.J.P. Taylor* (London, 1966).

Kaminski, Kurt, *Verfassung und Verfassungskonflikt in Preussen 1862 bis 1866, Ein Beitrag zu den politischen Kernfragen von Bismarcks Reichsgründung* (Königsberg, 1938).

Nirrnheim, Otto, *Das erste Jahr des Ministeriums Bismarck und die öffentliche Meinung* (Heidelberg, 1908).

Richter, Adolf, *Bismarck und die Arbeiterfrage im preussischen Verfassungskonflikt* (Stuttgart, 1935).

Ritter, Gerhard, 'Staatskunst und Kriegshandwerk, das Problem des "Militarismus"', in *Deutschland*, 3rd edn, Vol. 1 (Munich, 1965). English edn, *The Sword and the Sceptre, Vol. 1: The Prussian Tradition, 1740–1890* (London, 1972).

Winkler, Heinrich August, *Preussischer Liberalismus und deutscher Nationalstaat, Studien zur Geschichte der Deutschen Fortschrittspartei 1861–1866* (Tübingen, 1964).

The German question and the European system of powers before 1870

Barthel, Horst, and Ernst Engelberg (eds), *Die grosspreussisch-militaristische Reichsgründung 1871. Voraussetzungen und Folgen*, 2 vols (Berlin, 1971).

Becker, Otto, 'Der Sinn der dualistischen Verständigungsversuche Bismarcks vor dem Kriege 1866', *Historische Zeitschrift*, Vol. 169 (1949), pp. 264–89.

Becker, Otto, *Bismarcks Ringen um Deutschlands Gestaltung*, ed. Alexander Scharff (Heidelberg, 1958).

Besier, Gerhard, *Preussische Kirchenpolitik in der Bismarckära. Die Diskussion in Staat und evangelischer Kirche um eine Neuordnung der kirchlichen Verhältnisse Preussens zwischen 1866 und 1872*, with a foreword by Klaus Scholder (Berlin/New York, 1980).

Burckhardt, Helmut, *Deutschland, England, Frankreich: Die politischen Beziehungen Deutschlands zu den beiden westeuropäischen Grossmächten 1864–1866* (Munich, 1970).

Caroll, Eber Malcolm, *Germany and the Great Powers 1866–1914, A Study in Public Opinion and Foreign Policy* (Hamden, Conn., 1966).

Clark, Chester W., *Franz Joseph and Bismarck, the Diplomacy of Austria before the War of 1866* (Cambridge, Mass., 1934).

Craig, Gordon A., *The Battle of Königgrätz* (London, 1964).

Dehio, Ludwig, 'Beiträge zu Bismarcks Politik im Sommer 1866. Unter Benutzung der Papiere Robert von Keudells', *Forschungen zur brandenburgischen und preussischen Geschichte*, Vol. 46 (1934), pp. 147–65.

Dietrich, Richard (ed.), *Europa und der Norddeutsche Bund* (Berlin, 1968).

Eisfeld, Gerhard, *Die Entstehung der liberalen Parteien in Deutschland 1858–1870*, Studie zu den Organisationen und Programmen der Liberalen und Demokraten (Hanover, 1969).

Franz, Eugen, *Der Entscheidungskampf um die wirtschaftspolitische Führung Deutschlands 1856–1867* (Munich, 1933).

Frauendienst, Werner, *Der Jahr 1866: Preussens Sieg, die Vorstufe des Deutschen Reiches* (Göttingen, 1966).

Friedjung, Heinrich, *Der Kampf um die Vorherrschaft in Deutschland 1859–1866*, 2 vols, 10th edn (Stuttgart, 1916). English edn, *The Struggle for Supremacy in Germany, 1859–66* (London, 1935).

Gall, Lothar, *Der Liberalismus als regierende Partei, Das Grossherzogtum Baden zwischen Restauration und Reichsgründung* (Wiesbaden, 1968).

Groote, Wolfgang von, and Ursula von Gersdorff (eds), *Entscheidung 1866, Der Krieg zwischen Österreich und Preussen* (Stuttgart, 1966).

Hildebrand, Klaus, 'Die deutsche Reichsgründung im Urteil der britischen Politik', *Francia*, Vol. 5 (1977), pp. 399–424.

Isler, Rudolf, *Diplomatie als Gespräch, Bismarcks Auseinandersetzung mit Österreich im Winter 1862/63* (Winterthur, 1966).

Kessel, Eberhard, 'Gastein', *Historische Zeitschrift*, Vol. 176 (1953), pp. 521–44.

Kraehe, E., 'Austria and the Problem of Reform in the German Confederation, 1815–63', *American Historical Review*, Vol. 56 (1951), pp. 291–4.

Lange, Karl, *Bismarck und die norddeutschen Kleinstaaten im Jahr 1866* (Berlin, 1930).

Langewiesche, Dieter, *Liberalismus und Demokratie in Württemberg zwischen Revolution und Reichsgründung* (Düsseldorf, 1974).

Lenz, Max, *König Wilhelm und Bismarck in ihrer Stellung zum Frankfurter Fürstentag* (Berlin, 1929).

Lipgens, Walter, 'Bismarcks Österreich-Politik vor 1866. Die Urheberschaft des Schönbrunner Vertragsentwurfes vom August 1864', *Die Welt als Geschichte*, Vol. 10 (1950), pp. 240–62.

Lord, Robert H., *Bismarck and Russia in 1863* (Cambridge, 1923).

Lutz, Heinrich, *Österreich-Ungarn und die Gründung des Deutschen Reiches, europäische Entscheidungen 1867–1871* (Berlin, 1979).

Michael, Horst, *Bismarck, England und Europa, vorwiegend von 1866–1870* (Munich, 1930).

Millmann, Richard, *British Foreign Policy and the Coming of the Franco-Prussian War* (Oxford, 1965).

Mosse, Werner Eugen, *The European Powers and the German Question 1848–1871, with Special Reference to England and Russia* (Cambridge, 1958).

Muralt, Leonhard von, *Bismarcks Politik der europäischen Mitte* (Wiesbaden, 1954).

Naujoks, Eberhard, *Bismarcks auswärtige Pressepolitik und die Reichsgründung (1865–1871)* (Wiesbaden, 1968).

Oncken, Hermann, 'Die Baden-Badener Denkschrift Bismarcks über die deutsche Bundesreform (Juli 1861)', *Historische Zeitschrift*, Vol. 145 (1932), pp. 106–30.

Pollmann, Klaus Erich, 'Der Parlamentarismus im Norddeutschen Bund, Der konstituierende Reichstag des Norddeutschen Bundes', lectureship thesis (Brunswick, 1978).

Potthoff, Heinrich, *Die deutsche Politik Beusts, von seiner Berufung zum österreichischen Aussenminister Oktober 1866 bis zum Ausbruch des deutsch-französischen Krieges* (Bonn, 1968).

Pottinger, Evelyn Ann, *Napoleon III and the German Crisis, 1865–1866* (Cambridge, Mass., 1966).

Sandiford, Keith A. P., *Great Britain and the Schleswig-Holstein Question, 1848–1864, A Study in Diplomacy, Politics and Public Opinion* (Toronto, 1975).

Scheel, Otto, *Bismarcks Wille zu Deutschland in den Friedensschlüssen 1866* (Breslau, 1934).

Schieder, Theodor, *Die kleindeutsche Partei in Bayern in den Kämpfen um die deutsche Einheit 1863–1871* (Munich, 1936).

Schieder, Theodor, and Ernst Deuerlein (eds), *Reichsgründung 1870/71, Tatsachen – Kontroversen – Interpretationen* (Stuttgart, 1970).

Schüssler, Wilhelm, *Bismarcks Kampf um Süddeutschland 1866* (Berlin, 1929).

Schüssler, Wilhelm, *Königgratz 1866, Bismarcks tragische Trennung von Österreich* (Munich, 1958).

Stadelmann, Rudolf, *Das Jahr 1865 und das Problem von Bismarcks deutscher Politik* (Munich, 1933).

Steefel, Lawrence D., *The Schleswig-Holstein Question* (Cambridge, 1932).

Wandruszka, Adam, *Schicksalsjahr 1866* (Graz/Vienna/Cologne, 1966).

Wilhelm, Rolf, *Das Verhältnis der süddeutschen Staaten zum Norddeutschen Bund (1867–1870)* (Husum, 1978).

The Franco-Prussian War and the founding of the Reich in 1871

Becker, Josef, 'Baden, Bismarck und die Annexion von Elsass und Lothringen', *Zeitschrift für die Geschichte des Oberrheins*, Vol. 115 (1967), pp. 1–38.

Becker, Josef, 'Zum Problem der Bismarckschen Politik in der spanischen Thronfrage 1870', *Historische Zeitschrift*, Vol. 212 (1971), pp. 529–607.

Bonnin, Georges (ed.), *Bismarck and the Hohenzollern Candidature for the Spanish Throne, Documents in the German Diplomatic Archives* (London, 1957).

Clark, C. W., 'Bismarck, Russia and the War of 1870', *Journal of Modern History*, Vol. 14(2) (1942), pp. 199–202.

Dittrich, Jochen, *Bismarck, Frankreich und die spanische Thronkandidatur der Hohenzollern, die 'Kriegsschuldfrage' von 1870*, with an introduction by Gerhard Ritter (Munich, 1962).

Doeberl, Michael, *Bayern und die Bismarcksche Reichsgründung* (Munich, 1925).

Gall, Lothar, 'Zur Frage der Annexion von Elsass und Lothringen 1870', *Historische Zeitschrift*, Vol. 206 (1968), pp. 265–326.

Groote, Wolfgang von, and Ursula von Gersdorff (eds), *Entscheidung 1870, der deutsch-französische Krieg* (Stuttgart, 1970).

Halperin, S. W., 'The Origins of the Franco-Prussian War Revisited: Bismarck and the Hohenzollern Candidature for the Spanish Throne', *Journal of Modern History*, Vol. 45(1) (1973), pp. 83–91.

Hofer, Walter (ed.), *Europa und die Einheit Deutschlands, Eine Bilanz nach 100 Jahren* (Cologne, 1970).

Howard, Michael, *The Franco-Prussian War, The German Invasion of France 1870–71* (New York, 1961).
Kolb, Eberhard, 'Studien zur politischen Geschichte des Krieges von 1870', lectureship thesis (Göttingen, 1968).
Kolb, Eberhard, 'Bismarck und das Aufkommen der Annexionsforderung 1870', *Historische Zeitschrift*, Vol. 209 (1969), pp. 318–56.
Kolb, Eberhard, *Der Kriegsausbruch 1870, politische Entscheidungsprozesse und Verantwortlichkeiten in der Julikrise 1870* (Göttingen, 1970).
Lipgens, Walter, 'Bismarck, die öffentliche Meinung und die Annexion von Elsass und Lothringen 1870', *Historische Zeitschrift*, Vol. 99 (1964), pp. 31–112.
Lipgens, Walter, 'Bismarck und die Frage der Annexion 1870, Eine Erwiderung', *Historische Zeitschrift*, Vol. 206 (1968), pp. 586–617.
Lord, Robert H., *The Origins of the War of 1870, The Documents from German Archives* (Cambridge, Mass., 1924).
Morsey, Rudolf, 'Die Hohenzollernsche Thronkandidatur in Spanien', *Historische Zeitschrift*, Vol. 186 (1958), pp. 573–88.
Muralt, Leonhard von, *Bismarcks Reichsgründung vom Ausland her gesehen* (Stuttgart, 1947).
Rall, Hans, *König Ludwig II und Bismarcks Ringen um Bayern* (Munich, 1973).
Rein, Gustav Adolf, *Die Reichsgründung in Versailles, 18 Januar 1871* (Munich, 1958).
Steefel, Lawrence D., *Bismarck, the Hohenzollern Candidacy, and the Origins of the Franco-German War of 1870* (Cambridge, Mass., 1962).
Valentin, Veit, *Bismarcks Reichsgründung im Urteil englischer Diplomaten* (Amsterdam, 1937).

German domestic policy after 1871

Anderson, M. L., *Windthorst. A Political Biography* (Oxford, 1981).
Ashley, A., 'The Social Policy of Bismarck. A Critical Study with a Comparison of German and English Insurance Legislation', with a preface by G. Schmoller, in *Birmingham Studies in Social Economics* (Birmingham, 1912).
Binder, Hans-Otto, *Reich und Einzelstaaten wahrend der Kanzlerschaft Bismarcks 1871–1890, eine Untersuchung zum Problem der bundesstaatlichen Organisation* (Tübingen, 1971).
Blaich, Fritz, *Kartell- und Monopolpolitik im kaiserlichen Deutschland, Das Problem der Marktmacht im deutschen Reichstag zwischen 1879 und 1914* (Düsseldorf, 1973).
Blanke, R., 'Bismarck and the Prussian-Polish Policies of 1886', *Journal of Modern History*, Vol. 45(2) (1973), pp. 211–39.
Booms, Hans, *Die deutsch-konservative Partei. Preussischer Charakter, Reichsauffassung, Nationalbegriff* (Düsseldorf, 1954).
Bornkamm, Heinrich, 'Die Staatsidee im Kulturkampf', *Historische Zeitschrift*, Vol. 170 (1950), pp. 41–72, 273–306, repr. Darmstadt, 1969.
Cecil, Lamar, *The German Diplomatic Service, 1871–1914* (Princeton, N.J., 1976).
Constabel, Adelheid (ed.), *Die Vorgeschichte des Kulturkampfes, Quellenveröffentlichungen aus dem Deutschen Zentralarchiv* (Berlin, 1956).
Erdmann, Gerhard, *Die Entwicklung der deutschen Sozialgesetzgebung*, 2nd edn (Göttingen/Berlin/Frankfurt a.M., 1957).
Förster, Erich, *Adalbert Falk* (Gotha, 1927).
Franz, Georg, *Kulturkampf: Staat und katholische Kirche in Mitteleuropa von der Säkularisation bis zum Abschluss des preussischen Kulturkampfes* (Munich, 1954).
Goldschmidt, Hans, *Das Reich und Preussen im Kampf um die Führung, Von Bismarck bis 1918* (Berlin, 1931).
Hardach, Karl Willy, *Die Bedeutung wirtschaftlicher Faktoren bei der Wiedereinführung der Eisen- und Getreidezölle in Deutschland 1879* (Berlin, 1967).

Herzfeld, Hans, *Johannes von Miquel*, 2 vols (Detmold, 1938).

Kissling, Johannes B., *Geschichte des Kulturkampfes im Deutschen Reich*, 3 vols (Freiburg, 1911–16).

Lidtke, Vernon L., *The Outlawed Party, Social Democracy in Germany 1878–1890* (Princeton, N.J., 1966).

Lili, Rudolf, *Die Wende im Kulturkampf: Leo XIII, Bismarck und die Zentrumspartei 1878–1880* (Tübingen, 1973).

Maenner, Ludwig, 'Deutschlands Wirtschaft und Liberalismus in der Krise von 1879', *Archiv für Politik und Geschichte*, Vol. 9 (1927), pp. 347–82, 456–88.

Mann, Helmut, 'Der Beginn der Abkehr Bismarcks vom Kulturkampf 1878–1880, unter besonderer Berücksichtigung der Politik des Zentrums und der romischen Kurie', doctoral thesis (Frankfurt a.M., 1953).

Matthes, Heinz Edgar, 'Die Spaltung der Nationalliberalen Partei und die Entwicklung des Linksliberalismus bis zur Auflösung der Deutsch-Freisinnigen Partei, 1878–1893, ein Beitrag zur Geschichte der Krise des deutschen politischen Liberalismus', doctoral thesis (Kiel, 1953).

Mommsen, Wolfgang J., 'Das Deutsche Kaiserreich als System umgangener Entscheidungen', in *Vom Staat des Ancien régime zum modernen Parteienstaat, Festschrift für Theodor Schieder zu seinem 70. Geburtstag*, ed. H. Berding *et al.* (Munich/Vienna, 1978), pp. 239–65.

Mork, G. R., 'Bismarck and the "Capitulation" of German Liberalism', in *Journal of Modern History*, Vol. 43(1) (1971), pp. 59–75.

Morsey, Rudolf, *Die oberste Reichsverwaltung unter Bismarck 1867–1890* (Münster, 1957).

Oncken, Hermann, *Rudolf von Bennigsen*, 2 vols (Stuttgart/Leipzig, 1910).

Pack, Wolfgang, *Das parlamentarische Ringen um das Sozialistengesetz Bismarcks 1878–1890* (Düsseldorf, 1961).

Pauer, P., 'The Corporatist Character of Bismarck's Social Policy', in *European Studies Review*, Vol. II(4) (1981), pp. 427–60.

Pols, Werner, *Sozialistenfrage und Revolutionsfurcht in ihrem Zusammenhang mit den angeblichen Staatsstreichplänen Bismarcks* (Hamburg/Lübeck, 1960).

Röhl, John C. G., 'Staatsstreichpläne oder Staatsstreichbereitschaft? Bismarcks Politik in der Entlassungskrise', *Historische Zeitschrift*, Vol. 203 (1966), pp. 610–24.

Rothfels, Hans, *Theodor Lohmann und die Kampfjahre der staatlichen Sozialpolitik (1871–1905), nach ungedruckten Quellen bearbeitet* (Berlin, 1927).

Rothfels, Hans, *Prinzipienfragen der Bismarckschen Sozialpolitik* (Königsberg, 1929).

Ruhenstroth-Bauer, Renate, 'Bismarck und Falk im Kulturkampf', doctoral thesis (Heidelberg, 1944).

Schmidt(-Volkmar), Erich, *Der Kulturkampf in Deutschland 1871–1890* (Göttingen/Berlin, 1962).

Seeber, Gustav, *Zwischen Bebel und Bismarck. Zur Geschichte des Linksliberalismus in Deutschland 1871–1893* (Berlin, 1960).

Stürmer, Michael, 'Staatsstreichgedanken im Bismarckreich', *Historische Zeitschrift*, Vol. 209 (1969), pp. 566–617.

Stürmer, Michael (ed.), *Das kaiserliche Deutschland: Politik und Gesellschaft 1870–1918* (Düsseldorf, 1970).

Stürmer, Michael, 'Bismarckstaat und Cäsarismus', *Der Staat*, Vol. 12 (1973), pp. 467–98.

Stürmer, Michael, *Regierung und Reichstag im Bismarckstaat 1871–1880, Cäsarismus oder Parlamentarismus* (Düsseldorf, 1974).

Ullmann, Hans-Peter, 'Industrielle Interessen und die Entstehung der deutschen Sozialversicherung 1880–1889', *Historische Zeitschrift*, Vol. 229 (1979), pp. 574–610.

Van der Kiste, J., *Frederick III – German Emperor, 1888* (London, 1981).

Vogel, Walter, *Bismarcks Arbeiterversicherung, Ihre Entstehung im Kräftespiel der Zeit* (Brunswick, 1951).

Vossler, Otto, 'Bismarcks Sozialpolitik', *Historische Zeitschrift*, Vol. 167 (1943), pp. 336–57.

Weber, Christoph, *Kirchliche Politik zwischen Rom, Berlin und Trier 1876–1888. Die Beilegung des preussischen Kulturkampfes* (Mainz, 1970).

Winkler, Heinrich August, 'Vom linken zum rechten Nationalismus, Der deutsche Liberalismus in der Krise von 1878/79', *Geschichte und Gesellschaft*, Vol. 4 (1978), pp. 5–48.

Zechlin, Egmont, *Staatsstreichpläne Bismarcks und Wilhelms II, 1890–1894* (Stuttgart, 1929).

Zucker, Stanley, *Ludwig Bamberger, German Liberal Politician and Social Critic, 1823–1899* (Pittsburgh, 1975).

German foreign policy after 1871

Aretin, Karl Otmar Frhr. von (ed.), *Bismarcks Aussenpolitik und der Berliner Kongress* (Wiesbaden, 1978).

Bagdasarian, Nicholas der, *The Austro-German Rapprochement 1870–1879, From the Battle of Sedan to the Dual Alliance* (London, 1976).

Fellner, Fritz, *Der Dreibund, Europäische Diplomatie vor dem 1. Weltkrieg* (Vienna, 1960).

Geiss, Imanuel, *German Foreign Policy 1871–1914* (London, 1975).

Hallmann, Hans (ed.), *Zur Geschichte und Problematik des deutsch-russischen Rückversicherungsvertrages von 1887* (Darmstadt, 1968).

Herzfeld, Hans, *Die deutsch-französische Kriegsgefahr von 1875* (Berlin, 1922).

Herzfeld, Hans, *Deutschland und das geschlagene Frankreich* (Berlin, 1924).

Japiske, Nikolaas, *Europa und Bismarcks Friedenspolitik, Die internationalen Beziehungen von 1871 bis 1890* (Berlin, 1927).

Kennan, George F., *The Decline of Bismarck's European Order, Franco-Russian Relations, 1875–1890* (Princeton, N.J., 1979).

Kennedy, P. M., 'German Colonial Expansion: Has the "Manipulated Social Imperialism" been antedated?', *Past and Present*, Vol. 54 (1972), pp. 134–141.

Krausnick, Helmut, *Holsteins Geheimpolitik in der Ära Bismarck 1886–1890, dargestellt vornehmlich auf Grund unveröffentlichter Akten des Wiener Haus-, Hof- und Staatsarchivs* (Hamburg, 1942).

Kumpf-Korfes, Sigrid, *Bismarcks 'Draht nach Russland', 1878–1891* (Berlin, 1968).

Langer, William L., *European Alliances and Alignments, 1871–1890*, 2nd edn (New York, 1962).

Lutz, Heinrich, 'Von Königgrätz zum Zweibund', *Historische Zeitschrift*, Vol. 217 (1973), pp. 347–80.

Medlicott, William N., *The Congress of Berlin and After. A Diplomatic History of the Near East Settlement 1878–1880* (London, 1938).

Medlicott, William N., *Bismarck, Gladstone, and the Concert of Europe* (London, 1956).

Müller-Link, Horst, *Industrialisierung und Aussenpolitik: Preussen-Deutschland und das Zarenreich 1860–1890* (Göttingen, 1977).

Noack, Ulrich, *Bismarcks Friedenspolitik und das Problem des deutschen Machtverfalls* (Leipzig, 1928).

Novotny, Alexander, *Quellen und Studien zur Geschichte des Berliner Kongresses 1878*, Vol. 1: *Österreich, die Türkei und das Balkanproblem im Jahre des Berliner Kongresses* (Graz/Cologne, 1957).

Rassow, Peter, *Die Stellung Deutschlands im Kreise der Grossen Mächte 1887–1890* (Mainz, 1959).

Rothfels, Hans, *Bismarcks englische Bündnispolitik* (Stuttgart, 1924).

Rothfels, Hans, *Bismarck, der Osten und das Reich*, 2nd edn (Stuttgart, 1960).

Schüssler, Wilhelm, *Deutschland zwischen Russland und England. Studien zur Aussen-politik des Bismarckschen Reiches 1879–1914*, 3rd edn (Leipzig, 1943).

Stamm, Heinrich, 'Graf Herbert von Bismarck als Staatssekretär des Auswärtigen Amtes', doctoral thesis (Brunswick, 1978).

Steglich, Wolfgang, 'Bismarcks englische Bündnissondierungen und Bündnisvor-schläge 1887–1889', *Historia integra: Festschrift für Erich Hassinger zum 70. Geburtstag* (Berlin, 1977), pp. 283–348.

Stojanovic, Mihailo D., *The Great Powers and the Balkans, 1875–1878* (London, 1939), repr. Cambridge, 1968.

Strandmann, H. Pogge von, 'The Domestic Origin of Germany's Colonial Expansion under Bismarck', *Past and Present*, Vol. 42 (1969), pp. 140–50.

Taylor, Alan John Percivale, *Germany's First Bid for Colonies 1884–1885, A Move in Bismarck's European Policy* (London, 1938).

Townsend, M. E., *The Rise and Fall of Germany's Colonial Empire* (New York, 1930).

Turner, H. A., 'Bismarck's Imperialist Venture: Anti-British in Origin?' in Gifford, P., Louis, W. R. and Smith, A. (eds), *Britain and Germany in Africa: Imperial Rivalry and Colonial Rule* (Boston, Mass., 1967), pp. 47–82.

Waller, Bruce, *Bismarck at the Crossroad, the Reorientation of German Foreign Policy after the Congress of Berlin 1878–1888* (London, 1974).

Wehler, H.-U., 'Bismarck's Imperialism, 1862–90', in *Past and Present*, Vol. 48 (1970), pp. 119–55.

Winckler, Martin B., *Bismarcks Bündespolitik und das europäische Gleichgewicht* (Stuttgart, 1964).

Windelband, Wolfgang, *Bismarck und die europäischen Grossmächte, 1879–1885*, 2nd edn (Essen, 1942).

Wolter, Heinz, *Alternative zu Bismarck, die deutsche Sozialdemokratie und die Aussenpolitik des preussisch-deutschen Reiches 1878–1890* (Berlin, 1970).

Bismarck's dismissal – the final years

Eppstein, Georg Frhr. von (ed.), *Fürst Bismarcks Entlassung, nach den hinterlassenen bisher unveröffentlichten Aufzeichnungen des Staatssekretärs des Innern, Staatsminister Karl Heinrich von Boetticher und des Chefs der Reichskanzlei unter dem Fürsten Bismarck Dr. Franz Johannes von Rottenburg* (Berlin, 1920).

Gagliardi, Ernst, *Bismarcks Entlassung*, 2 vols (Tübingen, 1927/41).

Hank, Manfred, *Kanzler ohne Amt, Fürst Bismarck nach seiner Entlassung 1890–1898* (Munich, 1977).

Hofmann, Hermann, *Fürst Bismarck 1890–1895*, 3 vols (Stuttgart, 1913–14).

Mommsen, Wilhelm, *Bismarcks Sturz und die Parteien* (Stuttgart, 1924).

Nichols, John A., *Germany after Bismarck, The Caprivi Era 1890–1894* (Cambridge, Mass., 1958).

Penzler, Johannes, *Fürst Bismarck nach seiner Entlassung: Leben und Politik des Fürsten seit seinem Scheiden aus dem Amte auf Grund aller authentischen Kundgebungen*, 7 vols (Leipzig, 1897/8).

Röhl, John C. G., 'The Disintegration of the Kartell and the Politics of Bismarck's Fall from Power, 1887–90', *Historical Journal*, Vol. 9 (1) (1966), pp. 60–89.

Röhl, John C. G., *Germany without Bismarck. The Crisis of Government in the Second Reich, 1890–1900* (London, 1967).

Schüssler, Wilhelm, *Bismarcks Sturz*, 3rd edn (Leipzig, 1922).

Seeber, Gustav, *et al.*, *Bismarcks Sturz, Zur Rolle der Klassen in der Endphase des preussisch-deutschen Bonapartismus 1884–1890* ((East) Berlin, 1977).
Stribruy, Wolfgang, *Bismarck und die Politik nach seinev Entlassung (1890–1898)* (Paderborn, 1977).

INDEX OF NAMES

Achenbach, Heinrich von (1829–99), 88, 128
Albedyll, Emil Heinrich Ludwig von (1824–97), 156
Alexander II, Tsar of Russia (1818–81), 43–5, 47, 50, 55, 57, 117–18, 148
Alexander III, Tsar of Russia (1845–94), 147, 153–4, 215
Andrássy, Count Gyula (1823–90), 42, 56, 119
Antonelli, Giacomo (1806–76), 89
Arnim, Count Harry von (1824–81), 13, 30, 47, 96–7
Arnim-Kröchlendorff, Malwine von, *see* Bismarck, Malwine von.
Artois, Charles of, *see* Charles X, King of France
Augusta, German Empress and Queen of Prussia (1811–90), 17

Bamberger, Ludwig (1823–99), 32, 127, 131, 199, 200, 218
Battenberg, Prince Alexander of (1857–93), 148, 150
Baumgarten, Hermann (1825–93), 10
Bavaria, Prince Regent of, *see* Luitpold, Prince and Regent of Bavaria
Bebel, August (1840–1913), 35
Benda, Robert von (1816–99), 169
Bennigsen, Rudolf von (1824–1902), 66, 81, 84, 86–8, 90–2, 94, 99, 103, 108–9, 134, 168, 190–1, 221
Berlepsch, Baron Hans Hermann von (1843–1926), 203, 208, 211
Beust, Count Friedrich Ferdinand von (1809–86), 35–6, 41–3
Bismarck, *Herbert* Nikolaus von (1849–1904), 6, 51, 91, 141, 146, 149, 153–4, 158, 191, 221, 229–30, 232
Bismarck, Johanna von, *née* von Puttkamer (1824–94), 3, 6, 78, 229–31
Bismarck, Malwine von (1827–1908), 230
Bismarck, Countess Marguerite von, *see* Hoyos, Countess Marguerite of.
Bismarck, *Marie* Elisabeth Johanna von (1848–1926), 6
Bismarck, *Wilhelm* ['Bill'] Albrecht Otto von (1852–1901), 6
Bitter, Karl Hermann (1813–85), 111
Blanckenburg, Moritz von (1815–88), 28

Bleichröder, Gerson von (1822–93), 5, 76–8, 212
Blumenthal, Count Leonhard von (1810–1900), 5
Boetticher, Karl Heinrich von (1833–1907), 220
Boulanger, Georges (1837–91), 144, 183, 190, 201
Brandenburg, Count Friedrich Wilhelm von (1792–1850), 118
Bronsart von Schellendorf, Walter (1833–1914), 155, 185, 187
Bucher, Lothar (1817–92), 231
Bülow, Bernhard Ernst von (1815–79), 118
Bunsen, Baron Georg von (1824–96), 172
Burckhardt, Jacob (1797–1865), 130, 219
Busch, Moritz (1821–99), 84–5, 129, 172, 220, 231
Byron, Lord George Gordon Noel (1788–1824), 4

Camphausen, Otto von (1812–96), 76–7, 88, 92
Caprivi, Count Leo von (1831–99), 209, 217, 222–4
Chrysander, Rudolf (1865–1950), 220, 224
Clemenceau, Georges (1841–1929), 137, 142, 144
Comte, Auguste (1798–1857), 166
Courcel, Alphonse Chodron de (1835–1919), 141

Decazes, Louis Charles Élie Amanieu, Duke of Decazes and of Glücksb(j)erg (1819–86), 46
Delbrück, Martin Friedrich *Rudolf* von (1817–1903), 23, 32–3, 72–4, 76–7, 79–80, 84
Diest-Daber, Otto von (1821–1901), 63
Dietrichstein, Countess, *see* Mensdorff-Pouilly, Countess Alexandrine von.
Dinder, Julius (1830–90), 182
Disraeli, Benjamin, Earl of Beaconsfield (1804–81), 40, 55–6, 58
Döllinger, Johann Joseph *Ignaz* von (1799–1890), 18
Douglas, Count Hugo Sholto (1837–1912), 196

Eckhard, *Carl* Maria Joseph (1822–1910), 10
Eugénie, Empress of the French (1826–1920), 139
Eulenburg, Count Botho Wend zu (1831–1912), 92, 97
Eulenburg, Count Friedrich Albrecht zu (1815–81), 92
Eulenburg und Hertefeld, Count Philipp zu (1847–1921), 130, 195–6, 208, 227–8

Falk, Paul Ludwig Adalbert (1827–1900), 19, 22–5, 64, 90, 110–11
Ferdinand I, Prince (King) of Bulgaria (1861–1948), 150
Ferry, Jules (1832–93), 137, 142–4, 185
Fontane, Theodor (1819–98), 130, 219
Forckenbeck, Max von (1821–92), 87, 108, 165, 172
Francis Joseph I, Emperor of Austria (1830–1916), 42, 44–5, 119, 121, 222, 228–9
Franckenstein, Baron Georg Arbogast von und zu (1825–90), 108
Frederick I, Grand Duke of Baden (1852–1907), 89, 92, 214
Frederick II, 'the Great', King in, from 1772 of Prussia (1712–86), 54
Frederick III, German Emperor and King of Prussia (1831–88), 11, 86–7, 95, 109, 135, 147, 164–5, 168, 171–2, 189, 195, 197–200, 204
Frederick William I, King of Prussia (1688–1740), 203
Frederick William IV, King of Prussia (1795–1861), 20, 211
Freytag, Gustav (1816–95), 205
Friedberg, Heinrich von (1813–95), 77
Friedenthal, Karl Rudolf (1827–90), 111

Gambetta, Léon (1838–82), 131
Gerlach, Ernst *Ludwig* von (1795–1877), 23
Gladstone, William Ewart (1809–98), 55, 96, 141
Gneist, Rudolf von (1816–95), 66
Goethe, Johann Wolfgang von (1749–1832), 4, 50
Goltz, Count Robert von der (1817–69), 96–7
Goluchowski, Count Agenor Maria Adam (1849–1921), 228
Gorchakov, Prince Alexander Michailovich (1798–1883), 43, 46–7, 50, 58, 117
Gossler, Gustav von (1838–1902), 176

Hänel, Albert (1833–1918), 100
Hahnke, Wilhelm von (1833–1912), 196
Hammerstein-Gesmold, Baron Wilhelm von (1838–1904), 77, 167, 173
Harden, Maximilian [Maximilian Felix Ernst Witkowsky] (1861–1927), 224, 234

Hatzfeld-Wildenburg, Count Paul von (1831–1901), 103, 144, 153, 157–8
Hegel, Georg Wilhelm Friedrich (1770–1831), 123, 166
Heine, Heinrich (1797–1856), 4
Helldorf-Bedra, Otto Heinrich von (1833–1908), 196, 214
Herbette, *Jules* Gabriel (1839–1901), 209
Hinzpeter, Georg (1827–1907), 203
Hobrecht, *Arthur* Heinrich Ludolf Johnson (1824–1912), 92, 111, 124
Hödel, Max (1857–78), 93
Hofmann, Hermann (1850–1915), 220
Hohenlohe-Schillingsfürst, Prince Chlodwig zu (1819–1901), 30, 96
Hohenlohe-Schillingsfürst, Prince Gustav Adolf zu (1823–1896), 30, 141
Holnstein, Count Max von (1835–95), 91
Holstein, Friedrich von (1837–1907), 102–3, 144, 157, 220, 222–3
Hoyos, Countess Marguerite of [wife of Herbert von Bismarck] (1871–1945), 221

Ignatiev, Count Nikolai Pavlovich (1832–1908), 56
Itzenplitz, Count *Heinrich* August Friedrich von (1799–1883), 35, 63

Jacobini, Ludovico (1832–87), 115, 187

Kálnoky, Count Gustav (1832–98), 149
Kameke, *Georg* Arnold von (1817–93), 66
Kardorff, Wilhelm von (1828–1907), 75
Katkov, Michail Nikiforovich (1818–87), 151
Kessler, Count Harry (1868–1937), 226
Ketteler, Baron Wilhelm Emmanuel von (1811–77), 14–15, 17–18
Kinkel, Gottfried (1815–82), 16
Kleist-Retzow, Hans Hugo von (1814–92), 115, 192
Kohl, Horst (1855–1917), 220
Kopp, Georg von (1837–1914), 181–2
Krätzig, Albert (1819–87), 21
Krementz, Philipp (1819–99), 182
Krupp, Friedrich *Alfred* Heinrich (1854–1902), 227
Kullmann, Eduard Franz Ludwig (1853–92), 67

Lasker, Eduard (1829–84), 10, 63, 66, 70–2, 81, 85, 92–3, 101, 103, 105–6, 108–9, 162–3, 168–9, 172
Lassalle, Ferdinand (1825–64), 34, 39
Ledochowski, Count Mieczyslaw *Halka* (1822–1902), 182
Leo XIII, Pope (1810–1903), 89, 181–3, 187
Liebknecht, Wilhelm (1826–1900), 55, 58
Lohmann, Christian *Theodor* (1831–1905), 132, 166–7

Louis XIV, King of France (1638–1715), 235
Louix XV, King of France (1710–74), 123
Louis Napoleon, *see* Napoleon III, Emperor of the French
Lucanus, Hermann von (1831–1908), 220
Lucius von Ballhausen, Baron Robert (1835–1914), 16, 54, 78, 111, 120, 122, 136, 163, 206–7
Ludwig II, King of Bavaria (1845–86), 91, 98, 147, 223
Luitpold, Prince and Regent of Bavaria (1821–1912), 223

Machiavelli, Niccolò (1469–1527), 16, 36, 94–5, 153, 212, 222
Mallinckrodt, Hermann von (1821–74), 25
Manteuffel, Baron Edwin von (1809–85), 50
Marschall von Bieberstein, Baron Adolf (1842–1912), 208, 220
Marx, Karl (1818–83), 55
Maybach, Albert von (1822–1904), 92
Meglia, Pierre François de (d. 1883), 177
Melchers, Paulus (1813–95), 182
Metternich, Prince *Klemens* Wenzel Nepomuk Lothar von (1773–1859), 45, 123, 157
Milan I, King of Serbia (1854–1901), 148
Miquel, Johannes von (1828–1901), 100–1, 104, 168–70, 173, 230
Mohl, Robert von (1799–1875), 24
Moltke, Count Cuno von (1847–1923), 227
Moltke, Count *Helmuth* Karl Bernhard von (1800–91), 46
Mommsen, Theodor (1817–1903), 217–18
Mühler, Heinrich von (1813–74), 19, 21–3

Napoleon I, Emperor of the French (1769–1821), 97
Napoleon III, Emperor of the French (1808–73), 97
Nathusius-Ludom, Philipp von (1842–1900), 76
Nobiling, Karl (1848–78), 93

Oettingen, *August* Georg Friedrich von (1823–1908), 43
Orlov, Princess Catherine (1840–75), 3

Pecci, Vincenzo Gioacchino, *see* Leo XIII, Pope
Peel, Sir Robert (1788–1850), 110
Perrot, Franz (1837–1891), 76
Peters, Carl (1856–1918), 140
Pietro, Angelo di (1828–1914), 187
Pius IX, Pope (1792–1878), 89
Poschinger, Heinrich von (1845–1911), 220
Puttkamer, Robert Viktor von (1828–1900), 8, 111, 198

Radbruch, Gustav (1878–1949), 236

Radziwill, Prince Anton von (1833–1904), 21
Rantzau, Countess Marie zu, *see* Bismarck, Marie von.
Reuss, Prince Heinrich VII (1825–1906), 222
Richter, Eugen (1838–1906), 66, 86, 91, 131, 162, 187
Rickert, Heinrich (1833–1902), 101
Rönne, Ludwig Peter Moritz von (1804–91), 127
Roon, Count Albrecht Theodor Emil von (1803–79), 28, 62–3, 66, 136
Rössler, Constantin (1820–96), 190
Rothschild, Baron Meyer Carl von (1820–86), 5

Saxe-Coburg-Gotha-Kohary, Prince Ferdinand of, *see* Ferdinand I, Prince of Bulgaria.
Salisbury, Robert Cecil, Marquess of (1830–1903), 158
Schäffle, *Albert* Eberhard Friedrich (1831–1903), 166
Schleinitz, Count Alexander von (1807–85), 40
Schlözer, Kurd von (1822–94), 181, 187
Schnaebele, Guillaume (1831–1900), 144
Scholz, Adolf Heinrich Wilhelm von (1833–1924), 196, 197
Schweinitz, Hans Lothar von (1822–1901), 35
Schweninger, Ernst (1850–1924), 6, 231
Seydewitz, Otto Theodor (1818–98), 108
Shakespeare, William (1564–1616), 4
Shuvalov, Count Pavel Andreyevich (1830–1908), 56, 214, 216
Stauffenberg, Baron *Franz* August Schenk von (1834–1901), 66, 87, 108, 125, 172
Stoecker, Adolf (1835–1909), 195–6
Stolberg-Wernigerode, Count Otto von (1837–96), 92
Stosch, Albrecht von (1818–96), 86
Stumm-Halberg, Baron Carl Ferdinand von (1836–1901), 75, 227
Sybel, Heinrich von (1817–95), 10

Taaffe, Count Eduard von (1833–95), 121
Tacitus, Cornelius (after A.D. 50 – after 116), 220
Thadden-Trieglaff, Adolf von (1796–1882), 77
Tiedemann, Christoph von (1835–1907), 87, 94, 123
Treitschke, Heinrich von (1834–96), 170

Victoria, German Empress and Queen of Prussia [Empress Friedrich] (1840–1901), 199
Virchow, Rudolf (1821–1902), 165, 195

Wagener, Hermann (1815–89), 7, 63

Waldersee, Count Alfred von (1832–1904), 185, 195–6, 201, 214

Weber, Max (1864–1920), 83, 156, 160–1, 219, 226–7

Wehrenpfennig, Wilhelm (1829–1900), 25, 130

Werder, Bernhard von (1823–1907), 50

William I, German Emperor and King of Prussia (1797–1888), 11, 15, 17, 21, 23, 27, 30, 42, 44–5, 47, 50, 56, 62, 65–6, 73–4, 80, 86–7, 93–4, 96, 100, 111–12, 117–21, 125, 134–6, 142, 146, 165, 172, 174, 181–2, 188–9, 195, 197–8, 225

William II, German Emperor and King of Prussia (1859–1941), 153, 165, 195–6, 197–200, 202–16, 220–3, 226–8, 231

Windthorst, Ludwig (1812–91), 13, 25, 27–9, 70, 78, 85, 100, 108, 120, 174–82, 186–8, 194, 196, 210, 212

Wolf, Eugen (1850–1912), 143